a
love
story

SAILING
WITH
CAROL

Ron Ieva

ISBN: 1-4392-1703-3
ISBN-13: 9781439217030

Visit www.booksurge.com to order additional copies.

CONTENTS

Preface

"Sailing with Carol" is a sometimes humorous, always emotional journey through the first and last thirds in my wife Carol's life. It's a true story of unconditional love and passion, spanning nearly fifty years and chronicles her growth as a woman and as a sailor, revealing how the joy of sailing characterized our passage through time together. It's about a woman's soft nature and hard resolve, as well as her natural innocence, lusty passion, and zesty appetite for all that life offered. Lastly, it's about her courage and her heroic five year battle against the brain tumor that eventually took her from me.

As children growing up in Brooklyn, Carol and I lived across the street from each other. We were playmates and grew to become child-hood sweethearts, impatient to explore our love and the world outside the boundaries of our neighborhood. Even then, I knew she was unique and that as a couple, we would be linked for the rest of our lives. We spent countless hours at the shore where the Verrazano Bridge now stands. There, we dreamed of buying a sailboat that we would one day explore the world in, and in doing so, our lives became forever intertwined.

Sadly, Carol's family moved away. We were heartbroken and struggled to maintain regular but secret contact for several years while I was in the Navy and at college. Eventually, time, distance, and circumstances conspired against us and we drifted apart. But, to borrow a phrase I once heard, *I knew ours was a love by which all others in my life would be judged and found wanting.*

We eventually married others and almost two decades passed. Through all that time, we never stopped loving each other or wondering if at the end of our journeys through bad marriages and good children, we would be together again.

By 1986, I was divorced and Carol was separated. She found me living a mile from her parents' home where I had settled several years earlier in search of a link to her. Our reunion was joyful beyond words, and we instantly re-bonded as if those missing decades had never happened. We went on to share twenty-one immeasurably wonderful years together. For us, life was filled with love and adventure, and our compatibility was such that neither of us needed to compromise on anything of any importance.

Before then, Carol had never traveled outside America. She never dined in an elegant restaurant or in the company of ship owners, executives, or sea captains. In life, that wasn't at all important, but it was the world I lived and worked in and it spoke to her versatility that when thrust into such an arena, she could waltz through it with total self-confidence, but with a humility and grace that was distinctive to her unpretentious character.

We loved each other deeply and profoundly and constantly sought to express our love through intimacy, caring actions, and kind words. We were symbiotic in every way, something that was most apparent when we were on our sailboat. During those times, we experienced and dealt with all of life's extremes, and sailing became a metaphor for all other aspects of our relationship.

As we dreamed about when we were kids, we traveled all over the world. With Carol as my wife, lover, and best friend, I became a better person and better at everything I did. She had that way about her; she made you want to be better. She was my first mate aboard our two boats, *Ursaorion* and *Lastdance* and although we never became the blue water sailors we once dreamed we'd be, she sailed with me from New England to the Florida Keys for over twenty years. It was during those many voyages that she mastered her fears and honed the resolve that she would so desperately need in the final years of her short life.

Carol achieved most of the things she set out to do and left hundreds of friends and family with enduring memories of her many facets. Few will forget seeing her at the helm of *Lastdance* on a close reach or her beautiful smile that could at once embody her gentle nature and wanton passion. Fewer still, will forget her extraordinary bravery during the last years of her journey, least of all me because I witnessed her courage and experienced the selflessness that defined her.

It has been cathartic to write this book, but also very painful. Now, as I fight my own battle against cancer, Carol will forever be my inspiration and hero, and I pray for the faith to believe I will sail with her once again in another life.

Rich & Lori
    You were there from the
very beginning — thank you
for being good friends
        Ron
    S/V Lastdance

CHAPTER 1
FIRST LOVE

I was divorced, Carol was getting divorced. Twenty-four years earlier we grew up in Brooklyn where we played together as children, then fell in love as teenagers. We were now adults, and she just ended what she said was a suffocating marriage and had recently moved in with me. Carol the woman was even more beautiful than Carol the teenager, but I sensed she was different. She wasn't the adventurous, self-reliant girl I fell in love with a quarter of a century earlier. If she was different in that way, she could be different in other ways, and I wondered if having her move in so quickly was such a good idea.

Most of my concerns dissipated over time as I discovered her basic nature was unchanged. It became apparent during her contentious divorce that her marriage may have contributed to the guarded condition in which her adventurous spirit and insatiable curiosity had been suppressed. Still, I sensed the real Carol could percolate to the surface if encouraged. We were rediscovering each other with each passing day as we fell deeply in love again. In that environment, she slowly began to flourish and become herself; a grown up version of the teenage girl with boundless passion, wanderlust, and imagination. Thinking about these things as I lay in bed with her asleep in my arms, my thoughts drifted back to a time in Brooklyn when, after being playmates, we became adolescent lovers. I remembered the first time we made love and I drew her gently to me and smiled.

The big social event in our neighborhood in the early sixties was the Friday night confraternity dance. The guys went for pizza first and the girls went directly to the church school auditorium where the dance was held. You didn't take a girl to the dance; you went with the guys. You

danced by going up to a girl and saying, "Dance." It was more of a statement than a question. It was simple, but not for me because I was in love
with Carol, the skinny girl who lived across the street. When I was thirteen
and she was twelve, I did the unthinkable and asked her to go to the dance
with me.

"You did what?" my best friend asked.

"Nobody takes a girl, dummy. If anyone finds out she's with you,
some shithead is gonna try to dance with her, then one of the big guys will
kick your ass if you say anything."

"I don't care; I'm taking her!"

A day later she turned me down. With tears in her eyes, she said,
"I'm so sorry, Ronnie, but my parents won't let me go."

I ran with a rough crowd, which concerned her parents, but I was
still stunned and heartbroken. It hurt like nothing I'd experienced before
in my brief life. I was also embarrassed. *How could I face my friends?* I turned
and ran before she could see the tears welling up in my eyes and vowed
never to speak to her again. But even as I ran from her, I thought, *How will
I do that? She lives right across the street from me. We see each other every day. More
importantly, I am madly in love with her!*

Other than returning her persistent greetings whenever she saw
me, I didn't speak to her for almost a year. I went to school and worked at
shining shoes and hawking watermelons in Coney Island. I tried my best
to ignore her, but it was impossible not to be aware of her. Whenever our
paths crossed, she'd call out to me, "Hi, Ronnie." I'd see her beautiful smile
and wanted to notice her. I wanted to say hi and return her smiles, but I
didn't because her rejection still hurt.

Then, in the fall of 1961 while hanging out on a street corner with
my friends one chilly Saturday in October, I saw her. Actually, Mario saw
her first.

"Holy shit, who's the chick in the red sweater?"

Heads turned and a voice beside me said, "Oh man, look at this
babe!"

That got everyone's attention! More suggestive comments followed
as the pretty girl approached. She wore jeans, penny loafers, and a bulky red
sweater that bulged suggestively. I couldn't take my eyes off her. *Had she*

been away? I thought. She looked so grown up and radiant. To my surprise and those around me, I said loudly, "That's my girlfriend, Carol!"

I walked toward her and smiled. She smiled back and her whole face lit up. As she had done many times in the past, she said cheerfully, "Hi, Ronnie." Then, as an invitation, she said she was going to the Five and Ten Cent store.

"Can I walk with you?"

Without hesitation, she smiled and said, "Yes, I'd like that a lot."

My heart was pounding. She was beautiful and wasn't mad at me. More importantly, she still seemed to like me. *Why did I ignore her?* I knew then and there I was in still love with her, that I had never stopped loving her. As if reading my mind, she extended her hand to me, and with our eyes locked, she implored me to take it. I did, and I knew my life would never be the same again.

We stood facing each other for a long time, and I sensed a silence that a moment before had been the collective chatter of my friends. At almost the same instant they returned to their banter, my friend Danny yelled out, "Kiss her, turkey."

I did; briefly and tenderly and when I opened my eyes, I saw hers were still closed. She had a dreamy look on her face. I thought, "*Why do you still want me after the way I treated you? You could have any guy you want.*"

To my surprise, she said, "I've only wanted you, Ron. You're all I've ever wanted ever since we were little kids."

I had been speaking out loud, not just thinking those sentiments, and I smiled as I realized she was already turning my world upside down.

A few muffled howls rang out as we walked away hand in hand. I tried to be cool by casually saying, "Catch you later, guys," but my voice faltered and they laughed.

Joey said in an exaggerated falsetto voice, "Come back soon, Ronnie."

Carol simply drew me closer and looking back over her shoulder she said, "He won't be back anytime today, Joey."

More laughter and howls followed, but I knew they were directed at Joey. I smiled as I walked away with my girl.

We talked all afternoon about the things we'd been doing, and I told her how sorry I was for being such an ass. She looked at me with wisdom beyond that of a fourteen-year-old and said, "I know I hurt you, but I always loved you and knew you never stopped loving me."

This was heady stuff for a couple of kids, but it was only my first glimpse of how unconditional Carol could be.

We were inseparable, and even though Carol's parents didn't like me, they tolerated me. They imposed strict rules on where she could go and how late she could stay out. It didn't matter. We were happy to hold hands, take long walks, and explore our growing sexuality at our favorite place along Shore Road where the Verrazano Bridge was being built. Sometimes we'd watch workers high up on the towers and she'd ask me what they were doing. I knew just enough about suspension bridges to answer most of her questions, but I always wondered if she really believed me.

Many days we'd sit there for hours looking out at the bay. I'd tell her how I was learning to sail in school and how incredible it was to make a boat move through the water with just the wind. I told her I wanted to have a sailboat of my own someday and dreamed of sailing around the world.

"Don't you still want to do that?" she asked.

I kissed her cheek and said, "Yeah, I do, but I won't do it now that you're back in my life."

"Why not? Couldn't I go with you?"

I was astonished that a girl would even think about doing that. "You'd do that? You'd go away on a sailboat with me?"

"I'd go anywhere with you, Ronnie!" Then she added, "Could you teach me to sail?"

"I'm sure I could." That opened up a flood of questions from her.

"What kind of boat would we get? Where would we go? How do you find your way around?"

She listened intently as I answered each question except how to navigate.

"I don't know how to navigate yet, but I'll learn in school or when I join the Navy."

She then asked endless questions about how life would be for us when I was in the Navy. "Could we could have a military wedding when we got married? Could we have guys with swords make an arch for us like in the movies?"

"Yeah, of course we could," I replied. "I think only officers get to use swords, but I'm not sure if I'll be one."

She seemed disappointed for an instant, then brightened. "Oh, I'm sure you'll be an officer, I just know it."

I loved her enthusiasm, but eventually talk of sailing and questions about the Navy would trail off and we'd lie back in the soft grass and make out. It was there we first touched and explored our bodies, and it was not far from there we were married a quarter of a century later at Fort Hamilton, in a military wedding with my fellow officers making an arch of swords for us, just as Carol had envisioned.

When we weren't able to go to Shore Road, we spent hours on her front stoop playing chess, sometimes holding hands, and even sneaking in a kiss. But even then, we always talked of sailing or when I'd join the Navy and we'd get married and see the world together. Sometimes we'd watch *Adventures in Paradise,* a television series based on the book by James Michener, and we'd fantasize that I was captain of the *Tiki,* a schooner plying the South Pacific. Carol was my first mate, and we knew that someday we'd live the adventures we dreamed about. It was magical being with her, and I knew I would love her forever.

Early in the spring of 1962, we went to Palisades Amusement Park in New Jersey. Carol was allowed to be away from early morning until ten at night because her parents believed she was going with friends from her church and had no idea I would be with her. It was an adventure! We took the subway to Manhattan, which for us could have been the Orient Express on its way to Istanbul.

At the Port Authority Terminal, we caught a bus to the park in New Jersey. It was on the high palisades overlooking the Hudson River where it flowed past Manhattan on its way to the sea. Carol and I sat in the back of the bus where we held hands, kissed, and marveled at the sights of New York as we crossed the George Washington Bridge. Some of the younger girls from the group took fleeting glances at us and giggled. We didn't care; we were in love and had the whole day together.

Once in the huge arcade area, we split away from the group, agreeing to meet at seven o'clock for the ride home. It was heaven for us! We were anonymous; we could do whatever we wanted. For the first time, we were unmindful of the world around us, without fear of being seen by her parents or their friends from the neighborhood. It was fun to buy her cotton candy and take her on exciting rides. Unlike most of the other girls, she didn't scream like a sissy, but yelled like she was having the time of her life.

On the haunted house ride, I sat behind her in the partially enclosed car, which rode on tracks into what the sign said was the longest and scariest ride in the world. My legs were wrapped around her hips and my arms around her waist. I felt the weight of her breasts against the top of my clasped hands and my head spun. Then, looking down the front of her parka, I saw enticing cleavage over the top of her bra. As we waited for the rest of the cars to fill, I snuggled closer and kissed her neck, whispering, "You're so beautiful and I love you so much."

She turned and kissed me, and my heart pounded in my chest as I pressed myself more tightly against her.

The ride started and we crashed though swinging doors painted with a monster's face with pointed teeth. Once into the darkened house of horrors, Carol turned around and we kissed passionately, oblivious to the demons, devils, and skeletons that lurched out at us. She took my hand and put it tightly against her.

"Touch me, touch me here." I reached out nervously and touched her breasts, my hand trembling as I put it under her parka and gently caressed her through the material of her bra.

"Oh Ronnie. I love you so much."

I slipped my hand under the soft fabric and felt the warmth of her skin, and she pressed her hand over mine. I became dizzy as I caressed her, but a moment later the ride ended as the front car burst through the exit doors into the bright sunlight. As Carol hastily rearranged her disheveled clothes, I thought, *That was wonderful, but what happened to the longest ride in the world?*

The rest of the day was a fun filled trek through the park as we went on any ride that promised a thrill or the briefest moment of privacy. I couldn't get the memory of touching her from my mind, and we never missed an opportunity to kiss or exchange a knowing glance about what had occurred in the haunted house. Then, when alone under the cool shade of a tree, I looked into her eyes and simply said, "I want to do it."

With no explanation needed, she put her arms around my neck.

"Me too! Soon, very soon."

For the rest of the afternoon, my mind raced and my heart pounded as I imagined how it would be to make love to her.

Our summer days were spent at our place by the shore or going to the beach at Coney Island every chance she could get away. We barely tanned because we usually stayed under the boardwalk where we'd spend hours making out in the shadows, leaving the cool shade only briefly to mingle with our friends or go for a swim. It was the best summer of my life, and each day brought us closer and more intimate until we couldn't stand it any longer. We began to seek out a place to be alone. In the month since the haunted house at Palisades Park, we had enjoyed many heated encounters, some going pretty far, but we wanted more; we wanted to make love. We talked about it all the time, and although we were scared, we were deeply in love beyond our years and felt it was natural and inevitable.

On a hot summer day at our familiar place under the Coney Island boardwalk we kissed and held each other, then Carol began to cry softly. The tears pooled in her eyes and I asked her what was wrong.

"I didn't want to say anything, but I'm so upset."

She took a breath and said that she heard her parents talking about moving to New Jersey. My first reaction was panic, but after some thought, I told her that talking about moving and *actually* moving are two different things, and that for years I sometimes heard my own parents talk about moving to New Jersey, but nothing ever came of it.

Managing a smile, she said, "Really, you're not just saying that? Why didn't you ever tell me before?"

"No, I'm not just saying it. I never mentioned it because I never thought they were serious. Besides, your dad works in Brooklyn, so why would he move to New Jersey?"

"I don't know. I guess you're right."

I wiped the tears from her eyes. As I ran my hand through her hair, I put on my best smile, but I wondered what the future held for us. If her parents did move, we were too young to do anything about it. At sixteen, I couldn't even join the Navy, and with Carol at fifteen, I didn't think there was any place that we could run off to and get married. *No*, I thought, *they won't move, they can't.*

In the passing weeks, even just the thought of Carol moving added urgency to our desire to make love. Then an unexpected opportunity presented itself; my parents would be gone for a whole day. Living right across the street from me, however, she couldn't just stroll over and risk her parents or a neighbor seeing her enter my building when my parents weren't home, so an elaborate plan evolved. We met in my friend Bobby's building on 13th Avenue and went to his roof, then we crossed over a half dozen buildings to mine. We then went down to my apartment; not even the other tenants in my building saw her.

As soon as we entered the hall, I pressed her against the wall and kissed her, then, holding her hand, I led her down the flight of steps to my apartment. Once inside with the door locked, a flood of relief came over me. So many things could have gone wrong, but we were safe and alone until Carol had to go home five hours later, which was more time than we ever had completely alone. I asked if she was sure she wanted to do it.

In a trembling voice she replied, "Yes, I really do. Do you?"

"Yeah, I really do!"

Walking into the living room, I nervously turned on the television, but Carol stepped forward and turned it off.

"What are you thinking, Ron?" Then she kissed me.

The instant her lips touched mine my head began to spin. We were alone with just the ticking of the clock on the wall, and we were lost in time as we tenderly kissed. Remaining like that for what might have been a minute or an hour, I couldn't say, but we eventually walked into my bedroom hand in hand.

Silently, Carol surveyed the things in my room for a long time. Then, as her gaze fell back on me, I took her in my arms and we kissed with a growing urgency. It was like no other kiss we had ever shared before.

"Are you scared?"

She said nervously, "Yes, are you?"

I lied. "Yeah, just a little." I was *scared stiff* and could see she was too.

I fumbled with the buttons on her blouse and removed it. Without breaking eye contact, Carol reached back and unhooked her bra, leaving it loosely draped on her shoulders, her breasts still hidden. We kissed again as it fell to the floor between us. As our lips parted, she said, "Look at me!"

I lowered my gaze and became lightheaded and breathless.

"God, you're so beautiful," was all I could say as I stared at her.

For the briefest time, we stood facing each other just inches apart. Then, in one small stride, we were together, our bodies in contact and both overwhelmed by an almost mystical energy that bonded us for all time.

"What if I get pregnant?"

"I don't care. We'll get married."

I meant it because I knew beyond a doubt, nothing else mattered except spending the rest of my life with her. Hours later, holding my face in her hands and kissing me, she said, "This was more wonderful than I'd ever imagined."

"I feel the same, Carol." I kissed her softly, saying, "I will love you for forever and always."

Carol didn't get pregnant, but many years later, after living unhappy lives in unhappy marriages, we both wondered how things might have turned out for us if she had.

Living across the street from each other, I'd spend hours looking out my window for just a glimpse of her. If I saw her come out of her house, I'd fly down two flights of stairs to intercept her on the way to the grocery store or dry cleaners. We were always running errands together, and the local vendors knew us to be inseparable. If I went to the fish market or butcher shop without her, they would ask, "Yo, Ronnie, where's Carol?"

Frankie the butcher once teased us. "Hey, Carol, when lover boy came in without you last week, I asked him if you dumped him, and you shoulda seen him get pissed off."

Carol came to my rescue. She drew me close to her and said, "I'd never leave Ronnie." Then, shocking Frankie and the other customers, she kissed me passionately on my lips. Yeah, it was magical being with her!

On Easter Sunday in 1963 our world turned upside-down. We were going to Easter Mass together and meeting a block from our home so her parents wouldn't know she was seeing me. I watched her approach and knew something was wrong. As she got closer, she began to cry. She threw her arms around me, sobbing uncontrollably.

"We're moving to New Jersey."

Stunned, I could only ask, "When?"

Through tears she said, "October."

As we walked to church holding hands in silence, I thought, *October is only seven months away! What are we going to do?*

We spent every possible moment together that summer, sometimes coming up with wild plans to run away together, sometimes sitting silently by our favorite spot overlooking the nearly completed Verrazano Bridge. Even in our sadness her curiosity was insatiable. She asked questions about the bridge, ships in the harbor or sailing. We spent hours in Vinny's, a small pizzeria where we played the jukebox and danced to our favorite songs. She always picked her personal favorite for last. "Save the Last Dance for Me", by The Drifters.

In August, to celebrate her fifteenth birthday, I gave her an ankle bracelet and to my surprise, she gave me an ID bracelet. I took her to New York to see *Cleopatra* on Broadway, then to Mama Leone's for dinner. My friends thought I was nuts for spending that kind of money, but nothing mattered other than making Carol happy. Leone's was like entering a whole new world for us. We were a couple of jerky kids from Brooklyn eating in a real Manhattan restaurant, rubbing shoulders with exciting people from Broadway, maybe even some actors and actresses. We were probably seated at the worst table in the place, but like so many things about being with Carol, it was still wonderful. I tried to order wine. The waiter frowned, but being a master at his craft, he placed an empty Chianti bottle on our table for appearances along with two colas.

Knowing they'd be moving in a month, Carol's parents seemed to become more lenient and we took advantage of it, spending every day in September together. I should have been grateful for the extra time, but it actually made me angry. They had done their best to keep us apart, and letting us be together now seemed like a taunt because it made us realize how good things could have been. The days went by too quickly, then, on a sunny October morning, it was upon us. We cried unashamedly on her front stoop, and when it was time for them to go, her mom said we could have a few minutes to say goodbye inside. In her hallway, we hugged and kissed, making tearful promises to love each other forever.

"I'll always love you. I'll always save the last dance for you!"

Then she was gone, and the course of my life was altered forever.

We struggled to maintain contact, and Carol eventually found a classmate to act as an intermediary and we corresponded through precious letters and occasional pre-arranged phone calls. Time and distance were against us however, and I sensed I might be losing her. After joining the Navy, it became almost impossible for us to communicate by phone, and even letters were difficult to exchange. We drifted apart as Carol became more involved in her high school social activities and I spent long periods of time at sea aboard a submarine.

Almost a year later, I was struggling toward the end of my plebe year as a midshipman at Maine Maritime Academy. Other than my parents, no one ever called me, so it was a total surprise when I heard the pipe, "Midshipman Fourth Class Ieva, you have a telephone call."

As was required of all plebes, I double-timed it to the quarterdeck and reported to the Officer of the Deck, who directed me to the pay phone.

I spoke into the phone. "Midshipman Ieva speaking."

There was silence on the other end, then softly, "Ron, is that you?"

I closed the phone booth door.

"Carol, is that you, Baby?"

We talked for an hour. She said she had dated guys but still loved me and cried over me every night. She asked if I still loved her, and without hesitation, I said, "God, yes, of course I do."

Once again she found a friend to act as an intermediary so we could write and sometimes call. We were able to maintain contact, but I wouldn't get leave until Thanksgiving. I promised I would see her then.

I was alive again! She wrote me almost daily; sometimes I'd even get two letters written the same day. When Thanksgiving leave began, I hitchhiked five hundred miles to see her. Meeting at the train station in New Brunswick, we spent the day walking around in the chilly November air, occasionally ducking into a store or the library to warm up. She told me she still loved me very much but that she had sometimes dated out of loneliness. I asked her if she wanted to end our relationship and she cried softly. "No! I love you so much and want desperately to make this work somehow. I think of you all the time. We have to keep trying."

She had to go home in the afternoon, but we agreed to meet again that night in Manhattan. I got a hotel near the bus terminal, and when she arrived, we went to dinner, then back to the hotel for a few precious hours where we made love and promised each other that we would find a way for her to come and live in Maine that summer.

We saw each other once again over Thanksgiving and several times during my Christmas leave, but I could see she needed more time from me. Time was something I couldn't give her because after returning to school, we were going to sea for our annual three month training cruise. I wrote from all the exotic ports we visited, but Carol's letters became less frequent as she struggled to be true to me and still participate in normal social activities with her friends at home. We were drifting apart again, and there was nothing we could do about it. I saw her when I returned from our winter cruise, but she had changed. As we walked holding hands, I knew something was different; time had changed us. Even though our hearts were bonded forever, circumstances were ending the relationship.

In the summer, Carol once again called me and asked if I thought there was still a chance for us now that she had a job. Even though she had initiated the contact, I could hear doubt in her voice. Nevertheless, I still wanted her.

"Yeah, Carol, there'll always be a chance for us."

I was going to sea aboard a submarine for a month, but I said I would come to New Jersey as soon as we returned to port, and we agreed to meet at Seaside on the Jersey shore.

The time at sea passed agonizingly slowly. Although bursting with anticipation at the thought of holding her in my arms again, I was a little older and wiser and found myself doubting it could work. Midshipmen couldn't be married. *How can I move her to Maine? Where will she live? Where will we get the money?* But, I erased my doubts. All I knew was that she called me, and she wanted to try again. So did I.

Driving to Seaside, my hands sweaty, I experienced butterflies in my stomach for the first time. I wore my tropical white uniform, thinking I'd remind her of the days back in Brooklyn when as kids we'd talk of her traveling the world with me in the Navy. Unlike in years past when her face was full of love and joy at seeing me, she now looked distant, and there seemed to be little warmth in her embrace.

"What's wrong?" I asked.

"Why are you wearing your uniform?"

The instant she said it, I knew she had changed. Where we once talked of having a military wedding, she now seemed to be caught up in the sixties anti-military fervor. There was displeasure, even anger in her voice. Although we walked and talked, we only sometimes held hands and I knew for certain, it was really over.

For us, the strain of maintaining a long-distance relationship took its toll. Times had also changed, and I was out of touch with how a lot of young people felt about Vietnam and the military in general. It was no one's fault; it was just the way it was, but it broke my heart to know I had lost her. We didn't actually break up, but her letters simply stopped coming. Seven months later, I heard she got married. My world collapsed around me.

I finished school and went to sea and thought of Carol often on long nights in far flung places, wondering where she was and if she ever thought of me. On one frightening day in Vietnam, I had an eerie vision of her and was certain she sensed I was in danger. Strangely, it made me smile to think we were somehow still connected. A year later, I married Carol's high school classmate for all the wrong reasons, one being the notion that it would somehow keep me connected to Carol. After that, as if to end the final chapter of a book, I came off watch one night while serving aboard a destroyer in the Atlantic. I looked at the western horizon toward New Jersey and Carol. Unclasping the ID bracelet she had given to me ten years earlier and that I secretly still wore, I let it slip into the sea.

Five years passed quickly. I never got to buy a sailboat, but I had a son and gave up any dreams of sailing as I focused on my boy and my career. Still, every time we'd visit my in-laws in New Jersey, I'd find an excuse to go out for cigarettes or something, then I'd drive by Carol's parents' house, hoping I might get to see her. Looking back, I realized I'd spent fourteen years in an unhappy marriage, partially because we were ill-suited for each other, but also because I never got over Carol.

In 1978, I began jogging. It was an activity that strained my marriage even more as I immersed myself in the sport. By 1981, I was running two hours a day. It became my refuge, bringing me to a place where no one could intrude, and it was during those runs through country roads in Connecticut when my thoughts were entirely of Carol. My wife and I grew further apart almost daily, and in 1983 we got divorced. My ex-wife moved back to New Jersey to be close to her family, and after selling our home, I moved there as well to be near my son. I bought a condo not far from Carol's parents' home and continued my daily running, choosing a route that took me by their house. Several years elapsed, but I never saw Carol or her parents. Although I eventually gave up thoughts of seeing her, I never stopped thinking about her or wondering where she was or if she was happy or what she was doing.

Chapter 2
Her Voice

Fumbling with my keys, I rushed inside and after putting down the groceries, answered the phone on the fifth ring.

"Hello, Ron?"

I froze. Nineteen years had passed since I'd last spoken with her, but I knew her voice before she said another word. It was Carol. My heart was pounding. I almost stuttered. All I could say was her name.

"Carol?"

"Yes, it's me."

I collected my thoughts and said with an exaggerated casualness, "It's been a long time. How are you?"

"I'm okay, how are you?"

I didn't answer; instead, I asked how she found me. She said she knew I had married her friend and thought I might one day move to Somerset, so she always looked for my name in the phone book when visiting her parents. I felt a lump in my throat and thought of the years I ran by their house.

"When I saw you in the phone book a month ago, I called, but a young boy answered so I panicked and hung up."

Strangely, I found myself almost angry and with a slight edge in my voice I asked, "So why did you call now?"

"I had to. I just had to."

I hesitated a moment before replying, "That was my son, Christopher; he stays with me on Tuesday nights. I'm divorced."

"I'm separated. I'm at my mom's."

My knees felt weak as I thought, *She is less than a mile from me at this very moment.* I asked if she had children.

"Yes, I have four. Two boys and two girls."

My thoughts ranged from pure joy that she had called me to anger that she waited until she had four kids. I closed my eyes and did an instant replay of all the goodbyes we said in the past, then said, "I want to see you!"

"Are you sure you really want to?"

"Yeah, I do. Soon, today. Right now!"

She said she would think of something to tell her parents, and that brought my sanity back.

"Carol. Why are you calling me?"

Her voice trembled. "Because I've never stopped loving you and thinking about you."

I took a deep breath. "Look, we're adults, you're less than a mile from me, come here now because I'm not going to worry about your parents at this stage of my life. Just tell them you're coming to see me and be done with it."

"I'll be there in an hour, okay?"

Somewhat abruptly, I said, "Okay." Then after a moment's hesitation, I added more softly, "I'd like that very much."

"Me too, Ron. See you soon."

When she hung up, I wondered if it really happened. Was it really Carol? I felt bad about being harsh. Maybe her concerns about her parents had to do with her separation and legal issues. Then I thought, *It makes no difference. If anything at all is going to come of this, I know with absolute certainty, I cannot deal with sneaking around like we did as teens.*

I was nervous. I didn't know if she liked red or white wine or champagne, so I opened a bottle of merlot to breathe, then put a bottle of pinot grigio and champagne in the refrigerator. I lit a fire, selected some music. Wondering what she might like, I realized I didn't have a clue what her taste might be now. I thought about some of our old songs but rejected that as being too hokey. Instead, I put all of my George Winston LP's on the turntable and then laid out several Julio Iglesias records in case things got romantic. I showered and straightened up, then asked myself if this was just a vivid daydream or if it was really happening. A minute later the doorbell rang, jarring me back to reality.

Taking a deep breath, I opened the door and there she was. We didn't say a word at first; we just looked at each other until her eyes filled with tears. She just stood there and cried. I fought back tears of my own, then reached out and took her in my arms. We stood there holding each other until I said, "Come in, Carol. Come inside."

We talked, listened to music, and sipped champagne in front of the fireplace all afternoon and into the evening, but did nothing more than kiss and hold hands. When a George Winston recording of Pachelbel's *Canon* came on she began to cry softly and exclaimed, "Oh my God, that's the GE song!

Astonished, I asked, "Why did you call it the GE song? That's *The Canon*." Then I said, "I used to call it the GE song when it was used in a commercial years ago and always thought of you when I heard it!"

She looked at me, startled.

"Ron, I swear to God, my daughter Nancy would call me whenever that commercial came on, and as soon as I'd hear that music I'd think of you and wonder where you were!"

She said she always felt we were connected, and I told her about the strange vision I had of her when I was in Vietnam. She cried softly.

"I knew you were there, and one day I had an overwhelming feeling about you. Truthfully, I didn't sense danger, just that you were about to call me on the phone or something."

As I listened to her, a flood of memories cascaded through my mind like a waterfall and I thought, *How did I lose her? How did we lose each other?* The talk was wonderful, but I thought for all the years we'd been in love, the few times we made love always involved elaborate and clandestine arrangements. That day, I wanted her right there on my living room floor in front of the fireplace, but I couldn't help see the excitement in her face as she talked, so I let her go on. She was totally unlike the girl who lectured me about wearing my uniform years earlier at the Jersey shore. The woman in front of me now was a glimpse of my old girlfriend from Brooklyn and the warmth in her eyes was unmistakable. *No*, I thought, *the love making will wait until next time.*

Telling me about her life, she spoke volumes about her children, but nothing more about her marriage other than it was oppressive and she couldn't bear it any longer. I sensed she wanted to avoid talking about the years we drifted apart. That was alright for now, but if a new relationship was going to come of this, we couldn't avoid the reasons the old one failed. Eventually, we'd talk about it, but like the love making, not today.

She told me she was going to nursing school to become an RN, and when I asked her about it, she became excited and animated, and I listened with genuine interest. There was more than just talk of getting an education; she emphasized the mentoring aspects of her teachers, and when she spoke of her academic achievements, it was with an inordinate amount of pride, but also with much of the same humility I remembered from our teen years.

As she watched me cook dinner, she said, "Watching you preparing dinner in the kitchen makes me feel like it was my marriage that was the dream and this is the reality. Does that make any sense?"

"Yeah it does Carol. Almost twenty years have slipped by, and look, you've been here all afternoon and it's almost like those years have never happened."

I put my arms around her and we held each other tightly. I can't say with certainty what she might have been thinking, but given all the circumstances, I couldn't help wonder how such a complex situation might work. As I embraced her and took in her scent, I answered my own question: *It could work because we still loved each other.*

We opened a bottle of wine and ate dinner, talking about our lives until she looked at the time.

"I'm sorry, but I have exams in the morning. I should get going."

I wanted her to stay, but knew I shouldn't push it. Instead, I asked if I could see her the next day. She said she was seeing her kids for dinner, but thought we could meet for lunch at Ocean College. Without a thought of having to be at work the next day, I said, "Yeah, I'd like that."

We kissed goodnight and she was gone as suddenly as she had appeared. As the sound of her car driving away reverberated in my ears, I went inside and thought, *Did that really happen?* I saw the dirty dishes and wine glasses on the table and two wine stains on the carpet. *Yes it did!* I smiled, feeling better than I could remember feeling before.

Sitting in front of the fireplace where we spent most of the afternoon, I drank the remaining wine as the glowing embers in the hearth cooled. I thought, *So much soul searching to do. Be careful*, I cautioned myself, *you're still in love with a sixteen-year-old girl; This is a thirty-eight year old woman with four kids going through a messy divorce.* She also seemed different, quiet, and almost mousy at times, which was unlike the girl I knew and loved back in Brooklyn.

Earlier in the day, she had spilled a little wine on the carpet. She seemed overly fearful about it and kept apologizing until I shocked her by pouring some of my own wine on the carpet to show her it didn't matter.

"Are you crazy? Why did you do that?" she shouted.

"Because the carpet isn't important. I don't want you being upset about it."

I told her to spill more if she wanted to, but she just laughed.

"You're nuts, you know."

More important than any of that was my last thought before falling asleep. I had dreams and plans to go off on a sailboat, and having her back in my life could ruin those plans. But then I thought, *She used to be part of that dream; maybe we can share it again.* My head was spinning as much from my concerns as from the wine, but in spite of everything, I knew beyond a doubt that I still loved her and wanted her so much it hurt.

We met for lunch the next day and she talked of her exams. Again, I found her fascinating. Observing my genuine interest, she leaned over and kissed me for it. She had to get back to class and I had to get some work done, but I invited her for dinner the next night.

"Are you sure?

"Yeah, I'm very sure."

She smiled her old smile, and as she gathered her books, she asked, "Just for old time's sake or for now?"

I said, "For both, and hopefully for tomorrow as well."

We walked out to the parking lot, and for the second time in twenty-four hours, I watched her drive away and wondered if it was all a dream.

I had business meetings in Manhattan the next day, but after stopping at the markets, I came home early, showered, and opened a bottle of wine. I couldn't remember if Carol liked pesto, then chuckled out loud because pesto was non-existent in New York's Neapolitan kitchens in the sixties. With dinner ready to be cooked and the table set, I got the fireplace going and put George Winston's *December* on because she had liked it so much Sunday afternoon. Then I stopped and thought, *You're seducing her, maybe this isn't fair or the right time; she's vulnerable and not even divorced yet.* Remembering her passion and our lovemaking as teens, I rationalized my misgivings, *she's a woman not a child, and I want her badly.*

The doorbell rang, and any doubts I may have had about what she wanted evaporated in an instant as she put her arms tightly around my neck and kissed me with much more fervor than I anticipated. Still feeling archaically chivalrous, I felt a warning flag was in order and said, "Geez, don't do that again if you want dinner. I almost threw you over my shoulder and carried you off to my bed."

With her arms still around my neck, she tossed her head back and said, "Not on your life, buster. I'm hungry, and whatever you're cooking smells wonderful, so feed me first." Then, after kissing me again, she added, "Then you can whisk me off to your bed."

Sipping wine, we talked as she watched me put the finishing touches on the sauce while the gnocchi cooked.

"Green sauce. Is that an Irish thing?" she asked.

I laughed. "No, it's pesto. It's northern Italian, something neither of us knew about back in Brooklyn. I make it with fresh basil, olive oil, parmesan cheese, and pine nuts, but everyone has their own variation."

"I love that you cook. I hate cooking, but I don't mind doing dishes."

I replied absentmindedly. "Well, we'll make a good team then."

Her eyes welled instantly up as she stepped closer to me. "We always made a good team, Ron." Then, as tears ebbed from her eyes, she added, "I'm so sorry we broke up back then."

Before she could say another word, I took her in my arms.

"Look, I don't recall either of us breaking up with the other, so as far as I'm concerned, we're still going steady, right?"

Through tears she smiled and said, "Right!"

"Okay, no more tears. Have a seat while I get the pasta."

Toasting that we probably held the world record for going steady at twenty-three years, I watched as she tasted her first gnocchi dumpling.

"Well?"

She closed her eyes and moaned, "Mmmm, that is so good."

"Come on," I said, "be honest. I won't mind if you don't like it."

"No, I really love it. I wouldn't say so if I didn't because then you'd make it again, right?"

I smiled with satisfaction. "That's right."

With dinner finished, Carol started to clean up the table, but I embraced her from behind and kissed her neck, saying, "No, this time you get a free pass. We've been apart way too long. Tonight, I'll clean up after you leave."

She smiled coyly. "So you're throwing me out?"

"Well, no, but don't you have to go at some point?"

"I only have to go if you want me to. I told my mother I may not be home."

I kissed her neck again. Then, unclasping my hands at her waist, I raised them to caress her and said, "I want you to stay; I want you to stay more than anything in the world."

She leaned her head back against my shoulder, then put her hands over mine and pressed them to her.

"I've dreamed of this almost every night since the first time we made love in your apartment."

Turning to me, we kissed tenderly in the kitchen. Then, leaving everything where it stood, I shut all the lights as we went to the living room.

She went to sit, but I motioned her up. Standing just a pace in front of her, in the glow of the fireplace, I began unbuttoning my shirt.

She said, "Like in Brooklyn."

"Yeah, just like in Brooklyn!"

After hastily undressing, we stared at each other and as she had done years earlier; she left me breathless. She reached for me. I closed my eyes at her touch, which thrilled me in a way I hadn't felt since the last time we had been together. Then we made love in front of the fire with the same passion we shared more than two decades earlier. Afterwards, as she slept in my arms, the fire slowly burned out and the room chilled. I gently woke her. "Come on, wake up, let's get to bed."

Once in my bedroom, she said, "My things are in my bag. I need my jammies."

"You can use this bathroom; I'll get your bag, but no jammies. I want to feel you against me all night."

She smiled and put her arms around my neck. The feel of her body against me rekindled my passion. After kissing her, she said, "Hmmm, I haven't slept without jammies in a very long time." Then hastily added, "But I want to!"

Between Carol's classes and the time she spent with her children, it was difficult to see each other every day, but somehow we did, even if just for an hour or so. We talked frequently of the time we'd lost, so at the end of just two weeks, I asked her to move in with me. There were real obstacles and considerations. Foremost in her mind was what her children would think and how living with me might affect her divorce. In the end, we felt we'd already been apart too long, and with her parents' blessings, she moved in by the end of the third week. Our lives were forever changed in a way that only happens in fairytales.

Chapter 3
Can I Wear This?

Holding up the blouse, Carol asked. "Can I wear this?"

I said, "Do you mean do I like it?

"It's low cut. Do you mind if I wear it?"

"Sure, wear it. It'll look good on you."

She smiled nervously, then put it on.

I liked it immediately. "Wow, you look great, very sexy!"

She smiled again as she observed herself in the mirror. She did look great in it, but the exchange left me puzzled, and I realized I still had a lot to learn about this woman who, until a month ago, was only a vivid memory from a childhood romance. I watched her take off the blouse and, bordering between arousal and wonder, I was certain I wanted her back in my life again.

I asked, "Why did you ask me if you could wear the blouse."

"Never mind," she said.

"No, tell me. We've been through too much to have secrets."

She said her husband would never have let her wear something so low cut.

"Carol, you're a good person and a beautiful woman; showing some cleavage won't change that. Besides, you look hot in it and I like the way it looks on you! Do you like the way you look?"

Staring at me, she hesitated, then said, "Yes I do. I feel sexy in it."

I smiled. "That's because you look sexy it in! Now come here."

The following Sunday we drove to our old neighborhood in Brooklyn to visit my parents. It was all there: Carol's house, my apartment building, and the tree I had once tried to carve our names in as teens. Like us, it had all aged and changed. In doing so, it reminded us as much of the lost years as the joy and passion of our youth. Some doubts entered my mind and she sensed it.

"Is everything alright?" she asked.

I didn't answer her. Instead, I said we'd better get over to see my parents.

"Yes, I can't wait to see them again."

We walked along 13th Avenue passing many of the same stores we shopped in as teens. Carol even recognized a neighborhood character who seemed old even when we were kids, yet here he was still sitting in front of his bakery. I waved at him and he waved back "Hey, Ronaldo, long time. How are you?"

We talked briefly about the neighborhood, and he asked about my parents. Then, looking at Carol, he said, "Hey, whos'a the Madonna?"

Carol smiled. "You don't remember me? I used to buy bread here everyday."

It was like a light went on and a big smile filled his wrinkled round face.

He looked at Carol, and taking her hand, he said, "*Si*, I remember you!" Then, still smiling, he looked at me. "This was'a you chickadee!"

Putting my arm around Carol, I pulled her closer. "Yes, Mr. Gaidona, this was my chickadee!"

This brief exchange did more to bridge the gap of lost years than anything we'd done until then. It was a connection right out of left field; an old man from the neighborhood who remembered us as kids twenty-two years earlier.

Carol's reunion with my parents and brothers was joyfully tearful. They had always liked her, and I knew it had saddened them when we drifted apart as teens. We had a typical Sunday afternoon dinner with everyone shouting and competing for Carol's attention as my family did a verbal stroll down memory lane with her. For me, it was special to see her interacting through the din of voices and utensils clattering on plates, the way it always should have been. I watched her, knowing full well that I was already madly in love with her, and that somehow scared me.

We left Brooklyn, but instead of driving home, I headed into Manhattan. I had to talk to her, to be sure she really understood my plans to go sailing some day, but even as we drove, I knew it was probably too late. If it came to choosing between Carol and sailing, I knew I'd never let myself lose her again. Still, I hated that I might have to make a choice or give up my dream.

We went to a wine bar and laughed as we toasted Mr. Gaidona's memory. Then, after sipping our wine quietly a few moments, Carol asked, "Something is bothering you, isn't it?"

I said, "Do you remember what we used to dream about when we were kids sitting by the shore."

"Yes, of course, the bridge and having a sailboat."

"That's right. I've never given up on that dream, and my plan is to buy a boat when my son is finished with college and go cruising. I mean real cruising, not just weekend sailing around the bay."

A look of excitement came over her. "Really, Ron? Oh I'd love to do that," as if doing it was something that was already understood between us. I looked at her and thought half-jokingly, *Liar!* We stayed there for hours talking about sailing and faraway places. When we went home, she was eager to see all my cruising books and sailboat brochures before we went to bed. My last thought that night was that she really did seem excited. I began to think that maybe, just maybe I could have both worlds.

1986 was a difficult year for us. Carol was still going through a contentious divorce while trying to be an active mom and excel in nursing school. My own divorce had been finalized two years earlier, but I continued to deal with an endless stream of court motions over trivial issues. Nevertheless, it was also an extraordinarily happy time for us in many other ways. For one thing, we were together. If one of us had a bad time with an ex-spouse, the other would offer comfort in the form of reassuring words and a warm body in bed. What might have been an overwhelming problem during the day became insignificant in each others arms at night. Carol also finished nursing school that year, which was a real milestone for her. After making the President's Academic Achievement List several years in a row, she graduated Cum Laude. From a cautious housewife who constantly heard how stupid she was, she now emerged as a vibrant thirty-eight year old woman, eager to embark on a career. I was proud of her for such an accomplishment and could see the newfound confidence in her eyes.

In our very short time together, she was already evolving, and my only contribution was to encourage her to be herself. This was the woman I was meant to share my life with, and although I was enthralled with her beauty, my feelings for her went infinitely deeper. Carol was a confident woman of substance with a child-like innocence and a fascination with the world around her. She had a natural grace about her and a quiet nature that bordered on shyness, yet she could become seductive and wildly passionate in the blink of an eye.

Even sleeping, she captivated me. I woke one day for my morning run, a ritual I had been doing since 1978. Upon sitting up, I looked at her sleeping. Her eyes were closed, one breast exposed, the other an enticing rise under the sheet. As I looked at her, I recalled not only the lovemaking the previous night but also the tender kisses on my shoulder throughout all our nights. Then, without a thought of anything but an overwhelming need to embrace her, I slid back beneath the covers and pressed my body tightly to hers. Putting my arm around her, I whispered, "I love you."

She opened her eyes and smiled.

"I love you too, Baby." She began to close her eyes again, then they burst wide open. "Why aren't you going running? Do you feel alright?"

I pressed myself to her. "I feel fine. I feel really fine."

I did feel fine, but I didn't want to leave her. I never ran again.

Over breakfast months later, I read that Mama Leone's was closing its doors.

"How could they?" Carol asked.

It was a beautiful old restaurant in the theater district, an institution where thousand's of Broadway's biggest stars had regularly eaten. Now it was going to be torn down to make way for an office building. On the last Sunday of the last week they would be serving to the general public, we went back for the first time in twenty-two years. Even with reservations there was a one hour wait so we sat at the bar and ordered wine. Carol's excitement over being back there was infectious as she made nearby patrons privy to our fairytale romance. She even remembered the table we had been seated at two decades earlier, and the maitre de was only too happy to seat us there because, as it was then, it was still the worst table in the place. It made no difference. For us, like everything else we did together, it was magical.

Later in the summer, our friends, John and Denise, got married and had their reception at the officers club on Governors Island. As we danced, Carol said she loved the pomp and ceremony of a wedding on a military base. Still dancing, she asked if I remembered when we were kids and used to talk about being married at Fort Hamilton.

"Of course I remember," I answered.

We became caught up in the excitement of the moment and talked of our own romance while we danced on the patio, with the Manhattan skyline behind us. Still, I was reluctant to explore the subject of marriage and sensed her disappointment.

I still had some concerns and didn't know if she would even like sailing, let alone really go on a long cruise with me when I bought a boat. For me, talk of marriage was something to avoid right now. Still, there was a spark of adventure and spontaneity in her that always surprised me, and that night was no different. When the reception ended, we took the ferry back to Manhattan. As it arrived with a bump against the terminal, Carol asked if we could we go to Nathan's in Coney Island for hot dogs.

"Nathan's?" I asked incredulously. "We just had a five course meal and Nathan's is in the wrong direction. Besides, it's dangerous in Coney Island at night."

Looking at me with pleading eyes, she squeezed my hand. I knew arguments were useless, and forty-five minutes later, we were searching for a parking spot on Surf Avenue. Nathan's was where we stopped countless times as kids when returning home from the beach. The dogs and fries were still great, but it wasn't until we were standing at one of the dilapidated tables in the little alley off to the side that we realized how out of place we were.

Carol was in a nice dress and I was in a suit and here we were woofing down a pile of hot dogs in Coney Island at a time when there needed to be a cop on every corner. With our dogs and fries devoured, Carol cajoled me into taking her on the Wonder Wheel. We ascended one hundred fifty feet into the heavens on a machine that was built just fifty years after the

American Civil War! And if that wasn't enough for her, we made the next to last run on the Cyclone, an ancient wooden rollercoaster that we'd ridden as teens.

Tired and eager to get home, we walked toward our car. Carol suddenly yelled out, "Look, the carousel, we have to go on the carousel."

The building was unrecognizable, but there across the street where it had been for many generations before we were even born, was our carousel. I used to retrieve brass rings for her while riding on it decades earlier and wanted to get one for her now. We crossed Surf Avenue and gawked as the antique machine whirled around. Giant white chargers moved up and down on brass poles and the organ seemed to pipe out the same tune it had played in the past.

Entering the old building, I went to the attendant and asked, "How much?"

"We're closed; I'm just shutting it down."

I pressed a twenty dollar bill in his hand.

He said, "Climb aboard young lovers."

As we did, I saw there were no rings at the end of the arm extending out from the wall. "Where are the rings?"

"I put 'em away," he replied.

I waved a ten dollar bill and he inserted two brass rings in the snap at the end of the arm. As we had in years past, I climbed on one of the white chargers. Carol chose a black stallion behind me so she could watch me reach for the brass ring as the carousel went in endless circles.

The carousel began to turn and quickly gathered speed as the organ increased in tempo. I looked back and beamed as I saw Carol's face full of joy as her stallion rode up and down in an eternal pursuit of my white charger. A few revolutions later she yelled out above the sounds of the organ, "Go for the ring. Win me a ring."

I intentionally missed the first time and Carol laughed. "You old fart."

On the next rotation, I easily grasped the ring and held it over my head as if it was a golden prize, then yelled back to her. "Your turn!"

She grabbed it on the first try, and like me, she held it over her head. A moment later and eager to close up, the attendant brought the carousel to a stop.

"That's it, folks. I gotta go home."

My reward as we drove home while Carol slept was she never once let go of my hand. She clasped the brass rings in her other hand like they were made of gold, and I smiled the whole time, aware that I was truly happy for the first time in many years!

Summer was upon us and that meant sailing. I had previously chartered boats or sailed with a friend, but I was now considering a boat of my own. I wanted to sail more often, as well as test Carol's commitment. As we sometimes drove to boat yards, I looked for signs that she might be bored. I saw none. In fact, her enthusiasm seemed to increase. Then, on a Sunday morning while preparing breakfast, my friend Skip called from Connecticut to ask if I would crew for him that day.

"Can Carol come along?"

Skip said, "Sure," and after agreeing to meet at his marina by noon, I ran upstairs to wake her.

I felt a little guilty committing her without first asking, but she said she wanted to sail, so I thought, *What the hell? This is her chance.* I opened the shades and looked at her sleeping. She was beautiful. Her face angelic, her breasts rising and falling with each breath; it was impossible not to want her. I lay by her side and gently kissed her. She smiled a sleepy smile and reached for my hand and kissed it, then drew it to her. I wanted her badly, but if we didn't get going soon we'd be late.

"Princess, you have to get up; we're going sailing."

Still sleepy, she moaned as I caressed her. Then her eyes opened and she asked, "Sailing, how can we go sailing?"

After a brief explanation, she asked what time we had to be at Skip's boat.

"We have to be there at noon."

She frowned. "How long it will it take to get to there?"

"Maybe two hours," I replied.

Looking at the clock, she smiled wantonly as she pulled me to her. An hour later we showered together, then ran out the door woofing down buttered bagels and slurping coffee. Crossing the George Washington Bridge an hour later, Carol looked back to where Palisades Park once stood high above the Hudson River. Touching my thigh, she asked, "Remember the haunted house?"

I smiled, and after an hour of reminiscing about that day, we pulled up to Skip's marina in Norwalk, Connecticut.

Unlike the balmy day in New Jersey, it was windy in Connecticut. I estimated wind speed at over fifteen knots with higher gust. There were whitecaps on Long Island Sound, and I pondered if this was the best introduction to sailing for Carol. I didn't want her first experience to be boring, but I didn't want to scare her off either, and these conditions might prove to be a bit too much for her.

Skip and I were relatively experienced sailors, and *C-Shell*, a Bristol 30, was a seaworthy boat so I decided to give Carol a bit of excitement. We cast off and headed out. I cautioned her that it was going to get a bit rough and that if she got seasick, she should barf to leeward.

She said, "I don't get seasick, but what is leeward?"

I laughed. "That's the side of the boat away from the wind." I then added, "I'm glad you don't get seasick because I sometimes do."

Carol asked incredulously, "You get seasick?"

Somewhat embarrassed, I replied, "Yeah, but I've always managed it, even when in the Navy."

Sensing my defensive tone, she took my arm saying, "You must really love boats then, huh?"

"Yes I do, Baby. I like to think it's who I am."

She smiled, "I like that, Ron!"

By the time we cleared Sheffield lighthouse, we were feeling the full force of the wind and waves. Without sails up yet, *C-Shell* pitched wildly as we motored into four foot waves. Carol seemed to be doing fine as she propped herself against the cabin while I steered and Skip got the sails ready. He put on a harness and went forward to the mast to raise the mainsail and I headed *C-Shell* into the wind. We had already agreed to reef the main, especially with Carol aboard, but she seemed to be enjoying herself even when I steered the boat off the wind and we heeled considerably.

Skip returned to the cockpit, and I shut the engine. Even with just the reefed main, we were making three knots. He took over steering, and as I readied the jib, I answered a barrage of questions from Carol about what we were doing and why. I smiled, pleased with her, thinking that as we pounded into four and five foot waves, she wanted to know how I trimmed the sails. Once the jib was out, we were really flying on a starboard tack, taking waves right over the bow and port rail.

When one particularly large wave almost stopped the boat dead in the water and drenched us all, Carol asked, "Are we okay?"

Assured by Skip that we were fine, she smiled.

"Oh good, this is exciting!" Then over the noise of the wind, she asked if she could steer the boat.

Skip looked at me. I said, "Hey, it's your boat."

He looked at Carol. "Sure, come here."

I watched as he explained the effect of weather helm to her and how to steer by the compass and landmarks ashore. It occurred to me she wasn't just eager, but actually impatient to take the helm, and I thought, *What a woman! A few hours ago she was a sensuous siren in bed, now she is sailing into twenty knots of howling wind and pounding waves and laughing about it.*

Carol stayed on the helm for a half-hour. When it was time to come about and head home, Skip proved to be a generous host and offered to let her tack the boat to reverse our course. He explained the maneuver as a turn until the bow of the boat crossed the wind so that the wind would then be on the opposite side of the sails.

"We'll then trim the sails and go off on the opposite tack toward home."

In calm winds, this was a controlled and quiet process. In high winds and waves, it could be a noisy event as sheets were released and sails flailed wildly until they were trimmed. It could be intimidating to the novice sailor, and when not executed well in strong winds, it could fluster even an experienced hand. Skip explained all of this to Carol, then instructed her in the proper commands that she would call out to us, her crew. He told her that upon her command of, "Ready about," he and I would prepare to tack. When we each repeated her command in acknowledgment, she should then be sure we were clear of other boats, then give the command, "Hard a'lee." Skip would then release the leeward sheet as the bow came across the wind and I would rapidly sheet in the opposite line.

"Are you ready, Carol?" he asked.

I could see that she was nervous, but she looked at Skip and nodded her head, then bellowed out, "Ready about."

When Skip and I repeated the command to confirm that we heard and understood her, Carol looked around then yelled, "Hard a'lee," then she turned *C-Shell* into the wind.

When the jib was backed, Skip let go of the port sheet and all hell broke loose as the sail shuddered then flailed thunderously. The boat lurched through a wave and almost stalled as Carol became nervous and slowed the turn. She seemed frightened and looked to me for encouragement. I smiled and tilted my head to indicate she should continue the turn. Quickly regaining her confidence, she resumed bringing *C-Shell* to our new course. I trimmed the starboard sheet, and we began our run back to Norwalk.

After Skip took the helm, Carol and I snuggled in the cockpit. I asked, "So, what do you think about your first sail?"

"Oh I love it, Ron. This is so much fun!"

She talked excitedly until we got back to the dock, and I thought the day had been extraordinary. We had an exhilarating sail, and it was clear to me that she not only liked sailing, but she seemed to have the instincts and confidence to become a good sailor. For me, that removed the last vestige of concern about a future with her.

Chapter 4
URSAORION

We sailed several more times with Skip, and the more we did it, the more Carol liked it. Then, over breakfast one Sunday morning, she said, "We should buy a boat of our own."

I looked up from my cereal. "Really?"

She gave me her best smile and said, "Yes, really. What are we waiting for?"

I didn't need any encouragement. We spent the rest of the morning looking through boat classifieds. I wanted a traditional boat like a Cape Dory or a Bristol, but boats like that in our price range were scarce. Carol suggested we should drive around to marinas in the afternoon to get ideas about other boats. She was right; it was fun and we learned a lot, but more importantly for me, it was seeing her enthusiasm that made the day worthwhile.

With the arrival of fall, we went to boat shows and became even more determined to find a boat by spring. We needed a vessel under twenty-five thousand dollars that could accommodate all the kids at the same time for a weekend. The only late model boats I found that met that criteria were Hunter and Catalina, but these were not boats that would take us around the world. That day was far over the horizon so we reasoned that either would be a good choice for our immediate needs and to hone our skills.

We checked out boats everywhere; in the water, in dry dock, and even in backyards with cockpits full of dead leaves. We learned a lot in the process and refined our choices, eventually deciding on a Hunter 28.5 in a boat yard in Connecticut. The broker was in Northport, Long Island, so we took the ferry from Bridgeport to Port Jefferson. As we approached land, we left the warmth of the cabin and stood on deck in the winter chill, buffeted by the wind as we entered the narrow harbor inlet at Mt. Misery Point. We were greeted by a panorama of coves and anchorages to either side of the channel and as Carol snuggled tightly in my arms, we were already planning a visit there in the spring in our new boat.

The ferry continued another mile and a half to the terminal, which was adjacent to the beautiful Danford Inn and Marina. Carol became even more excited and asked if we could come here for a night by boat after anchoring out.

"Of course we can," I replied. "Maybe we could even have dinner in the inn."

"It looks so old; I bet they have four post canopy beds. Can we stay overnight?" she asked.

I smiled. "Sure," then jokingly added, "Maybe they even have mirrors under the canopy!"

With a devilish look, she asked, "Mmmm, have you ever had sex in a bed with a mirror on the ceiling?"

Hesitantly, I said, "Yeah, once back in my Navy days."

She smiled shamelessly. "Can we do that someday?"

I looked at her. "Oh yeah! With you it'd be a life experience!"

It was incredibly erotic to talk with her like that, and I drew her close as we explored the subject further while we waited for the ferry to dock.

Driving west on Route 25A to the broker in Northport, we discussed how much to offer for the boat. I said, "They're asking twenty-eight thousand. Let's offer twenty-five, that's about ten percent off the asking price."

Carol thought we should go lower so we agreed to offer twenty-two thousand. With that settled, she changed the subject back to the Danford Inn and canopy beds with mirrors. Twenty minutes later, we arrived at the dealership where Route 25A became Fort Salonga Road. We then kissed in the car for good luck and went inside.

After introductions, we went over the specifics of the boat and its equipment. Once we were sure of what we were getting, I offered twenty-five thousand, which the broker immediately accepted. Carol looked at me quizzically but said nothing. A half hour later with a contract signed, we walked out the door.

Carol immediately said, "Remind me not to talk about sex before we do business."

"Why not?" I asked.

"Because I thought we agreed to offer twenty-two for the boat."

I couldn't believe I did that. I thought, Of *course, the guy jumped at the offer.*

I said aloud, "Why didn't you say something in there?"

She seemed hurt and replied, "I thought you changed your mind because of the equipment or something. I'm sorry."

I realized I was passing off my own stupidity on her and that wasn't fair. I apologized, then said, "Hey, it makes no difference, we still got the boat!"

There was nothing we could do; we just signed a contract and had to live with my mistake. She hugged me. "Congratulations on your first boat, Baby." Then, tapping my forehead, she added, "It's kind of cute that we bought her after you were thinking with your little head instead of this one."

I smiled and congratulated her as well. "Let's go back to Port Jefferson. We'll go to the Danford Inn for lunch and celebrate with a bottle of champagne."

She replied seductively, "Why don't we just have lunch there, then go home for the champagne and to satisfy the passion the mere mention a mirrored ceiling has on you."

We drove back along Route 25A and, as we pulled into the parking lot, Carol jokingly asked, "Can you handle this?"

I smiled and asked, "What do you think?"

"Maybe we should skip the Inn and go right home?"

"Sounds tempting, but I'm hungry; let's eat first."

Then, walking into the restaurant, I said, "I have a better idea!"

We had a wonderful lunch, talking about all the places we were going to sail to in the summer, but we didn't go home. Instead, we bought a bottle of champagne, got a room, and celebrated our new boat in a four poster bed.

The rest of the winter passed slowly, but we poured over nautical charts and checked out marinas for *Ursaorion*, the name we had chosen for our new boat. With spring still two months away, Carol and I drove to Connecticut to see her. The boatyard was buried under a foot of snow as we traipsed around looking for her. We were excited beyond words, but not so much that Carol didn't find time to throw a snowball at me. In an instant, she was transformed to a little girl from Brooklyn as we hurled snowballs back and forth, laughing like kids.

It was a time of great excitement for us. After all, this was what we had dreamed of for most of our lives and it was all beginning to unfold. In the weeks before taking delivery of *Ursaorion*, we made frequent trips to boating stores to buy charts and things that we'd need to sail her to Staten Island. We spoke of nothing but our first voyage together, but then in typical Carol fashion, she sensed my son Christopher's disappointment that he and I wouldn't be bringing *Ursaorion* home.

After much discussion, she insisted that I make the trip alone with him. It was something that he and I had talked about long before she came back into my life, and she didn't want to ruin it.

I said, "Come with us."

"No, you need to do this alone with Christopher. Besides, it makes sense because I can drive you guys to Northport instead of us lugging our gear around in taxis and trains. Then I can meet you in Tottenville the next day."

I thought it was a wonderful gesture on her part and typical of her sensitivity.

Weeks later, as we prepared to depart from Northport, Christopher, who was fourteen at the time, said, "Dad, I know Carol wanted to come, but it was really nice of her to let us do this alone."

I told him it would be nice if he told her that himself, but I knew he might consider it being somehow disloyal to his mom. As we cast off lines, I told Carol we'd arrive at Tottenville Marina around four in the afternoon the next day, but that I'd call her when we got to Port Washington. She waved, then leaned forward and hurriedly kissed me goodbye once more. To my surprise, Christopher yelled to her, "Hey, what about me?" Before we drifted from the dock, Carol gave him a big hug and kissed his cheek. He smiled and said, "Thanks, Carol," and waved to her as we got underway.

As we motored out of Northport Harbor, I kept looking back at her waving from the dock. Christopher said, "Carol is really nice, Dad."

Surprised, I looked at him and said, "So are you, Chris, so are you."

Carol remained on the dock waving to us until we turned south around Little Neck Point and slipped from view. It was as if I was leaving her for a month, and I nearly turned the boat around just to see her one more time, but we had to make Port Washington by nightfall.

Leaving Northport Bay, we rounded the long, narrow spit of land that was West Beach. We raised sails and put *Ursaorion* on a broad reach out into Huntington Bay. The boat came alive as she sliced through the waves at six and a half knots and I turned the helm over to Christopher telling him to steer 315 m once we cleared R "8" at East Fort Point. Forty-five minutes later we rounded G "15" at Lloyd Point and Christopher hardened up to a close reach. As we sailed westward down Long Island Sound, I thought what a gift Carol had given us, as father and son made our first voyage together in our own boat. Three and a half hours later, we doused sails in Manhasset Bay and motored to the dock at Louie's Restaurant for dinner and an overnight stay.

The next day we were treated to a spectacular sight; the *USS Iowa* was riding at anchor in the upper bay and Christopher stared in awe as we raced passed the mighty battleship. Once under the Verrazano Bridge, we sailed inside Swinburn and Hoffman Islands, parallel to Staten Island's south shore. Three hours later, we rounded Ward Point at the southern most point of Staten Island and motored to Tottenville. As it came into view, there on the dock was Carol, waving and calling to us. The look of joy on her face made me tingle.

Tottenville Marina was on the Arthur Kill, a heavily industrialized waterway separating Staten Island from New Jersey. There were oil refineries and chemical plants, and it required a lot of motoring to get out onto the bay, but it meant new friends and a whole new social environment. Our new dock mates were mostly power boaters who seemed to have a distain for sailboats but Carol's good nature quickly won over even the most jaded of them and we were soon the only sail boaters in their tight knit group.

Ursaorion was assigned a slip furthest from shore where the deeper draft boats docked. This put us where the current was strongest, and to complicate matters, the slips were perpendicular to the current. Our new friends offered never-ending advice on how to dock our boat in these swift currents, and it didn't go unnoticed by me that Carol was always listening, while other wives chatted about shopping bargains and soap operas.

I practiced docking maneuvers when the current was at its slowest, then progressed to doing it at maximum flood or ebb. I'd get some disapproving headshaking from John, the marina owner, but also some approving nods from him as well. There was some friendly teasing by guys on the dock, but for the most part, few others took notice of our departures and arrivals. That changed one Saturday morning when Carol took the helm and I handled the dock lines.

Our routine had been such that I did all the marina maneuvering and Carol would take her turn steering once we were clear of obstacles. As we readied the boat, she asked if she could practice taking her out and docking. I was reluctant to relinquish my role, but the fact was, Carol was eager to learn and had a good instinct for boat handling. With a nod of agreement by me, she gave the order to cast off and smoothly took *Ursaorion* out of the slip into the fairway.

Once in the fairway, she brought the boat to a stop. Within seconds, *Ursaorion* was caught in the current's grip and began to yaw to port. Heads on the dock turned and I saw a flash of panic in Carol's eyes. I asked, "Do you want me to take her?"

"No, just tell me if I do something wrong."

An instant later she put the gearshift in forward and the helm over to starboard, briefly hitting the throttle as she had often watched me do. The burst of prop wash against the big spade rudder pivoted the boat so that our bow was once again pointing directly into the current. Carol smiled.

I said, "Take it out of gear and let the boat yaw again."

She did, and once again she recovered by using rudder and throttle.

"Do it again," I said. "Let her yaw to starboard this time."

She did, and again she recovered. A handful of guys gathered on the dock, most with their arms folded across their chest as if to say, "*What's this?*"

Carol said softly, "Everyone is watching."

"Yeah, just ignore them. Do it again! Do it five times each way."

Then I added, "I'm going below to pee."

Going down the companionway, I turned and asked, "Is that a problem?"

She laughed and said, "Yes it is, but go. I don't want you to wet your pants and have everyone think it was because I'm doing this."

I stayed below deck the whole time she practiced recovering from the yaw five times in each direction.

By the time I came on deck, a crowd had gathered. One of the guys yelled out, "Hey, Carol, can't you make up your mind which way you want to go?"

She flipped off her middle finger in his general direction and everyone burst out laughing. Tommy, the godfather of D-dock, said, "Guess she told you, asshole." Then turning toward us, he yelled, "Way to go, Carol girl."

She handled the boat and the heckler really well and I felt good for her, but I thought she should quit while she was ahead. She could just head out now and we'd go for a sail, but when I suggested it, she said she really wanted to be able to dock the boat and looked at me with eager eyes.

"Do you know what to do?" I asked.

"I think so. Yes, I'm pretty sure."

I said, "Okay, just don't forget to take it out of reverse or we'll crash into the dock.

She took a deep breath, eased up on the throttle, and an instant later we gathered sternway. A hush settled over the crowd as she deftly kept our bow into the current. When I thought she might be going too far, I whispered, "You might want to start your swing."

Without hesitation, she turned the helm enough to let the bow bear off, then put the gearshift in neutral. As the bow began to swing, she applied reverse and we gathered way. We swung faster, too fast. Before I could say a word, she turned the helm to port, put the gearshift in forward, and goosed the throttle just enough to slow the swing, but not remove sternway. She then went back into reverse and we glided into our slip as if she had been doing it for years.

"Damn," I said.

A brief lapse in her attention amidst the applause by her fans almost put our transom into the dock, but she quickly recovered and only a few of the pier head critics even noticed. I kissed her cheek, but not wanting to make too big a deal of her accomplishment and embarrass her, I simply said, "Take her out, let's go sailing."

As we motored down the fairway the crowd began to disburse, but a voice rang out, "Hey, Ron, guess you're out of a job, huh?"

In an exaggerated mocking tone, Carol laughed and then shouted back. "Captain Ron is always the captain; he's just got a real first mate now!" She laughed again, then accentuated her words with a jiggle and classic cheesecake pose which brought out a chorus of hoots

We had an idyllic summer sailing around Raritan Bay learning about the capabilities of our boat and honing our skills in fair weather and foul. The kids were with us every other weekend and if it fit in with soccer schedules, we'd take them sailing at every opportunity. Having them with us every other weekend was a lot of fun especially if we rafted with friends who also had kids. It made for tight sleeping quarters at night, but we made it work because we could then have the next weekend to ourselves. After so many years apart, we wanted time alone on our boat to enjoy intimate nights on deck under the stars or be free to lay in our bed under an open hatch in the moonlight. We would then make love and afterwards talk for hours about the places we were going to sail to someday.

CHAPTER 5
ITALIA

Luna's was one of my favorite restaurants in New York's Little Italy, but I might have talked it up a bit too much because when we arrived under the weathered green sign with the crescent moon, Carol asked in a disheartened tone, "This is it?"

Tugging on her hand, I said, "Come on, you're not gonna be disappointed."

We opened the door to a world of boisterous conversations, kitchen noise, and the clatter of utensils against dishes.

During dinner and well into a second carafe of wine, Carol asked, "Have you ever been to Italy?"

"No, but I've always wanted to go. We should go someday, maybe even charter a boat there."

Carol's face lit up and a barrage of questions followed.

"Can we really go to Italy? How long would it take to get there? Do you speak Italian? I've never been out of the country; do I need to get a passport?"

Her enthusiasm was testimony to her wanderlust; her cleavage a reminder of her capacity for sexual lust and I wanted to satisfy both.

I smiled. "Let's go then!"

In the spring of 1987, with her new passport in hand. we landed in Rome. There, we enjoyed three days of whirlwind romantic sightseeing and dined our way through the city's most popular restaurants. We left Rome all too soon, but on the way to Poistano, we stopped briefly in Pompeii, the ancient city that had been buried under volcanic ash for centuries. It was fascinating to see how people lived back then but it was the baths that captured our interest. There were dozens of well-preserved color murals on the walls painted more than two thousand years ago, depicting explicit sexual erotica. As I studied one particularly graphic image, Carol snuggled up to me from behind and putting her arms around my waist, she said, "Mmmm now that looks interesting. Too bad they don't have any private rooms here."

I turned and kissed her. "We do have a private room; it's waiting for us in Positano. Let's get going; it's getting late."

Positano is on the Amalfi Coast and sits on the face of a mountain that falls steeply to the sea. It is a village made for eating good seafood, drinking local wines, and romance! There, we spent a week in dreamy solitude. We strolled narrow alleys, dined in small trattorias and made love on our balcony at night. We also talked incessantly about our dreams and our future. From our hotel room halfway up the steep cliff, we could see the mountains of Capri in the distance and became increasingly impatient to sail there.

After leaving Positano, we negotiated the horrendous road traffic back to Naples. From there, we drove along the Via Nuova Marina to the charter boat waiting for us at Santa Luchia Marina at the foot of the old fortified town of Castell del' Uova. Carol strolled around the marina while I underwent a review of my sailing experience with the agent. Afterwards, we did a walk-through of the boat and discussed the weather forecast, which had been translated into English for us. The broker enthusiastically invited us to lunch, but I was eager to get underway, and after a hasty departure, we rounded the long breakwater before noon and set a southerly course for Capri.

As we motored clear of the harbor congestion, Carol said, "That was nice of him to invite us to lunch."

I laughed. "Carol, we've been in Italy almost two weeks. Haven't you learned anything? Men here are interested in one thing, sexy women! All he wanted to do was stare at your boobs over panini and wine!"

She laughed. "Get out; you think I look sexy today?"

Pulling her to me, I said, "You look sexy everyday and you know it, but right now take the helm, watch for traffic, and head her up; let's go sailing."

The Isle of Capri lay twenty miles to the south in the Tyrrhenian Sea. We could barely contain our excitement as we navigated through the busy marine traffic in the Gulf of Naples. High speed ferries of all descriptions darted about and large ships converged from every point of the compass. With the prevailing winds from the west and northwest, we were soon sailing on a broad reach, making six knots through the turquoise water. The farther we got from Naples, the clearer the water became, and even with our recent experiences in Rome and Positano, we sensed this would be the highlight of our vacation.

With only two days to spend in Capri, the broker secured a slip for us in the east basin at Marina Grande on the north side of the island. Marina Grande is actually the main harbor for Capri and has commercial docks as well as facilities for recreational boats. There, we did our first Mediterranean moor with our stern to the quay and our bow secured to a mooring. Fortunately, it was a weekday, so I found a spot with plenty of space between other boats. Tying up to a mooring made it much easier than anchoring, but even then I needed several attempts to get in.

Carol was eager to explore the town so after a romantic shower together in a unisex cabana, we took the funicular to Capri Town where we walked and drank our way through several carafes of local wine. The restaurants were outrageously expensive so we ate at a small trattoria near the marina, and because we were tired from the long day, we went back to the boat before ten o'clock. There in our cockpit, we drank wine and watched people strolling along the quay.

Carol said, "Italian women are so uninhibited, aren't they?"

"What makes you say that?" I asked.

"Just the way they dress and behave with men." Then she laughed and added, "Or don't dress!"

"Or don't dress?" I asked.

"Yes, don't dress. Tell me you haven't noticed half the women are braless and some women on boats today were topless."

"Of course I've noticed, but that's common in Europe, especially on the Mediterranean."

She smiled. "Do you like that, I mean a woman being uninhibited?"

I looked at her and said, "Yeah, I do like it, but where's this going, Baby?"

We were still discovering much about each other. After studying me a moment, Carol said, "I wish I could be like that. Uninhibited I mean."

"Well, sometimes you have to push the envelope to find new comfort zones, but I'm happy with you being just as you are." Curious, I then asked, "What is it you want to do?"

"Well, I'd love to sail or even sit here topless, but I could never do it unless I was really drunk I guess."

Then, with a lecherous smile, I said, "Why don't you enjoy your wine and start off slow, like sit there with your blouse open and let me ogle you?"

"You won't mind?" she asked.

I laughed aloud. "No, Baby, trust me, I won't mind."

A moment later, she sat in shadows of our cockpit with her blouse open seductively as she nervously talked with me.

"Feel good?" I asked.

She smiled. "Yes, very good!"

The next day we went on a tour to the Blue Grotto and Villa Jovis, which incredibly had once been a residence of the Emperor Tiberius. Splurging for an expensive dinner in Capri Town that night, we strolled back to the marina talking of love and our life together. After a breakfast ashore of strong coffee and lemon biscotti, we got underway and tacked our way into the Gulf of Naples against a fifteen knot northerly breeze. To my delight, Carol continued to push her inhibition envelope by sailing topless a few times until a ferry or another boat got too close. Watching her, I thought, *Life is beautiful!*

I asked her if she was doing it only for me, then said, "I love it, but I don't want you to be someone you're not."

"No, Ron. It's not just for you. I like pleasing you, but it's also for me. I've always felt this way, but I've been so uptight. I see women everywhere being comfortable with their sexuality, especially here in Italy, but even back home. I've never felt secure enough to let loose a little, but I do with you. Does that make sense?"

"Yes it does, and I'm glad you feel that way. Come here! You make it so easy to love you!"

CHAPTER 6
FIRST CRUISE

Like many boaters, our sailing was limited to week-ends and an annual two-week vacation cruise. Our interest didn't wane during the week, and we'd often spend evenings with a bottle of wine as I taught Carol to read charts and plot a course. When we covered basic piloting, she said what would come to be our customary comment regarding anything to do with math. "I wish I paid more attention to Mrs. Smith." We both laughed because Mrs. Smith had been our third grade math teacher.

In the spring, we put together an itinerary for a two week vacation cruise to Long Island Sound. Our plan was to leave our marina after work on a Friday and make a short trip to Great Kills where we'd anchor for the night. With just a week to go before vacation, we drove to the boat every night with stores and clothing for our voyage. At the end of each trek to the marina, Carol would ask, "Are you sure we have enough margarita mix and tequila?"

I laughed, giving her the same answer every time. "Yessss, Carol, we have enough for two months of heavy drinking with a college fraternity."

When departure day arrived, we scrambled home from work and we were driving across the Outerbridge Crossing to Staten Island by six o'clock. With the boat already fully loaded, we said goodbye to a few dock friends and got underway.

Not a zephyr of wind could be found, so we motored the twelve miles to Great Kills while listening to Jimmy Buffet, blotting out the sound of the engine and putting us in a vacation mood. Finding the channel in the dark, we then entered the almost totally enclosed little harbor and anchored *Ursaorion* by ten o'clock. Carol made snacks while I made a batch of margaritas, and we sat on the foredeck under the stars on the first night of our fourteen day adventure.

The music played a tropical beat as Jimmy sang songs of pirates past their prime and Havana daydreaming. Carol kissed me, then stood at the mast swaying to the music. I watched her intently, and under my stare, she slowly unbuttoned her blouse as she moved her head from side to side and I thought, *I could watch her for hours.* Her blouse fell to the deck and she took on a more alluring look as she embraced the mast and danced for me. I watched her for some time and couldn't help but wonder how I'd come to possess her. Then I smiled as I realized it was she who possessed me.

I was the breakfast maker ashore and afloat, so while Carol slept the next morning, I put on a pot of coffee and reached into the reefer to dig out eggs and bacon. It was still early, so I poured a cup of coffee and went into the cockpit to survey our surroundings. Great Kills Harbor is partially surrounded by Gateway National Park. If you didn't look west toward the yacht clubs and residential area, you would think you were in a secluded anchorage with woods on three sides and only the narrow channel to the south. True, there was a large mooring field with perhaps a hundred boats riding to mooring buoys, but if you squinted, this was a paradise right in the middle of New York City! I thought, *It might be fun to keep our boat here someday,* then wondered how one went about getting a mooring permit.

With that in mind, I went below to wake Carol but found her already awake and reading. She asked where I'd been.

"I've been out for a walk on the water, silly."

Laughing at my own words, I invited her to join me on deck. Still sleepy as she pushed back the covers, she plopped her head back on the pillow and rolled to her side. Her arms and thighs were aligned in perfect symmetry, and thinking of her dancing on deck the night before, I wanted to hold her in my arms again. I climbed into the V-berth with her. She sighed in contentment as we embraced, and pulling the covers over us, we lay there for almost an hour with hardly a word spoken between us.

Breakfast was al fresco in the cockpit. While eating, I shared my earlier feelings about the harbor. She agreed it was a lot nicer than being on the Arthur Kill, but added, "I wouldn't call it paradise. Maybe a nice refuge."

She then asked if we moved *Ursaorion* there, would I want to be in a marina or get one of the moorings.

"I don't know. I'll check it out, but a mooring might be fun and definitely cheaper."

I couldn't help notice the easygoing tone in her voice. She was a strong person, yet her voice conveyed an attitude of hey, "If this is where you want the boat, its fine with me."

Carol went on deck to remove the sail cover and ready the halyard and sheets while I checked the engine and the NOAA weather forecast on the VHF radio. She came below and stowed the cover, then quickly washed and stowed the dishes. Half and hour later, with her on the helm I prepared to raise the anchor. As I undid the snubber, I couldn't help but consider how smoothly we worked together, each knowing what was required of the other. We'd only had *Ursaorion* a few months, yet we were becoming a crew in the truest sense of the word.

Most of our anchoring evolutions were done with the throttle in idle so the helmsman could focus on using only the gearshift and rudder. We also used a few simple hand signals to avoid the common scene of the bowman yelling instructions and the helmsman shouting back. "I can't hear you; say that again."

Arm and index finger pointing up meant forward. Arm and index finger pointing down meant reverse, both signals being executed with the rudder amidships. If an increase in throttle was needed, it was indicated by a spinning motion of my hand. If helm was required, the same signals were used, but the arm was extended to port or starboard as required. Closed fist meant the gearshift in neutral.

I hauled in the anchor rode until it was straight up and down, then cleated it. At the same time, I signaled for Carol to go forward to break the anchor free. As she applied throttle, a slight vibration reverberated through the boat as *Ursaorion* tugged at the well set anchor. A moment later, it broke free. I signaled for neutral and hauled hard on the remaining chain, then facing Carol, I yelled in my best jaunty voice, "Anchor's aweigh." She knew this meant we were no longer secured to the bottom and that

Ursaorion was at the mercy of wind and current, so maneuvering the boat to avoid danger was now fully her responsibility.

As I coiled the rode and secured the anchor in its bracket, I smiled as Carol shifted into forward and applied throttle without any instruction from me. There was a barely perceptible lurch forward and we began to gather way. Walking aft, I joined her in the cockpit as she began a wide, sweeping turn that would take us to the entrance channel. Some folks on a beautiful moored boat waved as we went by and once we passed them, we could hear the man say to the woman, "Now why can't you do that?"

Carol beamed and softly asked, "Did I really do okay?"

"No, it wasn't just okay, you did great!" I kissed her cheek and told her to take us out.

She really had done well. I'd been sailing small boats for twenty-three years; Carol less than a month if you considered actual boat time. Nevertheless, she had an instinct for it and reinforced it by studying sailing books at every opportunity. More importantly, when experienced boaters offered advice or instruction, she paid attention to what they said. Then, once at home, she'd delve into my nautical books to separate fact from fiction. As she learned about sailing, I learned more about her. The more I learned, the more I liked, and I quietly hoped she felt the same about me.

The wind was from the southeast at only five knots. It was still early however, and the forecast was for continuing southeast winds, increasing to twelve knots by late morning. These were perfect conditions for a broad reach to South Street Seaport, so I decided to raise the main sail while still in the harbor. Carol searched for an open spot to head the boat up and then slowed to a crawl. When clear of several moored boats, she turned directly into the wind and promptly collided with a green channel buoy which neither of us had seen.

"Damn," I yelled.

I cursed under my breath as I ran forward to inspect for damage, even as the buoy continued banging its way along our hull. Fortunately, the only damage was some green paint on our hull, but it could have been worse, much worse.

"Damn it, Carol, you need to look before you turn. That could have been another boat. I've told you before, this shit is fun, but we're always just a dumb mistake away from disaster."

As her eyes moistened, I felt guilty and backed off. Carol was a smart woman and would one day be a good sailor, but she lacked experience and needed to be brought up short on mistakes like that. Nevertheless, I needed to soften my criticism and promptly offered an olive branch.

"Come on; don't go crying on me. This is just objective criticism. Just take it and move on because this boat crap is a constant learning curve, okay?"

She nodded and, without another word, looked about in all directions carefully and said, "I'm heading up."

I acknowledged her and stepped to the winch, preparing once again to raise the main. She brought the boat smartly into the wind and I hauled on the halyard, raising the sail to the peak. Once it was secured, Carol throttled up and steered a course for the channel.

We didn't speak about the buoy incident, but I watched her nervously look around in all directions and knew the lesson had set in. I glanced around at our position, then asked if she thought we might be approaching the channel a bit too closely to Crookes Point. Again, she looked around.

I said, "Look at the chart."

She looked at the chart and I pointed to where we were. She looked around again, then turned to starboard until we were steering almost due north.

By the time we entered the southwest leg of the channel we were an additional fifty yards from Crookes Point. Once fully in the channel, she turned to port and, still drifting to the right, she aligned us with the markers until she made the last turn to the southeast at the Green "9" buoy. This put us on a straight course for the remaining mile to the Great Kills entrance marker.

"Okay, why did you get farther away from Crookes Point when I asked you about it back there?"

"Because it gets shallow there!"

"Yeah it does, but that's not the only reason."

"Why then?" she asked.

"Do you want me to tell you or do you want to figure it out?"

"I want to figure it out, but can you take the helm while I look at the chart?"

I took the helm and without a word, she went to the chart. She looked back toward Crookes Point, then back at the chart again.

A second later she said, "I know. We were entering the channel on the inbound side. If we had been too close to Crookes Point, we might not have seen any incoming boats behind the reeds and could have crashed."

I smiled at her.

She smiled back. "I'm right. Right?"

"Yeah, Baby. You're right."

We got to the Great Kills entrance marker, a stone structure thirty-five feet tall surrounded by rocks with a flashing light at the top. When we rounded it, the wind was still southeast at around eight knots so I unfurled the jib and shut the engine. As soon as I did, Carol fell off the wind and set a course of 045m to the Verrazano Bridge. We weren't breaking any records in the light breeze, but we only had a twelve mile sail to Manhattan so there was no rush.

The boat was moving nicely with only the sounds of wind over the sails and water passing over the hull. I sat next to Carol and put my arm around her.

She said. "Don't apologize; you were right to get pissed-off at me. Turning without looking was a stupid mistake."

I said, "It was really careless, Carol." Then I laughingly added, "Besides, who said I was going to apologize."

We kissed and with few additional words, we sailed in the warm sun toward Brooklyn where we first fell in love a lifetime earlier.

The forecasted twelve knots of wind never materialized, so the best we could do was four knots as we approached The Narrows. Against the outgoing tide, that would put us in later than two o'clock, and I wondered out loud if we should crank up the engine.

Carol said, "Oh I'd really like to keep sailing; this is wonderful."

I knew what she was feeling. We weren't in a hurry; we were on a vacation voyage, a very short one, but a voyage nevertheless.

Arriving at South Street Seaport by three o'clock, we were assigned a place on their transient dock where several visiting boats were already tied up. This was a dilapidated series of floating pontoons secured to shaky pilings. The first pontoon was connected to shore by a narrow gangway that led to a wide open area littered with pipes, debris, and parts from machines, boats, and various restoration projects. I found the dockmaster and paid the outrageous hundred dollar fee. Only then was I told that there was no electricity. *Just great; welcome to New York,* I thought.

Back on the boat I told Carol we wouldn't have electricity, which meant no fans that night.

"So what. We're right here where all the sailing ships used to dock in the old days like the picture in your apartment in Brooklyn."

"What are you talking about? What picture?" I asked.

"The one you had on the wall in your bedroom."

It took a moment, but then I remembered a print from a calendar I once had, showing a row of old sailing ships with the Brooklyn Bridge in the background. "How can you possibly remember that picture?"

"I remember everything about your room from that day. You do remember that day, don't you?"

I smiled and drew her to me. "Of course I remember that day."

"You looked absolutely beautiful in my bed that day, and when I went to sleep at night, your scent was still on my pillow and sheets. I'll never forget that day with you, but calendars on my wall are not what I remember about that day."

"Oh yeah, what exactly do you remember about that day?"

I touched her breasts. "I remember these from that day!" After kissing her several times, I added. "And a lot of those."

She looked into my eyes. "I was always happy we made love that day, that you were the first."

"Me too, Carol. Me too."

She smiled. "I'm really glad you remember all of that, but if you still want to go ashore for a drink before we go to dinner, we'd better get going so save the frisky stuff for later."

Five minutes later, we were strolling to Pier 17 for margaritas. On the way, I said, "The other thing I remember about that day was that we planned it and made it happen like a precision commando raid. The roof climbing alone should have become a standard course of instruction at the CIA."

After two margaritas, we returned to *Ursaorion* to shower and then went to dinner at the North Star Pub. Afterwards, we went to Caroline's Comedy Club where we were treated to the best of New York's upcoming comedians. While strolling back to the boat sometime after midnight, my street senses kicked in as we came upon an obstacle course of derelicts under the elevated East River Drive. I told Carol if there was trouble, to make a run for the boat.

An instant later, there was a mumbling of foul language directed at us. In between several demands for spare change, two thugs placed themselves between us and the entrance to the dock where *Ursaorion* and safety waited. I could see the gate was wide open and thought, *Where the hell is the guard?* We walked around the troublemakers. They let us pass, but then followed us, along with two others who had joined them.

One shouted, "Hey, where ya going, fucker? We just wanna talk."

I was scared. I assumed we were going to be robbed at best or that they were going to physically attack us and go for Carol. We got to the fence but there was no guard. I closed the gate and looked for a way to lock it. There was none. As we walked briskly through the yard, I picked up a length of pipe and told Carol to run to one of the other boats on our pontoon and ask for help, then to call the marine police and Coast Guard on the VHF radio. She didn't want to leave me and hesitated.

I yelled, "Go, damn it!"

She ran down the gangway and across the moving pontoon floats. From out of the shadows a voice yelled out, "That ain't gonna help, scumbag; there's no way out!"

This was a nightmare. I felt better that Carol was out of harm's way and that I was free to fight without worrying about her. Pipe in hand, I backed down the gangway, which at this state of the tide was steeply inclined and seemed to be a good place to mount a defense. Then remembering the area above, I realized they'd have an endless supply of dangerous things to throw at me across the short distance between the dock and first pontoon. With that in mind, I backed up, careful not to fall as I stepped onto the second pontoon.

.The pontoons were bouncing and moving in the current and I figured that would work to my favor considering the thugs were probably drunk or high on drugs. Carol called out saying she reached the marine police on the VHF and a patrol car was on the way.

"Way to go, Baby," I yelled.

"What about you?" she yelled back.

"I'm okay; they haven't followed so far."

Continuing to back up until I was on the last pontoon, I was shocked to discover there were no other boats, just ours. Carol's head was poking out of the companionway and I yelled, "Where are the other boats?"

"I don't know, Ron. They must have left when we were at dinner."

I thought, *Geez, we're alone out here.*

I shouted for her to go below and lock herself in, feeling a tinge of relief as I heard the companionway hatch slam shut. The four thugs were still back by the gate shouting obscenities. They hadn't come close to the gangway, but until the cops came, I was going to stand there. If they approached, I was going to slam at least one or two of them with the pipe and hopefully knock them into the swift moving current. I heard the companionway hatch open and I called out, "Close the hatch, damn it." It closed once again and I yelled, "Now lock it."

A moment later, Carol was by my side. She had our emergency flare gun and extra flares.

"Here!" she said. "I don't think I can use it on someone."

I put the pipe down and took the flare gun from her, quickly inserting one of the flares into the chamber. Only then did I notice she was holding a heavy winch handle in one hand and a knife in her other.

"Go back to the boat."

"No. I'm staying with you!" she said.

Together, we stood our ground, her with a winch handle and knife, me with a 20mm flare gun. The thugs never ventured more than a few feet from the gate and when a police car finally pulled up, they faded into the crowd under the highway.

We watched as the cops went to the largest group, then another. When they went back to their car, one stayed and talked on the radio and the other came toward the dock. We walked toward him until I realized I still had the flare gun in my hand, something that wouldn't be a good idea for a cop to see on a dark pier after responding to an assault call. Taking several steps back, I laid it on *Ursaorion's* deck. As the policeman approached, he told us to step back to our boat. When we did, Carol put down the winch handle and knife next to the flare gun.

After telling him our story, he asked if we could identify any of the assailants. We said we couldn't, but that we weren't really assaulted, just harassed. He then assured us that those guys would not set foot on Seaport property, but that he would check in on us while patrolling the area. Then while taking our names as he wrote in his little pad, he saw our armament on the boat.

"You were going to use that flare gun to shoot a signal in the air for help, right?"

I hesitated. "Yes, sir, what else would I do with it?"

He said, "I don't even want to guess," as he turned and left.

It was only 1:00 a.m. when the cops left. The whole scary event had taken less than an hour, but it seemed like several. Shaken, scared, and knowing sleep would come hard, we considered leaving, but with the boat locked from below, we decided it was relatively safe. My biggest fear now was that someone would sneak down the dock and cast us off to into the river's current. Just in case, I ran a line from our outboard bow cleat to the end of the dock. I left it slack so it lay partially submerged in the water and couldn't be easily seen. If our regular dock lines were released, this one would hold us long enough to start the engine and get away.

Once in bed, the adrenalin dissipated and Carol began to cry.

"I was so scared."

"I was too, Baby, but you did real good. That was a brave thing you did."

She said, "I couldn't just stay locked up on the boat, not knowing what was happening to you."

I smiled. "The flare gun was brilliant; you were brave to bring it to me."

I put my arm around her. "Thanks, it went a long way to quelling my fear."

She got up on an elbow and asked, "Would you have used it?"

I looked at her and said, "Truthfully? One of the things that troubles me is that I was eager to use it! I was so pissed off that they put you in danger. Yeah, I would have used it."

She trembled. "I would have used the winch handle and maybe even knife if I had to. I may have moved to New Jersey, but I'm still a Brooklyn girl."

The next morning we went to the dockmaster and told him about the night before, complaining about the lack of security. He said they didn't have the money for security and there were no refunds! Carol shouted, "Asshole, a hundred dollars a night, and you don't have money for security. We could have been killed last night!"

Seeing we were getting nowhere, I told him where he could shove his docks, vowing never to return. Touring the sailing ship *Peking* later, we then made a half-hearted attempt to visit a few of the museum shops, but after the previous night, we just wanted to get away from there. Canceling our plans to go to Louie's for lunch, we went back to the boat and prepared to leave.

Getting underway at noon, we motored into the East River and under the majestic Brooklyn Bridge on our way toward Long Island. With no wind, we droned on under power until we cleared the Throgs Neck Bridge, connecting Queens with The Bronx. It was coming up on three o'clock and seeing we could make it into Manhasset Bay in a couple of hours, I called to Carol, "Hey, since we missed lunch at a Louie's in South Street, how about dinner at the Louie's in Port Washington?"

From down below I heard a cheery, "Aye aye, captain. That would be nice!"

Ten minutes later, we rounded Hewlett Point at G "29" and headed south into Manhasset Bay. A half-hour after that, we were tied up at Louie's dock. I gave Carol a big hug and said, "Considering all that's happened, you're like having a tough old sailor along, only you're pretty as hell and have great boobs!"

She laughed. "You're not too bad yourself, captain."

She kissed me softly, then told me to make margaritas while she washed up. Moments later as I squeezed limes for the drinks, I thought how lucky we were to be doing all these things together when just a short time ago, I didn't know where she was or what she was doing.

Dinner was great. We ended the night with a bottle of wine in the small gazebo at the head of the Louie's dock. The next morning I woke to a chilled cabin and the sound of rain beating down on deck. It was blowing hard from the northeast, so after putting on a pot of coffee, I started the heater. Its warmth radiated throughout the cabin and Carol moaned out a grateful, "Thank you, Baby. It's so cold. Where did summer go?" Then she asked in a pleading tone, "Do I have to get up?"

"No, stay in bed. I don't think we're going anywhere today."

Pondering our options over coffee, I considered that with twenty knots of northeast wind, even a short hop around Manhasset Neck into Hempstead Harbor would be rough. Looking at the chart, I could also see that once we got there we'd be in an exposed anchorage, so I decided to just move to the leeward side of the dock. There, the wind would be blowing us off the pilings and we wouldn't have to put up with the noise of our fenders worrying against the hull.

When Carol could no longer lie in bed as the aroma of coffee filled the cabin, I told her we were going to Plan B.

"What's Plan B?"

I smiled. "Plan B is what we do when it was blowing like snot outside." I added, "We'll stay put and find a nice place for lunch, maybe even go to a movie, then find another nice place for dinner or eat at Louie's again."

Smiling, she said, "Oh that sounds good," as she climbed out of bed.

I watched as she stood naked searching through the small pile of clothing for her bra. I thought, *She looks so delicately feminine, so beautiful; and yet, the night before last, she stood by my side ready to do battle with a winch handle and a knife.*

"Come here," I said.

She smiled and came to me, and I embraced her.

"I love you."

Kissing me with sudden passion, she said, "I love you too, Ron," then held me tighter and stifled a sob.

"What's wrong?

"Nothing is wrong; everything is right. I'm so happy we're together again and on our little boat just like we always dreamed we'd be." Then she coolly asked, "So what's for breakfast?"

"How about banana pancakes?" I replied.

"Yum, sounds great. So get into the galley and get cooking." She then went back to looking for her bra.

I said, "No bra."

"What?" she asked.

I laughed and told her I wanted to sit across the table from her at breakfast and watch her boobs jiggle.

She laughed. "You're such a pervert!"

"Pervert or not, you wear a bra, you don't get no stinking pancakes!"

Laughing again, she said, "Oh no, the dreaded pancake bribe!"

I dug out the pancake mix and bananas and watched her pull her sweatshirt over her head, my eyes fixed on her bare breasts, her eyes fixed on me with a devilish smile on her face. "You make me feel so desired...now go cook me banana pancakes. Maybe I'll give you a treat later."

The rain pelted our cabin top and the wind howled in the rigging, but with the heater on and galley stove going, it was very cozy aboard our boat. We talked briefly about the Seaport incident over breakfast, but it made Carol uncomfortable so I changed the subject. With the almost soothing sound of the rain on deck, we lounged around talking and reading, then played a game of Monopoly. Afterwards, we took a long, hot shower together in the confines of *Ursaorion's* small head. At one o'clock, we went ashore and walked in a light rain until we found a cafe to eat lunch. From there, we went across the street to the local movie theater and watched Mel Gibson annihilate hordes of bad guys in *Lethal Weapon*. Still raining, we returned to the boat. When the cabin was toasty warm again, Carol said she was going to take a nap. I sat at the salon table and picked up my book.

Again she said, "I'm going to take a nap."

"I heard you, Baby!" Then, I looked up from my book to see her suggestively smiling and gently moving her body.

"Did you forget I owe you a treat?"

A day later we departed Manhasset and sailed to Oyster Bay, then on to Northport as we played the winds, sailing along the north shore of Long Island. Carol was like a sponge, soaking up knowledge, and I could see her sailing skills were improving daily. She also became more comfortable with her sexuality and never lost an opportunity to show her seductive side. As the days passed, we sailed farther east and she'd often surprise me by coming on deck wearing only a flimsy tank-top. We'd kiss and tease each other until we anchored for the day. Once, after anchoring, we made love even before making margaritas, and Carol jokingly said, "I wonder what pre-margarita sex means."

I laughed, then got serious. "It means we really love each other, that's what it means!"

Our easternmost port before heading home was Mystic Seaport Museum, a partially restored, partially recreated whaling village on the shore of the Mystic River. Commercial marinas were plentiful, but since the Seaport offered transient slips, we wanted to stay there in order to experience a touch of what life was like in the nineteenth century. The village itself is a magnet for tourists during the day, but after closing, it transforms into a ghostly town, lit by gaslight lamps casting long shadows on the colonial buildings, docks, and narrow streets.

Sailing hard on the wind, we crossed Long Island Sound from Mattituck. I knew this area from my time aboard submarines and as we approached Fischer's Island Sound, I hoped Carol would get to see one. There were none to be seen that day and we continued sailing until we left the North Dumpling day marker, then Intrepid Rock to starboard. We then proceeded into the channel for Mystic, which began north of Ram Island Shoal.

Mystic channel is well marked, but it is narrow and requires careful attention as it snakes through shallows and moored boats, then on up to the railroad bridge. The river continued to narrow, but after transiting the bascule bridge in the village of Mystic, the Seaport unfolded to starboard.

I was excited, but Carol was completely thrilled as we docked in what could have been a journey back into time. Once we checked in, we toured the seaport all that afternoon and the next day, holding hands as we strolled the narrow streets.

At night, the only other people around were some folks off boats and the security guards, through whose gatehouse we used to leave and re-enter the village when we went out for dinner. After sundowners aboard *Ursaorion* our last night, we went to dinner at a nearby restaurant. The food was great and the drinks large, and when we left arm in arm, a bit unsteady on our feet, I laughed and said, "We're like a couple of drunken sailors returning to our ship."

Carol giggled. "We are a couple of drunken sailors returning to our ship."

Still laughing, we staggered through the cobblestone streets to the dock. I suggested we get some wine from the boat and go back to the gazebo in the middle of the wide grassy commons area. The whole village was in flickering shadows of varying hues cast by the gaslight lamps, making for a romantic and sometimes eerie setting. Walking hand in hand, I swung our arms toward the gazebo and said, "It's really dark there; maybe I'll have my way with you."

Carol laughed and called me a slut. Then laughing again, she slurred her agreement to the idea. "But furst let's gets the wime."

"The wime?" I asked, laughing.

"Yeah, thas what I said; les go gets the wime."

I retrieved glasses and a bottle of wine from Ursaorion and we walked back to the dark gazebo, sitting right in the middle on the polished wooden floor. I poured the wine, and we toasted our voyage. Then, lying side by side on our backs, we talked about how life must have been for people who lived in a village like Mystic. Carol pondered aloud how difficult everyday tasks must have been without things we took for granted like washing machines and gas stoves. Then, in one of her instant topic changes, she asked if I thought people fooled around back then.

"Of course they did, or none of us would be here now!"

Giggling, and still slurring, she said, "Thas why I lub to ask you stuff. You're so smart!"

I laughed hard, then we kissed passionately, interrupted a few times by a fit of Carol's giggling over her question about nineteenth century people fooling around.

Laughing intensely one moment, she became serious the next.

"I lub you so much, Ron!"

Then, as she kissed me fervently, I fumbled with the buttons on her blouse until it was open. She sat up, took it off, then unhooked her bra. I removed it and let out an audible gasp at the sight of her. Embracing, we fell backward to the floor again. We kissed a long and tender kiss, and as Carol turned her head to offer her neck to me, she shouted, "Whas that?"

Startled, I said, "What's what?"

She sat up, crossed her arms over her breasts, and with real fear in her voice said, "That!" as she pointed to the edge of the field.

I peered into the darkness and there, not fifty yards away, I saw a white apparition moving in our direction. It seemed to be a few feet high and slowly undulated as it came our way.

Carol said, "Oh shit, it's a ghost."

I said, "Don't be silly," but I didn't sound convincing because she stood up and backed away while calling for me come with her. With my eyes still glued to the object, I reached for her clothes and, in doing so, knocked over the wine bottle. The apparition stopped dead in its tracks.

Carol said, "Oh shit, it heard you."

"What the hell is it?" I said.

Whatever it was, it then pitched forward and gained speed. As it got closer, two red eyes became discernable. Mystified, and now getting a little scared myself, I gave up on gathering Carol's clothes and retreated with her. She let out a muffled sound as we backed against the far rail of the gazebo.

A second later, I half-laughed, half-shrieked, "Jump. Come on, jump quick; it's a big fucking skunk!"

Laughing hysterically, we ran far around the gazebo toward our boat, unable to catch our breath from running and laughing so hard. We looked back to see the biggest skunk in the world go under the gazebo, which was probably his home in the first place. As it crossed the grassy commons in the darkness, we had only been able to see its broad white stripes reflected by the flickering gaslight lamps and it truly looked like some strange apparition.

Carol was bare from the waist up, so I gave her my button-down shirt and we continued to laugh hysterically.

She said, "Go back and get my clothes and the wine glasses."

"Are you nuts? If that thing sprayed me I'd stink for a month."

I told her I'd get the stuff in the morning before the seaport opened. Holding hands, we continued walking towards our boat and I'd catch fragmented glimpses of her as we wove our way along the deserted docks under the flickering gas lamps.

On her, my shirt was more of an open robe than a shirt, and I could see the gentle curves of her breasts swaying with each step she took. I stopped directly under the subdued light of a lamp and stepped back to look at her. She looked beautiful. I took her in my arms and we could have made love right there on the dock. Instead, we walked to our boat clinging tightly to each other as if trying to make up for all the years we'd been apart.

I returned in the morning for Carol's clothes and the wine glasses, and with Mystic and the great skunk caper in our wake, we sailed in a fresh breeze on a westerly course toward Essex, a bucolic village on the Connecticut River with a long maritime history. Carol learned from the cruising guide that there was an old inn there with a restaurant and pub where an Irish group sang bawdy sea-shanties on Monday evenings.

Excitedly, she said, "It's Monday, we have to go. Okay?"

"Sure, Baby. That sounds like fun."

Essex was a twenty-eight-mile sail from Mystic. After tacking up Long Island Sound, it wasn't until two o'clock that we rounded R "8", a bell buoy that lined us up with the wide entrance of the Old Saybrook breakwater at the mouth of the Connecticut River. From there, we sailed up to the railroad bridge which was closed, so we tacked back and forth impatiently until it opened. Then, in a dying breeze, we coaxed three knots from *Ursaorion* to take us under the high I-95 bridge and on to Essex, two and a half miles farther up the river.

As we rounded Hayden's Point, the beautiful village unfolded before us and sounds of boat building and other activities wafted across the anchorage. Carol became visibly excited as we closed on Essex Island Marina where we hoped to find a transient slip. "Call them on channel 16," I said.

Carol continued to point out sights she recognized from the cruising guide. I laughed, thinking, *She is so animated and vivacious and can be so aware of her body, but at times like this, she is so innocent in her enthusiasm.* Both of these traits stirred my senses.

After contacting the marina on VHF, they directed us to a transient slip. In doing so, we discovered why the marina was called Essex Island Marina. It was really an island separated from town by the sliver of water we were then navigating. We followed the docking instructions and speculated on how we would get to and from town. Our question was answered by three blasts of a horn, signaling that a boat had her engine in reverse. We turned to look for its source and saw a small passenger ferry backing down as she began her transit from the marina to the town dock just seventy-five yards across the channel. Even that got Carol's interest and she said, "Oh this is going to be so much fun."

I called out to her. "Only you can get excited about taking a boat ride after being on our own boat all day."

We checked in, showered, then dressed for dinner. I wore my usual khaki shorts and golf shirt, but Carol looked enchanting in a long, wispy, turquoise skirt and a sexy white tank top with spaghetti straps. Again, I considered her contrasting images; *standing her ground alongside me on the dock at South Street or looking extraordinarily sensuous tonight.* I held her hand and smiled as she stepped off the boat, then kissed her softly and whispered, "You look absolutely beautiful."

"Thank you, Baby. From your lecherous tone I suppose you'd rather stay on the boat than go to dinner, but too bad, I'm hungry."

I laughed. "You're safe for the moment. I'm hungry too, let's go."

Once in town, we went to the Black Seal for drinks where we met Jack and Mary off a boat out of Milford, Connecticut. They were sailing to Mystic Seaport, so we told them about our close call with the resident skunk there, then talked with them about our respective boats and the night life in town. Mary slurred, "The main ting is, don't get drunk and miss the las ferry; it sops running at ereven-thirty."

We thanked her for the advice and after finishing our margaritas we then strolled to the Griswold Inn for dinner. "The Gris," as locals call it, was over two hundred years old. There was an elaborate sign over the entrance that proclaimed, "*Opened on the Fourth of July, the First Fourth of July.*"

After dinner, we went to the crowded taproom, which had to be one of the best bars in the world as far as nautical décor goes. It was originally a schoolhouse, but in 1801 it was moved on big log rollers to its present location and then connected to the inn. We ordered mugs of beer and sang along heartily with the rest of the patrons as an Irish trio belted out bawdy sea shanties.

The songs grew increasingly risqué and entertaining, and when we weren't singing, we laughed continuously. This was fun; I knew we were in our element where people chatted up one another as if they had been friends for years. I watched, amused as Carol was chosen from the crowd along with a young girl to go on stage and dance a jig with two of the singers while the third strummed his banjo and played a harmonica. Carol danced with wild abandon and a wide smile and when they stopped the music, they released the girl and asked Carol to stay on stage a bit longer.

I could see without the music and dancing she was slightly embarrassed, but when she looked my way, I smiled and tipped my drink to her and she relaxed.

"So, lass, you're a beauty! Tell me you're not already taken so you can run off to Tahiti with me on the morning tide!"

Carol giggled and pointing to me, saying, "I'm very taken."

The banjo player frowned and rolled his fingers over the strings. He asked if she was having a good time.

"Yes, I'm having a great time, but we have to leave soon because the ferry back to our marina stops running at eleven-thirty."

Letting out an exaggerated moan, he said to the audience, "Ere now, are we going to let this beauty leave us on account of a silly ferry? Who's got a boat and can give these folks a ride back to their marina?"

A dozen hands shot in the air with shouts of "Me, me!"

"It's settled then; you and your man can stay till closing, right?"

Carol laughed. "Right; that would be nice."

He turned his cheek and said, "Gimme a wee kiss here."

Carol kissed his cheek, and he held her hand to guide her as she stepped from the small stage while receiving a round of applause. Her smile went from ear to ear, and I felt good for her, really good for her!

True to her word, we stayed until closing and there was no shortage of offers to take us to the marina. We accepted a ride from a guy who seemed most sober, and fifteen minutes later, he deposited us on the other side of the narrow waterway. We slept late the next day then departed around eleven. When departing Essex, there is a wide but shallow cove to starboard named South Cove. Then, going further south and passing under the I-95 and railroad bridges, there is another cove. This is confusingly named North Cove. After passing through a narrow but well-marked entrance, it extends back almost half a mile and offers an anchorage with moorings in five and a half foot depths. If you had continued south on the river, you would come to another cove named South Cove. I thought, *Whew, navigator beware.*

Seeking a night of solitude but thinking it was too late to make a run for our next port, we took a mooring at North Cove and enjoyed a quiet night together. After dinner, we sipped red wine and ate Carol's favorite, dark chocolate, in the cockpit while pointing out constellations to each other using our pocket guide to the stars. Carol said, "You know I'd never leave you for any man, but if a spaceship came down and offered me the chance to go up there with them, I'd have to go." Then she quickly asked, "Would you go with me?" As corny as her question was, I could see she was serious.

I put my arms over her shoulders and replied, "I'll never lose you again, Carol, not even to little green men from Mars. Yes, Baby. I'd go with you." As preposterous as the whole conversation was, I knew I would go with her anywhere, and we fell asleep in each others arms with that thought in mind.

The plan for the next day was a forty-eight mile sail to Norwalk, so we woke at dawn and in the haste of getting underway, I fouled the mooring pendant in our prop. The only way to free it was to dive in the water and either cut it or untangled it. I dove on it for fifteen minutes without success and became chilled and exhausted from the effort and cold water. Carol insisted on taking a turn, and after putting on a long sleeve shirt to help keep warm, she dove beneath the boat. She was able to free it on her third dive and she climbed the swim ladder with a look of satisfaction that almost concealed her shivering. Free of the mooring pendant, we motored into the Connecticut River with Carol bundled in a large beach towel under the dodger. I turned south and thought, *She is really everything any sailor could want in a woman. What are the odds that I'd be with her again and that she'd also be this way?*

Once clear of the breakwater and with the wind at ten knots out of the northeast, I put *Ursaorion* on a westerly heading and said out loud over the sound of the engine, "There's plenty wind to sail." Without the need for further explanation, Carol understood my intentions. She took the helm and looked around to see if other boats were about. Then, after looking to the masthead to gauge the wind direction and seeing I was ready, she looked around once more, and then brought *Ursaorion* smartly into the wind. As she did, I hauled hard on the main halyard and raised the big sail. Then, when I let out on the traveler, she throttled back and shifted into neutral and said, "Falling off," and slowly turned to port until we were on our original westerly heading. The main filled instantly and *Ursaorion* gathered speed again. I waited a moment, then unfurled the jib and sheeted it in until it also filled. Carol propped herself up as our boat heeled while surging forward under the power of the large headsail, gaining speed with each passing second until we were making six knots as we approached Cornfield Point Shoal.

We sailed along the coast, passing several places along the way we considered spending the night, but with the wind kicking up to fifteen knots, we broad reached at almost seven knots and made the Norwalk Islands by four o'clock. This was where Carol had her first sail with Skip, so she wanted to take over the helm as we approached Cockenoe Harbor. Leaving Pecks Ledge to port, she entered the channel between Betts Island and Grassy Hammock rocks, sailing over some shallows near G "11" then R "12" where we joined the main channel into Norwalk. She headed up and we doused sails, then motored to Norwalk Cove Marina where we had first sailed together on *C-Shell*.

We had a great at dinner at DeRosa's but consumed too much wine and sambuca and both overslept the next morning. With our departure delayed too long to sail to Long Island as planned, we decided on Stamford where we enjoyed an uneventful night anchored behind the breakwater. Refreshed, we got an early start the next day and sailed all the way to the Statue of Liberty where we anchored near a dozen other boats. The anchorage was unprotected from the wakes of passing ships and tugs, but it was spectacular! With a gentle breeze out of the north, *Ursaorion* lay to her anchor with the dazzling New York skyline off our starboard bow and the brilliantly lit Statue of Liberty on our port quarter.

Except for the large tour boats that came increasingly close to the crowded anchorage, it was all very romantic and we enjoyed a late dinner in the cockpit surrounded by the magnificent vista. Opening a second bottle of wine, Carol came to my side so we could view the more romantic New York skyline together. Her scent was intoxicating, and in moments we were kissing passionately until she grew a bit uneasy under the extremely bright lights reflecting from Lady Liberty behind us. We went below to the privacy of our cabin, and after an hour of shared intimacy, we eventually drifted off to sleep to the gentle rocking of our boat.

As we slept, a shrill ship's horn penetrated the night, reverberating in our cabin and jarring us from our slumber. Our boat was brightly lit from outside, and I could hear the rhythmic rumbling of a ships engine getting louder. Jumping out of bed, we scrambled on deck, believing we were about to be run down by one of the cruise boats we had seen earlier. I stumbled into the cockpit. Carol halted halfway up the ladder behind me as we were caught in the beam of a probing searchlight on the vessel hurtling outrageously close to us. Hundreds of partygoers stared down at us in shocked silence as we stood in the bright light, both stark naked.

This was a dangerous and stupid maneuver on the part of the ship's captain, done only to give his passengers a closer view of the statue. We were in a designated anchorage, and as a professional mariner, he should have known better. I stared into his face as he stood on the bridge of the passing vessel. Still oblivious to my nudity, I was about to protest when instead, Carol gave him the international signal of two raised middle fingers while shouting, "Asshole!"

Some of the crowd on deck looked over their shoulders to the captain who stood speechless as he gazed down upon the bare-breasted woman flipping him two middle fingers. As quickly as we had been disturbed, the searchlight dimmed and the red, white, and green vessel was gone, leaving a large wake to roil the anchorage. As darkness returned, a voice rang out from an anchored boat behind us.

"That was good, lady, but if that son-of-a bitch does that again I'm going to shoot his sorry ass."

He might have been serious because there in the cockpit of a sailboat, stood a man with a rifle raised over his head. I fully sympathized with the guy, but I thought, *Shit, can we even pass through this city without a life threatening event happening to us?*

CHAPTER 7
GREAT KILLS

Over the winter of 1987, I applied to the Coast Guard for a mooring permit in Great Kills Harbor. It was approved and we were soon making trips to the area to inquire about the necessary ground tackle. We found Ruch's, a small marina that sold, installed, and maintained moorings. They also provided racks for dinghy storage, which solved the problem of getting to and from our boat. The following spring, we moved *Ursaorion* to her new home, mooring K-24, a six-hundred pound mushroom anchor about half a mile from the dinghy dock at Ruch's.

Located at the northernmost end of the harbor, it was secluded, but that was fine with us because it gave us a lot of privacy. There was a small beach less than fifty yards away with the rest of the wide arcing shoreline solidly bulkheaded. This would be very different from the nice slip we had at Tottenville, but we considered it to be yet another part of the boating experience.

The major downside was that we needed a dinghy to get to our boat. Believing it would be safer, Carol thought we should get an inflatable dinghy, but I didn't want to spend five hundred dollars on something I thought could easily puncture. Besides, I reasoned, an inflatable would mean we'd need to buy an outboard engine.

I said, "A good, hard dinghy can be easily rowed in almost any condition."

We scanned the classified ads in a local boating magazine and found a used hard dinghy for one hundred and fifty dollars. It sounded like a great deal, but when the guy dragged it out of his garage, I thought, *Geez, you don't get much for a hundred and fifty dollars.* It was all fiberglass without any supporting ribs, just a three quarter by two inch strip of wood for a gunnel. It had clearly seen better days, and I could see that Carol wasn't impressed. Although usually reserved in situations like this, she openly voiced her doubts about the dinghy. "Ron, I don't think this will hold both of us; it looks really flimsy."

I sized it up and began having my own doubts. The seller obviously wanting to get rid of the thing said, "Okay, a hundred dollars, and I'll throw in the oars!"

I said, "Deal."

We loaded our new toy into the back of the station wagon and I thought, *Damn it's heavy!*

I knew Carol wasn't happy with any hard dinghy, let alone this fiberglass eyesore. Nevertheless, as she did in most bad situations, she was willing to make the best of it saying, "Can I name it?"

"Sure, what do you have in mind?"

"How about a French name like, *Le Garbage?*"

I looked at her and frowned.

"Okay, I was just kidding. How about *Tonto?* You know, the faithful companion?"

I liked it. "Okay, *Tonto* it is!"

We took *Tonto* directly to Great Kills and struggled to carry the heavy boat from the car down the long dock to the dinghy rack. Carol griped, but I reasoned that in the future, we'd only have to slide it off the rack into the water.

"Do you wanna go for a ride and try it out before we put it on the rack?"

She said sarcastically, "No, it's dark; they'll never find our bodies!"

"Okay, Carol. You made your point, now give it a break. You'll see how good it'll be when we go to the boat Saturday!"

Saturday arrived, and I was eager to show Carol how we did it in Maine. We drove to Great Kills with two small duffle bags full of clothes and a fair amount of food for the weekend. Add to that a case of beer, ice, a case of water, and a bottle of rum and we were good-to-go! We slid *Tonto* from its rack into the water.

"Get in; I'll pass you the gear."

She said, "Not on your life! You get in first and I'll pass the stuff to you. If it doesn't sink, then I'll get in."

"It's not going to sink!" I exclaimed.

"Then why do you have lifejackets?"

"Because it's the law, now stop it."

Securing the painter to a cleat on the dock and in my most seaman-like manner, I stepped onto *Tonto's* un-ribbed hull. It bellowed downward like a loose drum. I thought to myself, *Shit, I've never been in a dinghy that did that.* Holding fast to the dock just in case, I put my other foot in, half expecting it to go right through the flexing bottom. It didn't, and I looked smugly up at Carol.

"See, smartass. Its fine, now pass everything to me."

Once loaded, *Tonto* seemed to give up an awful lot of freeboard, but I still felt confident we'd be fine.

"Okay, step aboard and sit on the stern thwart."

Carol was at best a hundred twenty pounds soaking wet, but once seated, the stern seemed dangerously low in the water. I rearranged some of the heavy stuff, moving water, ice, and beer toward the bow, but a voice sounded in my head, *You know better than this!* Voice or not, I was about to throw twenty-five years of sea going experience out the window. Carol offered me one last shot at salvation.

"Why don't we do this in two trips, Baby?"

"Two trips? It's almost half a mile each way to our mooring. Don't worry, we'll be fine." And with a gentle push off the dock, I rowed out into the harbor with Carol clinging to the lifejackets.

Shit, it's pretty choppy, I thought to myself.

Carol the mind reader asked, "Isn't it kinda choppy?"

"We're fine," I replied.

I continued to row, but incredulously, the gunnel bent with each stroke. I rowed harder. The gunnel bent even more, and worse, the screws holding the oarlock in place loosened. I thought, *What a piece of crap.*

Carol said, "It's getting choppier. I'm putting my lifejacket on."

"Good, put it on. How far to the boat?"

"We're about halfway."

Shit, I was getting tired rowing.

Another hundred yards and water began splashing over the bow as the chop increased. I thought, *Probably caused by power boats scooting around the harbor.*

I yelled out. "Damn power boats!"

Carol pointed to a nice inflatable dinghy, riding high and dry with an outboard engine, and she said, "You mean like that one?"

I ignored her and kept rowing.

"How far?" I asked.

"We're getting close."

"Close, what the hell does close mean? I'm rowing my ass off here."

She giggled softly. A moment later, a wave broke over the bow. It soaked our gear and added a lot of weight to the already heavy dinghy, further reducing her freeboard. *Son of a bitch, we're gonna sink*, I thought, as I rowed furiously.

Carol began bailing out water, but more was coming over the bow than she could bail, and we sank lower still.

"Throw the case of water overboard!" I shouted.

"Are you serious?"

Still rowing, I said, "Like a heart attack, and throw the beer and ice over too!"

We were shipping water with every wave, and as Carol did her best to jettison our provisions, we drifted right by *Ursaorion*. The one chance I had to reverse course and get back to our boat was lost when in turning *Tonto*, I got us beam on to the waves a millisecond too long and we were swamped.

Tonto began to sink quickly until her gunnels were not quite completely under water at which point, she hit bottom with a thud. We had drifted to the beach. Carol began laughing and said, "We should have waited a few more minutes before throwing the beer overboard."

I laughed as well, and we sat there like two fools in our semi-sunken dinghy in eighteen inches of water with clothing and grocery bags adrift as if floating in a bathtub. Then Carol shrieked, "The beer. Quick, get the beer!"

The case of beer floated not far away, the tops of the cans barely visible on the surface, until it washed up on the beach twenty feet from us. I got up, retrieved a six pack, pushing the remainder further up onto the sand. Then, sitting down with Carol in the swamped dinghy, I said, "Here, have a beer!"

A guy came by in a motor boat and asked if we were okay. We burst out laughing again and Carol said, "Do we look okay? Wanna beer?"

The guy looked offended and motored off shaking his head.

After finishing our beers, I walked all the way around the harbor to get our car while Carol watched our things. Several hours later, *Tonto* was in our front yard, its future forever sealed as a flower planter. We then drove to West Marine and bought an inflatable dinghy and a three horsepower outboard engine, both of which gave us excellent service for almost ten years. Carol never said, "I told you so," but she warned me that this was a story that needed to be told many times. She never missed an opportunity to tell it in dock bars and at boat gatherings from Maine to Florida but always in a manner that didn't humiliate or embarrassed me, which was just her way.

Carol continued to develop good boat handling skills, but she lacked the confidence to sail in the busy channel. Once in the harbor, however, she liked to take the helm and sail among the boats in the mooring field, saying it gave her a sensation of speed as compared to just sailing on the open bay. As she tacked her way through the moorings, we saw a group of boats that sometimes came into the harbor to take any available mooring. They partied all weekend, and although I sometimes thought they were loud and boisterous, Carol always liked the music they played and the fun they had.

I said, "It looks like they've taken a mooring near us again." Then added, "Shit, we're in for another loud night."

A few moments later, Carol said they might actually be on our mooring. I took out the binoculars and looked. Sure enough, they were on K-24. I went ballistic, and even though too far away for them to hear, I began yelling at them to get off our mooring.

Carol told me to calm down as she tacked *Ursaorion,* then approached our mooring at a fair turn of speed. As she closed the distance, I ranted aloud, but the people on the floating party just waved back. Then, in a drunken chorus, they yelled for us to raft up with them. I yelled, "Raft up my ass, that's my mooring; get the hell off my mooring."

Carol began to bear away from them, but I told her to get closer. Then, as she sailed down, their starboard rail only a boat length away, I heard one guy yell out, "Hey, it's a broad driving the boat."

That was it; I went bonkers. "Hey, asshole, I'm calling the marine police. Get off my mooring now."

After some grumbling by a few of the revelers, they then cast off our mooring, still tied to each other in a six boat raft-up. We watched as they drifted down on the first open mooring they came to whereupon they took hold of its pennant and began partying again as if nothing had happened.

Once we were secured to our mooring, I put the sail cover on and Carol made drinks. "What a bunch of turkeys."

Carol remained silent. I said. "What, you don't agree?"

"They're just having fun, Ron. Maybe it would be nice if we had boat friends again like we did in Tottenville. Wouldn't it be fun to raft-up like that with friends?"

"But Carol, just listen to them; we can hear their music from way over here!"

It wasn't so much that she said, "Yes, we can." It was more the way she said it, as if she liked it. I felt a little defensive. "So my music isn't good enough anymore?"

"I love the music you play, but sometimes I like dancing to something other than Jimmy Buffet and to be among friends."

Ever so sensitive to my feelings, even if I was being childish, she came to me and hugged me.

"Baby, I love you and wouldn't trade the times we have alone for anything, but maybe if we were at a marina again we'd make nice friends to sail with."

She disarmed me of course, and once I calmed down I said, "I guess you'd rather be back at a marina."

"That would be nice, but maybe one in New Jersey closer to home, and maybe one with a lot of sail boaters!"

Again, a bit too defensively, I said, "Wow, it sounds like you've got this all worked out." We talked it out over margaritas with the sounds of music from the raft-up drifting across the harbor and I admitted that I had occasionally considered going back to a marina as well.

"I guess we could still use the mooring for weekends, but it would be nice to have the security and comfort of a dock again and even make new friends. Okay, we'll look around at marinas over the winter and move in the spring!"

I wasn't prepared for Carol's reaction, which bordered on tears, and I felt bad that she had been unhappy on the mooring all this time.

CHAPTER 8
A REALLY BIG BOAT

Retiring from the Naval Reserve, I wanted to spend my last tour of duty on a ship, so in the spring of 1988, I requested and received orders to *USS Boulder,* an LST scheduled to do amphibious landing exercises for a month. Because I was eager to participate, Carol wrestled with how I could want to be with her, yet also be so keen to go to sea for thirty days. She wasn't complaining, she was confused, and I couldn't help but be impressed by her effort to understand me without being judgmental.

I tried to explain how seamen faced the dilemma of being drawn to the sea but also desired to stay home with their loved ones, but it sounded hokey. I showed her my favorite poem, *Sea Fever*, by John Masefield and after reading it only briefly, her eyes moistened.

"Carol, it's not that emotional."

"It is for me," she said

Then putting the book down, she recited the opening line from memory. "'I must go down to the seas again, to the lonely sea and the sky, and all I ask is a tall ship, and a star to steer her by.'"

She looked at me and held my hand. "I read that years ago and thought of you. I used to take my kids to the beach, and while they played, I would read poetry. When I read that poem, I looked to the ocean and wondered if you were out there somewhere." She put her arms around my neck. "I missed you so much, Ron."

I kissed her neck and whispered, "I missed you too, but we're together again, forever and always, just like I used to sign all my letters. I promise, after this, I'll never leave you again for such a long time."

After reporting aboard ship, I called her from one of the ever present pay phones on every Navy pier. It was almost eleven but she answered on the first ring as if she had been waiting by the phone for my call. She was full of questions about the ship and my quarters, and I answered each one because she was so full of enthusiasm. She teasingly switched gears and tantalized me by describing what she was wearing and all that I would be missing that night and every night for the next month.

USS Boulder went to sea two days later, and for the next three weeks we participated in amphibious exercises at Onslow Beach, North Carolina, with Marines. Returning to Little Creek at the end of the exercise, I was told we wouldn't be going to sea again before my tour was over, so I decided to bring Carol down to spend the last weekend with me. I made the airline arrangements and got a motel on the beach, and when I called to tell her, she burst into joyful tears because I would do it with only a week to go before returning home.

She flew down the next afternoon and our reunion at the airport was as if I had been gone for months. After a romantic dinner at Blue Pete's on Shipps Bay in rural southeastern Virginia Beach, we sat on our hotel balcony with a bottle of wine watching the surf and talked of things to do the next day.

"Could we go sailing?" Carol asked.

Sailing hadn't occurred to me, but I loved that the idea was hers. I kissed her cheek and said we could check out the Navy recreation marina at Naval Station Norfolk in the morning

After being checked out by the dockmaster the next day, we sailed into Willoughby Bay in a fourteen-foot daysailer. This was Carol's first experience in a small open boat. It probably would have been a better way to introduce her to sailing, instead of Skip's Bristol on a snotty day on Long Island Sound. While still in the sheltered boat basin, I explained that the person on the sheets would have to shift sides each time we tacked and I reminded her to duck under the boom when she did.

A moment later, we sailed into the bay in ten knots of wind and quickly heeled over in a gust, almost putting the gunnel underwater. Carol nearly panicked.

"We almost went over!" she shouted.

I laughed. "I don't think so, Baby. I'm sorry; I should have said you might also have to shift your weight in the puffs! This is different from a big boat; there isn't any ballast so the crew has to move around to keep things balanced."

After a few practice tacks, Carol regained her confidence and we ventured into Hampton Roads where waves added another dimension to her first open boat experience. When she got the knack of tending the sheets and shifting from port to starboard during tacks, I offered her the tiller.

"Oh I don't know, I might capsize us."

"Come on, you'll do fine. It's what sailing is all about; being close to the water in a fast open boat."

We changed positions and Carol was soon laughing aloud as she held tightly to the tiller in a series of maneuvers and tacks for the sheer fun of it.

"Oh, I love this! It's so much fun. Can we go further out?"

"You're really getting into it, huh? Okay, but stay out of the channel to the east, we'll round Fort Wool, and peek into Chesapeake Bay."

She asked, "Could we get to the ocean from there?"

"Yeah, but it's out of bounds for these boats, but trust me, I think the bay will be more than we can handle in this boat."

As I suspected, once we rounded Fort Wool the wind increased and things really kicked up. We began taking some water over the bow, so much so that I decided to turn around and head back into Willoughby Bay. Carol said she was having fun and wanted to go farther out and I got annoyed and shouted, "Turn around!"

My words stung her, and she brought us about without a word. The jib luffed wildly as the boom swung over, missing my head by inches. I glared at her as I trimmed the jib and got control of the mainsheet. "Take us back!" I shouted.

Once I calmed down, I added, "Okay, this is boat talk, so no damn tears. Firstly, you don't know shit about this boat. Number two, compared to me, you don't know shit about sailing in these conditions so you'll do what I say when you have my life in your hands. Number three, don't ever tack a boat without letting me know you're going to do it. The damn boom could have broken my neck!"

We sailed back in near silence. I felt really bad about my outburst, but Carol had to understand that fun on a boat could turn to disaster in an instant.

"I'm sorry I yelled at you, but it was very choppy out there and an open boat like this can be easily knocked down in waves like that. Then, when you came about without warning, the boom could have popped my skull or we could have easily been swamped. You violated everything I've taught you."

Her eyes were moist, but she kept her composure. "You've never yelled at me like that before."

I stared at her a moment. "I'm sorry, but you've never screwed up so badly before! I told you, this is boat talk. You can stay pissed off at me, or you can learn from it and we can enjoy the rest of our weekend. What are you going to do?"

I could see she was thinking about her response.

She said, "I'm sorry, I was just having so much fun. And I'm really sorry I came about without giving a command. That was a big screw up!"

I took her hand in mine. "Yes it was, but let's leave it behind and enjoy the rest of our weekend, okay?"

She smiled through moist eyes. "Okay, Baby."

On Sunday I brought her to *USS Boulder* for a tour of the ship and to have brunch with some of the other officers and the captain. Carol wore a modest dress, but she looked radiant in it.

"Do you think this is okay to wear on a ship?"

"Yes, Carol, you look wonderful!"

She was a nervous wreck as we drove to the base. This was a new experience for her and the formality of entering a naval base and boarding a warship did nothing to calm her. Once aboard and walking around, I pointed out various parts of the ship and answered her countless questions.

"Are you sure other women will be there? How does the ship carry so many Marines? What if the captain asks me a question? What should I say?"

I smiled and held her hand. "Relax, you'll be fine. Just be yourself."

Upon entering the wardroom, a sudden silence ensued as Carol stepped through the door. Looking stunning, she captivated all hands and became the center of attention. As the chatter picked up again, the assembled officers made small talk with her about her visit to Little Creek. A moment later, the captain came in and after introducing himself; he invited Carol to sit next to him, dispatching me to the far end of the long table.

From that vantage point, I observed her as if in a theater. There were a few nervous glances my way, but in a few minutes she transformed from a tense spectator to a carefree conversationalist as she bantered back and forth with the captain. When he asked her how we met, she told our story from the very beginning, and I smiled inwardly because I knew that once she left, I'd be taking some ribbing from them. Mostly, I was proud of how she adapted in what many would have felt was an intimidating situation.

Carol flew home that night, and I was discharged from *USS Boulder* the following Friday. It took all of my willpower to stay close to the speed limit as I drove across the Chesapeake Bay Tunnel-Bridge toward home. I had offered to take her out to dinner to celebrate the occasion, but instead, she insisted on making something very special at home. With a seven hour drive ahead of me, all I could think of was her waiting for me, and I wondered what she meant by "making something very special."

I pulled into our driveway at nine o'clock. Thinking the house seemed quiet and dark as I walked to the front door, it suddenly burst open and there she was, greeting me in a sheer chemise that took my breath away. She wrapped her arms around me before I could even put my bag down and we kissed in the doorway for a long time. Then, lifting her off her feet and with her legs wrapped around my waist, I carried her inside. I could feel the warmth of her body through the flimsy material, and I didn't want to let her go. As we stood there embraced, I once again vowed that I would never leave her for such a long time. She looked into my eyes, and with hers moist with tears, she asked, "Promise?"

I said, "Yeah, I promise!"

We kissed again, and looking around I said, "So what's all this?"

A dreamlike glow came from the fireplace which contained dozens of burning candles. On the floor directly in front of it was a pile of comforters, blankets, and big cushions from the couch. The coffee table was covered with a white cloth, and there was a sake bottle and two small cups and place settings with two crisp white napkins in holders.

She said with a sweep of her arm, "This is Carol's Ichi-Ban restaurant. Now go shower while I get dinner ready. Come back with your kimono on."

I tried to kiss her, but she patted me on the butt and said, "Go!"

Then, as I walked up the steps, she said, "Hey, sailor, the meal is free, but the chef expects a really nice tip."

I smiled and hurried along to my shower.

Returning downstairs wearing my kimono, I followed the wonderful aroma emanating from the kitchen. I expected to see her still wearing the lingerie as she prepared dinner, but instead, she was bundled in a robe.

Disappointed, I asked, "What happened to the sheer thing?"

Scurrying around with several pans, she said, "It's not for cooking, silly boy; do you want me to burn my boobs?"

I laughed. "No way, Baby! I definitely wouldn't want you to do that. Can I help you?"

"No. Go have some sake and make yourself comfy. I'll be right in."

As I sipped the warm sake, I lay against a big cushion and basked in the subtle warmth of the candles. A moment later, she came in with two big platters, one with a colorful assortment of sushi and sashimi, the other with a variety of tempura seafood and veggies. "Wow, this is incredible!" I said.

She had clearly put a lot of time and effort into preparing the meal. I leaned over to kiss and thank her, but she stood up saying, "One more thing," and then went back to the kitchen. When she returned, she was wearing only the sheer chemise again and carried a tray with another heated bottle of sake.

Sitting alongside me, she refilled my cup with the warm wine and then I filled hers and we toasted to being together again.

"Did you notice the sake bottle and cups?"

I replied, "Ah, I thought they were new."

I looked at them, and then burst out laughing as I realized the figures painted on the ceramic cups and bottles were classic Japanese erotica. I caressed her thigh and said, "You devil you!"

She kissed me. "I knew you'd like them!"

As we feasted, I thought, *God, she is so beautiful.* I'd been living with her for three years, yet I couldn't take my eyes off of her as we ate and talked. Everything about her excited me and as I watched her movements, I remembered something I once read about an Italian artist describing a beautiful woman. I told Carol it made me think of her.

She asked, "What did he say?"

"He said the summation of her parts was such that nothing needed to be added or taken away, everything worked in perfect harmony."

Then I added, "Whoever that artist was, he was describing you."

She smiled and said, "I love you, Ron," then kissed me softly.

Returning her kiss, I said, "I can't wait to be overly generous with your gratuity for the sensual meal you prepared."

CHAPTER 9
ROAD TO MARRIAGE

A month later and thirty thousand feet over the Pacific, we flew west for a vacation in Hawaii. It was a place we had fantasized about often when watching *Adventures in Paradise* on television as kids. We were going to spend several days on Oahu, and then meet up with our friends Tom and Diana on the big island of Hawaii. We stayed at the Royal Hawaiian and, even though I'd been to Hawaii many times, it was my first stay at that palatial hotel. It was a dream come true to be there with Carol.

During the day, we did all the tourist things including an outrigger ride near Diamond Head and surfing lessons at Waikiki. There was hardly a moment we weren't holding hands or touching each other and as we lay in the sand with the warm Pacific lapping at our feet, we kissed like we were teenagers at Coney Island. In the evening, we went to see Don Ho at the Hawaiian Village. Carol wore a silk muumuu and I wore a matching shirt. We looked like hokey tourists, but we didn't care. She looked stunning, and my matching shirt marked me as hers.

Don must have fallen on hard times because before the show he was greeting guest in his dressing room and posing for photos for five dollars. Carol was like a star-struck teenager and got right in line. I laughed. "I guess you want to see him."

"You know I do. Don't you remember I used to play his songs all the time?"

"Yeah, but the place is filling up and we won't get a good table."

She said, "Please, Baby. It'll just be a few minutes!"

A moment later, we were next in line, and when he saw Carol, he extended his arm to her.

"Whoa, come here to Uncle Don."

Carol looked ravishing, and he was enthralled with her. She took his hand and, without any inhibition, sat on his lap. I suppressed a smile as he looked at me and said, "Hey, brotha, don't get mad but your wife wants to sit on my lap."

I said, "It's okay with me, besides she's not my wife."

He smiled. "What's wrong with you, brotha? How come you don't marry this beautiful woman?" Then, sensing he might be getting into a sensitive area, he quickly changed the subject. "Okay, take a picture."

As she got up to leave, Carol gave him a big hug saying, "I'm Carol."

He said, "You, beautiful lady, I'll never forget and if this haole doesn't marry you soon, you call me, okay? Aloha."

Later, back on our hotel balcony Carol talked for hours about the Hawaiian Islands and how they were formed, about meeting Don Ho and his performance and then about us.

"I really love our life, Ron. So many of our dreams have already come true, but wouldn't it be wonderful to be married someday?"

Stupidly missing her point, I agreed that it would be nice; someday. At that moment, I was only thinking of her in my arms and how much I wanted her. Later, with her silk muumuu in a heap on the balcony floor, we went inside to sleep. I considered bringing up the subject of marriage, but regretfully didn't.

The next day we went to the Pearl City Tavern where I used to hang out in my sea going days. The food was always good, but the real attraction is the bar where dozens of monkeys play behind a glass partition. We had planned to do other things, but we got lightheaded on a variety of Hawaiian drinks while watching the monkeys behind the bar. She laughed like a little girl, and once again I thought of many facets. Her childlike amusement watching the monkeys, and her unbridled passion the night before on the balcony.

When she was a teenager, Carol had fantasized about a waterfall in Hawaii, but she couldn't remember its name or which island it was on. I knew of Waimea Falls Park near Haleiwa on the northwest shore and we drove there early the next morning. The parking area was empty, and as we walked to the falls, her eyes lit up. "That's it, that's the waterfall!"

"Are you sure?"

"Oh yes, Baby. That's it. Oh I can't believe you found it for me!"

She jumped in my arms and hugged me. "I didn't find it. It was the only one I knew of."

"It makes no difference, you found it, you found it. Come on, we have to go in!"

The forty-five foot high Waimea Falls is where divers re-enact Hawaiian warrior games by climbing the slippery rocks of the waterfall, then diving from various ledges into the deep lagoon below. Between shows, visitors can swim in the cool water and even walk directly under the falls, which for Carol was a childhood dream come true. The water was very cold, but it didn't inhibit her from swimming and once under the falls she reverted to her licentious side.

"Come here!"

I went to her and found it even colder standing under the falls. We kissed, then, with one last look to be sure we were alone, she hastily removed her bathing suit and stood before me.

"Carol, are you nuts?"

She said, "Take yours off!"

"This is crazy; it's broad daylight."

"No one is around. Hurry, I'm freezing."

I looked around to be sure no one had come by, then took off my bathing suit.

She immediately put her arms around my neck and drew me to her and we stood embraced with tons of cold water cascading over us for several minutes. I was getting numb with cold, but I tilted her chin up and kissed her softly on her lips. Above the thunderous roar of the falls, I said, "I love you, Princess."

"I love you too, Ron!"

After swimming back to the beach, we shivered as we walked back to our car and Carol questioned me incessantly about how the water could be so cold on a tropical island.

Drying off I said, "So what was that all about?"

"You mean getting naked under the falls?"

"Yeah. Not that I didn't like it, but sometimes you really surprise me."

She said, "You won't believe this, but when I saw a photo of that waterfall when we were kids, I wanted to do that with you."

I laughed. "We were maybe eleven or twelve years old then. You used to dream of being naked with me under a waterfall?"

She gave me a sly look and said, "Yes, and not just any waterfall, that waterfall! Then she added, "I used to think of doing more with you but back then, I wasn't sure what doing more involved."

At night we made love. Afterwards, she lay in my arms and as I held her, Don Ho's voice echoed in the recesses of my mind. *What's wrong with you, brotha? How come you don't marry this beautiful woman?* Remembering what Carol had said on the balcony about how it would be wonderful to be married someday. I thought, *What a dummy! You barely mumbled agreement; you must have made her feel like crap!* I wanted to say something to let her know I did want to marry her.

"Carol?"

No answer. I looked to her lying on my shoulder; she was sound asleep.

Our Hawaiian vacation was over but the subject of marriage came up very subtly in various forms over the next several months, but neither of us really addressed it head on. We had been living together for almost three years and it was abundantly clear we were madly in love. I was *absolutely* sure I wanted to be married to her, but we had settled into a comfortable relationship and simply hadn't seriously talked about it.

Then, one evening after dinner, Carol asked if we could talk.

"Sure, what's up?"

She came to me on the couch, took my hands in hers and asked if I believed she would sail around the world with me. I looked at her face and could see she was serious. In her eyes I saw the love of a woman who would truly go to the ends of the earth with me. In an instant I thought of all we'd done since she came back into my life and I knew beyond a doubt that she was part of my dream, not a threat to it.

Smiling, I said, "I guess this means you want to get married."

With a hint of tears in her eyes, she said in her own special way, "That would be nice, Ron."

I was almost speechless and couldn't think of how else to say it, but in my most sincere voice, I said, "I love you. I've loved you body and soul almost my entire life. Will you marry me, Carol?"

Tears flowed over her cheeks. "Yes, Ron, of course I will. It would make me very happy to marry you."

We talked for some time about the day in the wine bar in Manhattan. She said she knew I had fears of giving up my dream, even though it had always really been our shared dream.

"I knew the only way to quell your fears was to show you over time, rather than just tell you."

I said, "Well, even back then, I would have chosen you over any dream. Nothing else really mattered to me as much as being with you" Then added, "Let's open a bottle of champagne then get dressed and go someplace nice for dinner to celebrate."

She took my face in her hands.

"Why don't we open the champagne, get undressed, and just stay here to celebrate?"

We did just that, and looking back through the prism of time, we did more talking than lovemaking that night. We had always been able to express ourselves verbally, but that night, it was like we were reciting the most romantic poetry to each other.

In the following days we talked of little else but our wedding plans. As kids, we wanted a military wedding and Carol asked if that was still possible.

"Of course we can, I'm a naval reserve officer. If you want to, we can do it!"

With that settled, it made the location for the wedding and reception an easy choice, the officers club at Fort Hamilton. The Fort, as we called it when kids, was an historic Army garrison under the Brooklyn side of the Verrazano Bridge. We had played there as children, and we felt that it was yet another link to our past. It would be a perfect place to be married.

At the end of June, we went to Manhattan to choose an engagement ring and select wedding bands. Carol believed the engagement ring was silly, but I wanted her to have one. I thought of it as a symbolic way to blur the earlier course our lives had taken and recreate what should have been. She eventually agreed, but she chose one of the smallest and least expensive stones and settings.

"Ron, you said yourself, it's just symbolic. Besides, I'd rather spend the money on our honeymoon!"

She did insist on special wedding rings though, choosing a decorative nautical knot known as a Turks Head. It consisted of overlapping layers of three strands of gold intertwined with each other. She told me she had seen it in one of my sailing magazines when she first moved in with me.

I laughed. "So you've had this whole wedding planned from day one, huh?"

She gave me a devilish smile. "Yes, Baby. I've had it all planned since day one. Way back in 1958 when I was ten years old!"

The only requirement we had for a honeymoon destination was that it be romantic, relatively close by and it had to be on the ocean. We searched brochures and found dozens of resorts, then in a fit of inspiration, we booked the Bitter End Yacht Club on Virgin Gorda in the British Virgin Islands. It was an all inclusive resort accessible only by boat and emphasized sailing and water activities, offering private cottages rather than a hotel type environment.

Eight days before our wedding, Hurricane Hugo swept through the Caribbean with hundred and forty mile an hour winds and a sixteen foot storm surge! We tried to cancel the honeymoon but were told there were no cancellations because their facility suffered very little damage.

I said, "Shit, we might be living in tents when we get there."

Carol laughed. "Screw it, let's just go and make the best of it. If nothing else we'll have a great story to tell."

Again, I thought how lucky I was to have a woman like her, knowing that many brides would be in tears over such a turn of events.

Living together made the tradition of not seeing the bride on her wedding day a bit problematic. Our solution was to move *Ursaorion* from her mooring to our old marina in Tottenville and for me to move aboard. With that settled, we went forward with the many planning issues that confront any couple. We did everything ourselves and never argued or disagreed on anything, but Carol insisted on choosing the wedding march herself.

I joked with her. "What, no 'Here Comes the Bride'?"

She said, "You'll like it. I promise, but I want it to be a surprise."

I smiled. "Okay, Princess, that's fine with me." I didn't give it another thought.

After months of planning, our wedding day, September thirtieth, arrived. In dress white uniforms and swords, my ushers waited in the shadow of the Verrazano Bridge outside the huge guest tent overlooking the harbor. I sat in the bar with our childhood friends Danny and Mary, waiting for the ceremony to get started. Dan had been my best man at my first marriage and he was reminiscing about how I had wanted to bail out moments before the ceremony back then. He lifted his glass and toasted.

"This is the way it should have always been. Mary and me, Phil and Jo Ann, and you and Carol. *Cent' anni. Salud!*"

We drank, and I raised my glass to them.

"A hundred years to you and Mary as well."

The club manager came in a few minutes later. "We're ready, Commander."

As I walked outside I reflected on Dan's words in the bar. He was right; I did want to run off prior to getting married the first time. I knew it was a mistake back then but now, there was nothing in the world I wanted to do more than marry Carol. I removed my sword and took my place at the head of the canopy which was set up so our guest could observe the ceremony and still have a view of the bay and majestic bridge behind us. The music began and I choked back tears upon hearing the first notes. It was *The Canon,* or as we used to call it, "The GE song."

Carol's daughters, Jennifer and Nancy, were her bridesmaids, and after they took their place up front, her sons, David and Rob, escorted Carol to me. As she slowly strolled down the isle, she looked directly into my eyes and as always, she left me breathless. I smiled. She smiled back and we silently spoke the words, "*I love you,*" to each other. She was an angelic vision in a long white gown that accentuated her voluptuous body but tastefully hid the swell of her breasts beneath a translucent gossamer material. On her head was a wreath of small white flowers which added an air of maiden like innocence and it appealed to all my desires for her, yet was elegant and refined. She never took her eyes from mine, and I knew she had dressed entirely for me.

We finished exchanging vows with the sun setting in the western sky behind us and purely by chance, an outward bound cruise ship sounded its horn. We kissed ever so softly and our tears mingled as we realized our lifetime dream. My first words to Carol were, "Hello, Mrs. Ieva, I will love you forever and always!"

She smiled through tears. "Hello, Mr. Ieva, I love you too, Baby. Forever and always!"

As we posed for photos, our guest left the shelter of the tent and milled about outside. A moment later, my good friend, John Nash, gave the command for the culmination of any military wedding, the arch of swords

"Officers, draw swords!"

In one continuous motion, my ushers drew their swords and formed an arch. Carol and I walked through, and John, the senior officer, lowered his sword to block our path as is custom, requiring us to kiss until he removed his sword. Once satisfied with the duration and intensity of our kiss, he raised the blade, allowing us to proceed. Walking through the arch, he then gave the traditional gentle swat on Carol's backside with the flat of the blade and said, "Welcome to the United States Navy, Mrs. Ieva."

Like most wedding receptions, much of ours was a blur but I remember every dance and every glance I shared with Carol. She was beautiful beyond description and even after living together for more than three years, I wanted to take her to our room and make love to her as if for the first time. She sensed my impatience and as we danced, she laughed. "Down boy, you're looking at me like you're in heat."

I smiled. "I am in heat, but this is different from how I've ever wanted you before."

She whispered in my ear, "That's because I'm an honest married woman now."

Then she gently probed my ear with her tongue to let me know married and honest didn't mean dull and boring. As the dance ended, she laughed teasingly.

"Now be a good boy and I'll do more of that later!"

There it was again, the innocent maiden one minute and the wanton seductive woman the next. I loved knowing that about her as I watched her flit about the room talking with guest. I unknowingly said aloud, "What did I do to deserve her?"

A voice spoke out from behind me, "I don't know, Ron; you must have done something right for Carol to marry an ugly guy like you!"

It was my friend, Tom, who we had gone to Hawaii with.

"You lucked out big time, amigo; she's not only beautiful, but she's the sweetest gal I've ever known. You're a lucky man!"

"I know, Tom, I know."

Later, as Carol and I conversed with relatives, we heard the haunting opening notes of "Somewhere," a song from *West Side Story*. With knowing glances, we abruptly walked to the dance floor. It had been a difficult choice, but having selected, "Still Crazy After All These Years" by Paul Simon as our first dance song, "Somewhere" also had a special meaning for us and Carol wanted it played. As I took her in my arms with our guest watching, we danced and softly sang the words to each other.

There's a place for us,
Somewhere a place for us.
Peace and quiet and open air
Wait for us
Somewhere.
There's a time for us,
Some day a time for us,
Time together with time to spare,
Time to look, time to care,
Someday!
Somewhere.
We'll find a new way of living,
We'll find a way of forgiving
Somewhere.

There's a place for us,

A time and place for us.
Hold my hand and we're half way there.
Hold my hand and I'll take you there Somehow, Someday, Somewhere!

Carol whispered, "I'm so sorry I screwed up, Ron."

"Stop it. We both did, but that's all behind us now. We've found our *somewhere,* haven't we? I promise you, Carol, the rest of our lives will be as good as these past three years have been."

With tears of joy in her eyes, she whispered in my ear, "I want to leave now, Ron."

When the dance ended, we said hasty goodbyes and then snuck out of our reception, leaving our guest to enjoy the music and dancing. An hour later we were in the honeymoon suite at our hotel at JFK airport. I don't know how one night becomes more special than any other but our wedding night was truly special for us. Maybe because we'd found our place and our time and we knew that no one could ever take that from us again.

Landing on St. Croix the next day, our hearts sunk as we surveyed the hurricane devastation at the airport. Then, as we flew over parts of the island on take off, we saw areas where not a single tree was standing. Although we felt compassion for the suffering of the inhabitants, we couldn't help wonder if Virgin Gorda had suffered the same damage.

Fortunately, it had not! After a brief flight to Tortola, then a ferry to Virgin Gorda, we arrived with enough daylight to see that the Bitter End Yacht Club, being on the leeward side of a mountain, had been spared serious damage. Hours later, while lying in our hammock on our private balcony, we watched the sunset behind the mountains on the far side of North Sound and wondered what it must have been like during the storm.

In the morning we walked down the hill to the beach to see about using the boats. The larger boats were still unrigged from the hurricane, but we were assured they would be ready for guests later in the afternoon. Carol asked the dock attendant about the smaller boats on moorings. After introducing himself, Thomas said he could have one rigged in about fifteen minutes or we could take out a Boston Whaler and motor around.

She looked at me and said, "I'd rather sail, okay?"

"Sure, Baby. Let's go to the pool until Thomas gets it rigged."

Thomas smiled. "Okay, mon. See you in half an hour."

Forty minutes later, we left the dock and sailed away in a ten knot breeze, moving quickly through the crystal clear blue water. Taking turns on the tiller, we surveyed the extensive hurricane damage on the western shore of North Sound. It was unbelievable. Many homes were destroyed and dozens of large boats lay damaged hundreds of feet inland. When the wind diminished, we came about and ghosted back toward the yacht club at a lazy pace. My leg was dangling over the gunnel, one arm on the tiller and the other around Carol as she snuggled against my shoulder.

She said lazily, "I still can't believe we're married."

I looked into her eyes, then craned my neck and kissed her cheek. "Me neither, Princess. It seems like one minute there was nothing, and now it's almost like we were never apart all those years."

She looked up and we kissed fervently, sending a shudder through me, and I shifted my position.

She whispered, "Getting frisky?"

"You always make me frisky. I just look at you and I want you."

She pressed herself closer to me, and I looked around at the surrounding hills in the distance. "Some pervert could be looking at us with a big telescope from one of those windows."

"Do you care?"

I let the sails luff in the light breeze and drifting aimlessly, I took pleasure in her spontaneously wanton nature and her voracious curiosity to explore our sexuality.

Every day was like that and every night we dined and danced under the stars and conversed with the new friends we were making. We took out one of the thirty-foot boats with two other couples and sailed over to Mosquito Island to snorkel an entire afternoon away. Berndt and Celia, a couple from Germany we met at lunch, had never sailed, but they seemed content for the first few days to go off on their own in a Boston Whaler. Then at dinner one night Berndt asked if the club gave sailing lessons.

Before I could answer, Carol offered an invitation. "Hey, come with us tomorrow; we have one of the big sailboats and Ron will teach you to sail!"

I had been planning to spend the day in a secluded anchorage alone with Carol, but her spontaneity, fueled by rum drinks, precluded any chance of withdrawing her offer.

Thomas reviewed the chart and explained that the Dog Islands, and The Baths were as far as we could go. Fifteen minutes later, we were sailing in a warm twelve knot southwesterly breeze, passing Mosquito Island to starboard, our destination the Dog Islands. They are northwest of Virgin Gorda in Sir Francis Drake Channel and consist of six main islands. Great Dog, West Dog, East Seal Dog, West Seal Dog, Little Seal Dog and George Dog Island. After two hours of hull speed sailing, we anchored in fifteen feet of crystal clear water off George Dog Island. I sensed Berndt wanted some privacy with Celia and that was fine with me. Carol and I went off on our own and after snorkeling for an hour, we worked our way back to the boat and ate picnic lunches prepared by the club staff.

From The Dogs, we sailed over to The Baths on Virgin Gorda. The Baths are a natural collection exotic pools and grottos formed by enormous boulders creating caves and hidden rooms, penetrated by shafts of light in the sparkling clear water. Once there, we anchored and again went our separate ways, agreeing to meet back on the boat in an hour. After exploring several of the many pools, Carol and I found a grotto that led into a deep cave where the only light came from openings in the ceiling. There, we floated vertically in each others arms and kissed until our passions were awaken. Then, finding a submerged ledge to stand on, we made love with only our heads above the warm water of the grotto.

Two days later, we left paradise and arrived back in New York on a chilly fall day. Once settled into our home as husband and wife, we pondered what to do with *Ursaorion,* which was still sitting in a boat slip in Tottenville. Our original plan was to move her back to our mooring in Great Kills, then haul her for the winter, but it was October and temperatures were already dropping. We were both tired of having to use a dinghy to get out to the mooring, and Carol suggested we leave the boat in Tottenville, then haul her for the winter there. I agreed and added that we could then look for a marina in New Jersey for next summer.

CHAPTER 10

MORGAN

In the spring of 1990, we moved *Ursaorion* to Morgan Marina on Cheese-quake Creek in New Jersey. The locals called it Morgan Creek and it's only twelve miles south of Great Kills, so we could easily use our mooring for weekend visits. Morgan is a well protected marina about a mile up the creek from Raritan Bay. The entrance breakwater is narrow and there are two bridges to navigate before entering the creek proper; other than that, it's an easy entrance.

Maneuvering *Ursaorion* outside the jetties, I told Carol to call the bridge tender on the VHF radio so that I could focus on avoiding other boats and so she could become familiar with using the radio for bridge openings. We rarely had the opportunity to use the VHF radio for bridges, so not wanting to make a mistake over the airwaves, Carol took a deep breath and closed her eyes to briefly rehearse what she was going to say. As I knew she would, she sounded like an old salt, a very feminine old salt, but an old salt nevertheless.

After having her request acknowledged by the bridge tender, she put the mike down with a sigh of relief and asked me how she did.

"You did just fine, Baby."

She smiled with satisfaction as the highway bridge opened and we slowly moved forward. We easily navigated through the structure and on through the railroad bridge, then motored up the creek past tranquil marshes instead of the oil refineries on the Arthur Kill. Seeing wildlife in the marshes and huge turtles in the creek, we knew we had made the right decision to move our boat here. Then, once around the last bend in the creek, we saw the Garden State Parkway fixed bridge, which marked the end of the navigable channel for sailboats and the site of our new marina.

The current was running swiftly, more so than I had ever handled a boat in before. As I nervously backed *Ursaorion* into her slip, some guys came off their boats to assist us with lines. Once Carol had both stern lines tossed to our new dock mates, I felt better and thanked them for their help. Then, I heard a vaguely familiar voice. "Hey, this is the boat from Great Kills last year with the weird name and the broad steering."

It was them! Of all the marinas on Raritan Bay, we were not only at theirs, but we were also on the same dock. I grumbled below my breath as I secured our bow and spring lines and I could see that a congregation was forming on the dock to welcome us. We did a bunch of introductions, then beers were passed to us and I couldn't help but feel the first tinges of comradeship with them.

As more beers were handed to us with more welcoming words, I could see that it was my first mate who getting most of the attention. Then the guy who first shouted back in Great Kills about "the broad steering the boat," boomed over everyone and said, "Just to let you know, after we were on your mooring, some wives bitched about why they couldn't drive our boats, so thanks to you, Carol, we had to teach 'em."

He then raised his can in a toast to her. I was flabbergasted and couldn't conceal my smile as Carol thanked him and basked in her moment in the sun. A year had past and this rough sounding guy remembered her adept handling of *Ursaorion* under sail in close quarters. What a compliment!

We became quick friends with these good-natured people and sailed all over Raritan Bay with them, usually ending the day at Great Kills, where ironically, we'd all raft up on my mooring, sometimes with as many as twelve boats. As the years passed, they became our very best friends both ashore and afloat, and we spent nearly two decades exploring the far reaches of Long Island Sound and Chesapeake Bay with them.

Our first long voyage from Morgan was to Long Island Sound. After loading clothing, stores, and beverages, Carol brought aboard a mysterious box. She said it was a surprise. Whatever it was, it took up more space than I liked, but she was adamant about bringing it and said I'd be happy she

did. Still pondering the mysterious object, we departed Morgan and en-
joyed a short sail to Great Kills, along with *Tranquility*, *G-Force*, and *Adams*
Apple. We rafted on our mooring, and after dinner, we congregated aboard
G-Force for drinks and music.

Charlie always played fun music and Carol fit right in as she danced
almost non-stop. I could see that she was clearly enjoying herself more than
if we had been alone, and I smiled inwardly at our good fortune to meet
these people. *G-Force* was a cabin cruiser, and due to her wide open aft deck,
she had been earmarked as the official party boat. When Carol wasn't dancing with me that night, she was having a great time pole dancing using the
flying bridge ladder on *G-force*!

The next morning was bright and sunny and *G-Force* left along
with *Adams Apple* to go all the way to the Sand Hole at Oyster Bay. John
and I decided to stop at City Island that night, then catch up with them
at Oyster Bay where we planned on spending several days chilling out and
fishing. The wind piped up during the afternoon, which made for a rough
night on the moorings at City Island, making us wish we had gone to the
Sand Hole after all. We woke to a clear sky and a bright sun, but the wind
was blowing twenty knots, gusting to twenty-five from the north. This
was the leading edge of a front that was due to arrive that night, but with
our destination only fifteen miles away we decided to leave as planned and
make for the shelter of the Sand Hole.

The Sand Hole is an old quarry about half a mile long by a quarter
of mile wide. The entrance is defined by two narrow spits of sandy beach,
one jutting up from the south shore of Lloyd Neck, the other extending
down from the north. The south spit ends in a stone jetty that is submerged
at high tide. The north arm turns inward creating a narrow serpentine
channel into the anchorage. Carol and I had been to Oyster Bay before, but
never to this anchorage because of its menacing entrance. I knew this was
going to be a white-knuckle approach, so we were glad John had navigated
into this snug harbor in previous years. He assured me he had been there
many times and knew the way in so with *Tranquility* leading the way, we
slipped our moorings and set off with a reefed main and jib.

Once we got out of the lee of City and Hart islands, the waves
began to build considerably. Then once past Execution Rocks, I knew we

were in for a rough time of it as they built even higher when the tide turned. We were barely making three knots through the water, sometimes less when we got slammed by a big wave but we were getting some lift from the ebbing current, so after only four hours, we approached G"17" a bell buoy marking the shoals off Rocky Point on the west side of Oyster Bay.

Carol took the helm as we slammed into five foot waves, burying our bow, but she stayed on course for Lloyd Point two miles ahead.

I called John on the radio. "John, all I can see is a surf line up ahead. Did Charlie make it in there yesterday?"

"That's affirmative, he and Warren got in easily, but they checked out the entrance this morning and said it's pretty dicey because waves are breaking over the jetty."

"Oh that's just great. Okay, I'll call you again when we get closer. *Ursaorion* out."

I told Carol I was getting uncomfortable about running this inlet in the conditions.

She said, "Maybe we should just go into Oyster Bay for the night."

"I don't know, Baby. Let's see what it looks like when we get closer."

Even half a mile from Lloyd Point, the surf line looked threatening and I couldn't see a break in it where John said the entrance was. Ahead of us, *Tranquility* headed up into the wind and doused sails. I told Carol we should do the same so she put the gearshift in neutral and started the engine. A moment later, she yelled out over the wind, "Heading up!" As she brought us into the wind, I furled the jib, then dropped the main sail and secured it as we pitched wildly in the steep chop. Carol fell off the wind and got back on course about a hundred yards behind *Tranquility*. Inching our way forward, we now rolled heavily as waves pounded us on our port beam.

John called on the VHF. "*Ursaorion, Ursaorion, Tranquility*!"

"This is *Ursaorion;* go ahead, John."

"Captain Ron, stay close behind me. We have to line up exactly on the biggest tree on the beach. As soon as I clear the stone jetty, I'm going to turn hard right and run parallel to it, then snake around the sandy spit of land to port. Follow me. Okay?"

I was considering what he just said about lining up on the biggest tree when Carol asked, "When was he here last?"

"You must have been reading my mind, Baby."

We could now clearly hear the waves pounding against the stone jetty, but still saw only an unbroken line of seething surf with no sign of an entrance. The radio crackled with John's voice.

"Close it up, Ron. You want to stay right on my ass."

Carol looked at me and said, "If I get too close and he goes aground, I won't have room to stop or turn around."

She was right, of course, so I called John on the radio. "Captain John, when was the last time you were in here, amigo?"

There was a moment of silence, then his voice. "Three years ago!"

I thought, *Three years is a long time; the trees he was using as a landmark could have died and new ones grown. Shit, we could be using the wrong tree.* Carol didn't wait for me to say anything; she backed off the throttle. I called John and suggested we wait until things died down.

He said, "Too late. I'm already committed."

I looked through the binoculars and saw that *Tranquility* was between the northern spit of sand to his left, the breaking surf, and the stone jetty to his right.

A moment later, a large wave lifted her stern, then her hull disappeared, hidden by the back of the wave. Seconds later, she rose precariously as she raced toward the beach directly in front of her. Drawing on all of his skills, John turned hard to starboard at the last moment and I watched in awe as *Tranquility* glided safely behind the jetty, her motion easing considerably as she found smooth water. We still rolled wildly at idle speed just a hundred yards off the entrance and I pondered our options. Carol gave me a questioning glance.

I said, "I'll pass, how about you?"

She smiled and asked, "Oyster Bay?"

"Yeah, crank it up and steer for that green can buoy."

I called John on the VHF and told him we were going into Oyster Bay for the night and would try to hook up with them in the morning.

He said, "Okay, see you tomorrow."

His words were non-judgmental, but I could tell from the tone of his voice that I was in for some serious ribbing. I already had the nickname Captain Cautious, and this would certainly add to my reputation of being overly careful.

Turning into Oyster Bay, Carol negotiated the steep following waves, and we occasionally surfed at over eight knots down the face of them as they came rapidly from behind and towered above us. Cove Neck is a wide peninsula separating Cold Spring Harbor from Oyster Bay Harbor to the west. As we approached it, I considered which anchorage to spend the night. Looking at the chart, it was clear that with the wind out of the north, Oyster Bay Harbor offered more protection, so we rounded Plum Point on Centre Island and steered for the spires of town two miles away.

The town of Oyster Bay is located at the bottom of the U-shaped harbor, which is formed by Mill Neck to the west, Cove Neck to the east, and Centre Island jutting down from the north. A marina offered transient moorings, which included launch service so with the wind forecasted to blow hard all night; we opted to take a mooring rather than anchor. Having brought us all this way so far, Carol wanted to take us to our assigned mooring, so without a word, I picked up the boat hook and walked to the bow. As she carefully maneuvered us upwind in the stiff breeze, I smiled as she brought our starboard bow alongside the float pendant where I could easily snatch it with the boat hook.

Once secured, we breathed a sigh of relief. Knowing I was going to be getting some ribbing over this decision, Carol said, "I'd love to be partying with those guys right now, but coming in here was the right thing to do."

I smiled and hugged her. "Thanks, Baby, you're a good first mate and know just what to say to sooth my ego." Then, patting her ass, I said, "Now go make drinks while I put the sail cover on!"

Ten minutes later we sipped drinks in the shelter under the cockpit dodger and talked about the day. What began as a short fifteen mile sail had turned into a sometimes white knuckle adventure. I told Carol she made a good call by not getting too close to *Tranquility*, and we snuggled closer as she asked if I really thought she was a good first mate.

"You're the best. Really! I know I can count on you and trust you with my life." Then as I kissed her, I added, "And as I said before, you're very easy on the eyes!"

She smiled. "Flattery will get you everywhere, captain. Just for that I'm buying dinner ashore tonight!"

I laughed, "Oh boy, now that's a treat, but can I have my way with you when we get back!"

She kissed me and laughed. "I thought you'd never ask!"

By the next morning, the front had blown through and the harbor was like glass. Carol slept while I drank coffee in the cockpit. At eight o'clock sharp, I heard the call on the radio. It was from John, with Charlie and Warren yelling in the background.

"Good morning, Captain Cautious!"

John then asked, "Do you think it's calm enough for you to come to the Sand Hole this morning?"

Sounding defensive would only encourage them, so in my best serious voice I replied, "Yeah, I suppose I can handle it."

Warren yelled, "Maybe you should have Carol bring the boat in!"

"Good idea, Warry. Maybe I will."

John laughed and said to give them a call when we left Oyster Bay so they could come out in their dinghies to guide us in.

"Okay, John. You can figure we'll be there an hour from the time I call you. *Ursaorion* out."

Carol's voice rang out from the aft cabin. "Morning, Baby. Are they giving you shit?"

I said, "It's not as bad as I thought, but I'll probably be the brunt of their jokes for the rest of the trip." Then I asked, "Are you ready for breakfast?"

"Sure, whatcha making?"

"Take your pick, oatmeal or pancakes, but the bananas are already getting ripe so maybe we should use them?"

She came into the main cabin and, even with her hair all messed up and her eyes half closed, she looked beautiful.

She smiled. "What are you looking at? Haven't you ever seen a naked woman before?"

I smiled back at her. "Come here, naked woman."

She wearily plopped her head on my shoulders and put her arms around my neck. I drew her close to me and said softly, "I love you, Carol. I love our life together."

Her eyes glassed over. "I love you and I love our life together too, Ron."

We stood embraced like that a few minutes, then she said, "Okay, buster, now go make me some banana pancakes, I'm chilly and need to get something on."

Two hours later, I called John to say we were just getting underway, but there was no need to guide us in with the bay so calm.

He laughed. "Oh, no problem; we wouldn't miss it for anything."

We slipped the mooring and I went to full speed. At six and a half knots, we'd be there in less than forty minutes, not the full hour I told him earlier so maybe we'd get there before they came out. We made the four mile jaunt in just under thirty-five minutes. Then, just as we came within a quarter of a mile of the entrance, a parade of dinghies came roaring out from behind the stone jetty. They were blowing air horns and waving flags and one of the dinghies had a sign that said in big bold letters, "Follow Me."

Carol said, "Guess we're busted."

"Yeah, but make the best of it; jiggle your boobs and wave back!"

The tide was at mid-range and I made a mental note of where the deep water was in relation to the jetty on the right, the sand spit on the left, and the beach dead ahead. Carol brought up our camera and as we followed the dinghy parade through the hole-in-the-wall entrance, she took photos for future reference. Favoring the jetty side of the narrow unmarked channel, we made a ninety-degree turn to starboard when we were halfway between the jetty and the beach. After that, we had to stay uncomfortably close to the sandy beach as we followed its contours; first southeasterly, then in a tight one-hundred-eighty-degree turn to a northwest heading. Once clear of the sharp point of land, the anchorage opened up to a wide basin with eight to twelve feet of water all around. There, tucked nicely into the far western corner was our raft-up consisting of *G-Force, Adams Apple,* and *Tranquility.*

Lounging around for two days, we enjoyed the beautiful anchorage and the company of our friends. We also relished stolen intimate moments alone aboard *Ursaorion* and in our dinghy while we explored the winding creeks leading into the anchorage. At other times, John and Charlie taught me how to fish and dig for oysters, and we all feasted daily on the fresh caught bounty. Carol and I were getting a tiny sample of the cruising life we dreamed about, and at night lying in our bed, we fantasized about living like this in the Caribbean for months at a time.

Leaving Oyster Bay, we sailed east to Northport, then across Long Island Sound to Stonington, Connecticut, before returning to the Long Island side at Montauk. It was an idyllic time for us, and we grew closer with every passing day in a way that most couples never realize. I already knew the special nature of friendships built on being shipmates, but even for me, being able to strike this special bond with the woman I loved was truly extraordinary. We grew to depend on each other in fair weather and foul, and it became second nature to literally put your life in your lover's hands when a sudden squall turned a warm summer day into a brief but raging tempest.

As our cruise ended, *G-Force* and *Adams Apple* motored ahead with *Tranquility* and *Ursaorion* sailing slowly westward for one last rendezvous at Great Kills. It was there on the last night of our vacation that Carol revealed the surprise she had brought aboard in the box two weeks earlier. It was a small hand cranked ice cream maker and a large packet of vanilla ice cream mix. Everyone donated milk and the last of their ice and eight drunks never had more fun as we took turns cranking the handle. When it was ready, it was once again Warren who made a toast to Carol's resourcefulness. I was as proud of her then as I had been during some of the worst weather on the cruise.

Later, as we lay in bed, we talked about the nineteen year void in our lives when we were apart and could have been sharing times like this. We didn't do that often because it was too painful to wonder about *what might have been*. After all, we had wonderful children from our previous marriages and wouldn't change that even if we could. Nevertheless, we still sometimes wondered about how different life would have been for us. I turned to Carol and took her in my arms.

"What matters is that we're together now and that we had those special years as kids and this second chance to spend the rest of our lives together."

She kissed me and said, "The rest of our lives! I love the sound of that, Ron. I want us to live to be a hundred then, okay?"

I drew her to me and felt the warmth of her body, and we feel asleep happier and more content than ever before.

Chapter 11
Storms, Rocks and Englishmen

Jim, a long time friend and business associate, arrived from England to attend his daughter's high school graduation in Connecticut. We worked together for years and both got divorced during what we referred to as our company's nuclear winter. Afterward, we remained in close contact, so when he called to say he would be in America, we invited him to dinner.

Grilling steaks in our backyard, we overindulged in beef and wine, then talked over espresso and sambuca until three in the morning. Over a bleary-eyed breakfast, I told Jim that Christopher, who he hadn't seen in years, was coming over to go sailing with us and I invited Jim to join us.

He said, "Bloody hell, I can barely hold my coffee cup."

"Come on, you can rekindle your love affair with the sea and blow away your hangover."

He accepted our invitation and an hour later we were off to *Ursao-rion* with our hung-over Englishman chatting away with Christopher in the back seat. I carried the beer and rum, Carol managed the food, Christopher grabbed the clothing, and Jim clung desperately to a tube of SPF 40 sunscreen. He had never been sailing with me and seemed apprehensive, but became reassured after observing us go through our safety checklist and listen to the NOAA weather radio, which confirmed a favorable forecast.

Heading into Raritan Bay, I turned north toward the Verrazano Bridge to give Jim a view of the Manhattan skyline and the World Trade Center, where he had worked during his days in New York. While Christopher and I sailed, Jim chatted with Carol who provided advice from a mom's perspective, on dealing with American teenage girls and tips on tempestuous ex-American wives. Then, while sailing calmly in a freshening breeze, a small bundle of dark clouds appeared rapidly in the western sky. With nothing but clear blue everywhere else, Jim seemed surprise at the urgency at which I told Carol to go below and make sure everything was battened down.

He asked, "Ere now, what's all the fuss?"

Christopher offered to break out the foul weather gear.

"Good idea, Chris. Go ahead and set up the plotting board and turn on the LORAN."

Again, Jim asked what all the fuss was about. I pointed to the rapidly building dark clouds now filling much of the western horizon.

"That's a big thunder boomer. They come out of nowhere and it'll be on us in no time." Looking to where I pointed, Jim said, "Bloody hell, it was all blue skies five minutes ago! One minute it's margaritas and chips, the next minute it's white knuckles and salt spray is it?"

"That's the way it happens, amigo!" Then I added, "They generally don't last long. The biggest problem in a busy harbor like New York is loss of visibility."

As we prepared for the impending squall, I said, "Jim, you may want to stay below with Carol. When this happens, she keeps a plot of our position using the LORAN. Maybe you can watch and see how she does it."

He laughed as he collected his things and went below. "I'd rather watch Carol do anything instead of sitting in the rain with you. See ya, mate."

I yelled for Christopher to come up and help me reduce sail. After furling the big jib, we put a reef in the main just before the first strong gust hit. When the second gust hit along with torrential rain, it knocked us over, and before their voices were lost to the howling wind on deck, I could hear both Jim and Carol let out a loud "Whoaaa," as *Ursaorion* rolled over to thirty degrees on the inclinometer.

The wind blew in a series of powerful gusts, throwing *Ursaorion* around abruptly, but Christopher held her on a northeasterly course, which offered the most sea room and kept us out of the ship channel. Carol popped out of the companionway every few minutes to give me our position, course, and speed over ground from the LORAN plot she was maintaining. I was pleased that Jim was getting the chance to see both her and Christopher in action.

When it seemed the worst of the wind had passed and things quieted down, I went below to look at Carol's plot on the chart spread out on the cabin table.

Jim said, "I feel like a supercargo in this maritime drama; don't you have something for me to do?"

I laughed and said, "You're in charge of music."

Carol pointed to the bulkhead. "Tapes are in that locker!"

Mumbling assorted Liverpool curses, Jim rummaged in the locker to find a tape.

I said, "Jim, anything will be fine. Try some Jimmy Buffett."

He looked at me as if I had two heads. "And who in bloody hell is Jimmy Buffet?"

Carol and I laughed.

I was beginning to get queasy from being below deck in the pitching boat so as Jim continued to eyeball cassette titles, I climbed back on deck into the rain and gusty wind. I told Christopher we were coming up on Old Orchard Shoal Lighthouse and we should be seeing it off our port bow soon. Visibility was poor in the driving rain, but I scanned a wide arc in front of us to be sure we picked up the flashing six second light. Then, as our boat pitched in the waves, our speakers screamed to life at maximum volume to the sound of Wagner's, *Ride of the Valkyries*. Even over the howling wind and reverberating speakers, I could hear Jim and Carol laughing as they bellowed along with the music. Christopher smiled, and I shouted, "I must have a hundred Jimmy Buffett tapes and assorted others down there, but only Jim could find this one!"

The squall subsided almost as quickly as it came upon us. When Jim came back on deck, he looked around and saw that we were a long way from our original position, but precisely where Carol's navigation had us at on the chart.

"Bloody hell, I'm impressed."

Then looking at me and pointing to Carol, he said, "You want to keep this one, you know. She's very easy on the eyes, very sexy, and very clever she is!"

We got a thank you note from Jim in England a few weeks later:

Hi Mates,

I spent Saturday night in Manhattan in the same cheap hotel that had been the venue for my bachelors party twenty-one years ago—it is no longer cheap, but still seedy! I visited old haunts around midtown in pursuit of ghosts of my time as a New Yorker, but all I found were spirits by the glass. The following morning I caught the train for Connecticut and was at least prepared for the inevitable inclement reception and bittersweet reunion with Danielle. The storm we weathered in Ursaorion, Carol's counsel and the togetherness of the Ieva family provided me with a touchstone to reality in the soap opera of post marital warfare and Danielle's high school graduation hullabaloo. The fleeting moments with Danielle were over in a trice and as I sat on the transatlantic redeye clutching my British Airway's gin & tonic, my thoughts were of precious time spent with people I care for, in challenging circumstances. There is always a price, a penalty and a reward!

Love, Jim

P.S. Carol, if you ever get tired of Captain Bligh, come to England; it is a pleasure to know there are beautiful woman with brains and courage still among us!

Carol loved the compliments, but mostly she loved Jim referring to us as a family.

"I liked him the instant I met him. I like all your friends, Ron. Do you think we'll ever go to England and see Jim again and meet Claudi?"

I traveled to the UK often on business so I promised to take Carol with me someday, but at the moment, a new weekend was already approaching and I was eager to go sailing again.

We had sailed in and out of Great Kills, day and night hundreds of times, especially when we kept *Ursaorion* on a mooring there. Our weekend plan was to sail around Raritan Bay on Saturday, then spend the night on our mooring, then sail home late Sunday afternoon. As I grilled a salmon filet in our backyard Friday night, however, I looked out on the bay and thought, *It's a nice night; maybe we should jump start the weekend and sail to*

Great Kills. I suggested it to Carol during dinner and she immediately agreed, so as soon as we finished eating, we gathered our things and drove to the marina by sunset.

The wind was a gentle seven knots in the turning basin south of the bridge. As I held *Ursaorion* in place against the current, Carol stowed everything below, then came on deck to remove the sail cover and hank on the main halyard. The bridge opened, and after clearing the jetties, we stood out into the Bay. Carol took over the helm, and as I got ready to raise the main sail, she softly called out, "Heading up!"

Bringing us into the wind, I hoisted the main in a soft clatter of rigging and a gently luffing sail. A moment later she said, "Falling off."

She came left to a course of 060°m, which would take us right to the channel leading into Great Kills just seven miles away. A few moments later, I unfurled the jib and we sailed on a close reach making almost five knots, which would put us in around ten o'clock.

I took over the helm and Carol snuggled close to me in the glow of our running lights as we sailed in the darkness with only the sounds of wind, waves, and music. At nine thirty, we looked off our starboard bow expecting to see the flashing four second light atop the tower at Great Kills. In the dark, it would be important in helping us align with the unlighted channel markers running parallel to a rock jetty about twenty yards outside the north boundary of the channel.

My intention was to enter the channel from the south at G "3" as we usually did, rather than go to the channel entrance half a mile further to the east. Then, once in the channel, we'd fall off onto a broad reach and proceed west, guided by the flashing light at Crookes Point, which would also offer glimpses of the unlighted buoys. I looked at my watch; it was nine forty-five. I thought, *We should be seeing the flashing light from Great Kills by now.*

I said to Carol, "Maybe we got set back by the current more than I figured; let's give it five more minutes."

We settled back into our reverie, but I told her to keep an eye out for the light at Great Kills. Five minutes later she sat up. "I see it, there off our starboard bow."

We both stood up and looked for channel markers but saw none. A tiny alarm rang somewhere deep in my brain, but I ignored it. Great Kills was flashing every four seconds and was off our starboard bow, but it was farther to the south than I expected.

Alarm number two sounded, but I thought, *It's just a trick of perception from sailing at night.* Still, it concerned me so I let the jib luff to slow us down. A moment later, I made out the jetty silhouetted against the night sky half a mile in front of us and felt certain we still had at least half that distance to go before we got to the channel.

Carol said aloud with some concern in her voice, "At five knots we'll close that distance in just three minutes."

I looked at her and said, "I see you've been busy."

She smiled. "Mrs. Smith!"

As in times past, I knew she meant our third grade math teacher, and I became lost in the pleasant thought that we shared so much history. Then, I was shaken from my daydream by Carol's urgent voice.

"What's that sound?"

I said, "What sound?"

She yelled, "Surf, it sounds like water against a beach!"

I instinctively threw the helm hard to starboard, which turned us in less than half a boat length, instantly heading us into the wind. I continued turning until we tacked and were steering an almost reciprocal course. Carol sheeted in the jib and as we gathered speed, we saw red nun buoy R "6" right in front of us. I was totally disoriented and was about to tack again, but quickly realized what had happened.

I said, "Shit, I almost ran her on the rocks!"

I came to a southeasterly course to gain some sea room, and when I thought we were due south of the Great Kills Light, I headed up and told Carol to furl the jib. With the jib furled and just the main up, we drifted along at two knots as we took stock of what had just happened.

I had sailed right across the channel and out of it again on the dangerous north side. I had us heading straight for the rock jetty not twenty yards away when Carol heard the sound of waves against the rocks and sounded the warning.

"We almost bought the ranch, Baby. I don't know how we didn't run aground or hit the rocks; we had to be way out of the channel."

She asked, "How did we do that?"

"I'm not sure, but let's think about it after we get in; right now my knees are shaking. Start the engine."

Carol headed us into the wind and I dropped the main. We then motored to Great Kills Light and looked to the northwest until we could make out of the channel markers when the light flashed. I plotted the axis of the channel and we slowly crept forward on a course of 345°m until we could see R "2" along our starboard rail, then R "4" farther ahead. The flashing day marker opposite Crookes Point was also visible, and I gained some confidence and increased speed to three knots as the harbor lights ashore provided additional light, improving our visibility.

Twenty minutes later, we were safety tethered to our mooring. I shut off the engine and, in the dark silence, I said, "Drinks, make mine a double!"

Carol returned to the cockpit with two glasses of Gosling rum on the rocks.

I said, "Wow, you must be rattled to be having rum?"

She repeated her earlier question. "How did we do that?"

I clinked glasses and took a long sip of the dark rum.

"Okay, I've been looking at the chart; here's how I screwed up. For one thing, from now on if we enter a port at night, no short-cuts. We go in at the head of the channel, not half way down, regardless of how much depth is outside the channel." I took another swig of rum and went on. "When an inner alarm sounds in my brain, I need to listen to it. And finally, we shut off the music. As it is, I don't know how you heard the sound of the waves against the rocks with all the noise we were making. You saved our ass, Baby." Then I added, "From the position of Great Kills Light, I should have realized we were farther inshore and much closer to the channel than I assumed."

Carol said, "But you said you saw the jetty still a half a mile away!"

Pointing to the chart, I said, "Yeah, but once it was over and we were motoring safely down the channel, I could see it wasn't the jetty I had seen. It was a line of tall shrubs and bushes much farther back from the beach. I stupidly thought it was the jetty."

"We have to learn from this! It was a series of small mistakes, and I could have sunk the boat and seriously injured us or much worse. I'm so sorry."

She kissed me and began to cry softly, which surprised me.

"Come on, it's okay. It's over."

She said, "It's not that. I'll tell you later. Just hold me close and let's put some music on and look at the stars."

The double rums had the desired effect and we mellowed out as we noshed on cheese and crackers. I had a second drink, but Carol wasn't used to rum on the rocks and nursed hers as she slowly swayed to Jimmy Buffett singing one of her favorite songs, "Nautical Wheelers". She looked so sensuous with her eyes closed and her head moving from side to side. I just wanted to hold her and go to asleep.

"Come on, Baby. Let's crash."

She smiled. "You could have picked a better word."

I laughed and thought, *Even after all that happened, she still has a sense of humor.* We undressed and climbed in bed. Anything that might have been wrong with the world melted away as we embraced and I felt her body against mine. The open hatch above our heads brought in a soothing cool breeze and I said, "I love you, Carol."

She replied with a quivering voice, "I love you too, Ron, more than I could ever say."

After moments of silence, she asked if I was still awake.

"Yes, what's wrong?"

"Nothing is wrong; I just want to tell you why I cried before."

"Okay, so tell me."

"I see other couples at the marina and most of the men yell at their wives and blame them for everything, even for their own mistakes. I heard that crap for years."

I started to talk, but she put her finger to my lips.

"Let me finish. Tonight, you never even once said 'we'. You took full blame for what happened. I really appreciate that because I was afraid you might blame me for screwing up. You didn't, and it's one of the things I love about you, Ron."

Holding her tighter in my arms, I said, "It's not me. With anyone else I'd probably be like those other guys. It's you! You make me better than that. I'd never hurt you and especially not blame you for something I did. Besides, I've been doing this for more than twenty years, I should have known better."

She squeezed me and said, "It doesn't matter why you didn't blame me, all that matters is that you didn't."

Saturday was a beautiful day, and while waiting for the coffee to brew, I listened to the weather forecast: Clear skies, sunny with light and variable winds. *Not very exciting*, I thought. Then, with my book and a cup of coffee in hand, I went up into the cockpit to read and relax, leaving Carol to sleep longer. With no wind in the forecast, maybe we'd just stay on the mooring and chill out, maybe have lunch ashore and stroll along the beach. *Yeah*, I thought, *Carol would like that.*

It turned out to be a great chill-out day, and after walking for miles along New Dorp Beach, we had lunch at the Windjammer in Great Kills. As we got to the dinghy dock we saw that *Tranquility* had rafted to us. I laughed and murmured something about not getting naked on deck under the stars tonight.

Carol giggled and said, "You pervert, we can do that another time; it'll be fun to hang out with John and Gail. Besides, we can leave the hatch open and look up at the stars from our bed."

I laughed. "Only look at the stars?"

Rubbing my thigh, she said, "That depends who's on top; now let's go see our friends."

By late afternoon, two other boats joined us and we had a fun night talking and listening to island music and drinking too many margaritas. No one cooked dinner because each crew brought out endless trays of snacks while we played Uno and told sea stories.

The party dwindled to a close and everyone retired to their boats. As Carol and I undressed and got in bed, she said, "So who gets to look at the stars?"

I must have looked perplexed, so with a smile, she pushed me on my back saying, "It was your idea to look at the stars, so you get to look up!"

I did, and she looked beautiful as she swayed over me.

Looking seductively down at me, she said, "I've been thinking about this ever since we got in the dinghy this afternoon."

The next morning I woke to another brilliant sunrise and a warm twelve knot northerly breeze. The forecast was for more of the same all day and since we had spent all of Saturday on the mooring, I woke Carol and said I wanted to get underway early. She grumbled a bit but looked out the hatch.

"Oh it's so nice out and there's a good breeze. So what's for breakfast?"

We had a quick breakfast of coffee and toast and while Carol stowed things below, I prepared to get underway. She came on deck wearing shorts and a very flimsy blue silk top. I wondered, *Does she do that for my benefit or because it feels comfortable? Either way it drives me nuts.*

By eight o'clock, we were navigating out of the harbor for an easy day sail before heading home to face the work week ahead. Once in the channel, Carol unfurled the jib, and after clearing Great Kills Light, I steered an easterly course toward Ambrose Tower fifteen miles away. Ambrose marks the convergence of the main shipping lanes into New York. After an uneventful sail, we passed close aboard to what was then a hundred foot tall tower.

Carol asked, "How deep is the water way out here?"

I looked at the depth gauge. "It's seventy-six feet."

She seemed disappointed. "But we're so far out, is that all?"

"We're not really that far out; it's only about seven miles to Sandy Hook."

She said nothing more, but my curiosity got the best of me. I asked, "How deep do you want it to be?"

She said, "A thousand feet!"

I laughed and looked at the chart. "It doesn't get that deep for another hundred miles. Why do you want it to be a thousand feet?"

"I don't know; it would be so cool to know there's that much water under us. I'd love to dive in and float in water that deep."

I smiled and asked, "Would you float topless for me?"

She said, "I'd float naked for you, Baby!"

That image was enticing but there was no way I was going to sail a hundred miles out into the ocean in *Ursaorion,* but I told her to take the helm and I went below to check my Bowditch.

Returning to the cockpit I asked, "Have you ever been out of sight of land?"

She said, "No, of course not, except in bad visibility."

"Even now after years of going to sea and crossing oceans in ships, I still get a slightly eerie feeling the instant I'm out of sight of land. Do you want to do it?"

"Do what?" she asked.

"Go out of sight of land! The chart has the lighthouse on Atlantic Highlands at a height of 246 feet and our height is say, nine feet above sea level so the table says we'd need to go about thirteen miles farther out from here to lose sight of land and the lighthouse."

She said, "You're talking Greek to me. What does that mean in time?"

I thought a moment. "That's about two more hours out and about six to get back to Morgan, so we'll get back to the marina around seven tonight if we can keep making six knots." Then I added, "That'll make it a long day, but it's a perfect day to go. Do ya wanna do it?"

She smiled. "Yes! That would be nice."

Her excitement mounted and she asked if we would see dolphins or whales.

"We might see dolphins, but I really don't want to see whales too close to *Ursaorion.*"

"Why, do you think they could hurt us?"

I laughed. "Hurt us? Hell, even a small whale could sink us with just an accidental bump."

She looked a bit apprehensive, then said, "Let's keep going!"

"Okay, you take the helm; I want to plot a course that will keep us in the traffic separation zone."

"What's that?" she asked.

I explained that New York had six shipping lanes.

"The inbound and outbound lanes are separated by a wide zone in which ships shouldn't go."

Then, showing her the chart, I added, "There's no guarantee that a ship won't mess up and go into a separation zone, but we'll stand a much better chance of avoiding a ship if we sail in a zone."

She smiled and said excitedly, "I understand. Okay, let's go!"

From Ambrose, we sailed on a broad reach in the Ambrose-Hudson Canyon Separation Zone. The wind stayed steady at twelve knots from the north and after trimming the sails, we were making six and a half knots. Carol became giddy as she sailed in the deepening blue Atlantic and with each glance over her shoulder, land became lower on the horizon. After two hours, I plotted our position. I figured we were sixteen miles off Long Branch, which was already out of sight and almost eighteen miles from the higher Atlantic Highlands. Soon, that would also be gone, and except for a few fishing boats and several ships, Carol would feel what seamen have felt for thousands of years as they sailed to the ends of the earth.

I asked if she wanted a break, but I knew she'd want to stay on the helm.

"No, I'm fine! I want to be on the helm when we lose sight of land."

She then pointed east and said jubilantly, "Oh look, I can see the curve of the earth!"

As I often did, I considered her many facets and smiled as my mind wandered to the image of her the night before when she made love with lustful abandon. Now she was showing the same abandon but in a totally different way and for a totally different reason. Ten minutes later, I lost sight of the Highlands but said nothing. I wanted her to see for herself, and I watched her with my camera at the ready. A moment later, she turned and looked back over her right shoulder.

She yelled. "It's gone! Look, Baby. It's gone!"

I clicked off a series of photos to capture the moment, then looked around. We were almost totally alone on the deep blue sea.

"So what do you think?" I asked.

She said, "I wish there were no other boats around, but I still understand what you mean. It's almost scary not seeing land, but I'm not afraid. I know it's just over there."

"Are you sure it's in that direction?" I asked.

She hesitated, then looked down at the compass and said, "Yeah, smart ass, it's there to the west, but it feels strange not seeing it. I guess if we were going across the ocean it could be a little unsettling."

"Someday you're going to experience that. For now, let's head up and douse the sails."

"Why douse the sails?" she asked.

I chuckled. "Because you said you'd float naked for me."

Carol looked into the cobalt depths. "Will you come in with me?"

I laughed. "Hey, you're the one who wanted to float in a thousand feet of water."

I thought I had her cornered, but then she looked at the depth indicator and said in a scornful tone, "You'll have to keep sailing before I float naked, buster; it's only eighty-four feet!

I smiled. "Okay, can't fool you. Let's head for the barn."

I readied myself at the jib sheets and nodded to her.

"Ready about," she boomed in the stoutest sea going voice she could muster.

"Ready about," I answered in acknowledgement.

Looking around, she said, "Hard a' lee," then brought our bow playfully across the wind. I backed the jib, which brought the bow around even faster. Then, letting it go, I quickly sheeted in on the leeward sheet as we came to a starboard tack. The boom oscillated, then moved over to port as the main filled and *Ursaorion* leaped forward on a close reach.

I said, "A perfect tack!"

Carol said simply, "Thanks, but I gotta pee!"

It was almost one o'clock and we were sailing at six knots on a northwest heading. Carol came back on deck and kissed me, saying, "Thank you for that, Baby. What a thrill it was. Can we do it again someday?"

"Yeah, and we'll go farther out next time."

"I'd like that a lot, but right now I want to watch until I see land."

I gave her the binoculars, then settled in to enjoy my turn at the helm. Five minutes later, she said in a calm voice, "I see something. It's the Highlands, wanna see?"

She offered me the binoculars.

I shook my head. "No thanks, I can see it."

Sailing in near silence, Carol scanned for dolphin, but seeing none, she asked if it was okay to take a nap.

"Sure, Baby. I'll be fine."

Sitting on the leeward cockpit bench, she took off her top without any fanfare and rubbed on suntan lotion, the sight of which shook me from my peaceful daze. She always stirred my senses and I watched her intently as she lay back. Pulling her hat over her eyes, she said, "Please wake me if you see dolphins, okay?"

I said, "I promise." Then I thought, *It is magic sailing like this. There, lying in front of me on our boat, is Carol Dayton, my skinny little girlfriend, now all grown up and her name is Carol Ieva. It isn't a dream, it is a dream come true.*

CHAPTER 12
CHESAPEAKE

By 1992, sailing on Raritan Bay was becoming boring, especially after a winter storm wiped out Horseshoe Cove at Sandy Hook. It was part of Gateway National Park and had been the only undeveloped anchorage in the area offering decent protection. Even summer vacations to Long Island Sound began to lack adventure, so once Christopher was at the Naval Academy in Annapolis, Carol and I began talking about moving *Ursaorion* to Chesapeake Bay.

Compared to Raritan Bay and Long Island Sound, Chesapeake Bay was paradise! With more than eleven thousand miles of coastline, there were hundred's, perhaps thousands of anchorages ranging from urban Baltimore, to secluded coves where one or two boats could find a snug haven. We were almost convinced by the cruising literature alone and while at the Annapolis Boat Show in October, we visited a booth from a marina on the eastern shore at Kent Island Narrows. It was everything our marina in New Jersey wasn't. It had finger piers, a swimming pool, tennis courts, and showers, all at an annual price one third of what we were paying in New Jersey for just the season. To close the deal, they offered free dockage until April if we signed a contract. With the only downside being a three hour drive from our home, we signed and committed ourselves to a new adventure.

After crossing the Bay Bridge on our way home, we stopped at our new marina to pick out a slip. It was easier said than done. This was a six hundred slip marina spread over acres of waterfront with open slips scattered everywhere. Seeing that one dock had a preponderance of sailboats, we strolled over and eventually selected a slip with a wide finger pier, then called it in to the office the next day. All that remained was to move

Ursaorion south as quickly as possible because we didn't want to pay winter storage fees in New Jersey, and we were also hoping to sail on the Chesapeake before the end of the season in mid-November.

I had already used up all my vacation so our plan was to leave on a Friday night and anchor at Sandy Hook, then get a pre-dawn start Saturday and sail to Atlantic City eighty miles away. We could then make Chesapeake City on Sunday and leave the boat there until the following weekend. The logistics were a nightmare and everything hinged on the weather, car rentals and getting rides from friends. We knew the likelihood of so many variables falling into place was slim so as a back up, I found a delivery captain who came highly recommended by our new marina.

After reviewing his resume and testimonials of deliveries he had made, he then quoted us a per diem rate for himself and one crewman. We questioned the need for crew, but he was adamant about it. It was not cheap, but just as I was about to agree, I asked Carol if she would crew. I thought we'd save some money, but more importantly, *Ursaorion* wouldn't be totally in the hands of strangers.

"So, what do you think...do you want to crew?"

She thought about it, then said, "Sure, I'll crew! I can handle the boat and help with lines and do plotting."

The captain looked at me and said, "If that's good with you, Skipper, I'm okay with it."

I said, "I'm fine with it."

As an afterthought, I asked Carol, "How do you feel about doing the trip yourself?"

She said, "You mean alone, just me?"

"Yeah, you could do it if we could get someone to go along with you."

Carol thought for a moment. "No, Baby. I don't feel that comfortable yet."

I said, "Okay, Steve, let's see how the weather shapes up, and if you do the delivery, Carol will be your crew."

As the week progressed, we watched the weather forecast and by Thursday morning, we knew that Plan A was dead in the water. A cold front was moving in Friday with north winds at twenty knots, gusting to twenty-five, so anchoring at Sandy Hook was not going to be an option. The forecast for Saturday was worse, but it was supposed to moderate on Sunday, so we called Captain Steve and asked him if he would be available on Monday to take *Ursaorion* from Manasquan all the way to Kent Narrows.

He said, "Not if this shit keeps up. Have you seen it out there?"

I told him the forecast for Monday was much better and that if we could get the boat to Manasquan on Sunday, he should have good weather.

"Okay, call me Sunday. It's a more challenging trip. Is your wife still going to crew for me?"

"Yeah, she'll be fine. She's a good sailor, better than she thinks."

As forecasted, Saturday morning was blowing so hard I didn't think we would have made it out of the inlet at Morgan Creek. Even in sheltered Raritan Bay, twenty-five knots of north wind was piling up five foot breaking waves at the inlet. We drove down the coast to Manasquan and watched in awe as enormous steep waves crashed onto the massive jetties, sending spray thirty feet in the air and causing vibrations in the parking lot. As we drove back to our marina, I asked Carol if she was sure she'd be okay sailing with the delivery captain. She laughed and said she'd be fine as long as he didn't get frisky along the way.

I laughed. "Well, you better take a club or something, because you make everyone frisky!"

Conditions remained the same for the rest of Saturday, but things began to moderate by evening. Back at our marina, our dock mates happily started another impromptu farewell party for us. While sitting aboard Charlie's boat, our friend Sal came down the dock and seeing we were still there, he called out. "Hey, Ron, Carol, I thought you guys were leaving!" Sitting on Charlie's dock box, I passed him a beer.

Sal was a brash transit cop and a regular character on D-dock. With the crowd on *G-Force* yelling and joking, he blurted out good-naturedly, "Hey, Carol, no disrespect, sweetheart, but everybody in the transit authority is going to miss you!"

Carol said, "Yeah, why's that, Sal?"

Everyone looked at Sal.

He looked at me. "Man, no offense, but you're a lucky guy, amigo."

I said, "Yeah, I am, Sal, but what's your point?"

Once again, Carol questioned him. "So, Sal, why is everyone at the transit authority going to miss me?"

Sal laughed. "Why are they going to miss you? Ha, on account of the video cameras on the Verrazano Bridge."

By now I knew he was pulling her leg, but Carol took the bait.

"What cameras?" she asked.

Sal replied, "The Verrazano Bridge has video cameras to watch the harbor. I had camera duty once and saw you sailing topless. I tried to keep everyone from seeing you, but they already knew about your boat and switched the cameras so monitors all over the city could watch you."

Looking at Carol, I could almost hear the gears turning in her head. After a second of hesitation she dished some out some teasing of her own.

"There must be cameras on the Bay Bridge in Maryland, Sal. Can't you guys hook up to them and watch me sun these puppies on the Chesapeake?"

Everyone let out a howl and Sal laughed.

"Okay, sweetheart, you got me; I was just kidding."

I smiled. Carol handled herself with confidence in a crowd and it reminded me of the day back in Brooklyn when we walked away arm in arm from my street corner friends.

I was up before dawn on Sunday and listened for the sounds of wind in the rigging. There wasn't much so I climbed out of bed more optimistic than when I climbed in the night before. I put on the VHF and caught the NOAA offshore forecast: "Clear skies, wind fifteen to twenty from the northeast, diminishing to ten by late afternoon. Seas six to eight feet, diminishing to three feet by evening." I thought, *Damn, the wind is manageable but the eight foot seas concerned me.* I woke Carol, and after talking about the forecast, we decided to stick to the plan and go to Sandy Hook to see how things actually looked on the ocean.

We put on our harnesses and an hour later we were motoring toward Sandy Hook, eleven miles away. The wind and waves were right on the nose, drenching us with stinging spray that flew back over the dodger.

I only had an apparent wind instrument, so with twenty knots of wind showing and our boat speed at five knots, I estimated the true wind to be about fifteen knots. That seemed very manageable, especially if the forecast for conditions to moderate was accurate. The waves weren't bad either. They seemed less than half the size of the six to eight footers that had been forecasted for the ocean.

Approaching Sandy Hook, the waves became less steep and without white caps. Then, after passing Flynns Knoll, we encountered large ocean swells with a long period. They weren't breaking, except on the beach where they rose up to form towering breakers that thundered against the shore. I instantly thought of the scene at Manasquan Inlet the day before. Motoring into Sandy Hook channel, *Ursaorion* climbed high on the crest of the huge swells, then fell deep into their troughs, and I could swear our mast was sometimes below the crest. In any case, it wasn't a violent motion, just a long, slow rise and an equally long, slow drop. It was like nothing I'd been in before and not at all unpleasant, even for me who was prone to sea sickness. I decided the sea was definitely lying down after the tumultuous conditions from the day before.

Carol asked, "So what are we going to do?"

I said, "Take the helm, let's raise the main and see how we sail in this."

With the wind steady at thirteen knots, we moved along at about three knots with just the main. The sail was also dampening the roll quite a bit as we took the swells on the port quarter when on a southerly course.

I said, "Steer 180°m. That will keep us moving south, but also get us into deeper water where these swells should flatten out a bit. I'm going to call the Coast Guard at Manasquan."

I came back into the cockpit and repeated what the Coast Guard told me. The inlet at Manasquan was still dangerous, but conditions had been improving all morning.

"I say we go for it. It's about twenty-three miles to Manasquan and we can easily do six knots when we unfurl the jib, so we can be there in less than four hours. It's nine thirty now, so if we get there by one thirty and the inlet is still bad, that gives us a couple hours to linger around to see if conditions improve. If it looks good, we go in. If not, we still have plenty of daylight to get back to Sandy Hook or even the marina."

Carol smiled. "Okay, boss, unfurl the jib; let's get going, silly boy!"

I laughed. "Hey, that's silly captain boy to you, wench!"

With the jib unfurled and trimmed, *Ursaorion* raced down the coast, riding the crest and troughs of the large swells as if we were a sleigh on gently rolling hills. The beach communities along the shore clicked off with regularity, and we felt certain that the height of the swells was decreasing with each passing hour. We knew the wind was decreasing because our speed had dropped, and the apparent wind was down and I figured the true wind must be down to about twelve knots, still from the northeast. Arriving off Manasquan, we didn't think the swells were nearly as big as they were in the morning, but when they got to the inlet, they seemed to rise up and thunder onto the jetties and my mouth went dry.

Carol asked, "What do you think, Baby?"

I looked for a moment. "Geez, I don't know. It looks bad; let's furl the jib and hang out a while."

I called the Coast Guard, and they said the inlet was boisterous but navigable, and I thought, *Yeah, in what an aircraft carrier?*

With the jib furled, Carol tacked the boat back and forth a quarter of a mile off the inlet. I watched a sport fishing boat come out with some difficulty, pitching in great arcs as they punched through the waves.

I said aloud, "Going in is a lot more dangerous than coming out. We'll be surfing, and we could broach the boat and slam into the jetty or if those waves are big enough, they could even roll us. Let's wait an hour and I'll make a decision then."

At three thirty, the wind was about twelve knots and the waves at the inlet were smaller, but not as small as I would have liked. Still, I decided to go for it.

"We'll drop the main and fly just the jib, which should help keep the bow pointed downwind."

Carol asked excitedly, "We're not going to use the engine?"

"Yes, of course, but I want the jib to be pulling the bow downwind and keep us moving. Then I'll be able to throttle up quickly with the engine to maintain steerage if we begin to surf."

I explained that once we began surfing, the boat would be moving at the same speed as the water and we'd lose steerage unless we could travel faster than the water again so a force would act against the rudder.

Carol said, "Maybe we should go back."

"We can do this safely or I wouldn't try it, Baby. We just need to be on our toes and react instantly if the boat begins to broach."

She took a deep breath. "Okay, if you say so. What do you want me to do?"

"You tend the jib. Do everything I say and do it quickly. If I tell you to sheet in, don't hesitate, crank in fast. If I say sheet out, then sheet out, but watch me, okay?"

She said nervously, "Okay, I'm ready."

I dropped the main, then put the engine in gear, and we crept closer to the inlet to get a feel for the size and frequency of the waves in the shallower water. The closer we got the more thunderous they sounded against the jetties, but I knew they sounded worse than they were.

"Scared?" I asked.

"Yes, a little."

I smiled and said, "Me too, but let's go."

I turned *Ursaorion* around, and with the wind on our starboard quarter, Carol unfurled the jib and we slowly gathered speed. We were making three knots with the engine at only an idle speed, which gave me a lot of reserve power to keep from broaching. At a hundred yards, Carol looked at me and I could see a hint of fear in her eyes each time a wave crashed onto the jetty with a reverberating boom.

"We're going to be fine," I reassured her and she smiled bravely.

Ten yards from the inlet, the stone jetties were only seventy-five feet on either side of us and loomed ominously close as we fell into the trough of a wave.

"Okay, this is it. The next wave is going to lift us up, and we'll be surfing so hang on!"

A second later, our stern rose frightening fast as the wave slid under us. From then on, everything seemed to happen at warp speed. I could see people on the jetties watching and pointing at us and I thought, *Oh shit.* The wave continued to rise quickly, and we began sliding down its face. I felt the jib drawing well, so I didn't apply engine power as long as I still had steerage because I was afraid we'd slide down the wave too fast.

In an instant, we were surfing fast. Very fast!

I yelled, "No steerage!"

To prevent a broach, I had to sense which way the boat would turn before it actually turned. As we gathered speed, *Ursaorion* surfed between the two stone jetties on what I thought was an eight foot wave. There was a barely perceptible feel in the helm, and an instant later, I goosed the throttle forward. As soon as I sensed the rudder dig in, I twitched the helm to port, then to starboard while increasing the throttle.

I barked, "Sheet in. Now!"

Carol cranked the winch fast and hard, then stopped the instant I said. "Good!"

As we lost speed, I slowly throttled back and we slid into the inlet, surfing the crest of the quickly diminishing wave for almost a hundred yards.

Carol shouted, "That was fun!"

"Fun?" I asked. Then, breathing a sigh of relief. "Were you on the same boat as me?"

We furled the jib and motored to the Brielle Yacht Club where some folks off a beautiful forty-two-foot Grand Banks trawler took our lines.

Once secured, the man asked if we had just come in the inlet. I told him we had. He said they had come in a few hours earlier because his wife had been whining about the big waves the whole way down from Long Island.

"That's all Mama did," he said. "Whine, whine, whine. So I put in here for the night to keep her from crying like a little girl."

Not to be outdone, Mama stepped forward. "Listen to Captain Courageous. He thinks he's the old man of the sea, but ask him what happened when we came in the inlet. I'll tell you what happened, he peed his pants. That's right, Papa peed his pants!"

Carol and I laughed hysterically.

I looked at Papa. "Sorry, man, it just sounded funny."

"Hell, laugh all you want. I ain't ashamed. You ever been surfing on a thirty-five thousand-pound boat with no steerage?"

The forecast for Monday was better than expected. Northeast winds at twelve knots and clear skies. I called Captain Steve to confirm that he was good to go for the morning. He seemed surprised that we made it to Manasquan, but then asked if he could come by to check out the boat. Since Carol would be crewing, I thought she should do the briefing on the boat and equipment. For one thing, it would demonstrate to the captain that she knew what she was doing and I thought it would give her a shot of confidence. It would also give me a chance to observe Steve and make some judgments about his skills by the kind of questions he asked and his understanding of the systems.

Hours later, when they finished walking around the boat and Carol answered all his questions, he said, "Okay, I have to be back by Wednesday and I won't sail around the clock without my own crew so the best I can do is get you to Chesapeake City. One day from here to Atlantic City, maybe Cape May, and then another day to Chesapeake City. That's if the weather cooperates."

I said, "Shit, that really jams us up."

"Sorry man, but I don't sail at night with someone I haven't sailed with before."

"It's okay. I'm just trying figure a way out."

After a moment I said, "Okay, Chesapeake City on Tuesday is fine."

We shook hands and he said he'd be back at six in the morning and for Carol to be ready to go.

When Steve left, Carol asked what we were going to do.

"No problem. You go to Chesapeake City with the captain. We'll leave the boat at Schaefer's Canal Marina and I'll drive down and take you home. We'll return at the end of the week and then sail to Kent Narrows on Saturday. We can then get Christopher to give us a ride back to the car. Now, where do you want to go for dinner?"

After dinner we returned to *Ursaorion* and I sensed Carol was nervous about staying alone on the boat.

"If you really want me to stay, I will, but I'll have a three hour commute to work tomorrow."

"No, I'll be fine; I guess I should get used to it."

I held her in my arms and told her how well she did coming in the inlet.

She said, "I didn't do anything but sheet in the jib a little."

"No, Baby. You did much more than that. You were there and I knew I could count on you. I wouldn't have tried the inlet alone or with anyone else. We make a great crew!"

She hugged me tighter and asked if I was just saying that. I told her I meant it and that if we were going to go cruising someday, I had to be as objective about praising her ability as I was in my criticism of her faults.

She looked at me, and in her most seductive voice asked, "I have faults?"

In an overly-hesitant voice I replied. "We all have faults."

Before I could say more, she tightened her arms around my neck and slowly showered me with soft, tender kisses.

I moaned, "Are you trying to seduce me to spend the night here?"

She smiled coyly. "Oh no, Baby. Maybe just snuggle a little so you can tell me about my faults."

I responded to her kisses and, sensing I was weakening, she stepped back a pace. Without taking her eyes off mine, she unbuttoned her blouse teasingly.

"You do like to snuggle, don't you?"

Exhibiting such spontaneity made her irresistible, and I succumbed to her charms.

As we lay embraced hours later, I said, "So much for just snuggling a little." Then I added, "Be sure to close and lock this door tomorrow night."

"You're not worried about Captain Steve spending the night aboard, are you?"

"No, but we really don't know him and you, my lovely, are a very alluring woman so I wouldn't want him to get any ideas."

Laughing, she said, "Don't worry, I already have my outfit picked out for the whole trip; the same bulky sweatshirt and jeans to sail and sleep in, and I promise I'll lock the cabin door."

She looked at the clock and frowned. "I guess I'll be alright alone here tonight; you can leave if you want to." Then, she pressed her warm body gently against mine and added, "That is if you really want to go home to an empty house and sleep all alone."

I thought, *Even after the lovemaking, I still need her. It's just an hour longer to work from here, so what's the big deal between a two hour and a three hour commute in the morning?*

I kissed her and said, "Hold me!"

She smiled softly and purred. "Goodnight, Baby. Thanks for staying. I love you."

We were up at five thirty, and Carol had the boat ready to go when Steve arrived twenty minutes later.

"Good morning, folks!"

He wasted no time and told Carol to fire up the engine, then asked me to pass dock lines. As soon as I gave Carol the last line and a last kiss goodbye, Steve told me to push off his bow. I watched them pull away from the dock and motor down the Manasquan River until they went around the bend at Gull Island. I thought, *Push off his bow? Screw you, buddy, that's my bow!* Then for good measure, I said aloud, "And my wife!"

As I drove home to shower and change for work, I calculated that at six knots, they would be in Atlantic City by three o'clock. Then I laughed to myself as I thought, *If I don't hear from them by three-ten, I'll call the Coast Guard, FBI, and CIA!*

Carol called at four o'clock. Everything was fine and they were at the marina in Atlantic City. She said Steve was surprised that she had wanted to sail. He explained that a delivery captain generally motored along to keep a schedule, but being the owner, he let her sail and even taught her some racing sail trim tricks along the way. She called me again at nine o'clock to say she was back from dinner, but that Steve stayed behind at the casino. I laughingly chided her.

"Are you wearing your sweatshirt and jeans to bed?"

"Yes, Baby, and I'm locking the door to the aft cabin, but don't worry, he's been a perfect gentleman."

"Ah ha," I said. "Those are the ones you need to worry about."

She laughed. "No worries, I have my pepper spray. Okay, I'm going to sleep; we have a ninety mile day tomorrow. I miss you and can't wait to see you on the dock waiting for me."

"What time are you leaving Atlantic City?" I asked.

"Steve wants to get underway at five to catch the currents in Delaware Bay so we can get into Chesapeake City around eight tomorrow night."

"That's good for me because it's about a four-hour drive. I'll leave work an hour early and be there when you get in."

I missed her and thought I must be nuts making her sleep aboard our boat with a stranger. She had a separate cabin, and he came recommended and had a good resume but Carol was an attractive woman. *What if he came on to her?* I lay awake thinking that what bothered me most was that I even put her in the situation. I had a restless night, but was elated when she woke me at five in the morning.

"We're just getting ready to leave Atlantic City, but will be stopping in Cape May for fuel so we might be in a little later than eight."

"I'll be there on the dock whatever time you get in."

For me, sitting in my office, it was a totally unproductive day. I checked the chart every fifteen minutes, recalculating where they might be. Carol called from Cape May to say they topped off the fuel tank and we're about to get underway. They were right on schedule, and with sixty miles to go, if Steve calculated currents for Delaware Bay correctly, they would be in Chesapeake City around eight as planned. I thought to myself, *Now I know what she feels like when I go off on a business trip,* and I made a mental note to call Carol more often when I was away in the future.

At three o'clock, I said screw it, and left work. I wanted Carol to see me waiting for her when they arrived, so after breaking many speed limits, I found myself sitting down to dinner at Schaefer's Canal house two hours early. Eight o'clock came and went, but there was still no sign of *Ursaorion.*

The C&D canal pilot station shared a dock with Schaefer's, so I asked one of the pilots if there was a way for me to find out if they were in the canal. He said, "No, but the current is ripping east right now, so if they're coming from the Delaware Bay, they're bucking a two knot current." I thought, *So much for Captain Steve's current calculations.* There was nothing to do but wait. I watched a few tugs and barges go by, then a big ocean-going ship loomed ominously out of the night. I became concerned for Carol's safety. *Shit, what if they got hit in the dark by one of those ships?* I tried to sleep in my car but that thought kept me awake.

Then, at eleven fifteen while pacing the dock, I saw a tiny set of running lights approaching. I looked through my binoculars and could see Carol standing on the bow, ready to throw a line. I moved to take it as they approached and she waved and called out excitedly.

"Hi, Baby. We made it; did you see that big ship that went by?" Then she added, "It just missed us!"

I thought, *Just what I need to hear.* I took the line from her and secured it to a cleat, then ran aft to take a stern line from Steve. With *Ursaorion* secured, I stepped aboard and Carol gave me a big hug and kissed me solidly on the lips.

I said, "I missed you so much!"

She put her head against my shoulder and said, "I missed you too, Baby."

As Steve rigged spring lines, he laughed aloud. "You two are like a couple of newlyweds! I got your whole life history for the last eighteen hours, so I guess I should know better." Then he got businesslike again. "Okay, I've got an early day tomorrow, so can we close up the boat and get on the road?"

I also had an early day, so I went below to switch off the batteries. We were locked up and on the road by eleven forty-five.

Three days later, we drove to Chesapeake City to make the last leg of the journey to our new marina. With our gear stowed aboard *Ursaorion* we strolled up to Schaefer's for drinks and dinner, then ended the night with a bottle of wine back aboard our boat. In spite of talking into late hours, we were up early and underway by seven in order to have a favorable current for the fifty mile trek to Kent Narrows.

With the current beginning to run swiftly, we raised our sails and made a respectable six knots in just eight knots of northwest wind. It was still a bit chilly when we left the Elk River and entered Chesapeake Bay, but as we passed Worton Point in the late morning, the sun warmed considerably. We felt like explorers as we passed landmarks and rivers with historical and exotic names. The Sassafras and Bohemia Rivers evoked visions of colonial days and we excitedly made promises to return and explore them in the spring. Once past Poules Island, it was the broad expanse of the bay that impressed us most. There was so much to see and so many places to explore and this was just the upper bay. I thought, *Yes, we were going to like it here!*

At two thirty, we passed Swan Point and came to a course of 170°m, which brought us toward the Chester River. This approach would soon become familiar, but right now it was all new and our sense of exploration was heightened as we left the wide bay and entered the more confining river that would be our new home. With the current now beyond slack flood, we picked up some lift once in the river, and an hour later, we found the serpentine channel into Kent Narrows. It was a series of dog legs that ran on an east-west axis by Long Point, then turned sharply south into the narrows where the entrance to Mears Point Marina was located.

Once in Kent Narrows, sounds of music carried across the water and we were treated to our first waterside view of Red Eyes Dock Bar. As I looked for the marina entrance, Carol swayed to a catchy tune and made me promise to take her to Red Eyes for a celebratory drink once we got in. Finding our slip and with help from several willing men on the dock, we secured *Ursaorion* in her new home and met our new neighbors; Gene and Jane who greeted us with cold beers and an invitation to a party the following weekend. Then, with several hours to kill before Christopher was scheduled to drive us to our car in Chesapeake City, I did as promised and took Carol to Red Eyes.

Chapter 13
Annapolis

It was the end of October, but with many crews sailing as late as Thanksgiving, we decided to get in one trip to Annapolis before winter. Setting out on a beautiful fall day, we enjoyed a brisk sail across the bay, entering the Severn River in the fading late afternoon light. As soon as Carol saw the spires of town and the Naval Academy dome, she grew increasingly impatient.

"Oh look, Ron. It's beautiful. Can we come back again?"

I laughed. "Carol, we're not even there yet and you're already asking if we can come back. Besides, we've been here often."

She turned and scolded me in a mocking voice. "Not by boat, Ron. Not by boat!"

Finding a berth along the seawall, we strolled across Dock Street to the historic Middleton Tavern for dinner. What we didn't know was that after the dinner hour, the bar room spills over into the restaurant, and with the arrival of a band, a fair portion of Annapolis crowds into this popular pub. Many drinks later and when the crowd seemed like it couldn't get any bigger, a parade of collage students came in. Marching through the crowd in a conga line, they solicited items of clothing for a fraternity scavenger hunt. The crowd cheered when they called for a black bra, and just as the clamor died down, Carol, with several margaritas in her, shouted at the top of her lungs. "Hey, I've got one!"

The place nearly went silent and all eyes feel on her. The guy with the scavenger list looked at her admiringly and said, "I did say black, right?"

In a feat equal to Houdini escaping from a straight jacket, Carol nimbly removed her bra from under her sweater and donated it to the fraternity boys. The tavern crowd went wild as the kid held it over his head, stretching it out to show his friends that it was indeed black, and frilly lace to boot! Several men and one woman bought Carol drinks, which she eagerly shared with me, and every letch in the place pondered the charms hidden under her sweater. We stayed until last call, and afterwards, as we half-strolled and half-staggered across the street to our boat, several bar patrons whistled, and one yelled, "Lucky you, man!"

Carol smiled and hugging my arm, said, "I have so much fun with you, Baby."

The next morning, we had an early brunch with Christopher at Buddy's, then sailed back to Kent Narrows. As we approached Love Point in mid-afternoon, Carol stood in the companionway, and after looking to be sure no other boats were nearby, she removed her top and let the sun bathe her in its golden warmth.

I said, "God, you're so beautiful! What's got you so frisky?"

She said, "Well, last night was fun."

I laughed and asked if she meant donating her bra or afterwards back on the boat.

She looked at me seductively. "Both! I wouldn't have taken off my bra if I'd been sober, but then once I did, it was a turn on for the rest of the night."

As I steered the boat, I reached for her. She closed her eyes and slowly rolled her head back and let me caress her. Then, when I began to think of anchoring for a while, the sound of an engine broke my train of thought.

Carol heard it at the same time and opened her eyes. They became as wide as saucers and she pushed my hand away and covered herself.

"Oh damn, it's a cop boat!"

I looked back, and sure enough, a Maryland DNR Police boat was twenty-five yards astern of us. I wasn't sure if he could see Carol because our flag waving from our stern and me on the helm might have blocked his view. Not knowing what the law was regarding a woman being topless in Maryland, I told her to stay covered as the sound of the engine drifted to port.

Looking forward, I asked, "What's he doing now?"

"He's coming closer. What should I do?"

It occurred to me that she should simply go below, but she remained frozen under the dodger.

"What's he doing now?" I asked again.

She said, "Damn, he's waving." Then she asked, "What should I do?"

I laughed. "I don't know; maybe he wants you to wave back. You could go below you know."

Fully expecting her to duck below, she surprised me by suddenly dropping her arms, then boldly waved back to the cop. A moment later, I heard the boat rev up and with a toot on his horn; he peeled away and sped off to the west.

I looked at her incredulously. "I can't believe you did that!"

"I can't believe I did it either, but screw him, if he wants to be a peeping Tom, I got pissed off and decided to give him something to peep at."

"Yeah, but who knows what the laws are here; maybe he could have given us a summons or something."

She laughed and said, "Yeah, and I bet you would have put the ticket in our sailing album!"

I smiled. "I would have, but for now stay right there. I'll take a photo of you for the album instead!"

Now it's one of those great snapshots of a moment in time with a whole story to tell.

With the arrival of November, temperatures dipped into the forties, so we remained close to our marina, limiting our explorations to the Chester River. As with all the tributaries on Chesapeake Bay, the Chester offers dozens of smaller rivers and hundreds of coves to anchor in. Fortunately, we happened upon the Corsica. Like so many places I've been with Carol, it was magical, as much from her presence as the place itself. Her sense of wonder excited me, and I truly derived pleasure from seeing her happy. On this day, the Corsica River made her very happy.

Moving slowly along the south shore at the mouth of the river, we anchored behind a long spit of land that shoaled out to the red nun buoy marking the narrow entrance. It was somewhat secluded, but there was a dock, a small private lighthouse and some buildings. Still, it was sheltered from the chop on the Chester River and offered a spectacular panoramic view. As daylight faded, we sat in the cockpit bundled in sweaters and wool watch caps, drinking wine and holding hands. While watching a beautiful sunset, we heard the soft murmurings of what would be our first experience with migrating geese. There were thousands of geese! The sky became thick with honking geese. We marveled as they landed, completely blanketing the cove and shore, their honking becoming a subdued murmur as they settled in for the night. Except for four years sailing in Florida, we returned every fall to the same anchorage on the Corsica River to watch the geese, hold hands, and sip wine.

Winter came all too quickly. We skied a few times and went to a few indoor boat shows, but mostly we spent cold winter nights going over charts, cruising guides and planning voyages we would make the following spring. This was another side of Carol I loved, and it reminded me of our childhood. She had the same sense of wanderlust as me and she was always dreaming of faraway places. As I had so many times before, I tried to remember the first time I saw her when we were kids. I couldn't though. It seemed like she was always there. I do know that once I became aware I liked her; it was this adventurous aspect of her I liked most. Back then, I didn't think any of our friends felt that way. For everyone else, it seemed there was just the day and Brooklyn. For Carol and I, there was tomorrow, and the world. Then as now, there was no one else I wanted to share it with more than her.

Spring of 1995 came as fast as the previous fall had left us and along with our friends from O-Dock, we were among the first boats to sail from our marina in early April. We spent most weekends exploring new places with our friends, but every now and then Carol and I sailed off on our own. On Memorial Day weekend, however, we joined in a tradition that we've observed ever since; anchoring in Baltimore's Inner Harbor.

Baltimore Harbor technically extends as far east as Dundalk on the northern bank of the Patapsco River and Curtis Bay on the southern bank.

Inner Harbor is a small rectangular area at the terminus of the north branch of the river, west of Fort McHenry. In years past, it had been a bustling seaport within a seaport and ships from all over the world docked there to load and unload their goods. As container terminals expanded outside the city, Inner Harbor and the neighborhood around it decayed and became a dilapidated slum until a redevelopment project in the seventies revived the area. Now, with the Baltimore Aquarium, Maryland Science Center and Harborplace, a tasteful collection of shops and restaurants, the area became a popular tourist attraction to visit by car or boat. There is also the *USS Constellation*, an 1800's era sailing ship and the *USS Torsk*, a WWII submarine, all of which made this an exciting destination.

It was here we discovered Mama Jama, a reggae band Carol became a dedicated fan of. They played all over the bay, and we often planned our sailing trips to coincide with where they would be on any given weekend. With her love of dancing, Carol would groove for hours to their music, and when she exhausted me, she'd dance alone or with anyone who would dance with her. It was contagious, and she soon had most of our O-Dock friends joining us on Friday nights at Red Eyes or The Jetty, especially if Mama Jama was playing.

Carol's daughter, Nancy, occasionally came to the marina and after seeing this side of her mother; she learned to enjoy sailing with us even more. Like her mom, Nancy also loved to dance and one night at The Jetty, she got to see Mama Jama playing. I danced with Carol until my knees ached and for every margarita I bought, Nancy bought a tequila shooter in return. Mom and daughter were in rare form, but I was fading fast, and thinking this was a good opportunity for them to spend some time together without me, I opted to go back to the boat.

As I anticipated, Carol shouted, "It's only eleven o'clock!"

"I know, Baby, but I'm really tired. You and Nancy stay!"

Shouting above the noise of the bar and band, she asked Nancy if she wanted to stay. Nancy said, "Hell yeah, I'm having fun!"

Carol gave me a long and passionate kiss, then went back onto the dance floor while I finished my drink. Nancy joined her for a while, but even she took a break. Not Carol though. I happily watched her in her own world among the crowd on the dance floor, completely enjoying herself as she moved to the music. Nancy stood by me and asked, "Does she ever take a break?"

I laughed. "Only when the band does!"

Finishing my drink, I added, "Okay, I'm going back to the boat. Look out for her; she gets carried away."

Several hours later, I heard mother and daughter staggering down the dock, laughing and giggling as only two drunken sailors could. They climbed aboard *Ursaorion* making a lot of noise in their feeble attempts to whisper so as not to wake me. I came into the main cabin, and they burst out laughing.

"What's so funny?"

Laughing again, Carol said, "Your hair is pointy!"

I pushed back my hair. "That's what happens when I've been sleeping," making a point to emphasize *sleeping*.

"Did you girls have a good time?"

Carol giggled and said, "We had a great time," then asked for a beer.

Nancy said, "Your wife is a wild woman!"

"My wife? Hey, she's your mother!"

Nancy briefed me on what happened.

"After we left The Jetty, we were walking back to the boat when a beat up white car came to a screeching halt by us. The driver spoke with a Jamaican accent and asked us if we wanted to go to a party."

Carol yelled. "It was Orlando from Mama Jama!"

"Mom, I'm telling the story!"

Carol laughed. "Okay, so tell it already!"

Nancy went on. "Yeah, she got all giddy like a teenager and told him she was their number one fan! All I could see was a big grin on his face like he just hit the jackpot. It was almost an evil smile, and he kept trying to talk us into going to a party with him."

Carol laughed again. "Party pooper!"

Nancy shook her head and continued. "Then she said we should go to the party, but I smelled trouble and pot, so I told her we had to get back to the boat."

"She kept saying. 'Come on! Just for a little while,' but there was no way in hell I was getting in that car to go to a party with a strange Jamaican!"

I laughed and said, "Good thing I left you there to keep an eye on her, huh? What happened next?"

"After he drove off, I explained to her that the two of us were probably going to be the party."

Still thinking it was a joke, Carol pushed Nancy, then called her a party pooper again. She giggled again, then hurriedly went to the head. When she was gone, Nancy said, "She's disappointed with me, but I bet in the morning she'll be glad I talked her out of it."

"I'm sure she will. I told you, she gets carried away."

Nancy laughed. "Boy, did she ever want to go! She was like an excited little kid, not even thinking that anything bad that could happen. She was blissfully unaware that there could be anything wrong in going to a party with her favorite band!"

Then, from the head we heard the distinct sound of someone praying to the porcelain god.

I laughed. "Oh boy, her hair is going to hurt tomorrow morning."

We spent the following weeks exploring new places and revisiting old ones, but Carol always loved going back to Annapolis. When we weren't there or rafting up with our friends elsewhere, we'd go off to a secluded anchorage where oftentimes we'd be the only boat. We weren't hermits, but we just liked being alone sometimes. It made us feel like we were exploring uncharted new areas and sometimes we'd lie on deck under the stars and Carol would talk seriously of distant galaxies, UFO's and aliens. Whatever we did, we always talked about our dreams to go cruising someday, and I'd stop and think, *We're just like we were when we were kids back in Brooklyn!*

Over Labor Day weekend, our friends planned to sail to Swan Creek for a quiet holiday but Carol and I opted to go back to Baltimore instead. We left the marina and came to a course of 325°m, which would take us to Seven Foot Knoll at the entrance to the Patapsco River and then Baltimore twelve miles beyond. Taking a slip along the promenade seawall across from *USS Constellation*, we were close to the pavilions of Harborplace and

right in the thick of things. Although it was interesting to talk with folks
from all over the world, we found it noisy and crowded with hordes of tourists sitting on the wall day and night directly above our open hatches.

    With that in mind, we cast off lines the next morning and moved
out into the anchorage west of the water taxi dock and *USS Torsk*. There, we
dropped our hook and after enjoying a late breakfast on deck in the shade of
the World Trade Center, we then went ashore to visit the aquarium where
Carol gleefully watched the dolphins for hours. At night, we had dinner in
Little Italy, then went dancing at Power Plant Live, a collection of restaurants and night clubs located off the Harbor in Market Place.

    Later that night, we sat in the cockpit in the chilled air musing
over our day. Carol was wrapped in a blanket as we savored a bottle of wine
and marveled that we were sitting on our boat in the downtown area of a
major city surrounded by tall buildings. Carol kissed me and asked, "Think
anyone can see us?"

    I said, "I'm sure no one's in the office buildings, but those are hotels
over there, and I guess someone could see the boat if they were looking."

    "But could they see us?" she asked.

    "I don't know. There's some reflected light, but I guess not way out
here."

    "Kiss me!" she said.

    I turned to her and as always she took my breath away. She held
open the blanket invitingly, and I wondered if anyone looking out a window or walking along the promenade could see her, but I thought, *God, she
looks so beautiful*. We embraced in the chilly night air, surrounded by the
city on three sides and several other boats in the anchorage.

    I said, "Why don't we go to bed?"

    "We will, soon." Then she showered me with soft kisses.

    I was rudely awakened in the early morning by cold rain lashing
down upon me through the open hatch over our bed. Struggling to fully
open my eyes, I jumped up, closed the hatch, then stuck my head out the
companionway to make sure we hadn't dragged anchor in the unexpected
squall. Being chilly, I lit the propane heater, then returned to the warmth of
our bed. Carol snuggled against me and asked what all the noise was.

"The weather's gone to hell. We'll stay put until it improves or if we have to, we can spend another night here."

She snuggled closer. "If we spend another night here, remind me not to get frisky in the cockpit. It was nice, but it was so cold."

I laughed. "Hey, it was your idea, wench."

"Do you have any complaints?" she asked.

"No complaints from me!"

She smiled. "Good, can I stay in bed?"

"Sure, stay here as long as you want, but I'm wide awake. Shit, listen to that crap."

Even in the shelter of the tall buildings of Inner Harbor, *Ursaorion* strained at her anchor while being buffeted by the wind and rain.

Getting out of bed to a much warmer cabin, I shut the heater, then put some coffee on after tuning into NOAA weather. The report wasn't good. "Rain, heavy. Ending by late morning, wind east at fifteen to twenty knots, diminishing to ten to fifteen by afternoon; chance of an afternoon thunderstorm." I thought, *It's going to be a lousy day, but it could be worse: the wind could be right on the nose.* I preferred leaving that day, but I thought we should at least wait until the rain stopped. Reaching for my coffee and a book, I smiled as I decided not to decide just yet.

I read quietly until Carol's sleepy voice rang out from the aft cabin. "I smell coffee."

I poured her a cup of hot coffee, then said sarcastically, "Good morning to you too."

"I'm sorry. Good morning, Baby, but I need coffee; it's so cold in here."

"Come on, it's not cold; get your butt up and I'll put the heater on again."

As she threw on some sweats, I lit the propane heater, and within moments the cabin warmed noticeably. By the time Carol came out of the head a moment later, it was almost cozy.

Reviewing our departure options, Carol voted to stay. "Let's wait until the rain stops okay?" As an afterthought she added, "I still don't understand how the propane heater makes water."

I laughed. "Where did that come from?"

"You told me that once!"

"I know I did, but that was a long time ago. It's true, but what made you think of it just now?"

"I don't know. It just popped into my head."

I started to explain, but she said, "Not now, my brain is still drunk; tell me later, okay?"

I rolled my eyes and chuckled. "Okay, scatterbrain, I'll tell you when we're driving home. We've got one mushy banana left; how about banana pancakes?" Carol smiled a super-exaggerated smile, which I knew meant yes!

The rain stopped before noon so we got underway with the wind gusting to twenty knots out of the east. We motored to Lazaretto Point, where we were able to steer southeast down the Patapsco River. As Carol brought our bow into the wind, I raised the main with a single reef. I let out the traveler a bit and Carol killed the engine. A moment later, I rolled out the jib to the first reef point and we galloped off at nearly seven knots.

Ursaorion was a tender boat and even with the main and jib reefed, we had our rail in the water. Carol was on the helm and said, "I'm struggling here. She wants to head up bad. Should we put in a second reef in?"

"No, I think we're okay." Then I let out the main a bit. "The forecast has been right so far, so the wind should be diminishing soon and we only have another fifteen miles to reach the Chester River."

She said with some trepidation, "Okay, just be ready to let go of the mainsheet if I yell out."

An hour later we were due south of North Point and slamming into four foot waves. The wind was still out of the east but had diminished to fifteen knots with only an occasional higher gust. I relieved Carol on the helm because she was tired, but it also helped me ward off the queasiness I was beginning to feel as we got further out in the bay where the waves were bigger. She was right; the boat still had a lot of weather helm. We couldn't ease the main any further, so we plowed into waves and used muscle to keep her from heading up in the gust.

As I wrestled with the wheel, we took heavy spray and a few solid waves over our bow. Carol, who had tucked herself in the lee of the dodger, said, "There's a boat coming up on us fast."

I looked back and saw a sailboat well off our starboard quarter, but definitely coming up fast.

"We're busting our hump trying to hold a steady course and this guy is slicing through the waves like a hot knife through butter."

A few moments later, Carol yelled excitedly. "It's a Crealock, Baby!"

Looking astern again, I could see that, sure enough, it was a Crealock 37, the boat we planned to eventually buy and go cruising in!

"Damn, she looks beautiful, huh?"

Carol agreed, and we both watched intently as she quickly closed the distance.

Ten minutes later, the Crealock overtook us close-hauled under full sail.

"Beautiful." I said out loud. "Look at her, Carol."

I was captivated as I watched her clipper bow slice smoothly through the waves. As I stood and struggled with both hands on *Ursaorion's* helm, the man on the Crealock sat with one leg crossed over the other, just one hand on the helm and a cup of coffee in the other. He then added insult to injury by letting go of the helm briefly to wave to us. Carol waved back and yelled across the water, "Beautiful boat!"

The man nodded a final goodbye as he and his ship left us in his wake.

Entering the Chester River, the waves flattened considerably and we fell off the wind, steering almost due south toward our marina at Kent Narrows five miles away.

I said aloud, "We have years before we can go cruising, but it's time. I want that boat."

Carol looked up from her book. "What, Baby?"

"We've had *Ursaorion* ten years; we're not waiting any longer. We're going to buy the Crealock this winter."

Chapter 14

Lastdance

We understood market conditions for used Crealock 37's, so we believed we could afford a three to five year old boat. Built by Pacific Seacraft, they held their value well, and if in good condition, they were priced used for about what they sold for when new. They remained unchanged in basic design for twenty years so we went to the dealer in Annapolis to check out the interiors of new boats.

The Crealock 37 is small as far as thirty-seven foot boats go. They have an extremely fine entry forward, a narrow beam, and a canoe stern. They are strong and very seaworthy ocean going boats that could take us anywhere in the world and as Carol liked to say, "They're pretty!"

Actually they are beautiful, a perfect match of form and function, but I liked the way she said it. "They're pretty!"

Once at the dealer, we made it clear that we could only afford a used boat. They would broker *Ursaorion* for us but only if we brought her to their yard in Annapolis where they could show her more easily. With almost two months left to the sailing season we balked but our salesman Rod said they needed to have her surveyed and wanted to show her in November. Looking ahead to spring, I said, "We might be without a boat if we don't find a new one by then."

Rod smiled. "Ron, Carol, you will be sailing a Crealock 37 in the spring!"

Driving over the Bay Bridge, we shared our feelings.

Carol said, "I know we want a new boat, but *Ursaorion* has taken us to so many places, and we have wonderful memories of her."

I understood her feelings. "Carol, submarine or sailboat, a ship takes on a life of its own and it's always hard to walk down the gangway for the last time,"

"Yeah, but it's still sad."

"It is, but other crews will take her to new places, it's time for us to get the Crealock."

And so in the fall of 1995, we sailed *Ursaorion* for the last time. The wind was west at twelve knots and the temperature was in the forties, which was cold for October. We could have sailed the shorter sixteen mile route around Love Point, making Annapolis in four hours, but as we motored into the Narrows, Carol quietly asked if we could take the longer route through Eastern Bay and around Bloody Point.

I said, "That's eight more miles and you're already cold. It will take two hours longer."

In a forlorn voice she asked, "It's our last sail in this good little boat. Please, Ron?"

Looking at her bundled in a parka and foul weather jacket, her legs covered with a blanket, I smiled. "Okay, Baby. Bloody Point it is. Call the bridge tender and tell him we're standing by for the next opening."

She smiled and reached for the VHF radio. "Kent Narrows bridge tender, Kent Narrows bridge tender. Good morning this is the southbound sailing vessel *Ursaorion* standing by for your next opening."

The radio crackled, "*Ursaorion*, fifteen minutes."

Ten minutes later, as we drifted in the lazy current waiting for the bridge to open, I stepped away from the helm knowing Carol wanted to make this last transit. She was more connected to *Ursaorion* than me because she learned to sail in this boat. It held the same charm for her that a beat up old Lightening I learned to sail in held for me. We drifted closer to the bridge and Carol shifted into forward, turning into the current with only enough throttle to hold our position. I smiled and thought about how far she had come as a sailor and could see the self-confidence she had gained on the water was also evident in nearly everything she did ashore.

The horn sounded a shrill blast and the bridge began its awkward rise. Carol looked over her shoulder, and when she was certain it had opened wide enough, she throttled up and put *Ursaorion* into a slow turn.

We moved smartly through the narrow opening and out into Prospect Bay for a final sail in a boat that had given us a decade of good service and great memories.

Carol sailed the entire way to Annapolis, letting me relieve her only when she needed to use the head. She was tired but content when we arrived at the dock six hours later where we were greeted by Christopher. After removing the last of our personal belongings, we turned the keys over to the broker and said goodbye to *Ursaorion* for what we thought would be the last time. Christopher drove us back across the bay to our marina, and after a quiet dinner with him, he returned to the Naval Academy and we drove home. For the first time in ten years, we were without a boat.

Fall became winter and we spent countless hours looking at ads for a Crealock all over the eastern seaboard. We even looked at other well made boats like Caliber, Cabo Rico, and Island Packet, but seeing them only reinforced our desire for a Crealock 37. Putting almost everything aside, we focused our attention to naming our yet to be found new boat. This was serious stuff because this would be our last boat and we would own her for the rest of our seagoing days. Whatever name we chose, it would be what countless friends, old and new, would come to know us by.

Our naming requirements were straightforward. First and foremost, it had to be linked to us. It had to be succinct and sound clear over the radio. It should preferably be one word and finally, we didn't want anything with a play on words like *C-Shell* or *Y-Knot*. After independently developing our short list, we sat in front of our fireplace with a bottle of wine on a cold Sunday afternoon to name our still un-purchased boat.

I asked, "How many names do you have on your list?"

"Just one," she replied.

"Just one?"

"Yes, just one!" she said again.

I looked into her eyes and saw what looked like steadfast determination.

"Do you wanna go first?"

She smiled like she had a good poker hand. "No, you go first."

I took a sip of wine. "Okay, here's my list in order of preference!" I laid a sheet of paper on the floor with three typewritten names on it:

1. *"Somewhere"*—From the song in Westside Story.
2. *Carol Lee*—For you.
3. *Barcanostra*—Italian, meaning Our Boat

She gave me a radiant smile. "You'd really name the boat after me?"

"Of course I would; it would make a great name."

"I'm really touched, Ron, but I don't want it. I want this."

She put an index card on the floor with a single hand written name on it in her own script, and said out loud. *"Lastdance."*

I was puzzled for a minute.

Carol said, "We both had the same idea, a song from when we were kids. Mine is "Save the Last Dance for Me*,*" by the Drifters."

Then she touched my hand and said, "And I did save the last dance for you, Baby."

I just stared at her.

She said, "Don't you remember, Ron?"

My eyes welled up. "Of course I remember. It was the last thing you said to me the morning you moved to New Jersey. You said you'd always save the last dance for me."

I put my arms around her and held her to me.

Through soft tears she said, "I did, Ron. I saved the last dance for you."

Once we composed ourselves, I said, "But the name in the song isn't one word."

She squeezed my hand. "So what, just think, people will ask us what it means, and we can tell them our story."

I smiled. "I like it! *Lastdance* it is! Now all we need is a boat to go with the name!"

We spent the rest of the winter looking at listings for a new boat, but there weren't any Crealock 37's on the market we could afford. By early March we began to wonder if we'd find a boat by spring. Carol thought we should look at other models and I had to agree that maybe a Crealock wasn't in the cards for us. We found a Caliber 38 for sale by the owner in Norfolk, Virginia and we began a dialogue with him. Two weeks later, we went there to look at the boat.

Driving to Virginia, we talked about some of the advantages of a Caliber over a Crealock. It was almost two feet wider in the beam and had a square transom which gave it a lot more interior volume, allowing for creature comforts such as a separate shower stall in the head and a big Pullman bed. I knew Carol liked it and I agreed that it would clearly meet our needs, but she could see my heart wasn't in it. She suggested several times that we turn around and go home, continuing our search for a Crealock. I thanked her for the thought, but said we may as well at least look at the boat.

"Hey, maybe Blue Pete's is still there, so if nothing else, we can have a nice romantic dinner!"

The Caliber is a good little boat to be sure and this one was in great shape and in our price range. I could see that Carol liked it, but I wasn't crazy about giving up on a Crealock. Nevertheless, we talked about putting a deposit on her. Again, I hesitated. I told the owner I wanted to give it some thought and talk it over with Carol alone. We strolled down the dock and she stopped.

"You don't want it, do you?"

I looked at her then at the boat. Her gaze followed mine and together we just stared.

I said, "It's just another boat!"

Carol replied, "I don't know much about the seaworthiness and construction things that you know about but I like the interior."

"Look at this boat, then close your eyes and picture the Crealock and tell me what you think?"

She did as I asked, then opened her eyes and said, "An RV with sails!"

I laughed. "Well, the naval architect term is a block coefficient of one. Even if the boats are close to the construction criteria we wanted, the Crealock is as you've often said, 'Pretty!'"

Ever unconditional, Carol said, "Let's tell them no thanks and go find Blue Pete's!"

A month later our broker called me at work.

"Ron, I have a new thirty-seven that just came in!"

I hung up on him.

He called back. "Hey, Ron, Rod here again. I think we got disconnected."

"We didn't get disconnected, I hung up on you!"

"Why'd you do that?"

"Because I told you I can't afford a new boat, that's why!"

"Listen to me, this boat is almost in your price range, but you've got to get here first thing tomorrow morning. Every salesman is contacting prospects even as we speak. Can you come?"

"Rod, don't jerk my chain. What do you mean by almost in my price range?"

"All I can say is a deal fell through on this boat and we can make this happen. Can you be here?"

Even though I agreed to be there, I really didn't believe a new boat was in the cards, but I was hooked.

I called Carol at work and told her.

She laughed. "So we're not even going to consider a new boat, huh? Can I go with you?"

"Of course, that's why I'm calling, to see if you can get off from work."

I told her even though I didn't think we could afford a new boat we should at least go check it out.

"Alright, but you sure sound excited; I'll see you at home around six, okay?"

I then called Christopher and left a message for him that we would stop by and have lunch with him at the Naval Academy the next day.

We drove to Annapolis that night so we could be at the broker's office first thing in the morning. After dinner at Maria's, we went back to our hotel and poured over brochures of the Crealock 37. We drank wine and talked about everything from interior fabrics to the kind of oil lamp we wanted and then went to bed excited and full of expectations. Even though they didn't open until nine o'clock, we were at the broker's office at eight and there on stands in front of the building, was *Hull # 313*. She was definitely brand new, and we hastily climbed aboard. The cabin was locked so we couldn't go below, but it didn't matter. As I stood on her deck, I was totally absorbed with the thought that this beautiful little ship could be ours.

She was cutter rigged with both headsails on roller furling and her canvas was the dark navy blue we wanted. Her ports and winches were chromed bronze and her teak looked magnificent in the morning sun. As I sat behind the helm, Carol's voice broke my reverie. "Where are you, Ron?"

"What?"

She smiled. "Where were you? You seemed like you were in a trance."

"I was. I was daydreaming we were sailing in turquoise blue waters and you were sitting right there in the cockpit sipping a sissy drink with a little umbrella."

We went back to the car to warm up. Carol asked if maybe our broker was full of crap about all the other salesmen contacting other buyers.

"Yeah, probably." Then looking at my watch, I said, "I suppose one of us should be up there by the office door, just in case he wasn't full of crap."

Carol said, "It's so cold out and besides, it's a work day. No one else will come here."

I thought, *She's probably right, but it would really piss me off if someone drove up and got to be first in line after we had been sitting here for almost an hour.* While Carol waited in the car, I took first watch at the broker's front door.

When our salesman arrived, I was still the only one in line. Carol chuckled as we sat alone in the office and she softly asked, "So where do you think the horde of other buyers are?"

I said, "Okay, so maybe we got reeled in with the sales pitch."

Laughing, she drew on her Cherokee heritage and referred to the old Tonto/Lone Ranger joke, saying, "We got reeled in? What you mean, we, white man?"

I gave her a gentle kick under the table as Rod came in with the paperwork.

After pouring us coffee he got right to the point.

"Here's the deal," as he nodded toward the new Crealock in the boat yard. "That boat was sold, but the sale fell through. If we can close a deal this morning, she's yours for one eighty-six!"

Carol coughed and kicked me under the table.

"Rod, I told you our limit was a hundred fifty!"

"Yes you did, but that was for a five-year-old boat. I know you've done your homework on these boats; you have to agree that one eighty-six is an extraordinary price for a brand new Crealock 37."

I knew he was right, but she was still thirty-six thousand more than I wanted to spend and I couldn't mask my disappointment.

"Can you leave us alone a few minutes to discuss it?"

Rod told us to take our time as he left the room, and as soon as the door closed, I told Carol I was sorry I dragged her down there.

She took my hands in hers. "Is it a good price for the boat?"

"It's a great price, but I didn't want to spend that much because we'd have to finance more than I want to."

Always practical, she asked, "Is it more than you want to spend or more than we can afford?"

"It's more than I want to spend because the extra thirty-six thousand will probably add three hundred a month to the loan payment."

Carol laughed. "Ron, be serious. We could stop drinking wine and save that much!"

For the first time since the salesman called me a day earlier, I really thought it could happen.

"Are you serious, Baby, you'd be okay with that?"

Still holding my hands, she said, "You've been dreaming about that boat your whole adult life. She's a beautiful little ship, and like you said, they hold their value. Let's see if we can manage it?"

I hugged her and said, "Okay, we'll see how the numbers look."

They wouldn't budge on the price, but I had to agree, it was a great price and I hadn't expected them to come down. As we worked out numbers and continued to negotiate, I could see this was going to be a stretch for us, even after they offered a high trade-in on *Ursaorion*. As I pondered their final offer on *Ursaorion's* trade in value, Carol broke the impasse. "Let's sell the house!"

I looked at her, stunned. "Sell the house?"

"Yeah, we say we want to go cruising someday, so if this is such a great deal but the payments are a little high, we can sell the house and rent a cheaper apartment!"

"Are you serious?" I asked.

"I'm very serious," she added. "I always thought we'd have to sell the house someday to go cruising, right?"

Still stunned, I only said, "Yeah, right."

The salesman tapped me on the shoulder, and pointing to Carol, said, "Ron, whatever you decide, you want to keep this one!" It was the second time in our relationship someone had said that and I smiled inwardly, pleased that others saw what I always knew.

I said aloud. "Sell our house or not, Rod, I've always wanted to keep this one."

I thought for the hundredth time how lucky I was to have a second chance with Carol. That she loved sailing and that she was so unconditional about almost everything. I vowed I would repay her in every way possible and never disappoint her.

I turned to Rod and simply said, "Deal."

Over the next hour we signed all the preliminary paperwork, and the owner of the dealership came in to congratulate us. Before we left the office to scrutinize our new boat, Rod suggested we look through the catalog and pick out a font so when we chose a name, he would arrange to have it painted on her stern.

Carol said, "We already have a name. *Lastdance!*"

Then, looking through the catalog, she settled on a bold script and as we had previously agreed, she said, "Make it one word; Lastdance."

Something we hadn't discussed was the official home port, which also had to be painted on the hull. Carol quickly resolved that. "Annapolis, I'd like the homeport to be Annapolis!"

Rod looked at me for confirmation.

I laughed. "Why are you looking at me? This is the woman who said to sell our house, remember?"

He said, "I sure do. Okay, Annapolis it is."

Five minutes later, we sat alone in the main cabin of *Hull # 313*. As I surveyed our new boat by probing around in lockers, Carol talked about decorating the salon. I silently cringed when she mentioned lace curtains but then I thought to myself, *Hey, asshole, she can put up pink polka-dot curtains if she wants.*

At eleven o'clock, as much as we hated to leave, we drove to the Naval Academy to meet Christopher for lunch. Meeting at the entrance to Bancroft Hall where all four thousand midshipmen live and eat, Christopher said, "So what's up? How come you guys came to town on a weekday?"

I smiled. "We've got some good news!"

After hesitating, he took on an astonished look. "I'm going to have a little baby brother?"

We burst out laughing and Carol said, "Christopher, I'm forty-eight-years-old, there are no baby brothers in the cards."

Christopher chuckled. "What do I know? From the way you said you had great news that's what came to mind. Besides, you don't even look thirty-eight!"

Carol gave him a hug. "Flattery will get you everywhere, you handsome devil."

"So what's the great news?" he asked.

Almost in unison we said, "We just bought a new Crealock 37!"

His eyes lit up. "Wow, really? A new one?"

He seemed as excited as we were and as we walked into the massive dining room, Christopher selected a table for us and moments later, four thousand midshipmen marched into the mess hall in a silent and orderly procession. Over lunch we told him everything about the new boat, and we made plans for him to join us when we took delivery several weeks later.

We drove to Annapolis the following week and with some take-out food, we enjoyed Easter dinner aboard *Lastdance.* We made several more trips to load gear and simply bask aboard her after she was launched. She was the subject of our conversation every night during and after dinner until the day finally arrived for us to take delivery. Nancy joined us and we got a ride over to Annapolis from a friend at our marina. Then, after picking up Christopher, we drove to the boat yard full of excitement and anticipation.

Purely by chance, *Ursaorion* was tied up right behind *Lastdance*. She had been sold and her new owner was taking delivery the next day. It made the moment somewhat bittersweet, but as Carol tied a bouquet of flowers to the bow of *Lastdance*, out thoughts went to the future. The flowers had been her idea, and it added an air of festivity to our departure and helped overcome any sadness we felt saying goodbye to *Ursaorion*. She had served us long and well and now it was time to move on

I was nervous as hell as I planned how to get our pristine new boat out of the tight spot she was in without banging into another boat or a dock piling. We were tied starboard side to the main dock with a boat in front of us and *Ursaorion* behind us. To port, another boat was in a slip, so I would have to kick our stern out, then back down slowly, being careful not to drag our starboard side down onto our old boat. I looked at Carol and knew she saw the nervousness in my eyes.

She smiled. "You've done this a million times. This is a piece of cake for you, captain."

I smiled back faintly. "Maybe so, but not with a two hundred thousand dollar boat!"

Taking a deep breath I said, "Carol, Christopher, double-up the bow and stern lines." That would allow them to cast off and take in the lines from the boat. As soon as they did, I told Nancy to take in both spring lines and Carol to standby to cast off the stern line.

"Christopher, keep a turn around the cleat with the bow line so I can warp the stern out."

I shouted, "Everyone ready?"

They voiced their acknowledgements, and with a nod toward Carol, she took in the stern line. When it was clear, I put the rudder hard over to starboard and the engine in forward and with the bow line preventing any forward motion, the prop wash slowly pushed our stern out. When we cleared *Ursaorion's* bow, I told Christopher to take in the bow line, then backed down slowly, sliding gently into the fairway.

Once clear of the other boats, I called for Carol to come aft.

"What, Baby?" she asked.

"Take the helm; you take her out."

She took on the same nervous look I displayed a few minutes earlier, but I knew she could do it and I wanted Christopher and Nancy to see her do it.

"Are you sure?" she asked.

"Yeah, I'm sure."

Then, using almost the same words she said to me earlier, I added, "You've done this maneuver often with *Ursaorion* and this boat handles much better."

As she stepped behind the wheel she whispered, "Yes, but this boat is so much bigger."

I moved aside and thinking back to my earlier comment, I said, "Yes she is and don't forget she's also ten times more expensive but don't let that worry you."

Carol laughed faintly. "Thanks, that's just what I needed to be reminded of."

Without any further hesitation, she spun the helm to port, put the engine in gear, and goosed the throttle. *Lastdance* responded instantly, her stern spinning to starboard smartly. Carol waited for the boat to settle down, then repeated the maneuver. Again, the stern swung to starboard with hardly any forward motion. She repeated the maneuver once more until our bow was pointed out of the fairway. Bringing the rudder amidships, she then slipped in gear and we slowly motored into Back Creek.

Christopher and Nancy came back to the cockpit.

Nancy said excitedly, "Mom, that was incredible the way you turned the boat around."

Carol beamed silently as we motored past flashing R"2E". Once in the Severn River, Christopher took the sail cover off and I rigged the main halyard. The day was perfect with a cloudless blue sky and the wind at twelve knots from the north. I was eager to sail, not motor our new boat home and as soon as we were under sail with the engine secured, Carol offered the helm to me. After a half-hearted suggestion by me that she sail first, she said. "No, Baby. I'll get more pleasure from watching you."

What happened next had served as a harsh lesson about the dichotomy of boating; one minute it was all fun and enjoyment, the next minute it can turn to tragedy. With all three sails set, we ran before the wind out the Severn River. We were in great spirits and couldn't have asked for better conditions as our new boat performed flawlessly. Clearing the flashing R "4" marking the shoal at Greenbury Point, we came onto a broad reach, steering about 165°m for Tolly Point. Moments later, the VHF radio crackled with a voice full of fear and urgency, and we became riveted to the exchange:

Boat: "Coast Guard, Coast Guard…Mayday, Mayday. Man overboard, my friend just fell overboard. He went under. Help, Mayday, Mayday"

USCG: "Vessel calling mayday, this is US Coast Guard Station Annapolis. Switch to channel 22 Alpha. If you cannot establish contact on 22 Alpha, switch back to channel 16. Over."

Boat: "Okay, Okay, I'm switching!"

USCG: Vessel hailing US Coast Guard. What is the name of your vessel, source of your distress, and what is your location? Over."

Boat: Coast Guard, I'm on a sailboat off Greenbury Point. My friend fell overboard and went under. Please hurry!"

I yelled, "Geez, that's right behind us!" Everyone turned to look. I shouted. "Ready about!"

Christopher jumped to the winch and acknowledged my command. An instant later, Carol did the same on the other sheet.

I yelled, "Hard a'lee."

Lastdance responded instantly and turned rapidly to port, and as we crossed the wind, Carol eased the windward sheet, then let it fly as Christopher hauled in hard. Seconds later, we were off on a starboard tack making six knots back toward Greenbury Point and the vessel in distress. Carol then trimmed the staysail as Christopher scanned ahead with binoculars. He quickly spotted a small sailboat adrift by the Yellow "A" marker, its mainsail halfway up the mast. The radio crackled again…

USCG: Vessel in distress off Greenbury Point, a Coast Guard vessel is approaching your position and has you in sight, and a Coast Guard helicopter will be on the scene in three minutes.

Boat: "I see your boat, please hurry; he fell over and went under.

By this time, several boats were converging on the scene including the marine police and a harbormasters boat. A minute later, the Coast Guard helicopter arrived and civilian boats were waved off, probably for fear of running over the man who fell overboard or concern over the danger of collisions.

I said, "There's nothing we can do. Let's come about and get out of their way."

Once again, we came about and headed for Kent Narrows, our mood now somber. Here we were laughing and enjoying life and our new boat. A mile behind us, a man was dying. We later heard that the man fell overboard because of a wake from a fast moving passing boat. It seems he banged his head as he fell and his body wasn't found for almost a week.

CHAPTER 15
COMMISSIONING WEEK

We spent the next three weekends doing shakedown cruises, learning the nuances of sailing a cutter rigged boat and making a list of new equipment we wanted. At the top of the list was an anchor windlass. For ten years I had easily manhandled the relatively light anchor on *Ursaorion,* but *Lastdance* had two anchors, a forty-five pound CQR and a thirty-three pound Bruce. Each had an all chain rode and they were proving too much for me to haul up by hand even on a clam day!

With the new windlass installed, we began a two week vacation by sailing to Annapolis for Christopher's graduation from the Naval Academy. Even before we bought *Lastdance,* we envisioned spending graduation week at City Dock in Annapolis so we would be right in the thick of the festivities. Our plan was to sail over Monday morning when the docks were empty in order to get a good spot along the seawall. There, family and friends would have access to nearby parking and could easily socialize with us aboard *Lastdance.*

Well stocked with food, beer, wine, and a case of champagne, we woke at dawn only to be greeted by a thick shroud of fog. Carol wanted to wait until it lifted, but I'd been dreaming about this for four years and wasn't going to let some fog screw up our plans. As I broke out our brand new GPS and read the instruction manual, Carol prepared breakfast, but again voiced her opinion that we should wait a few hours. Plugging in waypoints, I said, "We'll be fine."

With running lights on and a fog horn ready, we bundled in foul weather gear and got underway at six thirty. Turning north, Kent Narrows

faded into the mist behind us, and we could barely see the channel markers ahead when we entered the channel. Carol steered in the pea soup fog
by compass, while I used the GPS to plot our position on the chart and I
thought, *Shit, the current is setting us outside the channel.* Instinct told me to
stick with the compass course but I went with intellect and followed the
GPS. I directed Carol to make a few course corrections and we made it into
the river without incident. From there, the current ran pretty much due
north, which was what we had to steer, so our primary concern was other
boat traffic. Running the engine just above idle killed our time but kept us
at a safe speed and was quiet enough that we could hear other boats.

Carol steered and sounded the horn one prolonged blast every two
minutes. We would then listen for any replies or the sound of nearby engines. I plotted our position every six minutes, and just when I told Carol
she should be seeing Green "3", she called out that she could see it close
aboard.

She said, "If it had been ten yards farther away I never would have
seen it."

I re-calculated our waypoints to put us right on the buoys ahead of
us. I said, "The GPS has us moving three knots over ground."

Carol asked when she should be seeing the next buoy.

"Red "2" is exactly two miles north of us, so if we maintain three
knots, we'll be on it in forty minutes."

The fog was still thick as cotton. As we approached the mouth of the
river, I became concerned that we might now be getting set to the west by
the current as it spilled into the bay, so I began plotting positions every three
minutes. The first plot put us well to the east of the long shoal north of Love
Point. We were also east of the Rock Pile, a flashing thirty-five foot tall day
marker, but we were still nervous about navigating in the white out condition and wouldn't be comfortable until we saw Red "2". At latitude 39° 03.8,
Longitude 76° 15.9, I had us about two hundred yards south and three hundred yards east of it. I felt comfortable that we could turn west and proceed
out into the bay, but Carol would have none of it until she saw Red "2".

I put the GPS in Course-To-Steer mode. "Okay, Baby. Use the GPS
and go find Red "2"; we should be seeing it in about six or seven minutes."

I took the helm, and she scanned in front of us with the binoculars. Almost exactly six minutes later, she excitedly called out, "I see it. I see it!"

A moment later, it passed down our port rail as we turned southwest and came to course 260°m. An hour and five minutes after that, we changed course to 190°m, which would keep us close to Kent Island and out of the ship channel. Carol took the helm again, and I told her to watch her depth as we were skirting the shallows to the east.

"If the depth goes below fifteen feet, turn right." Then added, "We should be at the Bay Bridge in an hour, so let's stay on our toes and listen for traffic."

It wasn't just big ships I was concerned about; they were confined to the channel, which ran under the center span of the bridge. Tugs, barges, and pleasure craft could be virtually anywhere, so we listened intently and sounded our own horn every two minutes. Carol steered with a look on her face that was all business and I was really proud of her. Her concern in this pea soup was valid but I could see she wasn't afraid and as she glanced from compass to GPS to the depth instrument, I marveled at how fast she had become a competent sailor.

To the northwest we heard a faint horn. We waited for additional sounds but heard nothing. I looked at my watch. The seconds passed, and at exactly two minutes, another prolonged blast of a horn sounded.

"That's a ship underway, and it's getting closer."

Carol said, "Oh shit."

"It's okay; it's still far away. Slow to idle."

I plotted our position twice. We were well to the east of the main ship channel. The fog signals were getting closer, and as the minutes ticked by, I strained through binoculars to see a shape or running lights. A moment later, we heard a securite call over the VHF. It was the southbound ship giving his position at Green "95" off Sandy Point by the Bay Bridge.

"He's way over to the west in the ship channel," I said.

We breathed a sigh of relief and increased speed to three knots again. "What's that noise?" Carol asked.

I listened intently, and although we couldn't yet see the bridge, I recognized the sound of cars overhead on its roadway. I plotted our position again and had us just a quarter of a mile north of the bridge. I told Carol to turn west as doubt set in about the height of the span this far east.

The eastern channel span had a vertical clearance of fifty-eight feet and we needed forty-nine, so I got apprehensive about transiting any of the spans east of the channel. I changed waypoints, and a few minutes later, we saw the massive bridgework. Without waiting for me, Carol turned toward it saying, "Even with the GPS, I don't want to lose sight of it in the fog again, okay?"

I said, "That's good, you did the right thing."

As we approached the span, the fog thickened. We lost sight of the towers to our left and the highway span directly overhead, but we could still hear the sound of cars passing far above and behind us, indicating that we were safely through the bridge.

Carol said, "I'm steering 210°m, is that okay?"

I looked at the chart. "Yeah, stay on that course and I'll call up the next waypoint."

I made a mental note to prepare a route the next time we used the GPS.

"Okay, come to course 270°m. We have a four and one-half mile run andwe're going to be crossing deep water where tugs and barges can go, then the main channel where ships might be so let's stay alert."

We heard horns and power boats moving about but nothing seemed close until a large sailboat under sail crossed astern of us moving at a fast turn of speed. He had running lights on, but made no sound signals and I thought,, *Idiot!* Then we came very close to hitting flashing Red "90", which was our next waypoint and I thought, *Our next toy will be radar.* Forty minutes later, I plotted our position, and we were just half a mile east of Greenbury Point at the entrance to Annapolis.

"Hear that bell?" I asked.

It was a rapidly ringing bell, then a faint horn sounding a short, a prolonged then a short blast. I looked up the signal in the navigation rules book.

"It's a vessel at anchor; go to idle speed."

We both heard it now; it was getting louder.

"Go to neutral."

Carol immediately took the engine out of gear, and we slowed almost to a stop. She looked to me, then blew the horn.

There it was again, the rapidly ringing bell followed by a horn sounding a short, then prolonged, then a short, but much closer now. I few moments later, it appeared right in front of us not fifty yards away! It was a Navy YP patrol boat, used by the Naval Academy for training. We drifted south until we were astern of it. I told Carol, "Slow ahead."

We crept forward and the anchored YP faded back into the fog, only the sound of its bell and horn to remind us where it was or that it had even been there. The GPS had us coming up on my next waypoint which was Green "5." As I strained to look for it, the fog dissipated into a thin mist over the course of thirty seconds, then bright sunlight as we burst into Annapolis Harbor. We were both stunned and looked back.

I said, "It's like we stepped from a dark room out into daylight."

Carol asked, "How did that happen?"

I mumbled that the air was warming in the afternoon sun and the water out in the bay was cooler than in the harbor and the dew point must have been exceeded. She looked at me with some doubt and said, "I'll accept that for now, but I want to read up on it when we get in."

At two thirty, we motored passed the mooring field south of the Naval Academy and removed our foul weather gear. By the time we got into City Dock, we were in t-shirts. The seawall was totally empty so we picked a spot with a ladder to make it easier for guest to board *Lastdance*. Hundreds, maybe thousand's of tourist were already strolling the picturesque downtown waterfront area.

Carol said out loud, "These people have no idea what we just went through."

I laughed. "No they don't. They probably think we were out for a nice sunny sail."

Then I added, "I'm ready to forget the trip, so make me some rum, wench."

Carol scowled. "How about please?"

"Sorry, Baby. Make me some rum wench...please!"

When we tidied up *Lastdance* and relaxed with a couple of well-deserved drinks in the cockpit. I told Carol how much I had depended on her.

She beamed. "Did you really trust me?"

"Yes, of course I did. You're really a good sailor."

She came to my side of the cockpit and we kissed as I held her close to me and we sat in comfortable silence. It had only been a twenty-four mile trip, but it had been an adventure, and we felt very pleased with ourselves.

The rest of the week was a succession of parties, dinners and military ceremonies, one of which was The Color Parade, a tradition dating back to 1871. It is the oldest special parade at the Naval Academy and all four thousand midshipmen participate in it. After marching from Bancroft Hall to Worton Field, the outgoing honor company passes the colors to the new honor company. With Christopher being a brigade midshipman officer, his mom was entitled to be escorted to her seat by a midshipman usher. Upon our arrival, we were pleasantly surprised as another midshipman took Carol from me and escorted her as well. It was an incredible honor for her, and as she walked arm in arm with the midshipman, tears streamed down her cheeks. It was a noble gesture by Christopher, one that Carol never forgot.

The week ended on graduation day with Christopher being commissioned a second lieutenant in the U.S. Marines. He now had his own life to live, and he was starting out with all the hard fought advantages anyone could hope for. My life had been very good being a father, but now I was going to share the rest of it with Carol. It was going to be more than good, and nothing else mattered in the entire world but being with her.

Christopher reported for duty at the Marine base in Quantico, Virginia, and after seeing my parents off; Carol and I sailed north to Baltimore to rendezvous with our friends for a Memorial Day raft up. We arrived to find six of our friends anchored between the Baltimore Aquarium and the World Trade Center, and with Carol handling lines, we rafted alongside *Seawoof.* Hours later, our holiday flags caught the attention of a boat anchored nearby and after a brief chat, we discovered the crew of *Lay Back* were all Navy submariners, one of whom dove into the murky harbor water and swam to Lastdance for a beer.

That was Captain Harry; he immediately adopted Carol who invited him to raft his boat to *Lastdance*. Harry was eager to comply and once again, dove into the harbor and was soon rafted to us, much to chagrin of our friends. The problem was that Harry and his buddies allegedly had some hookers aboard their boat the night before, so I asked him if he could tone things down.

He said, "Hell yeah, no problem, but tomorrow two of my twin sisters are coming and they get kinda wild, but if things get out of hand, I'll break away from your raft up and anchor alone again."

I thought, *What does he mean by two of my twin sisters?*

The next day, Carol called down the companionway to me. "Hey, Ron, you really want to come up and see this."

Harry was approaching in his dinghy with two striking young blondes. They didn't look anything like him, but they were definitely twins. Boarding *Lay Back*, the girls stowed their gear and after introductions to Harry's crew, they stripped down to only their panties and dove into the harbor. We were all astounded, but the twins continued to swim and frolic in the water, oblivious to the hundreds of onlookers afloat and ashore. I reached for my camera and began clicking off photos. Carol smiled as she watched. I chuckled. "Don't get any ideas, wench!"

She said, "Don't worry, Baby. Even if I was twenty years younger and had a few margaritas in me, I still wouldn't swim in this water, with or without clothes!"

The twins were completely uninhibited and casually pranced around *Lay Back* topless. Carol got them to pose for a photo with me, something most if not all of the other guys wished they could do...pose for a photo with two topless twins! Their wives would have none of it though, but for me, in addition to being fun, it gave me a glimpse into yet another facet of Carol; she wasn't a jealous woman, and that could be worth more than gold!

Lay Back cast off early the next morning and our raft up broke up a little later. As our friends headed back to Kent Narrows, Carol and

I sailed south with plans to anchor at Solomon's Island, and then go on to explore the Rappahannock River in Virginia. There was a gentle west wind, but we motored out of the Patapsco River in order to charge our batteries, which had become low after days of running the stereo, lights and blender while at anchor. A mile past Seven Foot Knoll, and with the batteries fully charged, we shut the engine and in eight knots of west wind, sailed south on the east side of the ship channel. After passing under the Bay Bridge, I laughed to myself, thinking, *Even though we were just there for a week, I wonder how long it will take for Carol to ask if we can spend a night in Annapolis.*

It didn't take long. She looked south into the light haze and casually asked, "How long will it take us to get to Solomon's Island?"

I said, "Who cares, we're on vacation right?" Then added, "We're making four and a half knots, so maybe another eight or ten hours."

I smiled as a barely perceptible pout crossed her face, and I could almost hear the wheels turning as she pondered what to say next. Then, looking through the binoculars, she asked, "Is that Annapolis over there?"

I laughed out loud.

"What's so funny?" she said.

I laughed again. "I guess you're not very creative today, you know damn well that's Annapolis."

She turned and snuggled up to me, and in her best purring tone said, "Wouldn't it be nice to take a mooring and go into town for dinner, maybe go to the Middleton Tavern, then sip some wine under the stars at night?"

I gave her my best serious look. "Are you trying to bribe me with sex?"

She kissed me. "Who said anything about sex, I'm just talking about wine and stars and maybe some dark chocolate from the candy store on Main Street!"

I maintained our course as we approached Green "1" off our starboard side. This was where we usually turned west toward Greenbury Point to go into Annapolis. I thought, *It's worth going an extra couple of miles out of the way to see how long it takes her to say something.* Twenty minutes later, I looked at her out of the corner of my eye as she gazed westward to the

Severn River. She lowered the binoculars and had such a forlorn look about her, I just couldn't tease her another second.

"Ready about!"

Carol jumped to her feet and put her arms around my neck.

"I knew you'd turn. I just knew it!"

I kissed her. "Were not turning anywhere until you get your lovely ass over to the winch to tend the sheets." She was exuberant and with one hand on the leeward sheet, she repeated my command, "Ready about!"

"Hard a' lee." I yelled.

A moment later, we were sailing north-northwest close-hauled on a port tack and Carol was jumping about like the little girl she could instantly become. She was full of excitement as we closed on Greenbury Point and sensing her impatience, I said, "We'll douse the sails at the entrance marker and motor in."

She smiled. "Oh good; I was afraid you were going to spend the afternoon tacking all the way in."

I put my arm around her. "So, still want to go out to dinner?"

"Yes, of course. I know I said the Middleton Tavern before, but I feel like some Italian now. How about Maria's?"

We took the second mooring in the front row where I knew she loved to be so she could hear and see Annapolis up close. From there, it was a short dinghy ride to the dock, and we could also easily hear the music from Pusser's. Once secured to our mooring, Carol got our shower gear ready as I paid the harbormaster who had come over in his patrol boat. A moment later, we were in our dinghy on our way into City Dock to shower. People imbibing tropical drinks at Pusser's waved as we went by and Carol returned their greetings as if they were long lost friends.

Back on *Lastdance,* we had cocktails. Then, as we made our way back into town, I observed her closely. It was like she was seeing it all for the first time, and the look of wonder on her face made me feel guilty for teasing her earlier. I thought, *What a small thing to change plans if it made her so happy.*

I yelled over the sound of the outboard. "Hey, how about I buy you a drink at Pusser's after dinner?"

She beamed. "Oh I'd love that; can we really?"

I promised we would, and a moment later, she was all business as she tied our dinghy to the dock.

Anything could be a romantic experience with Carol, but dinner at Maria's that night was especially so. After finishing our meal with tiramisu and sambuca, she said, "Let's do Pusser's some other time; I want to go back to the boat."

"But I promised to take you. Are you sure?"

She took my hand. "Yeah, let's go back and have some wine and chocolate."

"Oh shit, we forgot to stop for the chocolate!"

She smiled. "Do you think I'm just another pretty face? I got a bag while you were still in the shower before. It's back in the reefer just waiting for us to open some red wine." Twenty minutes later, with a gentle breeze cooling the night, we sat in the cockpit and snuggled as we munched on dark chocolate and sipped a nice Cabernet while talking about our lives and the future.

Carol smiled slyly. "Think anyone can see us?"

CHAPTER 16
ASIA AND EUROPEAN TOUR

I was launching a new project at work that required me to travel for almost a month. Not wanting to be away from Carol for such a long time, I arranged to bring her with me for part of the trip and once everything was confirmed, I told her about the project over dinner. I watched her cheery face fade into a deep frown when I said I had to travel for month.

"A whole month?" she asked.

"Yeah, a whole month, I can't wait to go!"

She looked at me surprised and hurt. "You can't wait to go?"

"Yup," I said. "It will be great to get away for a whole month."

She sat speechless, not believing I would say such a thing.

Placing my hand over hers, I smiled. "So if you want to come along, you'd better start packing!"

"I can come?" she asked, tears welling up in her eyes.

"Unless you'd rather stay here and be rid of me for a month."

She came to me and sitting on my lap, put her arms around my neck.

"I never want to be away from you, definitely not that long. Are you sure I can go?"

"Yeah, I already cleared it with Dan; we just have to pay for your plane tickets and direct expenses."

Carol was beside herself as I told her about the places she'd be going to. "First, we'll stop in Japan, then Hong Kong and Singapore, spending four to five days in each place. From there, I have to go to India, and you're going home."

Her frown returned.

"Be patient, there's more! From India, I fly to England where you'll meet me again."

"Oh boy, can we see Jim and Claudi?"

"Yes, of course. He'll be working with me in Europe,"

"From there we go to Germany, then we fly home together. Well, what do you think?"

"I'm so excited," she said.

After dinner, we opened some wine and talked well past midnight about all the places and things she wanted to see and do. I told her she'd be on her own most days and some nights, but she was undeterred.

"I don't care, I just want to go there with you and know we'll be sleeping together at night."

Carol met most of my business associates in New Jersey over the years and many had been to our home for dinner. She had always been an excellent hostess, making them feel genuinely welcome, so it was no surprise she was received with open arms wherever we went. Wives of friends took her sightseeing during the day. In the evening, we were invited to homes and restaurants and Carol did an excellent job exploring their customs and cultures with ease and diplomacy.

One of her curiosities whenever we traveled was to visit old haunts from my days at sea. In Singapore, I took her to the now elegant Raffles Hotel, which during my seagoing days had witnessed hard times. We also went to Bugis Street! Carol heard the name mentioned in sea stories many times over the years so she knew it was an unsavory place. Back in the day, it had been notorious for every variety of vice and had been popular with seamen from many nations on shore leave and American troops on R&R during the Vietnam War. Its appeal even attracted locals to the many food stalls offering al fresco dining from food carts until the early hours of the morning. Some stalls served exotic specialties such as, "Penis of Bull with Noodles," which was considered to be an aphrodisiac for men. At its peak, Bugis Street was rife with con men, pimps, and street vendors selling their wares. Hookers sat on balconies overlooking the carnival atmosphere on the street below which began every night with an actual parade, loosely translated as the Parade of Hookers.

That was the Bugis Street Carol wanted to experience. It was what I prepared her for, but when we exited the taxi, we were greeted by rows of fancy boutiques and gourmet food shops. Disappointed, she asked, "This is where you used to hang out as sailor?"

Laughing, all I could say was, "Believe me, things were very different back then. I don't know what happened here?"

Strolling the sedate sidewalks, we eventually found a seedy bar that retained some of the color and character of yesteryear. We then spent several hours drinking Tiger beer and eating satay, which were bite-sized pieces of beef, goat or chicken, skewered and marinated in exotic spices, then grilled over charcoal. As I watched her, I thought, *Last night, she dined and drank champagne in the elegant Raffles Hotel and today she is perfectly comfortable in a seaman's bar drinking beer and eating satay with me.*

While I worked the next day, Carol did some sightseeing on her own. Returning to the hotel in the late afternoon, there was a note for me at the front desk from her:

Hi, Baby, I signed up for a tour to Malaysia, will be back very late tonight. Have to go, bus leaving. I love you...Carol

Walking to the tour desk, I said, "My wife is on the Malaysia tour. What time does the bus get back?"

"Ah, that is long tour. Fourteen hour, include dinner. Bus be back to hotel eleven thirty."

The woman gave me a brochure and asked which lady was my wife.

"Mrs. Ieva."

She looked at her manifest. "Ah, yes, very nice lady. Very beautiful like movie star."

I smiled and thanked her and wondered what Carol got herself into. I went to the bar for a drink and read the brochure:

Fourteen Hour Malaysia Tour. All Visas arranged. Pick up and drop off at your hotel. Visit Malaysia's most historical city, which has seen the rise and fall of major empires that extended their influence to this region. The legacy of the Malay Sultanate, Portuguese, Dutch and British is evident in Malacca's medieval charm, picturesque buildings, multi—racial population and narrow streets. This tour includes a visit to historic site such as

CHENG HOON TENG TEMPLE—oldest Chinese temple in Malaysia. Lunch at private home in stilt village and dinner included. US $ 148.00.

As adventurous as Carol could be, I was surprised she would go off on her own to another country. Even though it was a tour, I felt it showed moxie, especially since it was her first visit to Asia. As I sipped my drink, I once again counted myself lucky to have her and contemplated how good those nineteen missing years would have been with a woman like her.

Alone for the evening, I took a taxi to East Coast Park where a row of uniquely Singapore restaurants specialize in chili crab and seafood. After a dinner of spicy crabs and several beers, I returned to our hotel by eleven o'clock and waited in the lobby bar for Carol's tour to return. When the bus pulled up and unloaded its passengers of mostly sleepy elderly tourist, Carol's voice stood out above the din of weary travelers. She was excitedly talking with two women. I smiled at her and when she saw me she yelled. "There he is! There's my husband, Ron!"

Carol and I hugged, and one of the women said, "Well, young man, we certainly know all about you."

I chuckled. "I hope it wasn't all bad."

"No, not at all. Your wife told us all about your long love affair."

I smiled. "I hope you all enjoyed the tour. Goodnight, ladies," and putting my arm around Carol, I whisked her away toward the elevators. Back in our room, we snuggled in bed, both too tired for anything more than a few soft kisses.

A moment later, she asked, "What's that awful smell?" She took a whiff of me. "It's you!"

"Sorry, Baby. It's one of the perils of eating chili crabs. Don't worry; it'll be out of my system in a day or so"

I liked to surprise Carol, so I had arranged for us to spend two extra days in Singapore at the Shangri-La Resort on Sentosa Island. We lounged on the hotel's sandy beach and allowed ourselves to be pampered with daily body massages by beautiful Malaysian women wearing exotic sarongs. When not doing that, we used the resort's fast little sailboats to race each other, sometimes capsizing as we laughed hysterically. Carol didn't beat me, but my victories were hard won as she aggressively matched my maneuvers. On one such outing, she came right along side me, causing our boats to bang into each other as we darted for the imaginary finish line,

"Stop it." I yelled.

She shouted, "I'm sorry, but don't capsize. I think I saw a shark back there!"

I looked back and shouted. "A shark? Where?'

She pointed. "There!"

Not ten yards away I saw an unmistakable dorsal fin cutting the surface above a dark shadow.

"Holy shit! Come on, stay with me and go right into the beach!"

At the last second we pulled up the dagger boards, running the boats up onto the sand! The shark hadn't pursued us, but still, once on solid ground I told Carol to put some real urgency in her voice if she saw anything bigger than a goldfish in the water the next time.

Our room had a private balcony with a chaise lounge and double hammock overlooking a tropical garden and the Straights of Singapore. After dinner on our last night, we lay in the hammock looking up at the brilliant stars. Carol said, "I used to look up at the stars and wonder where you were and if I was seeing the same ones as you, like in the song 'Shang-hai Breezes'."

As our words evolved into intimacy, we moved to the lounge and afterwards; we lay embraced with only the sounds from the garden, nearby jungle, and waves gently washing ashore on the beach.

The next morning, Carol boarded a flight for home and I went on to India to finish up the Asia leg of my business tour. A hectic week later, I sat in Gatwick airport waiting for her flight from Newark with my friend, Jim, who hadn't seen Carol since the day we took him sailing years earlier in *Ursaorion*. He and his wife Claudie had a full social calendar prepared for after business hours, the first of which was dinner at a place with the unlikely name of Tiddy Doll's in Shepherd's Market. Carol wore a new dress she'd bought while at home and she looked ravishing in it.

"Wow, you look beautiful!"

She asked if I thought she would be overdressed.

"Not at all, it's perfect for the occasion."

I thought, *It's not so long ago that she would have asked for my permission to wear such a revealing dress, the way she had when we first got together.* I was pleased she was now confident in me and self-confident in herself to wear clothes that complimented her.

To help Carol adjust to jet lag, we went to dinner at seven o'clock, which according to Jim was in the middle of the afternoon and explained why we found ourselves at a table for four in a nearly empty restaurant. Then, as our second round of cocktails arrived, the place slowly began to fill up and a large group of men in dark suits arrived and sat at the adjacent table. As we ordered dinner, Jim and I, with our ears tuned by years of maritime business travel, concluded the men at the next table were speaking Russian. To confirm it, with the arrival of their wine, they began their ritualistic toasting to some worthy cause or glorious moment in Russian history.

Jim explained to Carol, "Their tortured culture is riddled with guilt, which prevents them from drinking without a good reason or a passable alibi." Then he added, "We, on the other hand, with two Americans, a French woman from Bordeaux and a Liverpudlian, have no such inhibitions and can drink freely without proclamations of victory in battles long past."

Carol nodded a tentative understanding of what Jim just said, but looked at me and shrugged.

The food arrived and along with our Slavic neighbors, we settled down to eating, talking and drinking wine, complemented by music from somewhere overhead. By the time we'd finished desert, the four of us were definitely feeling the effects of two rounds of cocktails and two bottles of wine. Nevertheless, Jim still ordered a round cognac. At the next table, our Russian friends did the same and began making toast again, becoming more boisterous by the minute. Then, totally out of character and without preamble; Carol stood up on wobbly legs and extended a hand across the sea toast of her own saying simply, "Sheers!"

Jim, Claudie, and I burst out laughing, but twenty heads at the next table turned toward Carol in silence. An old guy at the far end of the table stood and said something in Russian, then held his glass high. A man at our end of the table looked at Carol and said in perfect English.

"The admiral says you are a most beautiful lady, an oasis to a man in the desert; cheers to your beauty and your health and the health of your children and their children!"

The entire table stood and said, "Nostrovia."

Their voices then trailed off mumbling in Russian as Carol drank her wine and then clapped her hands over her head.

I laughingly said, "Easy, Baby. You're jiggling. I think the old guy wants to take you back to Russia with him."

For the next half hour, we engaged in a game of toasting tennis as both tables competed with creative drinking toast, interspersed with gusty Volga folk songs from the Russians. Jim opened up a dialogue with the two men sitting closest to us. They revealed they were from the British Foreign Office, hosting a Russian military trade delegation. Once Jim explained our seagoing backgrounds, they pointed out the admiral among the visitors. He was the old guy at the end of the table so taken with Carol. Armed with that information, I stood, raised my glass and addressed the group. I announced I was a former American naval officer and had visited Russia many times on business. I then proposed a toast of my own, mentioning that I had served in submarines as well as other items I thought might be of interest, that when translated, struck a chord with the admiral, who then offered an even longer counter toast.

We drank again, and I asked the Foreign Office guy what the admiral said. He leaned close to me and said, "The admiral wants to dance with your wife."

Carol heard the word dance, and there was no stopping her.

"I love to dance!" She exclaimed as she got up and walked to the end of the long table.

All eyes were on her as she went to admiral and taking his hand, walked him out to the dance floor. There was silence among the delegation as they watched Carol and the old admiral dance. When the music ended, he bowed and thanked her, then brought her back to our table and thanked me.

His entourage remained nearly silent with only occasional whispered murmurings, but the admiral shouted something in Russian and raised his hands, which caused a burst of boisterous chatter and yet another toast. Jim leaned over to me and jokingly whispered. "I think Carol has their full attention. While they're all looking at her boobs, now would be a good time to ask them to reveal any military secrets you may want to know."

Before they departed, the admiral and I exchanged embraces with goodwill messages written on the backs of business cards and he even autographed the back of a photo of Christopher in his Naval Academy uniform. Carol and Claudie were the recipients of many embraces and kisses from the admiral's entourage, blowing kisses to those out of reach, but saving their final goodbyes for the admiral himself before he walked off into the night.

Finishing up the week in London, we agreed to meet Jim at Gatwick Airport Monday morning for the flight to Hamburg. Carol and I then rented a car and drove to Stonehenge. This was a spiritual journey for her as she had been reading about the Druids all her life and had dreamed about visiting the mysterious stones for many years. From there, we drove to Tintagel in Cornwall, about one hundred and fifty miles away on the west coast of England. It was the mythical home of King Arthur, and we spent the night in a romantic bed and breakfast overlooking the ruins of the thirteenth century castle on the beach.

Carol could hardly sleep from anticipation of touring the fortress the next day. I sensed her leave the bed several times and go to the window to stare at the castle below. Once from the darkness, she asked, "Are you awake?"

I smiled and answered. "Yes, Baby. I'm awake."

She asked, "Are you thinking about King Arthur too?"

I looked at her silhouette, naked in the moonlit window. Her hips were perfectly rounded, her breasts as perfect and enticing to me now as they were the first time I saw her thirty years earlier. I thought of her body and its capacity for pleasure.

"No, Baby. I'm definitely not thinking of King Arthur at the moment."

I went to the window and embraced her, then kissed her neck. "I want you. You can pretend I'm King Arthur or Sir Lancelot or even Robin Hood, but I want you right now!"

After a breakfast of eggs, sausage and scones with clotted cream, we walked the rugged path to the castle ruins which are set on a dramatic headland that is almost an island connected to the mainland by only a slim finger of land. Over the centuries much of the castle had fallen into the sea but it was still worth the steep climb up the weatherworn steps to see what is left of the stronghold. Carol's childlike enthusiasm was contagious, and as we walked the ruins where knights once fought great battles, she conjured up visions of those events for me. I thought. *Here on the ruins of this castle, she's a picture of innocence.* Then, looking toward our hotel on the mainland, I though, *There, just hours before in that very window, she was a quintessential lustful woman.* I loved her all the more for it.

A day later, we met Jim at Gatwick Airport and were soon on our way to Hamburg. There, Jim and I would do presentations for several days and Carol and Claudie would be entertained by our good friends Ernst and Anna. Ernst is an engineer of the first order but his real calling is extending hospitality. In typical Ernst fashion, he informed us they were going to his farm in Rostock for two days. "Ja, Anna and I we show Carol and Claudie the countryside and the farm, then we return in two days time for SMM."

Carol looked shocked and whispered to me, "What the hell does he mean S and M?"

I laughed. "Carol, he said SMM. It's short for Shipbuilding, Machinery, & Marine technology which is the other reason we're in Hamburg."

She wasn't sure what all that meant but she felt if I was okay letting this big German and his wife take her and Claudie to the former East Germany for two days, she was game.

"Trust me, you're going to love it but be prepared to drive very fast, eat a lot and drink a lot of beer and wine."

"What do you mean drive fast? How fast? Is he safe to drive with?"

"Yes, he's very safe. They all drive very fast on the autobahn but Ernst keeps it under two fifty."

"Two fifty! My God, he's going to drive two hundred fifty miles an hour?"

"No, silly, that's kilometers per hour."

Carol breathed a sigh of relief then asked, "What's that in miles per hour?"

I did a quick mental calculation. "About a hundred fifty miles per hour!"

Carol laughed and said, "Oh get out."

Claudie chimed, "Oh, Carol, Ernst has zee big Audi, and he is very good driver, trebien, no? Not crazy like my Zjim."

Two days later after Jim and I finished up the presentations and while Anna entertained Carol and Claudie, Ernst took us back to our hotel so we could check-out. I missed Carol and was disappointed that she was still out but I would be seeing her soon in the most interesting hotel she ever stayed in.

SMM was the largest marine industry trade show in the world and on the social side of the event my company threw an annual party for clients aboard *Das Feuerschiff*, an old German light ship converted to a restaurant and pub with rooms for overnight guests. Ernst helped Jim, and I check into our new lodgings and then we all waited in the cozy pub for our ladies to arrive. Two rounds of foamy pilsners later, we heard their voices as they made their way along the main deck to the pub. Carol's voice was not much louder than the others but her excitement about staying aboard this ship for two nights was unmistakable.

Her face lit up when she saw me, and we embraced like we had been apart of months, which drew an exaggerated but good natured snicker from Jim. After we settled down and ordered wine for the ladies, Carol pinched me. "Ernst did drive a hundred fifty miles an hour! Wow, it was so exciting, I couldn't believe we were going so fast."

I watched and smiled to myself as she monopolized the conversation, telling us about the visit to Rostock and all the things she had eaten and the farm Ernst and Anna had there. I thought back to those early days when she first began to meet my friends, *She had been so quiet and shy; if they could only see her now.* Ernst and Anna left us on our own for the evening, but Jim and I already made plans for an interesting night out in Hamburg and we agreed to meet back in the pub at eight o'clock for a drink before going to dinner.

I brought Carol down the narrow passageway lined with pipes and electrical conduits to our room, hoping she wouldn't be disappointed when she saw it. The shiny brass nameplate above the door read, *"Zwei Lightsmen."* Meaning the room had been for two electricians. It was a cramped tiny cabin with bunk beds and there was barely enough room to turn around in. A desk was built into the bulkhead and the toilet and shower were smaller than the one aboard our sailboat.

"Well?"

She said, "Well what?"

"Well, I checked us out of a four-star hotel and brought you here for two days, that's what!"

She put her arms around me and in a serious tone said, "Ron, I would go anywhere with you, don't you know that by now? Besides this will be fun sleeping on an old ship, maybe it's even haunted?"

I smiled and kissed her, a little disappointed in myself for not knowing she would react so well to the room.

Surveying the bunk beds, she looked at me with a devilish smile. "We have hours before dinner. Do you want to take a nap?"

I asked, "Who's on top?"

She pressed her body to me and said, "I want to be on top!"

I looked at the upper bunk bed and nodded to it. "Are you sure you can climb up there?" Kissing me softly, she said, "That's not what I mean, silly boy."

Hours later, we met Jim and Claudie in the pub and ordered drinks.

"Okay, ladies." Jim said. "We have a bloody great night planned for you. First, we're going to The Old Commercial for dinner. It's a three hundred year old seafood restaurant where Ron, and I go at least once every time we come to Hamburg. Then we're going to a cabaret in the Reeperbahn."

Carol asked, "What's the Reeperbahn?"

"It's not for the bloody feint of heart, that's what it is. You tell her, Ron!"

I laughed, thinking it unusual for Jim to suddenly get shy.

"I've told you about it before, Baby. It's where all the cabarets and live sex shows are, and the street with the hookers in the windows."

Carol said with genuine enthusiasm. "Wow, really? Let's skip dinner!"

Then Claudie offered her own thoughts. "Carol, I sink et es nosting, just some people fooking on zee stage." The she added. "Zjim, I want to go to Herberstrasse."

"What's that?" Carol asked.

"Carol, et es where zee hookers sit in zee window and zee men look at them to buy." Carol looked at me and said, "Can we go there, I want to see it too?"

I thought, *Oh boy, this is going to be an interesting night.*

Dinner at The Old Commercial was great, but we passed on their exceptional desserts because Carol and Claudie were eager to get over to the Reeperbahn. In fairness, Jim and I had been there before so the novelty factor wasn't driving us mad with curiosity. In the taxi, Carol asked endless questions.

"Is there really a live sex show? Is it safe to go there? How close can we get to the stage?"

I laughed, and said aloud. "Listen to Mother Teresa here. Carol, chill out, we'll be there in a few minutes and you'll see for yourself."

Like most red light districts in Europe, cabarets in the Reeperbahn offered entertainment that ranged from seedy sex shows to elaborate productions with mature adult themes. Not being sure where Carol's American based morals might be in that spectrum; Jim chose a cabaret offering the latter. Still, it was a memorable variety show for all of us, especially for Carol who had never seen naked people performing live on stage. There were other acts without any sexual content to round out the experience but with three rounds of drinks costing four times more than back at *Das Feuerschiff* pub, we decided to leave.

Once out on the street, Claudie asked. "We are going home, not to Herberstrasse?"

Carol chimed in and slurred, "Yeah, les go to Herbies dresser!"

I laughed. "It's not Herbies dresser."

Carol giggled. "Who cares whose dresser it is, I wanna see the girls in the windows!"

I looked at Jim. "I'm game. They can see it and call it a life experience. Do you remember which way it is from here? I think it's toward St Pauli and the river."

After getting our bearings, Jim agreed and pointing left, said, "That way," and we walked down Davidstrasse a block from Reeperbahn and there it was!

Herberstrasse was only one block long and closed to automobile traffic. Brothels line both sides of the street, and hookers sat behind large hinged windows. If a man stopped to look, the woman opened the window and negotiations begin. If they agreed on a price, he went inside with her and another woman took her place. At each end of the street, there was a solid wooden wall with an entrance. As we approached it, we were confronted by a sign in several languages that read, "ATTENTION - NO WOMEN PERMITTED!"

Jim said, "Ah, right. Bloody hell, they wouldn't want a bunch of tourist gawking."

Claudie asked, "We cannot go in?"

Jim, who was getting tired, said, "No, Claudie, it's not permitted."

Carol pouted and then asked, "Can Claudie and I peek inside."

Jim, with a drawn look on his face but ever eager to please, went in to look around. Seeing no police, he came back out and said, "Okay, we all go in. Claudie, you and Carol walk between me and Ron. We walk in the middle of the street and we go straight through to the other end and then get right out. No stopping, okay?"

They agreed and we went in with Carol and Claudie walking between Jim and I. Everything went fine until one of the hookers spotted the girls and all hell broke loose. She opened her window and unleashed a tirade of what had to be obscenities. This was followed seconds later by other windows opening and more abuse being heaped upon us in several different languages. We ràn for the exit!

Laughing hysterically, we scrambled through the narrow exit on the far end of the street. Fleeing like common criminals, we ran back to Reeperbahn where we caught a taxi to our floating hotel. We couldn't stop laughing and finally the taxi driver asked in heavily accented German. "You vent to a comical show?"

Jim replied, "Yes! Bloody hell, we were the show!"

Back at *Das Feuerschiff* and once down in our tiny cabin, Carol kissed me and said how much fun she had.

I said, "It was fun, wasn't it?"

She summed it up by saying, "We're so good for each other, aren't we. I can be curious about places with hookers in windows and you don't make judgments about me."

"I feel the same, Princess. You're so unconditional and considering what a pirate I am; I am so lucky to have you!"

She laughed, and as she undressed, she asked, "Do you want to be on top?"

Remembering the afternoon, I smiled and said, "Sure, I'll be on top!" Then, teasingly, I looked at the upper bed and said, "But I'm not sure I can climb up there."

She scowled. "I told you this afternoon, that's not what I mean, silly boy!"

Laughing together, we kissed and both climbed into the lower bed. I took her in my arms, but between our earlier lovemaking and the beer, wines, and cognac, neither one of us got on top; we just feel asleep the way we always did, in each others arms.

Graduation from junior high school – 1963

194

Graduation from Maine Maritime Academy – 1968

Wedding Day; an arch of swords just as she asked for
when we were teenagers. – 1989

Carol sailing our first boat Ursaorion on Long
Island Sound – 1986.

Carol at Marina Bay, Fort Lauderdale, FL - 1997

Carol sailing *Lastdance* on Chesapeake Bay - 1996

Carol sailing *Lastdance* off Miami Beach - 1999

Ron and Carol: A happy couple on Biscayne Bay – 2000

Chilly sailing to Duck Island Roads, Connecticut - 2001

Carol on *Lastdance* anchored in Inner Harbor, Baltimore - 2003

Ron and Carol Good Life: Another bountiful dinner
aboard Lastdance – 2003

Sailing the Ionian Sea in Greece - 2003

Exploring the caves of Megenisi, Greece - 2003

Carol loved to dance with her tambourine - 2004

Cockpit Table: During Carol's last sail, I carved our
names in a heart on Lastdance's cockpit table – 2006

Chapter 17
Florida

Dan was the vice president of sales, I worked in marketing. We had a some-times contentious relationship so I was totally surprised when he invited me dinner and asked me to consider working for him.

I stopped in mid-bite of my steak. "You're kidding?"

Then, sensing this might be one of those defining moments in a career, I thought it would cost me nothing to say yes at that point.

"Yeah, Dan. I think I'd work for you. What do you have in mind?"

He said, "Another day. Right now I just needed to know if you would."

It was strange to say the least, but I left it alone as he suggested.

Whatever happened, it would involve Carol and I valued her opin-ion, so I told her about my chat with Dan.

"Work for Dan?" she asked incredulously. "Did he say what he wants you to do, or if we'd have to move?"

"No, that's all he said, nothing more. It's weird, but that's all I know. I'm meeting with him again when he gets back from London, so maybe I'll find out more then."

In a manner I was getting used to, Dan got right to the point the minute I sat down in his office three weeks later.

"Miami. I want you to run Miami for me. Actually, the whole southeast territory, but mainly the cruise business in Miami."

I was stunned. "Dan, I've been in this business twenty-five years, but I have no experience in the cruise end of the industry. None! You have to know that, so why would you want me to run it?"

Dan had built his reputation in Miami. When he was promoted and came to New Jersey, we were doing business with every major cruise ship company. Now, two years later, we'd lost two major clients and a third was at risk.

"I know what you're thinking. You're thinking we're screwed in Miami. Well, we are screwed in Miami. I need someone to train the sales team to sell engineering value. That's how I won the business; that's how we need to get it back. Are you interested?"

I hesitated, thinking about the implications.

He said, "I just need to know if you're interested. If you are, I'll put a compensation package together. In the meantime, you and Carol take a trip to Miami and look around. Just say you're on vacation; you know the drill. Wadda ya say?"

"Okay, but no commitments. I want to talk about it with Carol, but I'm interested."

Carol was peeking out the window as I pulled into the driveway, and I wondered how to tell her we'd have to move if I took the job. I walked in and she hugged me then excitedly said, "Well?"

I laughed. "What, I don't get to take off my coat first?"

She went behind me and took off my coat and hung it in the closet then came back and again said, "Well?"

"Miami, he wants us to go to Miami."

I tried to read her reaction. She looked at me impassively for a moment, then turned on her heels and fled out of the kitchen. It was a reaction I wasn't prepared for. I thought, *Shit, if she feels that strong about it, I won't take the job.*

I was about to go into the bedroom to tell her, but she wasn't finished with her theatrics. Closet doors opened and closed, then I heard strange flopping footsteps on the floor.

"Carol?"

A moment later, I burst out laughing as she came through the doorway wearing a bathing suit, sunglasses, diving mask with a snorkel on top of her head, and swim fins, and with a suitcase in each hand, she said, "I'm ready, Baby. When do we leave?"

After we stopped laughing, she went back to the bedroom to change, saying she had a bottle of champagne chilling in the refrigerator, which I took as my cue to open it. When she returned, I told her everything Dan had said. I added that this would be a challenge, but it would also be a promotion and a big bump in salary which would bring us closer to an early retirement and cruising.

"Damn, I didn't even think about that, we'll be able to sail year round down there."

She hugged me. "Congratulations, Ron, I'm so proud of you."

We sipped champagne, and I told her we wouldn't have to be there until September and we wouldn't have to make any decision until Dan came back with a compensation package.

I explained the situation in Miami, and we talked about pros and cons. The fact was, other than family issues, there weren't any cons.

I said, "I'm content to stay in New Jersey so if you change your mind, all you have to do is tell me, and I'd tell Dan no."

She promised she would, but then added. "But I'd really like to go; we can have so much fun together and like you said, we could sail all year and go to the Keys. Let's do it, Ron!"

"Are you sure, Carol?"

"Yes, Baby. I'm sure, but it's your career, so if you feel it's not right for you, then tell him no."

While we waited for Dan to put a package together, New Jersey was hit with a snow storm and Carol joked that he was controlling the weather to influence our decision. During those cold winter nights, we read books and cruising guides on sailing to Florida, and then in early March, we flew there as Dan suggested. By the second day, Carol fell in love with Fort Lauderdale and we agreed to focus our house hunting there. Then, while eating lunch at the bar at Pier Sixty-Six Marina overlooking the Intracoastal Waterway, she got all misty eyed.

"This is the place, Ron; I really feel this is the place for us."

I started to agree with her, but she began to sing softly. "'There's a place for us, somewhere a place for us...'" It was our old song from *West Side Story,* and I got choked up as she sang it. I reached out and took her hand.

"I love you, Carol. I missed you so much all those years, but I'm so thankful for the wonderful times we've had these past twelve years. I promise they'll be many more."

Before returning to our hotel, Carol wanted to look at some of the shops on A1A for something tropical to wear for dinner. Afterwards, at the corner of A1A and Las Olas, she yelled, "Oh my God, it's the Elbow Room."

She pleaded with me to go in for a drink because it had been in the movie *Where The Boys Are.* One drink became two as she told me about the entire movie. We finally left after I promised her we would return when we moved, as if it was already settled I was taking the job.

Waiting on the balcony for Carol to finish dressing for dinner, I looked at the incredible array of yachts docked along the piers. Out on the waterway, watercraft of every description moved about in all directions and loud cigarette boats with scantily clad women passed right under our hotel with pleasing regularity. A cluster of southbound sailboats waited for the 17th Street Causeway Bridge to open, and I envisioned us aboard *Lastdance* doing the same. My reverie was broken by her voice behind me.

"I'm ready, Baby. How do I look?"

She looked stunning in a beautiful sundress. It was silky with flowers printed along the hem and below the bust line, and it flowed easily over her curves, accentuating her body.

"Wow!" I exclaimed. "You look beautiful, what's keeping those puppies in?"

She asked, "Too much cleavage?"

"No, not at all. Have you seen the way women dress to go food shopping around here? No, Princess. You look great. Maybe a bit too sexy for a baby christening back home, but very appropriate for here."

"Are you sure, Ron? This is like the start of a whole new life for us and I want tonight to be special."

I repeated that she looked beautiful and she gave me one of her radiant smiles.

"Come on, we have time for a glass of wine on the balcony, you have to see the line of sailboats waiting for the bridge to open."

We had dinner at a small restaurant on A1A, right across from the beach. All the waitresses wore white halter tops and blue sarongs and they all had intricate tattoos at the base of their spines. As exotic as the waitresses looked, I thought Carol looked even more so. There was a slight sea breeze blowing wisps of her hair about, and I thought it made her look like a model in a TV ad. As we talked about how good life could be in Florida, I looked at her as if we were still newlyweds. I couldn't make up my mind if I wanted to rush back to the hotel with her or take her dancing after dinner.

Instead, we sat along the oceans edge holding hands, our shoes off and our feet lapped by the small waves. She slowly reclined back onto the sand and pulled me to her, and we kissed passionately. There were people wandering about the beach in the dark but she didn't seem to care as she took my hand and put it to her breasts.

I said, "You're feeling bold tonight!"

"I feel very bold tonight, very bold and very sexy."

I caressed her softly and as we kissed I asked, "What does this remind you of?"

She instantly said, "Hawaii," then she closed her eyes and moaned with pleasure at the memory.

I kissed her softly. "It's time we went back to the room!"

Hours later, in the dark shadows of our balcony overlooking the ICW, we sipped wine and watched boats moving along the waterway. We talked about where we would put *Lastdance* and the possibility of buying a small power boat to cruise around the canals. She became excited. "Oh could we? That would be so much fun. We could get one with a bimini and go to restaurants by boat. Wouldn't it be great if we could get a place right on the water?"

As always, I loved to watch her when she got like this and it gave me immeasurable pleasure to see her so animated.

With the decision made that Fort Lauderdale would be our new home, Carol asked if we could drive to Key West. I hadn't been there since the mid-sixties so in the morning we got an early start and headed south to Captain Tony's! We were like a couple of teens driving with windows wide open and the cassette player loudly cranking out Jimmy Buffet music. We knew it was going to be almost impossible to turn down the job and we concluded that Dan had cleverly counted on how we'd respond to this little trip. In Key West we walked Duval Street and watched the sunset from Mallory Square along with other tourists, and we snobbishly felt like locals because we felt we somehow belonged in Florida, as if it was our destiny to live here.

Back in New Jersey, we were greeted by yet another snow storm and our interest in moving to Florida increased substantially. I met with Dan for business briefings and by the time he offered a compensation package, I was sure I wanted the job. That night, I discussed it with Carol over a bottle of wine and we decided we'd go to Florida and we toasted to a new chapter in our great adventure.

The months went by fast and we found a townhouse to rent in Plantation, about twelve miles west of Ft. Lauderdale. With that settled, we then focused on relocation issues in New Jersey because in addition to the normal task, we also had to move *Lastdance*. We wanted to sail to Florida but my company didn't have a policy on moving big boats. We eventually reached an agreement that they would give us two weeks of relocation time if we used my vacation time for the remainder. Carol and I decided we wanted to make the most of the voyage and stop at points of interest along the way, so in addition to the allocated two weeks, we planned on an additional two full weeks from my vacation.

The official start of hurricane season is the first of June, so summer was not the best time to cruise the East Coast. We had no choice, however, so we wanted to depart Chesapeake Bay as soon as possible. We set our departure date for the June twenty-eight. While I went to work, Carol spent a lot of time with her kids, but she also made frequent trips to Maryland to load our boat with the bulk of our clothing and stores.

The moving truck hauled away our things, and after teary goodbyes with friends and family, our friend, Jane, drove us to Maryland. Carol cried over leaving her children the whole drive south. I did my best to tell her there would be opportunities to visit them and for them to visit us, but as the miles clicked by, I wondered if this was a mistake. She had sacrificed so much to be with me, and I didn't want her to be unhappy. I vowed that if it really made her sad, we'd go back to New Jersey, even if I had to resign and find a new job. My thoughts were interrupted as we pulled into the marina. Carol seemed better and as I had observed in the past, she displayed the ability to recognize when one door closed and another opened, accept a situation and move forward. With our gear stowed and *Lastdance* fully loaded with fuel and water, there was nothing to do but socialize with our friends on the dock.

There was always a dock party of sorts on Friday night at the marina and that night, it was a going away party for us. By nine o'clock, an unusually large crowd had gathered, which caused the dock to literally shake, and we wondered if it might collapse. We were touched by the number of people who came to see us off. All brought gifts of wine, rum and tequila, enough that I figured would last us through our first year in Florida. I sensed that most of the emotion over us leaving was directed at Carol, and more importantly, I could see that she felt it as well. I smiled and thought, *Wherever she goes in my life, she turns casual acquaintances into friends.*

The party slowly came to a close and only a few dock mates remained. Sitting on *Bliss* with our good friends Jane, Gene, Barbara, and Jeff, we recounted the many wonderful memories we shared with them in anchorages all over Chesapeake Bay. I wasn't sure we'd ever be back and it was difficult to say goodbye but with a planned departure at six thirty in the morning, we reluctantly called it a night. Carol cried as we walked down our dock to *Lastdance*. Once aboard, I asked her if she was sure she wanted to go to Florida.

She looked at me puzzled and asked, "Don't you want to go?"

"Yes, I do, but you being happy is much more important to me."

She smiled. "I want to go, Ron. It's just so sad to leave family and friends. Don't you have mixed feelings like that?"

"Yeah, I do, but when I see you crying, I assume there's more to it than that."

She smiled and put her arms around my waist. "I'm from Venus, remember? I get emotional like this, but I really want to go to Florida. It's our great adventure and I want to share it with you, so stop fussing and take me to bed. Who knows, maybe you'll get lucky tonight."

I woke at five o'clock, but I let Carol sleep. As I boiled water for coffee, I prepared the boat and monitored the NOAA weather forecast. At six o'clock, I gently woke her and said I'd take us out if she wanted sleep in.

"No, Baby. I want to be on deck when we leave, I just need some coffee and a granola bar."

Fifteen minutes later, I fired up the engine, and we took in dock lines that we normally left secured to the pilings for our return. She looked at me as I retrieved the leeward bow line, and I was surprised that such a small act evoked deep emotions in both of us. I went back to the cockpit and gave her a big hug as she fought back tears.

"Is my first mate ready?"

She smiled and answered me with a crisp, "Aye aye, captain!"

"Okay wench, I'll take in the stern line, you take off the starboard bow line."

A moment later, I slipped the gearshift into forward, and we silently began our journey.

Ships Log: 28 June 97—Underway at 0630, bound for Fort Lauderdale. Winds NNE, 6 knots. Barometer—1033 Mb. Forecast—Clear skies, winds light and variable, chance of afternoon thunder storms. Florida or Bust!

The log is short and concise, but it doesn't reveal the emotion of leaving everything we knew behind. Still, we didn't fully come to grips with the extent of our connection to this place until we transited Kent Narrows. One minute we were in the turning basin waiting for the seven o'clock bridge opening, the next moment, we passed under its open span, and as we had hundreds of times before in years past, we waved a thank you to the faceless bridge tender in the tower. In another moment, our festive mood changed as the full weigh of our leaving struck us when the bridge sounded the forlorn closing signal on its loud horn. It was if a massive door had shut on us and we could never return.

"Know what today is?" I asked.

She looked at me puzzled for a moment then her face transformed into a big smile.

"It's the day we got our wedding rings!"

I put my arm around her shoulder. "We're going to be alright, Princess!"

Motoring the whole first day of our twelve hundred mile voyage, we hoped it wasn't a harbinger of the days to come as far as getting time under sail. The next two days were uneventful, but we got some sailing in, which was much more enjoyable than hearing the constant drone of the engine. Either way, without an auto-pilot, it was essential having Carol to stand her share of watches on the helm. In Norfolk, we stayed at Waterside Marina where we picked up a life raft and met our friends, Dick and Virginia, for dinner. So far, we'd been on a part of Chesapeake Bay we had cruised before but after getting underway the next morning, we entered the Chesapeake & Albemarle Canal. It was new territory and we reveled in the things we saw as we motored to Coinjock, VA.

Several days later, we left the Pungo River in southwest winds of fifteen knots. By the time we entered the Pamlico River, the wind increased to twenty knots, and it began to rain hard. Carol steered as I put a reef in the main and we tacked our way to Goose Creek where we were able to sail a southerly course through the wide tributary, then the narrow, three mile long land cut. We were low on diesel, but as long as there was wind, we continued sailing for the fun of it and to conserve fuel. This was a rural area, but at the Hobucken Bridge, there was a Coast Guard station and some industry, and we must have been a sight sailing by at six knots.

It was still raining hard and visibility was less than a mile when we entered Bay River. Carol fell off onto a broad reach until we got to the junction of the Neuse River where once again, we had the wind right on the nose. She needed a break on the helm, but it was back to short tacks as we came to a course of 220°m, so she stayed on the wheel while I handled the sheets during the tacks. I relieved her at Maw Point Shoal so she could go below and warm up and I remained on a starboard tack all the way to Horton Point. Tacking once again, we then rode almost all the way to our destination of Oriental.

When Carol came back on deck to relieve me, the wind was still blowing over twenty knots, driving the rain nearly horizontal. At the Flashing Green "1" marker, I doused sails, and we motored into Oriental Harbor where we sought shelter behind the long breakwater. Unfortunately, there was no room at the proverbial inn as more than a dozen boats occupied the small anchorage; all were tugging hard on their rodes.

Carol circled the anchorage several times as I stood on the bow looking for a safe spot, but there wasn't enough room. The sky was getting darker from storm clouds and the wind seemed to be picking up with each gust. Carol shouted that she was going to go further into the harbor to look for a fuel dock and maybe an open slip at the marina. From the bow, I watched her thread her way through the anchorage, carefully avoiding anchor rodes beneath the surface.

There was a fuel dock on the eastern side of the harbor, and I quickly made lines ready as Carol maneuvered to turn us around so she could approach the T-dock into the wind. Fortunately, it stopped raining, which made things a little easier because the area near the fuel dock was very crowded. She seemed nervous.

"Do you want me to bring her in?"

She said. "I'd rather stay on the helm than handle the lines in this wind."

I put out extra fenders just in case.

She laughed. "You don't trust me?"

I yelled back to her. "I trust *you*; it's the dock I don't trust!"

A moment later, Carol laid us softly alongside. I got a bow line around a piling then stepped off the boat and took the stern line from her, quickly securing it to a cleat. We took up the whole T-head, our bow and stern extending beyond its ends, so we rigged spring lines fore and aft just as the dock attendant conveniently emerged from the small shed by the fuel pumps.

"Hi, we needed diesel and a slip for the night."

He said. "Y'all just made it. I'm closing up here in two minutes and we ain't got no slips for y'all."

A woman on a powerboat just inside the T-head shouted to him. "Oh, just fuel him up, Smitty, and stop giving the man a hard time!"

Then she yelled over to Carol, "Nice going, honey. That was a nice docking you made." The woman and Carol started chatting while I helped the attendant bring the diesel hose to our fill connection, again asking him if we could spend the night.

"Can't y'all read the sign? This here dock is for fueling up only."
I said. "Yeah, but it's after five o'clock, and you said yourself you're closing." There's no room in the anchorage and it's blowing like snot out there. We'll be gone from the dock before you open!"

"Can't do it, yer blocking these here boats!" he replied.

The woman chatting with Carol got off her boat and came toward us, and my first thought was that she was now going to complain because we blocked her view or something. Instead she said, "Smitty, what's wrong with you? Why don't you let these nice people stay the night? My God, it's getting ready to storm!"

She was joined by her husband. "Hey, Smitty, they're fine where they are. We don't mind." Then turning to the boat on the other side of the T-head, he yelled, "Hey, Raul, you okay with this boat here for the night?"

A dark-skinned man popped his head up from below. "Sure thing, man."

Under this barrage of opposition, Smitty relented. "Okay, okay but y'all got to be out of here by eight o'clock sharp, and it's going to cost you seventy-five cent a foot."

That's how we came to know Chuck, Jennifer, Raul, and Kathy, four of the nicest folks we've ever met. Jennifer invited us to join them for happy hour drinks aboard their boat and from there we joined them for dinner and many more drinks. It was like we knew them our whole lives, but as we all staggered and laughed our way back to the dock, I said we'd be leaving first thing in the morning and wanted to thank them for everything and say goodbye.

Chuck said loudly, "You can't leave! Tomorrow is the Fourth of July and the Croaker Festival and they'll be fireworks an all."

We explained that we were on a tight schedule, but they wouldn't hear of it. Raul and Kathy joined the fray, and when I said we had to be away from the fuel dock by eight, they said if we couldn't find a slip at the town dock or room in the anchorage, we could raft up to one of them. I searched for more excuses, but becoming impatient with me, Carol banged on the table and shouted, "Stop it. If there's a croaker festival tomorrow, we're staying!" Then giggling, she added, "What the hell is a croaker any-way?"

Over nightcaps, we learned that a croaker is a fish that makes a sound by vibrating muscles against their swim bladder. Raul tried to make a croaker sound and we all laughed and joined in imitating the fish for which a whole festival was named. True to our word, we left the fuel dock before eight o'clock and motored to the town dock at the head of the harbor. Surprisingly, we found an open space. We went to the Croaker Festival and shared a great day and evening with our new friends, then got underway in the morning for the next leg of our journey.

Our desire to see new places kept us on the ICW most of the time, but we ventured out along the coast when the wind was favorable and the weather settled. During those times, we found sailing at night tiring but sailing around the clock out on the ocean then bought us time to linger and sightsee in places like Charleston and Hilton Head. Carol was clearly enjoying this routine as much as me and the more we depended on each other in handling the boat, the closer we grew in our relationship. With no television, we read a lot and also did more interactive things together. Nights at anchor, we played board games and spent hours talking about boat stuff, our children, and the probability of intelligent life in distant galaxies. We made love a lot, and then we'd stretch out on deck at night and hold hands as we looked at the stars, and sometimes we'd say nothing or we'd say everything. It didn't matter, as long as we were together.

Our voyage was interesting and fun but also exhausting and I got to see the full extent of Carol's stamina in fair weather and foul. Days were often hot and uncomfortable, but she never complained and it was her attitude that made the journey a fun-filled adventure rather than just a voyage. When we ran into afternoon thunderstorms, she would defer to my judgment on how we should weather each one, but then she would marvel at the beauty of these violent displays of nature as if she was watching a holiday firework display. I'd nervously laugh and say, "Carol, we're the only boat out here and we have that big aluminum mast sticking up in the air; stop saying how pretty the lightening is!"

The only time Carol lost her cool was during an overnight stop in Georgia. While still in South Carolina, we planned to motor to the Savannah River, then go out on the ocean at Tybee Roads. From there, we could make the hundred mile sail along the coast to St. Mary's Inlet, then spend a night on Amelia Island in Florida. After a wonderful dinner in Beaufort at a café in a renovated old bank, Carol was reviewing a bad weather alternative route on the ICW and noticed Moon River, south of Savannah.

Ever the romantic, she announced, "Baby, we have to stay on the ICW and anchor in Moon River!"

"Where is Moon River?" I asked.

She walked off the miles on the chart and frowned. "Wow, it's farther than I thought, maybe about forty-six miles south of here."

"We agreed we didn't want to mess with the swamps in Georgia, right?"

"I know, Ron. But this is special. Please can we do it?"

I considered the time we'd lose, but I could see she was really excited.

I was about to agree anyway, but she pressed her body to mine and said, "And if I can buy an Andy Williams recording tomorrow morning, I promise I'll make you glad we went."

This was getting out of hand. Waiting for the stores to open would delay our departure until after ten in the morning. "Carol, you said it's forty-six miles; if we wait for the stores to open, we won't get in until at least eight at night."

"Oh, please, Baby. How can we anchor on Moon River and not play the song?"

I laughed. "I didn't even know there really was a Moon River, let alone think about anchoring there!"

Her arms went around my neck, and she kissed me softly and whispered, "Please."

I melted easily. "Okay, we'll do it, music and all!"

She laughed. "You're such a push over. A little rub against you with my boobs, a kiss or two and you'd do anything, wouldn't you?"

I got serious and looked into her eyes. "Carol. Boobs or not, I'd do anything to make you happy, anything!"

Smiling seductively and looking toward our bed she asked, "Anything?"

We were at the marina in downtown Beaufort just south of the Ladies Island Bridge. As I prepared the boat for departure, Carol went into town to look for a recording of "Moon River". She was back aboard by ten forty with an Andy Williams cassette and we were underway five minutes later. Leaving Parris Island behind us, we entered Port Royal Sound and motored through lowland rivers, creeks, and marshes and the whole time, Carol hummed and sang "Moon River".

"Carol, we killed three hours waiting for the stores to open this morning so you could buy the cassette; why don't you play it?"

She smiled. "I am playing it, in my head. I want to save the cassette for when we get to the river."

Averaging better than six and a half knots, we entered Skidaway River by five forty. An hour later, Carol maneuvered us around the marked shoal southeast of Marsh Island and into the mouth of Moon River. There was only marsh nearby, but we could see homes and docks farther up the river on the western shore. She chose to anchor close to Marsh Island to keep us away from any early morning river traffic as well as give us privacy, but we both wondered about insects and alligators.

With the anchor set, Carol went below for a bottle of wine. She returned wearing only a white cotton dress, and with the sun setting behind her, I looked with delight at the silhouette of her body and it stirred my senses. She sat by my side and we quietly drank the chilled wine in the cockpit and with my arm around her, she told me how happy she was to be there. Then, as the sun dipped below the tree line, she hit the stereo remote and there, anchored on Moon River, Andy Williams sang for us.

> *"Moon river, wider than a mile*
> *I'm crossing you in style some day*
> *Oh, dream maker, you heart breaker*
> *Wherever you're goin', I'm goin' your way*
>
> *Two drifters, off to see the world*
> *There's such a lot of world to see*
> *We're after the same rainbow's end, waitin' 'round the bend*
> *My huckleberry friend, moon river, and me"*

Embracing, we kissed softly and with her warm tears on our cheeks, I drew her closer to me. "That's us, Princess. Two drifters off to see the world."

As wonderful as the moment was, the mood dissolved when ravenous mosquitoes appeared and began feeding on us. We hurried below, and I saw that while getting the wine and changing into the flimsy dress, she also prepared a romantic table setting for dinner. I lit the oil lamp and poured more wine. Carol took the ingredients for her shrimp scampi out of the reefer and the cabin was quickly infused with the pleasing aroma of sautéed garlic and scallions.

Later that night after dining at the best restaurant in Georgia, I asked my beautiful first mate to dance. With "Moon River" playing again, we waltzed to a song we first danced to thirty-six years earlier and a world away as teenagers back in Brooklyn. When the music ended, Carol hit reverse with the remote, and as it played again, we danced more slowly and kissed more passionately. I told her I was really glad we came to the river. She smiled and said, "Good, because I didn't forget my promise."

She unbuttoned my shirt and removed her dress, and hitting reverse again, we danced magically in the soft glow of the oil lamp.

Departing early the next morning, we continued south on the ICW with thoughts of going out St. Catherine's Sound onto the ocean. An hour later, an updated NOAA weather forecast called for severe thunderstorms all day with winds gusting as high as fifty knots, and I considered going back to Moon River. Instead, I decided to look for a safe anchorage in St. Catherine's Sound, sixteen miles away. I thought if we could outrun the bad weather, we could anchor briefly in one of the many creeks there, and if necessary, even spend the night. Then, as we motored rapidly up the Ogeechee River, we got whacked by a monster thunderstorm with high winds and driving rain, which reduced visibility to almost zero.

This was not good! There were commercial fishing boats around with their net booms in the down position, and I didn't want them running into us as we all moved about in the near zero visibility. Carol put on her combination harness-lifejacket and went up on the bow to look for the entrance to Florida Passage which was a mile and a half west of Flashing Green "93". The only other marker was Green "95" along the marshes on the south bank of the river, but we never saw it in the driving rain. I figured I had already gone more than one and a half miles and was about to turn around when the rain let up. A few moments later, Carol spotted the Flashing Red "98" marking the elusive entrance.

Assuming there might be a lot of traffic in Florida Passage, I decided to wait for another break in the rain for visibility to improve. While I held our position within sight of the flashing red beacon, Carol took visual bearings on the light, then plotted our position with the GPS so that, even if visibility decreased, we could still hold our position. I was glad we waited out in the river because several large shrimp boats came barreling out of the passage and were barely visible in the shroud of rain and mist. Then, when the rain nearly stopped, I said, "Let's go for it." I pushed the throttle forward and *Lastdance* quickly gathered speed.

Florida Passage is arguably about five miles long before it becomes the Bear River, which runs for another three miles before emptying into St. Catherine's Sound. Regardless of its name, it is a twisting, tortured waterway with no less than ten smaller tributaries off its marshy banks. About four miles into the Passage, with a sweeping S-turn in front of us, terror struck from those marshy banks as we encountered a barrage of flying cockroaches, or as the locals call them, palmetto bugs.

Cockroach or palmetto bug, it was like a scene from a horror movie. At first there were a few, then a horde came thundering out of the marsh to starboard.

"Carol, go below!" I shouted.

She needed no further encouragement and as she slammed the hatch behind her, I thought I saw one of the thumb size creatures follow her down. They were gone as fast as they appeared, and with shivers of revulsion, I brushed away the remaining few that tried to hitch a ride aboard *Lastdance*. I called Carol on deck. She was truly fearful, but I needed her to take the helm so I could walk forward and get rid of any that might be there.

"Oh God, will they come back?" she asked.

"I don't know. I hope not; they make my skin crawl. I've only seen them in Vietnam."

"How could you stand it up here?" she asked.

"I had to, I couldn't just leave the helm and let us crash, but geez, it still gives me the creeps."

As if pestilence wasn't enough, we got hit with another thunderstorm, this one worse than the first. In spite of the cockroach attack, Carol still plotted our position every five minutes and had us coming up on Red "104", which we could just barely make out. Still, it showed that we were keeping ourselves to the middle of the channel using the GPS, which was a good thing because several fast-moving shrimp boats had already passed us.

Carol directed my attention to the chart and shouted that she didn't think we should go as far as St. Catherine's Sound. She was afraid there would be a lot of boat traffic there and visibility might deteriorate further.

I agreed. "Okay, look for a place for us to anchor off the river."

A moment later, she shouted. "Kilkenny Creek," it's a mile ahead just after Flashing Red "106" on the right, directly opposite Green "107" on the left."

"Good girl," I shouted over the heavy drumbeat of rain on the bimini.

Kilkenny Creek was deep, so we tried to anchor close to shore to be away from shrimpers with their lowered booms, which tripled the space they occupied in a channel. Even as we circled, two fast moving shrimpers came out of the mist and into the creek.

I shouted. "That's it, this place sucks! We need to find another anchorage, one of those guys will run us down in this visibility and I don't have a clue what they do at night."

Frustrated and tired from the ordeal since leaving Moon River, I said, "Go below and look in the cruising guide and see if there are any marinas around."

A moment later she shouted excitedly, "You won't believe it, but there's a marina about two miles up this creek, maybe a little less!

"Does it have enough water for us?"

"Yes, it says it has eight feet alongside. Should I call them?"

"Yeah, go ahead. See if they can take us and ask for approach directions. I don't see anymore markers on the chart."

I slowly motored up the creek, careful to keep in mid-channel and listen for approaching boats. Carol yelled up the hatch. "They can take us and the only hazard is a shoal that comes out after the small creek on our left so stay to the right side of the channel. And get this; it's only fifty cents a foot!"

The docks emerged from the rain and as we got close. My first thought was this was a scene out of dueling banjos. Still, it was better than being run down by a shrimp boat, and we'd have shore power to run the fans.

The marina consisted of a long, floating dock running parallel to the creek. There were small boats on the inside of the dock and several larger transient boats on the outside so we tied up behind a big trawler from New York. Someone came out in the rain to help us with lines and once I checked in, I could see it was actually a nice place. As we got the boat squared away, the sun came out, and we opened up hatches and port-holes and although the humidity hung on us like a damp rag, I began to think, *What the hell, it wasn't such a bad day.* Carol wasn't quite so affable about it and said some of the characters hanging out at the dock gave her the creeps.

Showering in the marina, we returned to *Lastdance* only moments before the rain started again. This was no thunderstorm but a constant downpour so with the boat closed up again, we had a dinner of left-over scampi and a not so bad packaged pasta mix. Later that night, as we played strip Scrabble with torrential rain still beating down on the cabin top, the fans suddenly stopped.

"What the hell?" I said aloud.

I got up and looked at the power panel. "Shit, we lost shore power!"

Carol asked, "Is it the whole marina or just us?"

I looked through the porthole and saw the dock lights were still on, as were the lights on the trawler in front of us.

"I think it's just us. Maybe the power cable came out?"

Looking out the forward porthole, I froze. Two guys in rain coats were standing close to our power cable, which was out of the receptacle box and lying on the dock almost at their feet.

"Shit, Carol, our power cable is out of the receptacle and there's two guys standing right by it."

She got up to see. "I'm scared. Do you think they might have done it accidentally?"

"Maybe, but what the hell are they doing standing there in this friggin' rain to begin with?"

Without the fans on, the cabin was fast becoming oppressive. I had to do something, but I was a little scared myself.

"I'm going to go plug it in. You stay here and watch, but lock the hatch behind me. If anything happens, call the police on the cell phone and radio, but do not come out of here like you did at South Street! Tell me you won't unlock the hatch or leave the boat!"

She looked terrified, but she knew we couldn't stay below with everything all closed up and no fans on.

"Okay, I promise not to leave. If they do anything I'll call 911 and use the radio."

Putting on my shorts and foul weather jacket, I then took my gun out, chambered a round and stuck it in my jacket pocket.

"Oh, no. Why are you taking a gun?"

"Carol, we're out in the boonies here on a dock with two fucking guys who are standing in a downpour and may have unplugged our power cord to lure me onto the dock, that's why!"

She was near tears. "Baby, I'm scared, don't go, okay? Forget it. We'll be alright without the fans."

"No, we can't stay with everything closed up and no fans. I'll be fine, just watch from the porthole."

Opening the companionway hatch, I could hear the men talking in garbled heavy Southern drawls. I went onto the dock and slowly approached them and the power receptacle.

One of the men said aloud, "I s'pose it's gonna rain all night. Maybe we should just leave."

Then, seeing me advancing, he said what sounded like, "Hey, mister, whatcha doing out in this crap, it's raining hawgs and dawgs out here."

I said, "My power cord came out of the receptacle."

They both looked down and one of them said, "Well hell, y'all shoulda just yelled over, I would have plugged her back in fer ya."

I said, "That's okay, I'm out here now." Then, with one hand on my gun, I leaned over and plugged the power cord in. Saying goodnight to the men, I began to back away. As I did, one said to the other, "Screw this shit, it's gonna rain all night, let's just go."

I watched them climb into a small open boat on the inside of the floating dock, start up the engine, and head up the creek into the night. I felt like a complete fool out in the rain holding a loaded gun when all I had to do was just ask them to plug in the cord. That's when Carol screamed.

My mind raced, *Shit, they lured me off the boat and someone else broke in to get at Carol.* I bounded over the rail and boarded *Lastdance* just as she opened the hatch while letting out another scream.

Scrambling to get out, she yelled, "Get him, hurry get him!"

I jumped below with my pistol drawn and seeing no one in the cabin, I ran forward and pulled open the door to the head. No one was in there.

I yelled, "Carol. Get who?"

She peered down over the hatch boards. "He's on the quarter berth, shoot it, do something, or I'll never sleep on the boat again. God, he's so big!"

I yelled again, "Damn it, who's so big?"

She yelled, "The fucking roach, right there on the cushion!"

There, on the quarter berth was the biggest insect I'd ever seen. I instantly remembered when Carol ducked below earlier in the day and I thought I saw something go in with her. I let out a squeal and instinctively backed away. Carol again yelled for me to do something.

"Don't let it get away. I'll never be able to sleep on this boat!"

"Okay, okay...let me think!"

The gun was heavy in my hand, but sanity prevailed and I put it down being sure to put the safety on. I looked for something to do battle with and saw one of Carol's flip-flops. I hit the bug squarely and very hard, but it had no effect. I retrieved a plastic plate from the galley sink and whacked the monster twice; still no effect. It just sat there and in my mind, it seemed to pant like a dog.

"Carol, come down here."

"Are you nuts, no way, buster," she yelled.

I said, "Come on, nothing kills this thing, I'm going to scoop it up and throw it on deck and you don't want to be there when I do!"

Even just saying it made my skin crawl, but I couldn't think of anything else. She came below and stepped far away from the quarter berth.

"Why don't you try to capture it in a cup or glass?"

"Good idea for a firefly, but we don't have a cup or glass wide enough; look at the size of that thing. Shit, you wanted me to shoot it! Get back in case he tries to fly."

In one motion, I scooped it up and flung it into the cockpit, and quickly closed the companionway hatch.

The fans were on again and one three inch flying palmetto bug was back in the wild.

I laughed. "I can't believe you were screaming for me to shoot it."

Then looking at her, I laughed again. "And I can't believe you ran up on deck in just your panties! Those two guys should have stayed a few minutes longer!"

"Oh my God," she said. "I wasn't even thinking. I just wanted to get away from that thing."

"Hmm, did I ever tell you that you look very sexy when you're half-naked and scared? Come here, I deserve a reward for slaying the dragon!"

She said, "You're not touching me with that hand ever again, buster."

I had to wash my hands several times with soap, then rinse them with alcohol before I could claim any reward. Even then I had to promise that we would always keep the companionway screen on at all times!

After twenty-six days of cruising, we arrived in Ft. Lauderdale! We had a hard fought forty mile trip south from Lake Worth, tacking all day against the two knot Gulf Stream current and a twenty knot southeast wind which kicked up big waves. It was late in the day and we were both exhausted, so we decided to take a mooring at Las Olas, rather than spend an hour navigating the many bridges on the New River where our new marina was. Carol broke out the blender to make margaritas. I got the grill going and in our own little world, we celebrated our journey until we couldn't stay awake any longer.

The next morning we took the dinghy ashore, and after paying for the mooring at the municipal marina, we walked down Las Olas Boulevard to the beach so Carol could dip her feet in the ocean! I watched her prance around in ankle deep water like a kid and all I could think of was how strong and determined she could also be. I asked myself if I could I have made this trip without her? Probably not, but even if I could have, I wouldn't want to. It was the sharing of the adventure with her that made all the difference. My thoughts were broken by her voice calling to me.

"Come on, wuss, get your feet wet!"

I laughed. "Call me a wuss, huh?

Laughing again, I caught her in a bear hug, then kissed her as I picked her up and walked into deeper water.

"Stop, Ron. We're going to get wet!"

"So who's the wuss now?" I asked.

Half-laughing, half-pleading, she said, "Come on, stop; we have to go to breakfast!"

The waves now lapped at our thighs, thoroughly soaking our shorts, but she stopped protesting and tightened her arms around my neck, then she kissed me passionately. I told her I loved her more than life and if no one was on the beach I'd make love to her at the water's edge like we did in Hawaii.

She wiped tears from her cheek. "I love you too, Ron!"

Then, poking me in the belly, she added, "And I love when you get crazy like this! That was so exciting that day in Hawaii, wasn't it?"

I didn't care if anyone was on the beach; I caressed her and said we should skip breakfast and go back to the boat.

She laughed. "Ha, not on your life. I want breakfast at a restaurant on A1A, then we'll go back to the boat."

The forty-five minute trip up the New River through the heart of Fort Lauderdale was like nothing we'd ever experienced. First, you'd have to understand Carol to appreciate the added dimension she brought to anything we did. She was vivacious and tantalizing and watching her point out beautiful homes, restaurants and dock bars was a treat to behold, even after all the years we'd been together. Combined with her enthusiasm, her body movements could communicate a penchant for either simple fun or passionate lust, sometimes both at the same time. Now, as I navigated up the narrow river, I was constantly distracted by her as well as the specific shore attraction she happened to be pointing to. I didn't know if I should laugh or tell her to sit and be quiet.

Settling into our new dock at Marina Bay, we met Butch, the gregarious bartender at Rick's, the marina tiki-bar & restaurant. Marina Bay is an almost perfect rectangular notch off the New River, just west of the I-95 Bridge. It was an old Florida kind of place, and we became regulars at Rick's, spending almost as much time there as traversing the river to go for weekend sails to Miami. If bad weather kept us from sailing, we'd be happy hanging out at the marina, especially at night when they had live entertainment, whereupon Carol would dance for hours.

We made a lot of friends at Marina Bay, but we weren't crazy about living in Plantation. The townhouse was great but within weeks after moving in, we were sitting on our balcony one Sunday morning sipping coffee. It overlooked a wide courtyard and pool and Carol commented how beautiful the property was, but there was something in her tone that begged me to probe her thoughts.

I asked her, "You do like it here right, Baby?

She patted my hand and said, "Who wouldn't, it's beautiful?"

I smiled. "But?"

She looked at me and said, "I could live here forever but this development could just as well be in Scottsdale, Arizona or Ponca City, Oklahoma. It's just not Florida."

At first, I wasn't exactly sure of what she meant. Then I thought of our marina and places we had seen in the Keys, even nice old sections of Miami like Coconut Grove, and I came to understand. From then on, in between sailing, work and entertaining customers, we searched for a new place to live. We wanted to be in Ft. Lauderdale on the water in order to keep *Lastdance* in our back yard so we focused our search on the canals off Las Olas Blvd. Seven months later we moved into Laudonnaire which was definitely an old Florida kind of place on Isle of Venice just off Las Olas. It had twelve apartments, eight boat slips, a heated pool, and a tiki-bar. Aside from meeting neighbors who would become lifelong friends, the decision had a colossal impact on our lives many years later.

Before we moved, friends from Marina Bay invited us to a nautical scavenger hunt in Fort Lauderdale. I wasn't excited about motoring *Lastdance* through crowded canals and waterways to chase down clues, but Carol wanted to participate so we signed up. Going to our marina the night before the event, we found Rick's crowded with regulars as well as sailors off a Navy ship in port for the weekend. I knew Carol wanted to stop there, but we went directly to our boat so we could get up early the next morning for the event. As we prepared to go to bed, loud reggae music from the bar carried down to the docks and Carol, who was already restless from the beating drums asked if we could go up for just one drink.

"Okay," I said. "Just one drink!"

We were given a big welcome at the bar by Butch. "Hey, you came back; I saw you guys sneak by before!"

Carol ordered a beer. I was about to order a rum and coke, but I asked Butch what the sailor beside me was drinking. "That's a Rum Runner. If you drink three of them and can still walk, you don't have to pay. You wanna try it?"

I laughed and was about to say no and order my usual rum and coke, but Carol said, "Have one; I want to taste it."

I liked it.

Carol said, "Yuk, too much rum."

We danced a few dances and I went back to my drink. Carol danced alone, then with two very drunk sailors young enough to be her sons. When the music stopped, she came to bar and drank the last of her beer.

Looking at my drink, she said, "If you're going to nurse that drink all night, I'll have another beer."

I laughed, but it came out more like a giggle. "I'm not nursing my drink, this is my second one!"

It was Carol's turn to laugh. "What happened to just one drink?"

I giggled again. "I dunno. I guess the first one makes you stupid."

She sat in my lap and Butch brought her another beer and another rum runner for me. Carol said, "Oh boy, are you going to be okay?"

The last thing I remember was saying, "Yeah, I'm fine."

Carol woke me the next morning and I felt like there was a ball of lead in my head that ricocheted around my skull every time I moved.

"Holy shit I feel like crap. How did I get back to the boat last night?"

She laughed but looked concerned. "Butch helped me bring you back. You lost the contest, so you owe him fifteen dollars for the three rum runners!"

I couldn't even get out of bed without feeling nauseous, and I could see that Carol was disappointed we weren't going to the scavenger hunt.

"I'm sorry, Baby, but I can't even move here. Why don't you call Clive and see if you can ride with them or on another boat?"

"Are you sure? I don't mind staying with you."

"What, and watch me sleep and barf all day? No, if they have room or can find you a spot on another boat, you go with them, and I promise I'll meet you at the party at four o'clock."

Other than to use the head, I stayed in bed until three o'clock. Even then, I felt weak and my brain still hurt. Nevertheless, I promised Carol I'd be at the post-rally party, so I showered and took a taxi to 17th Street causeway where the finish line was. Carol saw me walk into the tent and ran to me. After a warm hug and kiss, she asked if I was okay, then showed me a small trophy she won for getting the most clues correct. I couldn't believe how happy it made her and I was glad I urged her to participate in the event.

I nursed a ginger ale and Carol introduced me to some of the crew from the boat she was on. They were all men!

I poked her and said, "Now I see why you're so happy, five guys and you in a Hooters tank-top all day!"

She kissed my cheek. "Don't worry, Baby. You know I always save the last dance for you. Besides, you wanted me to go!"

The owner of the boat then came up to us and introduced himself.

"You must be Ron. Hi, I'm Anthony. Let me tell you, your wife knows every line in every Jimmy Buffett song. She gave us the right answer to every clue, and we would have won the rally if we didn't make a few wrong turns."

I smiled. "You should have let her steer the boat; she's a good sailor."

Anthony looked at Carol hesitantly.

Carol sheepishly said, "I was steering when we made the first wrong turn."

I laughed hard, which made my head hurt. "How could you do that? You just set women's seamanship back a hundred years."

Anthony came to bat for her. She made a wrong turn at a very confusing junction. Then he added, "It was the wrong turns made by other crew members that cost us the rally, but hell, we all had fun."

As we walked away, Carol giggled. "You try steering with five men staring at your boobs all day and see how you do!"

I laughed. "Hell, I'd really be nervous if five guys were staring at my boobs all day!"

CHAPTER 18
HELLO COLUMBUS

After Labor Day, most of the talk at the marina was of the Columbus Day Regatta. Carol wanted to sign us up and join the flotilla of boats that were going, but over drinks with our friends at Rick's, I said, "We don't race."

Everyone laughed. "We don't race either. We just go for the party!"

Someone shouted, "Yeah, three hundred boats race, three thousand boats party, mostly topless! You and Carol have to come!"

I looked at him. "Why do I get the feeling that it's not me you want to see prancing around topless on *Lastdance?*"

A chorus of laughter followed, then they began chanting, urging me to sign up. Looking to Carol, I caught a look on her face that said, "*Party pooper.*" I shrugged. "Okay, okay, we're in, but just for the party!"

A month later, we left Marina Bay bound for Miami along with five other boats; two power and three other sailboats. We stayed close to each other going down the river but once at Port Everglades inlet, *Dagger* and *Emily,* the two powerboats, sped south. Along with *Joy, Empress,* and *Second Chance,* we enjoyed a more leisurely pace, sailing just a quarter of a mile off the beach in twelve knots of east wind! I could see that Carol really enjoyed doing stuff like this with others, and I secretly wondered if it was because I was boring. I pushed the thought from my mind and took pleasure in seeing the contrast between her steering *Lastdance* at a steep angle of heel and Terry over on *Joy,* who was reading a romance novel and hadn't left her spot against the cabin, since we left Fort Lauderdale.

Arriving off Miami with the wind still onshore, we all sailed into Government Cut and ran west, wing and wing alongside towering cruise ships docked on Dodge Island. Carol loved it and gleefully waved at passengers on the ships, ceasing only when we doused sails in the turning basin at the end of the channel. We then motored south of the Dodge Island Bridge to Miamarina, which is part of Bayside, an eclectic collection of restaurants, bars and shops similar to Baltimore's Inner Harbor.

As we entered the marina we were greeted by a festival like atmosphere and Carol's eyes lit up.

"Oh this is so much fun. I love coming here; just listen to the band. We should move the boat here."

Seconds later, she asked, "Do you think we could get a slip here?"

God she could make me laugh. "Carol, listen to yourself. Calm down."

Still laughing, I called the marina on the VHF and was greeted by a heavily-accented voice giving us docking instructions.

Once secured in our slips, our three thirsty crews marched off to The Conga Bar, an outdoor cafe on the water where our powerboat friends and their guest were already beyond the social drinking stage. They offered us chilled mojitos and friendly taunts.

"What took you so long; we've been here for hours?"

By our third round, everyone was dancing and toasting life, the sea, our women, and any other women who happened to be within earshot! While I was making a fool of myself along with the other guys, Carol was having a great time, but was becoming borderline wild as she danced, telling anyone at the bar who would listen, that mojitos were now her official drink!

Following late afternoon siestas, we had a boisterous dinner at Lombardi's, then turned in early from the exhaustion of being on the water all day and too much pre-regatta celebration. With a dawn departure from Miamarina for the sailboats, we motored past high-rise condos then under the Rickenbacker Causeway. There, we hoisted sails and swept past Key Biscayne into Biscayne Bay. Our powerboat friends soon overtook us and raced ahead promising to get a good spot. Then, with only the sound of the wind across our sails and the ripple of our wake, we glided through turquoise water, bound for Elliot Key, leaving Miami and our inhibitions behind.

To get to Elliot Key you must traverse Featherbed Bank, which runs across Biscayne Bay from Boca Chita Key to Black Point. You have to be sure of your navigation here as this is part of Biscayne National Park with protected coral and sea grass. If you run aground and damage any of the coral or sea grass, you can be fined thousands of dollars, so Carol took over the helm and I navigated using both GPS and frequent visual bearings. Once clear of Featherbed, we steered for what we believed was a forested island. We soon realized that the forest was really thousands of masts in the anchorage. I didn't know how we were going to find our friends, but Don on *Joy* called me on the VHF and told me to follow him. I'd never seen so many boats, let alone so close together. In between closely anchored boats, there were people swimming and in dinghies and every manner of paddle craft, so I took over the helm.

That was fine with Carol, who was eager to check out the bizarre scene unfolding before us. We followed *Joy* as she carefully eased her way through boats that were anchored impossibly close to each other and through throngs of people in the water. There was no way to describe this other than to say it was not for the shy or timid because you could almost pass a beer to the boat alongside you.

Our two powerboat friends were already anchored and rafted together. *Joy*, a heavy forty foot Passport, went outboard of *Dagger* along with *Empress*, the smallest boat in our group. *Second Chance* and *Lastdance* rafted outboard *Emily* to balance the raft. It occurred to me that the anchorage was totally exposed with considerable fetch in every direction except the east. I shuddered to consider the mess this could quickly become if a nasty squall blew up, and I briefly contemplated anchoring alone on the far fringe of the anchorage. Carol however, had already set up our outdoor speakers and was swaying to the sounds of Jimmy Buffett singing "One Particular Harbor". I'd just have to monitor the weather forecast and put out all our fenders.

With our six-boat flotilla securely rafted, a huge Jolly Roger was raised from *Joy's* mast. The other boats in our raft-up hoisted their own banners. I raised our own colorful string of flags that ran from the top of our mast to deck level. Drinking liberally from a pair of five gallon margarita coolers, our group of middle-aged sailors settled down to enjoy our surroundings. The weather was perfect. We socialized with our friends and with strangers from nearby boats as hundreds of dinghies filled with women, most wearing only bikini bottoms, paraded slowly around the anchorage. I thought, *Except for that one day with Captain Harry's twin sisters, boating was never like this on Chesapeake Bay*

After several margaritas, Carol and I went exploring in our dinghy. We slowly threaded our way through thousands of anchored boats, swimmers and revelers in every manner of watercraft. This was not the sanctuary of our cockpit, so Carol was at first uneasy to be riding through the anchorage, but she quickly grew accustom to the whistles and wolf calls directed her way. Any self-consciousness was put to rest as we came upon huge rays gliding gracefully in the shallows. She was fascinated with their effortless motion, and tried to reach down and touch them and I had to caution her that although not aggressive, they could be very dangerous creatures. We also saw several small bull sharks on the ocean side of Elliot Key, so we opted to avoid snorkeling that day for the same reason. Once we returned through the deep narrow cut to the bay, we were greeted by tantalizing aromas from thousands of grills drifting across the anchorage. Moving as fast as we dared with so many people in the water, we rushed back in time to participate in our raft's pot luck dinner.

As darkness settled on Biscayne Bay, we were treated to a spectacle that could have been the source of inspiration for Jimmy Buffett's song, "Stars on the Water". One by one, then in rapid succession, thousands of anchor lights came on from the colossal fleet. Those on sailboats were high atop mast and those on powerboats were closer to the water, all of which made an awe inspiring sight.

Exhausted, individuals and couples began to fall asleep where they sat. Those who were still able, drifted off to their beds below deck. Carol and I could still navigate our way back to *Lastdance* and the comfort of our bed and as we lay under the open hatch and looked at the multitude of stars above us, we talked for a long time about how much fun we had. Fortunately, I had the good sense several times during the long day to rub sunscreen on her, front and back. She now thanked me, whereas earlier, she had jokingly accused me of trying to fondle her amidst the thousands of fellow boaters.

I chuckled and whispered, "Okay, so I knocked off two birds with one stone." Then, as I applied soothing aloe lotion to her chest, I snickered and said, "But this is purely medicinal."

After a community breakfast on Elliot Key the next morning, we got underway with the wind again from the east at twelve knots. We sailed north toward Miami for two hours, then we went out to the ocean using Biscayne Channel, which joins Cape Florida Channel where it enters the sea several miles north of Fowey Rock. These deep channels are carved out of a coral reef, so the area outside the waterways is very shallow with coral rising almost to the surface. A cluster of vacation and fishing homes called Stiltsville exist on these state-leased shallows, and sailing through here is like driving down a rural street lined with homes.

Once on the ocean, we steered a course to Fort Lauderdale that arced out into the Gulf Stream, giving us a lift from this fast moving river in the sea. *Lastdance* is not a fast boat, but with the wind increasing to fifteen knots and help from the current, we logged record speed, sailing from Cape Florida to Port Everglades in just over three hours, averaging nine and a half knots!

With Thanksgiving approaching, we provisioned *Lastdance* for a trip to Bimini, but a cold front with northerly winds in the twenty to twenty-five knot range stopped us once again. These conditions make for a very bad Gulf Stream crossing, so we spent two days in Key Biscayne's No Name harbor with a dozen other boats, waiting for a weather window. It was not to be! We were running out of holiday time, so on the third day with a chilly wind still blowing out of the north we opted to go to Key Largo.

Leaving Key Biscayne with twenty-five knots of wind out of the northeast, we reefed the main and flew the small staysail as we broad reached the entire thirty-five mile trip to Key Largo. Channels through reefs and shoals along the way often forced us to jibe, sometimes putting the wind directly astern, but we were able to sail all the way through Barnes Sound, right up to the entrance to Jewfish Creek on Key Largo. This is considered the true beginning of the Keys, and with its own colony of saltwater crocodiles, we decided to not do any swimming there!

Thanksgiving Day found us anchored in a small cove off the main channel surrounded by mangroves. We had hoped to have an al fresco dinner in the cockpit but with the wind at twenty knots and the temperature still in the sixties, we opted to eat in the warmth of our cabin. Carol shifted gears from first mate to chef and prepared a bountiful Thanksgiving dinner in the small galley. We had fresh baked turkey breast with all the trimmings and she even produced a ravioli course in keeping with my family tradition. In the warmth of our oil lantern, we ate a leisurely meal, and as always, we talked about life and love as we slowly consumed our feast along with two bottles of a very smooth merlot. Later, while listening to George Winston's *December* album, we huddled under a blanket in the cockpit, sipping the remaining wine while we watched the sun set.

Lingering at anchor the next morning, we then motored to the marina-motel on the east side of Jewfish Creek, immediately south of a small bascule bridge. Once secured in our slip I said, "Enough with turkey leftovers, we need some seafood! How about we take a taxi and go to The Quay for dinner tonight?"

We had lunch there on our way back from Key West the year before and I thought this would be a good opportunity to revisit it. Before dinner we took advantage of the marina facilities, especially their pool. Call us weenies, but we worried about the salt water crocodiles, so a refreshing swim in a heated pool felt great.

Carol was like a dolphin. Her swimming was unhurried, graceful and even erotic and I loved to watch her. As she swam a slow methodical back stroke, she watched me watch her. Smiling, she then came to me and put her arms around my neck, wrapped her legs around my torso, and I walked through the warm water, kissing and whispering sweet nothings to her. As we talked and kissed, it was only the voice of an elderly woman sitting by the pool that broke our trance.

"Honeymooners?"

Shielding our eyes from the sun, we looked to the source of the voice.

I said, "Excuse me?"

This time a man spoke. "Don't mind my wife; she just asked if you were honeymooners."

I laughed. "No we're not, we just feel like it."

Carol said, "We're together thirty-five years!" She then smiled and added softly to me, "Well, we are, sort of."

It was true. It often felt like we had never been apart and the whole exchange reminded me of a similar chat we had with a waitress many years earlier in Hawaii.

We had a drink with the couple before we went to dinner and told them the real story of our relationship. The woman was nearly in tears, and as I had often heard before, the man laughed and said I got the better end of the deal. They were from Chicago and were married fifty-two years, which was longer than we'd been living. They were amazed that we had sailed down on a boat, so we invited them aboard *Lastdance* for a quick tour. Teresa said, "My God, Louis, he has two paintings of her on the boat. Why don't you have a painting of me?"

Lou shrugged and looked at me and jokingly said, "Men like you are trouble makers!"

Later, as we rode in a taxi to the restaurant, Carol said we should have invited the couple to dinner with us. Squeezing her hand, I said, "Are you nuts? I want you all to myself tonight. Besides, they probably go to sleep at nine o'clock."

After sipping mojitos at an outdoor table, we went into the dining room for dinner and without being concerned about driving, I had a few drinks too many. We were having fun reminiscing about the Columbus Regatta, but our conversation triggered something still on my mind, and I just blurted out, "Do you think I'm boring?"

Carol looked at me and laughed. "Boring? Now who's nuts? Why would you ask that?"

"Well, you seem to prefer doing things with crowds of people. Like when we used to be on a mooring in Great Kills, you wanted to go to a marina and meet people and going to Columbus Day with a group. Stuff like that."

"Ron, you're not boring! My God, I have so much fun with you. I love when we have time alone, but you know me, I love to party and get a little crazy and there's no way I'd do that without you there. Think about it, you're the same way, Baby."

It was true, as much as I loved being alone with Carol, I liked the camaraderie of friends as well. I thought, *Why didn't you see that before, dummy?* Maybe it was because Carol was so beautiful or the occasional teasing of others like Lou earlier in the day saying I got the better end of the deal.

Her voice broke into my thoughts. "Ron, you said a long time ago that we have to be ourselves. I love you, Baby, and if you want us to avoid being with friends, I will, but it's not me and it's not you either. I'm sorry if I've hurt you, but I never would have thought this bothered you,"

She was right, of course, and with just those few sincere words from her, I never gave it another thought.

I woke the next morning to a forecast of a seventeen knot easterly breeze, which if it held, could take us all the way to Miami. Carol slept and I read while sipping coffee in the cockpit until I saw Lou sit at a table by the pool. I invited him aboard.

"Are you sure?" he said.

"Yes, no problem, come on join me."

He laughed. "You know, being on your boat was the biggest thrill we had the whole trip."

I said, "If we had the time, we'd take you and Teresa for a sail, but we need to head for home. Then I added. "Hey, when you get to Key West, you should take Teresa for a nice dinner cruise. There's a big sail boat there that does sunset dinner cruises. It's a catamaran, so it's really stable so folks can enjoy dinner. You should surprise her and do it, Lou!"

Before he could answer, Carol stuck her head up the companionway. "Good morning." Then added, "You should listen to my captain and take Teresa on the dinner cruise, Lou!" He laughed and said he would.

When Teresa came down, we joined them for breakfast by the pool, but although we enjoyed their company, we had to get going so after saying goodbye, Carol backed out of our slip and they waved to us as if we were their children. I told Carol I wondered what Teresa was saying to Lou at this moment as they watched her handle the boat. As soon as we cleared the bridge, I hoisted the main with a single reef and unfurled the jib. Jewfish Creek is sheltered by trees and mangroves on both banks, but we still caught enough wind aloft to move *Lastdance* along at four knots. As always,

Carol loves to steer in situations like this because even at four knots, she likes the sensation of speed that comes from being close to objects, especially land. We entered Barnes Sound where the wind picked up and we quickly accelerated to six knots.

Carol stayed on the helm for the next six miles until we cleared the high Card Sound Bridge, taking us into Little Card Sound, then Card Sound.

"Okay, captain, she's all yours. I need to use the head.

I laughed. "I thought you'd never ask."

As I took the helm, I thought, *This is sailing…eight to twelve feet of clear water and we're moving more than six knots.* The sensation was of flying low over a sandy beach and as long as the wind held, we could sail like this all the way to Miami, thirty-two miles to the north.

Carol called out from below. "Having fun? Want something to drink?"

We were fast approaching Cutter Bank and I knew she'd love sailing through the mile of very narrow channel with just one foot of water immediately outside on each side. "Yeah, get me an iced tea please. Then come up here, we're about to go through Cutter Bank."

Cutter Bank is west of Broad Creek, which opens to Hawk Channel and the ocean. A strong flooding current can push a boat out of the narrow waterway, so even though there was no southbound traffic, I hugged the eastern side of the channel. We were suddenly hit by a strong gust of wind and *Lastdance* quickly began to head up. I put the wheel hard over to port, but there was too much weather helm and we continued to turn into the wind. I thought, *Shit, were going to be driven aground.* Carol, who was just stepping into the cockpit with two cans of iced tea in her hands, quickly sized up the situation. Dropping the iced tea, she let the main sheet fly free, instantly spilling the wind, enabling me to regained control.

"Holy shit, we almost bought the ranch. That was quick thinking, Baby. You saved our asses!"

She smiled and jiggled her boobs. "And you thought I was just another pretty face!"

The rest of the sail was glorious but uneventful and by three thirty, we passed under the Rickenbacker Causeway Bridge. Twenty minuets later,

I headed up into the wind and doused our sails in front of Bay Front Park, and we motored into Miamarina. Our friend Carlos was on duty and handled our dock lines. As usual, he flirted with Carol who brazenly returned his flirts with equal enthusiasm. In reality, Carlos was a real gentleman in his late seventies, with a head of thick snow white hair. He had been a pilot in Peru and came to America during World War II to join our air force. Unfortunately, not being a citizen, he spent those years on the ground, then remained here after the war. As he plugged in our power line, he asked us why we didn't get an annual slip there since we came so often. I told him we just hadn't thought about it, so he told us he would drop off a brochure and application if he didn't see us when we came back from dinner.

Over dinner at Lombardi's, Carol said, "I did mention it, you know!"

"What did you mention?"

"I mentioned we should move the boat to Miamarina."

"I don't remember you saying that?"

"It's okay, but I mentioned it when we stopped here on our way to the Columbus Day Regatta. Remember now?"

"Yeah, I guess so, but I'm sorry, Baby. I didn't think you were serious since we knew we were going to move *Lastdance* to Laudonnaire."

I said, "Let's see how we like the boat in our backyard for a while, then maybe we can move her here for a few months and maybe even Coconut Grove for a few months. It would be an hour drive, but then we wouldn't have to spend forty minutes on the ICW to get to the inlet."

Carol beamed at the suggestion that we could move around like that. "Oh that would really be nice, Ron. We could sample it all, maybe even the marina in Miami Beach."

I smiled. "Sure, we could get slips on a monthly basis. Then, if we don't like being down here, we can always return to Laudonnaire."

Bayside livened up around noon when a Brazilian band began to play and Carol couldn't contain her excitement. I knew she wanted to stay, but we had a twenty-seven mile sail ahead of us and had to get underway. With the wind at twelve knots from the southeast, we motored out of Miamarina and on through the Dodge Island Bridge. Once in the ship turning basin, we hoisted sails and sailed out the main channel where Carol put aside thoughts of the carnival at Bayside and once again became enthralled at the sight of the cruise ships.

"Why do you get so excited when you see a cruise ship?"

She looked back at me. "Oh, I don't know. I guess because they're so big and there are so many people on them and everyone looks like they are having fun."

"Carol, we've lived here for almost a year. Why haven't you asked if we could do a cruise? I mean shit, these are my customers. It's what I do for a living. Do you wanna do a cruise?"

She hugged me. "Oh could we?" Oh, I'd love to, Baby!"

I told her I'd check it out as soon as I got back to work and kissed her as we sailed along, dwarfed by the huge ships to starboard.

In the last week of December, Bayside took on a wild carnival like atmosphere as restaurants and shops prepared for the annual Orange Bowl Parade and holiday celebrations. Miamarina was a zoo as hundreds of transient boats arrived for the New Year Eve celebrations. Tables were set up on the docks and people displayed all manner of mostly Latino foods including a group of Cubans who had a whole roasted pig! Carol and I strolled around and were greeted by total strangers, mostly speaking Spanish, but all offering us mojitos or a plate of roasted pig or chicken.

The dock hands were scrambling to get the correct transient boats into their assigned slips, and our friend Carlos became flustered and asked us to please watch the open slip beside us and to call him if any boat, but *Premium Time* tried to go in it. Later, while below in the galley making drinks, I heard Carol shouting.

"Are you *Premium Time?*"

The reply was an energetic shout in return. "Yes we are!"

Then I heard Carol's voice again. "How come it says *Happy Hour* on your stern?" *Hmmm, time to go on deck,* I thought.

I asked, "What's up?"

Carol said, "This boat is trying to come into the slip for *Premium Time.* You better call Carlos." I thought, *Assholes,* then went below and called Carlos on the VHF.

A few minutes later the confusion was cleared up. It seemed *Premium Time* had engine problems so everyone in his party came up from

Coconut Grove on *Happy Hour,* which belonged to one of his guests. They were clearly pissed at us, and one guy shouted above the din of music, "Thanks for squealing."

Carol was hurt and said, "Hey, we're sorry, but think about it, we were really looking out for you!"

She then offered them a bottle of champagne from our cooler. As with most people who've encountered Carol, the crew of *Happy Hour* succumbed to her friendly temperament and we were invited to join their party. That's how we met Mike and Liz. They became great friends, and we sailed to many places with them during our time in Florida.

CHAPTER 19
LAS OLAS

I woke early, but Carol wasn't in bed, which was very unusual. Walking into the living room, I found her sitting at the large window overlooking our courtyard with its many tropical plants, flowers, and *Lastdance* in her slip, just yards from our front door. Palm trees swayed gently in the breeze and clouds reflected off the still waters of the canal, and even though I couldn't see her face, I knew from her posture that she was happy. For me, that was all that mattered.

"Good morning, Princess. Like the view?"

She turned with a smile. "I love the view, come here!"

I went to her and she put her arms around my neck and thanked me for moving.

"I know we're going to love living here, Ron. Just imagine waking to that view every morning. I'm not sure I still want to move *Lastdance* to Miami."

"Well, there's no rush. Let's see how we like it here and give it some thought in six months or so."

We sat there a long time talking about all that we'd achieved, not just in material things but in the quality of our life as well. It was one of those infrequent times we asked ourselves, "What if?" As in what if we had never separated. It was a brief departure down a road we could never alter and I was the one to change the subject. "So, is it going to be breakfast at the Floridian or do we start a tradition and have breakfast out back?"

She smiled. "Oh could we? That would be wonderful to do that every morning, then maybe go for a swim!"

Except for when a cold front came through in the winter, we did that almost every morning for next three years. We were often joined by our neighbors, Rick and Susan, who came to Florida by way of the Caribbean, after sailing their boat *Windbird I* from California. David and Linda were also early risers and appreciated good coffee and croissants. They built their boat *Tenacity*, a beautiful Lyle Hess designed cutter with bright work and craftsmanship that looked like fine furniture. It was from Linda that I learned the art of varnishing and from whom Carol gained an even greater desire to achieve more lofty sailing goals.

In 1999, Hurricane Floyd tested our mettle as it raced toward us with frightening speed and ferocity. It was a Category IV hurricane with hundred and fifty-six mph winds and all the forecast models said it would make landfall at or near Fort Lauderdale. We had a meeting of boat owners at Laudonnaire and decided that even with this monster storm, the major threat on our protected canal was not waves, but wind and storm surge. The strategy we adopted was to move the boats to the middle of the canal and secure them to each bank with as many long lines as possible. That would keep them away from the pilings and allow for a large vertical rise and fall from any storm surge.

Although everyone was responsible for their own boat, it became a collective effort to do the job well. As the wind increased and the first intermittent bands of rain arrived, Carol and I got *Lastdance* secured with a total of sixteen, five-eighth inch lines, each, fifty feet long. Using our dinghies, David, Rick, and I secured them to pilings on each bank of the canal while Carol, Linda and Susan secured them to cleats and winch drums on the boats, adding heavy chafing gear on each line. We did this to *Lastdance*, then *Tenacity* and *Windbird I* with help from Tory and Andy, two young brothers from California who came to Florida by way of the Panama Canal in their Westsail 28.

Again using the dinghy, we then deployed our two bow anchors and a stern anchor and as we manhandled these heavy anchors and chain amidst the increasing wind and rain, I stopped and looked at Carol.

"Look at you," I said. "Your fingers are scraped, your nails are broken, you're hair is matted and looks like shit, but you're working to save our boat like a crusty old sailor, and still, you're the most beautiful woman I've ever known."

Kissing me quickly, she laughed. "Flattery will usually get you everywhere, but right now, row the stinking boat so I can let go of this yucky chain."

After removing all sails and electronics, we then tended to our apartment, which was on the first floor and would certainly be flooded by even a modest storm surge. All of our paintings and most of our books and other valuables had already been taken to a hurricane proof storage facility. Carol then had the idea to put our remaining things into our two dinghies, which we dragged up from the dock and put in the living room. If we did get flooded, she reasoned, the dinghies would float and keep our things dry unless the water rose too high.

With Floyd due to hit late that night, all of coastal southeast Florida was under a mandatory evacuation order and our area was already nearly deserted. Matt and Susan kept their boat at Laudonnaire and invited everyone to spend the night at their home in Weston, fourteen miles inland. As we prepared to leave, Arne and Craig, two young neighbors from overseas, decided to remain behind, saying that they'd never seen a hurricane. We tried to talk them out of it, but they were determined to stay. Carol's maternal instincts kicked in and she broke out two of our lifejackets, a handheld VHF radio, and two emergency beacons. She then warned them about flying debris and cautioned them to stay away from windows. It was almost comical as these two young virile guys stood nearly at attention as Carol adjusted their lifejackets and scolded them about being so foolish as to ride out a hurricane.

With the wind a steady forty-five miles an hour and gusting to fifty-five and higher, we took one more look at *Lastdance*. Carol shed tears as we watched our beautiful boat heel over, her lines straining with each powerful gust. I checked my handheld wind gauge with each blast of air and with the wind howling as it blew through the rigging of hundreds of sailboats on the canal, I yelled. "That one was sixty-two, we'd better get going!"

"Just sixty-two?" she shouted. "What will it be like when it reaches a hundred and fifty?"

Then, burying her face in my shoulder, she said aloud, "We're going to lose *Lastdance,* aren't we?"

"I don't know, Baby. I can't imagine what a hundred and fifty mile an hour winds will be like, but we've done all we can do; it's time to go."

Driving west, I considered my early concerns about Carol's desire to sail and then of the thousands of miles she had eagerly cruised with me. I smiled and drew her closer to me, knowing that her enthusiasm in preparing *Lastdance* for Hurricane Floyd wasn't to please me, it was to save our ship! This was an aspect of her that no one outside the seafaring community could ever understand. She had long since become my shipmate, forming yet another powerful bond between us

Our caravan drove through the deserted streets of downtown Fort Lauderdale, and as the strengthening wind buffeted our cars, tree branches flew through the air like large darts. Once at Matt and Susan's home, it was anything but a hurricane party as we followed the progress of the storm on television. Our mood was somber, and we all wondered how things were back at Laudonnaire. I was touched at how emotional everyone was over their boats, which objectively speaking, were just assembled bits of fiberglass and wood objects, yet we fretted over them even though everyone was insured.

Between the screaming winds outside and concerns for our boats as well as Arne and Craig, it was at first impossible to sleep. Nevertheless, we were all exhausted from twenty-four hours of arduous storm preparation, and one by one, we dozed off. The last report I saw had Floyd's eye wall passing over Eleuthera. It made a slight turn to the northwest but was still on course for Fort Lauderdale with one hundred and fifty-five mph winds. I thought, *We're screwed*.

Matt excitedly woke me when the latest storm update came on. Miraculously, sometime during the night, Floyd's course changed abruptly to the north-northwest then a more northerly track. The report confirmed it had slammed into the Abacos with fifty-foot waves and a twenty-foot storm surge, but it would miss Fort Lauderdale! I woke Carol with the news and she cried with joy, but she was horrified as we heard about the destruction in the Bahamas. She had a caring nature and truly felt the pain of others and she wanted to volunteer her services as nurse in the Bahamas. Rightly or wrongly, I talked her out of it because for one thing, it had been years since she did any clinical nursing. Instead, she got involved with a friend in the Red Cross and raised money.

Chapter 20
Key West

As unexpected as my transfer to Florida had been four years earlier, the news that I was being transferred back to New Jersey was a complete surprise. We had mixed feelings, and I even considered resigning, but it was a big promotion, and in the end, we agreed to go back. Knowing that it might be our last chance to sail to the Bahamas, I then scheduled a full three week vacation for the first time since coming to Florida. Carol and I poured over charts and cruising guides and after speaking with our friends David and Linda who had been there many times, we decided on the Abacos as our destination.

Our plan was to sail directly from Fort Lauderdale to West End on Grand Bahama Island. If the wind was unfavorable or if a front came through, we'd go to Miami instead. Crossing the north flowing Gulf Stream in opposing winds can make for an uncomfortable if not a treacherous voyage so if the wind was from any northern quadrant, we'd wait for a safe window at an anchorage on Key Biscayne. Departing from that far south would also enable us to reduce the course offset we'd have to factor in for the Gulf Stream and could even make for a quicker passage.

Lastdance was fully provisioned by departure day and I monitored NOAA weather radio from work but I was disappointed when the forecast called for light and variable winds and a cold front on the way. This was not the best forecast for sailing across sixty miles of open ocean, so I was already considering the Miami option. I called Carol at her office and she immediately sensed my frustration.

"I'm sorry, Baby. So what do we do?"

I said, "If not for the cold front I'd wait here, but I suppose we should scoot down to Miami, which will give us more options."

"Whatever you think," she said. Then asked, "Tonight or tomorrow?"

I said, "Let's still leave tonight okay?"

"Okay, you're the captain. See you when I get home, I love you."

I hung up and thought to myself, *How many wives would so casually set off on a twenty-five mile night sail after a day at work?*

I was impatient and drinking an iced tea at our tiki bar with neighbors when Carol got home from work. As she darted into our apartment, she yelled out to no one in particular, "Tell him to calm down. I just wanna change. I'll be right there!"

We all laughed! She came out ten minutes later wearing white shorts and an alluring new blouse. As she walked toward us, my mind wandered and I briefly considered leaving in the morning, thinking I'd rather spend the night in our apartment with her instead of motoring to Miami for six hours.

She was at my side and broke the spell with a soft kiss. "Well, let's go. Do I have to wait all night for you?"

David said in his most charming tone. "My, my, Carol, darling, you look exceptionally beautiful this evening. Why don't you stay here with us and let this cantankerous old fart of yours go away by himself?"

She laughed. "Ha, he'd be lost without me."

We cast off lines and our friends called out bawdy farewells as we silently glided down our canal past palm trees and people who waved at us from some of the many boats on the waterway. I found it oddly inspirational whenever we'd catch an occasional glimpse of our mast and flags reflected in windows of homes along the canal and I hoped it was a sign that we would have a great vacation.

Carol hugged me and we kissed. She said, "Three weeks together sailing in the Bahamas, I'm so excited."

"Me too," I said.

"By the way, David is right, you do look exceptionally beautiful."
I was rewarded with another kiss, then another.

"Keep that up and we'll be anchoring here for the night!"

We missed the Las Olas Bridge opening, so it took us over an hour to get to Port Everglades. With only the slightest breeze, I said, "It still looks like we're going to be motoring, so it's your call, go outside along the coast or take ICW?"

Carol pondered the choice. "It's still rush hour and the bridges on the ICW will be slow. It'll be less stressful outside, and maybe I'll let you peek inside this blouse you like so much. Let's take the coast!"

"Good reasoning." I agreed! And with a lecherous smile on my face, I turned *Lastdance* east and motored out the inlet.

We turned south and I maintained a leisurely five knots to keep the engine noise low so it wouldn't intrude on our music. Carol made some snacks of cheese, crackers, and artichoke spread, and we noshed as we motored down the coast less than a mile off the beach. She sat by my side, and with one arm for the helm, I placed the other around her shoulder and drew her close to me. We could see people still lingering on the sandy beaches as the sun set behind the high-rise apartment buildings.

I whispered softly, "I love being with you. I love doing things together and going to places with you!"

She snuggled closer. "I know, Baby. I love being with you like this too!"

We kissed, caressed, and fondled our way south, arriving at the Miami entrance after midnight and then proceeding up Government Cut to Miamarina where we took a slip for the night.

After securing *Lastdance,* I noticed the cabin lights had darkened. When I went below, I expected to find Carol already in bed, but I was pleasantly surprised to see her lounging in the salon, wearing a seductive baby doll that barely contained her. I stood motionless, absorbing the setting she had created. A bottle of champagne was chilling beside our fluted glasses and Carol looked enticing in the flickering light from several strategically placed candles. She hit the remote and Jeffery Osborne singing, "Baby Stay with Me Tonight," began to play softly on the stereo.

She smiled seductively and said, "Happy vacation, Ron."

I woke in the morning and immediately listened for wind. I thought, *There's nothing, not a sound.* I turned on NOAA weather and heard a forecast that was worse than the day before. Winds were still predicted to be light and variable and the arrival of the cold front was more imminent. *Damn,* I thought, *we're going to be stuck here a few days.* I made coffee and went up to the office to check in and take a shower. When I returned, Carol was still asleep. She had kicked off the sheets as the morning sun flooded through the hatch above our bed and warmed the cabin. The image of her stopped me in my tracks. I thought, *Why am I always so surprised by what she does to me? Even in her sleep, she's so beautiful, innocent, and wanton, all at the same time.*

In watching her, I knew it was much more than those things that made me love her so deeply. There was the elusive but powerful chemistry that bonded us since childhood of course, but also her gentle nature, sense of wonder and her unconditional love. As I looked at her serene face, I hoped I made days as joyful for her as she made for me and I silently promised to be kinder and more caring, every chance I got.

With no wind in the forecast, I let Carol sleep. Half an hour later, upon hearing me stirring around in the galley, she woke with an exaggerated yawn as she climbed out of bed. Even after our previous night of lovemaking, she stirred my senses again as I watched her pull a t-shirt over her bare breasts.

"Coffee will be ready in five minutes. Go shower, I'll have some oatmeal ready for you when you get back."

She kissed me with eyes still partially closed, then lazily gathered her things and went off to shower still half asleep.

When she returned, I joined her with a cup coffee as she sat at the salon table to eat the oatmeal I prepared.

"It's not instant, is it?" she asked.

"No, does it taste like instant?" I replied.

I smiled at this ritual we went through whenever I made oatmeal for her. It began fifteen years earlier when she first lectured me on the evils of instant foods. I can still hear her. "There's no nutrition or fiber, and who knows what chemicals they put it."

From then on it was slow stirred old fashioned Quaker Oats or else.

She finished her oatmeal and sipped her coffee.

"So what's the plan, captain?"

"There's no wind in the forecast and a cold front is moving in tomorrow so we may as well hang out for a few hours, maybe eat lunch here and leave in the afternoon for Key Biscayne to wait for a weather window."

"Can we go to No-Na-Me?" she asked.

I laughed. "Yes, we'll go to No-Na-Me."

No-Na-Me was really No Name Harbor. The first time we went there, Carol thought the name was dumb so she renamed it, No-Na-Me and marked all our charts accordingly.

Like me, my first mate was not a shopper. We shopped only when we needed something, but at a place like Bayside, it was fun to browse through the many interesting stores and eateries. After strolling around the arcade hand in hand for an hour, we ended our tour with lunch at Lombardi's, one of our favorite restaurants in Miami. Then, while walking back to the marina, we heard a familiar voice call out from behind.

"Hey, it's my good friends the lovers!"

It was Carlos. He was wearing his familiar outfit of clean pressed jeans and a crisp white long-sleeve shirt. Carol gave him a big hug.

He smiled and said, "You get more beautiful every day. Why don't you stay here and be my girlfriend?"

Carlos and Carol exchanged their routine flirts, and then he was all business.

"Are you staying for the night?" he asked. "If you are, I can move you to a better slip you know."

He was always accommodating and considerate, almost to a fault, but he carried himself like an aristocrat and never took a tip. He called us the lovers because he said we were always holding hands and stealing kisses from each other, just like he and his wife. Telling him about our vacation cruise plans, he cautioned us about the approaching cold fronts.

"Fronts, as in more than one, Carlos?"

"Si, there is a series of cold fronts approaching. If you're thinking of making a crossing, you should wait because it's already too late to leave.

"Bummer, I heard just one front arriving tomorrow."

"No, amigo," he said. "There are several, but maybe you'll get a window in between them."

He suggested we wait it out at the marina.

"Not at these prices, Carlos. We've been strolling around and just had lunch. We're going to head over to No Name Harbor and anchor until the weather passes."

Carol corrected me. "It's No-Na-Me!"

Carlos looked perplexed so I explained, and he laughed.

"Si, No-Na-Me sounds much better, but you could get stuck there and be bored."

Then he giggled. "No, I'm sure you two never get bored."

We all laughed and he said he'd help us get underway.

As Carlos cast off our last line, I shook his hand, and we waved goodbye. Carol took us out of the marina into the channel that ran close to the adjacent bridge. She then motored in front of Bay Front Park and on to the confusing intersection of the ICW, Miami River and Dodge Island Cut. Once clear of the junction, we entered the channel east of Claughton Island. From there, the channel narrowed as it turned toward Virginia Key, and then under the high Rickenbacker Causeway Bridge into beautiful Biscayne Bay.

Reading a book the whole time, I looked up only when we came out of the shadow of the bridge into the bright sunlight again. I watched Carol deftly maneuver our little ship, one moment checking the compass, the next, her surroundings. I smiled at the confidence in her eyes as she steered from her perch on the cockpit bench which allowed her to see over the dodger without standing on her toes. She had one hand on the wheel, the other holding the boom for support and although all business, I delighted at the figure she cut in her bathing suit. I thought, *It's always how I think about her. I'm pleased by her confidence and skills, yet aroused by her sexuality at the same time.*

As I returned to my book, I said softly, "Do you know what you do to me?"

She looked at me, and over the noise of the engine, said, "Speak louder, I can't hear you."

I smiled. "I'll tell you later; pay attention to where you're going."

I then stared hungrily at her body, letting her know that whatever it was I said had something to do with sex. Looking ahead, she smiled and said out loud, "Pervert."

With the bustle and excitement of Bayside behind us, we headed for the relative solitude of No-Na-Me Harbor on the south side of Key Biscayne, in Bill Baggs Park. No-Na-Me offers excellent shelter and easy access to Cape Florida Channel, which runs southeast to the ocean about seven miles south of Miami's Government Cut. For that reason alone, many sailboats going to the Bahamas prefer to leave from there, rather than Miami.

Carol drifted closer to Key Biscayne until we were at Flashing Red "4", which she rounded and then proceeded into Cape Florida Channel.

"How close can I get to shore?"

I checked the chart before answering. "Stay fifty yards off until we get to the entrance, then go in at a right angle. Don't cut the corner!"

I returned to my book again until I heard the engine throttle back, and I knew we were close to the entrance. Ten years earlier aboard *Ursaorion*, I taught her what I had learned twenty years before when I asked my teacher how fast I should maneuver when in close quarters.

"Just fast enough. Just fast enough!" was his reply.

I went to the bow to get the anchor ready and Carol slowed to idle as she searched for a spot away from the dozen boats already at anchor. People sat lazily in cockpits and waved as they watched *Lastdance* coast silently by. I thought, *I must be vain, but I love that we almost always have the prettiest boat in an anchorage.* I waved back and asked how much scope they had out so I could gauge their swing radius. Most replied that they had between seventy and eighty feet. Moments later, Carol chose an open area and said, "I'm showing ten feet."

She knew I'd want that information so I could estimate how much scope to let out. Pleased that she anticipated me, I said, "Good. This looks fine."

She pointed us into the slight breeze, then gently put the gearshift in reverse and stopped our forward motion.

As we moved slowly astern, I let go the anchor and with a rattling of chain, we slowly gathered sternway. I signaled for neutral and we drifted back until I saw the fifty foot mark. Locking the wildcat, the chain became taut. I watched a moment, and after assuring myself that the anchor wasn't dragging, I signaled for reverse and let more chain out until we had eighty feet out. This was probably more than we'd need, but with several fronts coming through, I thought it best to use an 8:1 ratio while there was still room, rather than worry about dragging anchor at night with the wind howling.

I signaled with two close fists that the anchor chain was secured to its cleat and the rope snubber rigged. Carol immediately throttled up the engine while still in reverse to deeply set the anchor. The chain became taut and without any evidence that we were dragging, I made a slashing motion across my throat and she throttled down, putting the engine in neutral. Then, as was custom for the first mate aboard *Lastdance* when anchoring, she went below to make drinks.

"What a wench!" I shouted, and then needlessly added, "Put some Jimmy on!"

A moment later, I smiled at her choice of songs as Jimmy Buffett's voice bellowed from the cockpit speakers, singing, "One Particular Harbor". I rigged the bimini for shade and Carol returned to the cockpit with a beer for her and rum on the rocks for me, and we toasted our first full day of vacation.

By day five, we were still anchored in No-Na-Me Harbor with a forecast for more of the same nasty weather. One crew got inpatient and tried to make the crossing. They came back nine hours later with a torn main sail and a sea sick crew. Word soon spread around the anchorage that they had a very rough time of it, with seas out in the Gulf Stream as high as ten feet. I was bummed out because we were almost a week into our vacation and running out of time.

I decided to give it one more day. If the forecast didn't improve dramatically, we'd have to make a decision. Several hours later we sat in our cockpit having lunch with Barry, a seasoned single-hander sailor off *Desnia*, the sailboat anchored beside us. We'd been alternating boats for evening cocktails and dinners with him, especially since he seemed to have an endless supply of Gosling rum.

"So what do you think of the forecast?" I asked.

He said, "I'm staying put. I went ashore this morning to the light-house and could see it's really nasty out there."

Then, referring to the wind, he said. "It's going to blow like this for another two maybe three days, then we'll need another day for the seas to settle down. I'm not on a schedule, so there's no sense in getting my brains knocked out."

Agreeing with his logic, I said, "That's it then, we go to plan B."

Carol smiled. "What exactly is this particular plan B?"

"This plan B is we stay here for the next two weeks and drink all of Barry's rum!"

He laughed. "For the pleasure of Carol's company, you can drink every last drop, but I'm afraid I'd bore you both to tears. Why don't you go south, even if the wind blows all week you'll have an easy passage to Key West."

Carol's eyes lit up and she couldn't suppress her enthusiasm. "Oh I'd like that, Baby! How long will it take to get there?"

"Three days," I said.

Barry chimed in saying, "I hate to see you guys go, but you could still leave this afternoon and make it to Pumpkin Key, then go out Angel-fish Creek tomorrow."

I broke out a chart and laid it on the cockpit table. It was only twenty-two miles to Pumpkin Key, and with twenty knots of north wind, we could be there in less than four hours. It wasn't the Bahamas, but we'd be sailing and seeing new places. Plan B became plan A, and once we finished lunch, we made *Lastdance* ready to sail and weighed anchor.

Carol took us out of No-Na-Me and turned west in Cape Florida Channel. Soon after passing Flashing Red "4", she looked around to be sure we were clear of any boats, then yelled, "Heading up."

She brought *Lastdance* directly into the wind and I raised the main with a single reef. As soon as it was secured, I nodded and at her command of, "Falling off," I let the mainsheet run out and watched it fill as we gathered speed. Carol then brought us on a southerly heading, then shut the engine. I unfurled the jib, and as I quickly trimmed it, we accelerated until we were running before the wind at almost seven and a half knots.

Sailing on the relatively flat waters of Biscayne Bay in those conditions was exhilarating. The sensation of speed is far greater than you might think because even though there is a bit of a chop, we could still see the bottom racing by, especially as we sailed over shoals and reefs. As expected, we made Featherbed Bank in less than two hours. Then, just as we entered its narrow channel, we were joined by several dolphins much to Carols delight. She reached out and tried to touch them for as long as they stayed alongside us but the moment we left the channel on the south side of Featherbed, they darted off along the bank toward Sands Key. An hour later, we raced through another narrow channel across shallow Cutter Bank but instead of anchoring behind Pumpkin Key, we ducked behind the larger Long Arsenicker Key.

We were anchored and sipping margaritas by five twenty, only three hours and twenty minutes since leaving No-Na-Me. Carol made hors d'oeuvres, and we wrapped ourselves in a light blanket in the cockpit and watched the sun set. As if she was responsible for the bad weather she told me how sorry she was we couldn't go to the Bahamas.

"It's okay, Baby, we're together and doing the same things we'd do over there. We're spending time alone and we'll be exploring things ashore, so what's the difference if we're in the warm Keys or warm Bahamas, as long we're not freezing our asses off up north?"

Snuggling closer, she wrapped her arms around me. "I don't know about you, but we're almost freezing our asses off here; I'm ready to go below."

Waking soon after sunrise, I found the wind still out of the north. It was a more reasonable fifteen knots and the forecast was for more of the same throughout the day, diminishing to five knots in the evening. We got underway at nine o'clock, and after a bumpy passage out of Angelfish Creek, we were sailing south in Hawk Channel at six knots, just an hour later.

Passing Rodriguez Key around noon, it had warmed enough for Carol to peel off her sweatshirt and then her tank top as we raced southwest on a broad reach. I loved watching her sail like that, so full of confidence and so eager to please me. She knew I love photographing her and I knew she loved being photographed and I thought of a time when she'd hastily cover up if another boat came within a mile of us, but no longer. Life in Florida had diminished her inhibitions and as I watched her at the helm, I thought of a heavily accented line from an ex-New Jersey governor doing a tourism commercial, "So purrfect together!"

Hours later, we changed course at Alligator shoal to enter the anchorage at Indian Key. Carol had been napping and I woke her.

"Baby, wake up. We're here."

She rubbed the sleep from her eyes. "Where is here?"

I laughed. "Indian Key, silly." Then I added, "I need you to take the helm while I get the anchor ready, so you might want to get a top on; there's a few boats at anchor."

Taking the helm, she said, "What if I don't want to?"

I looked at her quizzically. "What if you don't want to what?"

"What if I don't want to put a top on?"

I was sure she was bluffing to see what I'd say, so I turned and went forward to prepare the anchor, saying, "Suit yourself, but I bet you chicken out. This isn't Columbus Day."

Half a mile southwest of Indian Key, Carol was still topless when she headed us into the wind and I doused our sails. Then, with as much calm as she could muster, she motored toward the anchorage.

With a smug look on her face, she said, "Still wanna bet?"

I looked around. There were three boats anchored to starboard and two to port and some smaller power boats moving about.

"Yeah, I'll bet. What do you want to bet?"

She smiled and said, "How about a day at a spa when we get to Key West?"

"And what do I get?" I asked.

She considered my question. "You could have the same thing or I'll buy dinner."

I was sure she'd chicken out, but I added a stipulation. "Okay, it's a deal, but you have to stay like that until we're fully anchored and you get our drinks."

I saw a hint of hesitancy cross her face, but whatever inspired her to be so brazen took control again.

"Okay, it's a deal!" she said.

As I walked to the bow, Carol brought us slowly in between the two groups of anchored boats. As often happened when entering an anchorage, *Lastdance* drew a lot of attention. This time, however, the casual admiring waves by crews on nearby boats reflected an interest level we'd not seen before. I saw that Carol was sitting, not standing as she usually did when at the helm. I laughed to myself thinking it was a small concession to our wager, so I said nothing. She remained indifferent and almost cavalier as she brought us to a stop, and I casually called out to nearby boats, asking how much scope they had out.

Someone on the boat nearest us shouted back. "Seventy feet!"

I acknowledged them with a cheery wave.

With our anchor well set, I surveyed our surroundings. A few folks simply stared while others feigned a lack of interest as they craftily glanced over the tops their books at *Lastdance* and the first mate at the helm. After shutting down the engine, true to her word, Carol stood and went below to make drinks. Jimmy Buffett's voice soon drifted softly from the speakers singing "Nautical Wheelers." A moment later, she was back on deck with my drink. She then sat back with her beer, slowly shaking her heard in time with the music.

"Okay, you won. I owe you a day at a spa in Key West. You can put a top on now if you want."

She just sat there humming along with the music, oblivious to everything until she finished her beer. Standing, she then went below for another and nonchalantly asked me if I was ready for a refill.

I said, "Sure," and wondering what this new found lack of modesty was all about, I handed her my glass.

When she came back up with our drinks, she had a tank top on, and I asked if she was getting cold.

She smiled. "No, but I won a day at a spa and did what I set out to do."

I looked at her puzzled. "What was it you set out to do?"

"I was reading about Key West, and there were photos of all these women walking on Duval Street topless during Fantasy Fest, so I set out to not make a big deal about being topless on a boat. Women all over Europe,

Miami Beach, and even Sandy Hook, New Jersey, do it, so I thought I'd force myself to do it, and I did."

Then she looked alarmed and asked if I was bothered or mad over it.

"Hell no. Not at all, Baby. You looked damn fine! You just never cease to surprise me, and that's one of the things I love about you."

Before sunset, Ted and Anna, the owners of *Lost Pilgrim*, a forty-seven-foot ketch anchored nearby, rowed over to introduce themselves and invite us to their boat for cocktails. I accepted and thanked them, saying we'd be along shortly. As they motored off to invite the crew from another boat, Carol emerged from below.

"Oh my God, I'm so embarrassed. Do you think they saw me before?"

"Carol, everyone in the anchorage saw you! Come on, you know sundowners like this are common in every anchorage we've ever been in. Besides, what happened to everyone in Europe does it?"

She smiled. "You're right, screw it!"

"Good girl, now find something nice to wear, put together a cheese tray, add the dolmades in the reefer and get a bottle of wine while I get the dinghy ready."

The party aboard *Lost Pilgrim* grew to eight couples and went on for hours. There was little mention of Carol's spectacular arrival other than several comments about how well she handled *Lastdance* when we anchored. I sensed her tense up at those times, but by her second glass of wine, she relaxed considerably until one of the women said that her husband tried to video the whole maneuver. Giggling, she added, "But don't worry, honey, I told him I'd break his knuckles if he did."

I looked at Carol and detected a hint of embarrassment, but then the bravado surfaced and she smiled. "Oh, why'd you do that? We would have loved a copy!"

Everyone laughed and more drinks were poured and we had a great time telling bawdy sea stories until well past midnight. Rowing back to *Lastdance*, Carol giggled. "Do you think they'll all be telling sea stories about today in their next port?"

"Oh yeah, I'm sure they'll be talking about it for a long time!"

After Indian Key, we spent a quiet night in Boot Key Harbor, departing from there at dawn the next day. Then, with fifteen knots of northeast wind, we made the forty mile run to Key West in just over seven hours, arriving off of Whitehead Spit at two o'clock in the afternoon. I had been sailing the last five hours while Carol slept so after waking her, she took the helm and headed up onto a close reach past Fort Taylor. Key West is an adventure! We'd been there several times by car but there is something about arriving by boat that stirs the imagination. This is not the Key West of yesteryear, but even as a shadow of its former self, its risqué side is not for the timid. We planned to spend five days here, which would give us a full week to get back to Fort Lauderdale, even allowing for bad weather.

I surveyed the channel ahead and decided to stay on this tack until we reached Tank Island. There, we came about onto a port tack and sailed the remaining half mile to Key West Bight, where our marina was located. There were boats of every description going every which way, including a large cruise ship coming up astern of us from sea. Carol was getting nervous, but I told her we'd be fine. We already passed where the cruise ship would be docking, and all she had to do was keep us close hauled for another five minutes, at which time we doused sails and called the marina for a slip assignment.

After checking in at the marina office, we showered and dressed, and then went to the Sunset Tiki-Bar for drinks and to plan dinner. Sunset was at six-thirteen, and Carol insisted we go to Mallory Square for the ritualistic sunset celebration. The bartender told us we could see the sun dip below the horizon from we were but Carol wouldn't hear of it.

She clasped my arm. "Please, Ron. It has to be from Mallory Square."

I learned long ago that when Carol did that, there was no sense in arguing, so that evening and for the next four evenings, we watched the sun set into the sea from Mallory Square.

In the morning, while Carol slept, I made a pot of coffee, then walked over to the nearby Hyatt Resort to arrange for her spa treatment. I had no idea how complicated this could be. There were different types of massages, facials, manicures and pedicures, not to mention saunas, aromatherapy, and mud baths. The prices for these services precluded doing them all, so I chose the two hundred and fifty dollar package which bought a sauna, a full body massage, a facial, a manicure and a pedicure. Told all of this would take about three hours, I made a ten o'clock appointment so Carol would finish in time for us to stroll around and find a nice place for lunch.

When I returned to the boat, Carol was up and having coffee.

"Hi, Baby, where'd you go? I was getting worried about you."

"I went to make arrangements at the spa for you."

She seemed surprised. "You didn't have to do that, Ron. I really wasn't serious about the bet."

"Hey, I was serious. You won fair and square. Had I won, I would definitely be collecting."

"But I've never been to a spa. I won't know what to do."

"You don't do anything, silly, they do it all. Besides, you've had massages in Singapore."

Handing her the brochure, I said, "You have a ten o'clock appointment, but they want you to be there fifteen minutes early, so wash up and I'll walk you there, then meet you when you finish at one o'clock."

"That's three hours! What are they going to do to me?"

"I'll tell you on the way. Come on, you only have an hour, and it's going to take fifteen minutes to walk there, so hurry and get ready."

"Was it expensive?"

"Carol, don't worry about it. I want you to enjoy yourself, now get ready!"

I felt like I was walking my child to her first day at kindergarten and teased her about it. "I'll see you at one o'clock." Then I laughed. "It's okay, dear, Daddy promises to come back."

I remained there until as she was escorted from the reception area through the luxurious doors that concealed whatever happened in a spa. Dutifully, I was back ten minutes early in order to be there to greet her when she came out. When she did, she literally glowed.

"How was it?" I asked.

"Oh it was incredible. Wonderful! So all I have to do is sail around topless every now and then and you'll treat me to more of that?"

I laughed. "No, Baby. That was a one time bet, but feel free to sail around topless or treat yourself to a spa anytime."

We ate ashore daily and visited every bar on Duval Street, pouring most of our money into the coffers of Captain Tony's, which is the original Sloppy Joe's, made famous by Ernest Hemingway. During one late night visit to this unique bar after too many Papa Dobles drinks, Carol made me staple several of my personal photos of her from my wallet to the ceiling and rafters. Years later, they were still there, alongside thousands of other risqué photos, business cards, and personal memento's that have become part of the eclectic décor of this great old saloon!

As we lay in bed our last night with *Lastdance* gently tugging on her lines, I told her I couldn't decide if our morning departure had come too soon or not soon enough.

"We've consumed more alcohol and conch fritters in five days than we have in the last five months; I'm ready for a long rest."

She rolled on her side to face me, and sounding very serious, she asked. "You're not sorry we came here, are you?"

"No, not at all! We've had so much fun, I love doing stuff like this with you; I'm just exhausted."

I took her in my arms, and we kissed tenderly.

"I love you so much, Carol."

And with a gentle kiss and electrifying touch, she whispered, "I love you too, Ron."

The voyage north was without incident. We stopped in Boot Key Harbor again and the next day, we sailed all the way to Rodriguez Key where we anchored for the night and grilled the conch we had purchased in Key West. The wind was from the west the next day at fifteen knots and made good speed up Hawk Channel, so much so we even considered going all the way home. Once east of Key Biscayne, however, we realized how tired we were, so we abandoned that idea and ducked into Government Cut. There, we took a slip at Miami Beach Marina where we had docked *Lastdance* for three months the previous year. It's a neighbor to Monty's, a great restaurant with an outdoor tiki-bar and there we came to know Liz, a medical student and one of the world's great bartenders.

Carol took a long shower at the marina club house while I secured *Lastdance* and gave her a quick wash down to remove a weeks worth of salt residue. She returned from the shower but was impatient to see if Liz was working and to order stone crabs so we agreed to meet at the Tiki-bar. Twenty minutes later, after a hot shower of my own, I strolled into the lounge area feeling clean and refreshed. Except for the piped in reggae music, the place was unusually quiet, even for a week night. I easily found Carol at a corner of the bar with a beer and a tray of crab claws, talking with a guy.

She saw me come in. "Hi, Baby. Look at these crabs!"

"Wow, you did good!"

I kissed her and said hello to the guy she was talking with.

"This my husband, Ron. Ron, this is Matt,"

Then she called out. "Hey, Liz, he's here!"

Liz waved and came over and I gave her a big hug over the bar and ordered a beer, then dug into the crabs, offering some to Matt.

"No thanks, I've already eaten. You wife has been telling me you two go way back."

I laughed and said, "Oh boy, you got the whole saga, huh?"

Matt said, "Yeah, you ought to make a movie about it. It'd be a hit, trust me, I know!"

We chatted twenty minutes longer, then Matt got up and said he had to go. As soon as he was gone, Liz came over and said to me in a conspiratorial voice

"You better watch your woman. That was Matt Dillon, and he chatted up Carol the minute she sat down!"

Carol grabbed her hand. "What did you say, Liz? Who was that?"

Liz repeated herself. "That was Matt Dillon I'm telling you!"

Carol exclaimed. "Oh my God, are you serious?"

I laughed. "See that's the problem with women. One minute he's just some guy, then you find out he's a movie star and you go bonkers."

Carol ignored me. She was giddy as a school girl. "I can't believe I was talking with Matt Dillon. My God, I'm old enough to be his mother."

I thought of teasing her by saying he only wanted our stone crabs, but instead said, "You're a beautiful woman, Baby. Any guy would want to talk to you."

She kissed me. "You sweet-talking devil you. You really know how to make a girl feel desired."

She then asked Liz, "Do these crab claws have the same effect as oysters?"

We both smiled when Liz said, "I see nothing's changed with you two, huh?"

Even as we ate our crab claws, the wind increased ominously and by the time we got back to *Lastdance*, it was blowing over twenty knots from the north.

I said, "Geez, it has been blowing out of the north like this off and on for weeks."

Carol thought it might moderate by morning but the NOAA forecast didn't agree with her.

"Damn." I said. "The forecast is for twenty knots from the north all morning, gusting to twenty-five before moderating in the afternoon. I guess we can stay close inshore, but we're still going to get bounced around."

Carol said, "Maybe we should just motor up the ICW."

"Baby, we've sailed almost the entire three weeks from Fort Lauderdale to Key West and back, I'm not going to do the last twenty-five miles motoring up the ICW."

In exaggerated agreement, she said, "Whatever you want, dear," then mumbled, "it must be a Mars thing."

The morning was beautiful with a bright blue sky and hardly a cloud to be seen, but the loud clanking of halyards against masts in the marina confirmed what I already knew. NOAA was right. It was blowing like snot out there and chilly, but I kept focusing on the part of the forecast that called for conditions to moderate by late afternoon. I made some oatmeal and woke Carol.

"Come on, sleeping beauty, get your butt up, we're going home."

She got out of bed and let out a loud shiver.

"Listen to that racket out there, and who turned off the heat? What's it blowing?"

I said, "NOAA says twenty-two knots, gusting higher and right on the nose from the north."

She asked, "Are you sure you don't want to motor up the ICW?"

"Yeah, I'm sure. It won't be so bad if we stay inside the stream."

I poured her coffee, and as she sat down, she said, "Okay, but you're the one who gets seasick." Then she asked. "Is this instant oatmeal?"

As always, I laughed and said, "No, Carol. It's the real stuff."

Once on deck, I saw that NOAA wasn't completely right. The wind was more northeast than north which meant the waves would be more onshore as they were pushed by the easterly component of the wind. With the wind out of the northeast, tacking would be more problematic because we'd be steering away from our destination when on port tack. Still, it was only twenty-five miles to Fort Lauderdale, and we'd easily sailed in these conditions many times before. This would be a glorious sail for the last day of our vacation.

We left the marina at nine in the morning under a single reefed main and our small staysail. Racing out Government Cut, we could feel the large swell rolling in the inlet even before we reached the fishing pier at South Pointe Park. When I saw huge waves breaking against the north jetty with spectacular plumes of spray I said, "Get the harnesses out!"

Beyond the jetties, large waves could be seen crashing against the range markers south of the channel. I thought, *Where in hell is this coming from?* The height of the swell increased until at the end of the jetties, we were rising up the face of them at a steep angle then diving down the backsides at exhilarating speed. Once out of the lee of the north jetty, the waves grew even bigger and hit us on our port bow, sending huge plumes of spray back at us and solid water across our deck. The wind howled and Carol sat in the shelter under the dodger. I yelled for her to be sure her harness was clipped to the cockpit pad eye. She held it up for me to see that it was, and then she double checked mine.

I've experienced seasickness my whole life, but it seems to have diminished with age. That day, however, the combination of waves, crabs, beer, and mojitos the night before, was churning away at my stomach, and even though I was occupied with steering, the symptoms came on fast. I tried staring at the horizon, but *Lastdance* was like a bucking bronco on a roller coaster. Our movement was a series of sharp jerks, coupled with a long slow rise and falling motion, which I attributed to smaller breaking waves atop of big swells. We weren't even a mile out and I got sick fast! Not just vomiting but also dizziness, so much so that I wasn't steering well, and we took some heavy rolls as waves slammed into us broadside.

"Carol, take over!"

She was worried about me and shouted, "Why don't we turn back?"

I looked back. The waves at the rock jetties seemed huge, and I didn't want to risk surfing into the inlet in those conditions.

"No, I'm feeling woozy, and I'm not sure either one of us could bring us through the inlet."

She asked, "What about Port Everglades, won't it be bad when we get there?"

"I thought about that, but the NOAA forecast said conditions will moderate considerably. It'll be okay by the time we get there." I hoped they were right.

We changed places, and for the next seven hours, Carol steered *Lastdance* through dozens of short tacks as we worked our way north. The only help from me was to handle the sheets when we tacked. We short tacked because I wanted to keep about a mile offshore in deeper water. There, the waves would be smaller than in the shallows where they slowed and bunched up on each other, growing in height and steepness. Any farther out and we would then encounter really big waves in the Gulf Stream where the north moving current opposed the wind.

If I hadn't been seasick, this would have been just another exciting sail and once we got into deeper water, I could see it was becoming just that for Carol. In between spasms of vomiting, I yelled, "Having fun yet?"

She gave me a big smile as our bow broke through a wave, inundating her with a cascade of spray. She yelled at the top of her lungs, "Arrrgghh! Yo ho ho, a pirate's life for me!"

As the hours went by, conditions began to moderate and I felt a little better. "Want me to relieve you?"

She looked at me and shaking her head, shouted, "No, I'm okay. You still look lime green!"

"Do you have to pee?" I asked.

She laughed and yelled over the wind, "I already have, twice!"

I put my head down again until she shouted a familiar, "Ready about."

We came onto a starboard tack with Fort Lauderdale's high rise condos appearing closer with each series of tacks.

By two o'clock, we were off Hallandale Beach. The wind had diminished to a steady seventeen knots but the waves were still big and we were being slowed as we punched our way through them.

Carol shouted, "We're underpowered!

I looked at the sails, then the wind gauge. "I think we should leave a reef in the main, but do you want me to take out the jib?"

The moment I said it, we both sensed a threshold had been crossed. It wasn't just the question. I had asked for her opinion before in these situations before, but it was always in the way of caution, such as, "Should we reef?" This was a subtle but significant difference. I was calling on her to decide to increase sail in windy conditions. True, it wasn't a storm, but still, it marked a new level in my confidence in her sailing skills.

Although barely perceptible, Carol's voice took on a new tone of authority and nodding her head, she shouted, "Furl the staysail and unfurl the jib!"

The small staysail came in and out came the big jib and once trimmed, our speed increased dramatically. Up until then we had been averaging just three knots toward our destination, but now we were moving almost twice as fast and pointing higher.

An hour later, Carol asked, "Do you feel well enough to shake out the reef in the main?"

"Yeah, I'll get it. Do you want me to relieve you after I do?"

She shook her head. "No, Baby. I'd really like to finish the trip myself."

Understanding how she felt, I smiled an acknowledgement, and then shook out the reef in the main and we instantly gathered more speed. Instead of retreating back to my perch under the dodger, I sat alongside her and put my arm around her shoulder, kissing her cheek as she focused on steering. "Who sent you to me?"

She looked at me puzzled. "What do you mean?"

"I mean you're so good for me in every way, what god sent you back to me? What made your parents move to my street in Brooklyn? What made you love me?"

She smiled. "It was destiny. I told you, we've been together before. We'll be together again."

As we approached the inlet at Port Everglades, we tacked for the last time. Carol told me to unfurl the staysail. "Once we turn down the channel, we'll be on a broad reach and I want to go in under full sail."

I smiled again, knowing exactly how she felt. She was tired and wet, but she had completed a challenging voyage and she wanted to finish it in style. There was no better way than to enter port under full sail, behind the helm of a beautiful ship like *Lastdance*. I unfurled the staysail. We heeled a few degrees more until at the mouth of the inlet, Carol fell off the wind and we sailed down the middle of the channel, our headsails billowing like two big clouds.

Chapter 21
Leaving Paradise

In between work and sailing, we squeezed in two house hunting trips to New Jersey. On the last day of the last trip, we found a large townhouse in Boonton, right up the street from my office. From the back windows, it had a view of the distant Manhattan skyline and a mix of wooded hills and suburban towns in the foreground. For the first time in my career, I could walk to work!

With its antique shops, historic cemeteries, and Main Street that wound its way through a series of curves and hills, Carol loved the old town. We signed the lease and had lunch at The Reservoir restaurant to celebrate. Carol was excited and it was good to see her so energized as we talked about how nice it would be if she could find a job in town, and we could have lunch together everyday.

With the last of our household goods on the moving truck, we moved aboard *Lastdance* and the burden fell on Carol to prepare for the voyage north. Our plan was to take advantage of the prevailing winds and Gulf Stream by making a series of three day coastal passages to Beaufort, North Carolina, where we would take the ICW to Norfolk, Virginia. From there, we'd go back on the ocean at Cape Charles, and then sail north along the Delmarva peninsular. We would then cross Delaware Bay and go up the New Jersey coast to Manasquan, where we planned to spend a few days visiting Carol's kids. After that, only a fifty mile leg remained from Manasquan to New York, then another short sail to our new marina in Stamford, Connecticut.

In all, this would be a voyage of almost one thousand nautical miles, so adequate provisions, fuel, and water had to be organized and stowed.

Older charts needed to be updated and new ones purchased and inspections of the boat and her safety equipment made. Most of this was done by Carol, and she did it well because she knew that such a voyage held the promise of fun and adventure but also risk and danger.

As our departure date of May 15 loomed near, our plans came apart. My replacement, who was being transferred from Rio de Janeiro, couldn't be in Miami for at least another month and I couldn't leave until he arrived. We considered delaying our cruise north but that would put us into hurricane season, so we decided to hire a delivery captain. Again, the burden fell on Carol to do the research to find a captain and crew. She checked resumes and references, then did telephone interviews and when she had a short list, we met with them aboard *Lastdance*. One captain stood out far above the others, and we selected him and agreed on a May 5 departure date.

I suggested that Carol fly to New Jersey, and I would follow a month later, but she wouldn't hear of it saying, "I want to be here with you."

Then, with the clock ticking, I came home from work and she announced our new plan. "I arranged for the moving company to keep our stuff in storage for another month and we'll move into a hotel. When you can leave, we'll drive to New Jersey together and take our damn sweet time doing it."

"What about *Lastdance?*" I asked.

"Oh, that's easy." With a look of self-satisfaction she added, "We fly up and take delivery in New York, then sail her to Stamford ourselves. Then fly back here!"

She had everything covered and a week later, after going through a system and equipment checklist with our delivery captain, we stood on the dock with our neighbors, my arm around Carol's shoulder, and watched as they took our beautiful ship away.

The captain kept us apprised of his daily progress and when he made Atlantic City, Carol and I flew to Newark, arriving a day before *Lastdance* was due at Great Kills where we still maintained our old mooring. They called as they past Shark River and said they were close-hauled in a twelve knot breeze, making better than six knots so we estimated they'd be at Great Kills by four o'clock.

We had plenty of time, but we were excited beyond words as our taxi fought the afternoon traffic on the Staten Island Expressway. We stopped at a market and bought a couple of steaks, some breakfast stuff, and a few bottles of wine at a liquor store, then went on to Gateway National Park and walked over the dunes to Crookes Point. There, we waited for our boat. An hour and forty minutes later, Carol let out a yell, "That's her, they're here!"

I looked closely and saw she was right and we hugged as if someone was returning our child.

I called the captain on the cell phone and gave him instructions to K-24, then added, "It shoals up badly by the green daymarker, so favor the red nun buoy close to where we're standing as you enter the cut."

A few moments later, our beautiful ship sailed almost silently by with a whoosh of air across her sails and the sound of water rippling along her hull, and she entered the safety of the harbor. We took the launch out to her as she made fast to K-24.

"She's a good ship," the captain said. "Very seaworthy. We hit some real snotty weather a few times and just reefed her down, and she behaved like a clipper ship."

He turned over the log book and we settled our account with him and in less than an hour, he and his crew boarded the launch on their way to a taxi and the airport. Carol and I hugged, then looked around to be sure everything was in good order.

"Do you want to put clean sheets on the bed or open the wine and make some snacks?"

She said, "I'll get the sheets. You get the wine and snacks."

Having sailed *Ursaorion* out of Great Kills for many years, it now seemed strange being aboard *Lastdance* on K-24. As we drank our wine, Carol asked if I ever thought about keeping her there instead of a marina in Stamford.

"Yeah, but then I remembered how confining Raritan Bay got for us in *Ursaorion*. Heck, even John and Gail moved *Tranquility* to Connecticut. Let's see how we like being on Long Island Sound. If we don't like it, we'll move here for a season or even back to Chesapeake Bay."

Carol agreed. "I guess we'll get to see more of Joe and Julie and maybe Rhonda will come sailing with us more often."

"Yeah, and don't forget DeRosa's. We can eat at DeRosa's once a week if we want! Don't worry; we'll have fun there, even if it's just for a season."

We woke before dawn and got underway in the dark in order to catch a favorable current through New York. An hour later, in the first light of morning, we approached the Verrazano Bridge. If timed right, you can pick up a favorable flood current from the Narrows all the way up the East River, through Hell Gate and on to the Throgs Neck Bridge. From there, the ebb begins in Long Island Sound, and you can ride that eastward for another six hours more or less.

Once through the Narrows and in the Upper Bay, the breeze increased to eight knots from the northwest. With only the words, "Let's sail," Carol looked about, then headed up into the wind. I raised the main and trimmed the sheet and with the sun reflecting off the shimmering towers of the World Trade Center, I unfurled the jib. And just like that, as if we'd been transported back in time, we were sailing silently, just like people did thousands of years ago!

The wind increased as we approached The Battery, but being westerly, I said. "We're going to be in the lee of the tall buildings as we sail up the East River."

Reminding me that we had a flight to catch, Carol asked, "Should we start the engine?"

"No, we have plenty of time, lets see what it does if we go way over to the east side of the river, maybe we'll catch gusts that funnel down the cross-town streets."

I took over the helm because I'm a little better at playing the puffs and lulls. Then, as we passed under the Brooklyn Bridge, *Lastdance* began cycles of heeling over in the gust, then standing up in the lulls as we weaved in and out of the wind shadows of the tall Manhattan buildings to port. We slowed considerably during the lulls, but still maintained enough way to carry us to the next gust. *Lastdance* would then heel and surge forward, sometimes getting up to six knots before hitting the next calm spot. Even with the heavy commercial traffic, I felt we could sail safely like this as long as our speed didn't fall below two knots, but just in case, Carol had the starter key in place and was ready to start the engine.

Once we passed Mill Rock, the wind steadied as we entered Hell Gate and approached the Astoria railroad bridge. Carol went below to calculate an ETA at Stamford. A few minutes later she called out, "Hey, at this speed, we should be there around noon. If you don't need me, I'm going to take a nap. Can I get you anything before I do?"

"Yeah, I saw some cans of iced tea in the reefer."

Handing up a can, she asked, "Think we'll have time to go to DeRosa's for dinner?"

"I don't think so. Our flight's at nine o'clock, so we need to turn in the rental car and check in no later than eight. Let's save DeRosa's for next time. We can eat at the airport."

She gave me an exaggerated pout. "Eat what at the airport, flavored cardboard?"

I laughed then said, "Hey, how about Tony's in Newark?"

As exaggerated as her pout had been, her smile was more even so. "Oh, yes, let's go there!"

"Okay, wench, Tony's it is." Then I added, "But we'll need to buy mints before we get on the plane." She smiled knowingly. Tony's is a great Portuguese restaurant in the Ironbound section of Newark, and there is never a shortage of garlic in their food.

Carol's navigation was right on. We passed through the Stamford breakwater shortly after noon and then proceed up the channel to our new marina, which we had mixed feelings about. The main marina was on the west branch of the Rippowam River. We had been assigned a slip in the small annex on the east branch of the river. It was comfortably situated behind a hilly hook shaped peninsular known as Ware Island but Carol didn't like being isolated from the main marina. I liked the park like setting, and we heatedly discussed the merits of both opinions over garlic-laden shrimp and grilled squid at Tony's, before flying back to Florida.

The weeks rolled by and we were just getting used to living in a hotel when it was time to leave. We attended a large farewell party given to us by my co-workers at Carol's favorite club, Howl-at-the-Moon, in Ft. Lauderdale. The party began at seven in the evening and ended at two in the morning and Carol was at her best as she sang along with the dueling pianos and made me dance until my legs grew too tired to even stand. The last party was the most difficult. Our neighbors at Laudonnaire took us to a quiet but lengthy dinner at Martinis, on Las Olas Blvd. We grew to love these good friends who became family to us during our four years in paradise. As difficult as it was to leave them, we knew that most of the friendships wouldn't end with our departure.

Once back at our hotel, Carol cried. I took her in my arms and comforted her and she said, "I'm sad about leaving, but excited about seeing my kids and going off on another adventure. It's always like that, isn't it? We're sad to leave old friends, but happy to make new ones and see new places?"

"Yes, Baby. For as long as people have traveled. Let's go to sleep. We have an early day and a long drive ahead of us."

I took her to our bed, partially shedding a few tears and a few laughs, and as we've done almost every night for the previous fifteen years, she fell asleep in my arms.

CHAPTER 22
HOME AGAIN

Life was good in Boonton. I liked my new job, and we reconnected with our old friends in the tri-state area. Our families were close enough for weekend and holidays visits and the only downside was that Carol couldn't find a job in town. We could be at our new marina in an hour and we spent more time with our Connecticut friends Joe, Julie, and Rhonda who lived up the road in Norwalk.

With Carol's friendly smile, we quickly got to know our dock mates who were great folks except for one curmudgeon who lived on a trawler in the slip beside us. It turned out that he wanted two power lines but was only willing to pay for one. We soon discovered that he'd unplug our shore power after we left on Sundays, then plug his in all week. He would then put ours back in before we returned the following weekend. The first time we found food spoiled in our refrigerator, we assumed the power had gone out. After asking others on the dock about it, someone told us it was probably the guy in the trawler because word was, he had used other peoples shore power in the past.

The second time we found food spoiled, Carol became furious and wanted to catch him in the act. "That son of a bitch ruined two good steaks on us."

"Yeah," I added somewhat tongue-in-cheek. "And we had no ice for drinks!"

We pretended to leave that Sunday, but we watched from the parking lot for half an hour. Sure enough, the guy came out of his boat, pulled out our plug, and replaced it with a cable from his trawler.

I got pissed off, but Carol went ballistic. She charged down the dock, retrieving a trash bag from the dumpster. A few folks who had been sitting on their boats tagged along and watched as she banged on the hull of the trawler. When the cabin door opened, she yelled, "Hey, asshole, I've got something for you." She then dumped the smelly contents of the trash bag onto his deck. A chorus of hoots and laughs rang out and one woman yelled, "You go, girl!"

I unplugged his power line and with my leatherman tool, bent back the prongs, and tossed it onto his boat with a thud.

Getting right in his face, I shouted. "Screw with my boat again and I'll rip your lungs out."

Carol chirped in. "We saw you unplug our power line; you ruined our food!"

He looked at us dumbfounded and having been caught red handed, only managed to stutter out, "Wha...what?"

Andy, another live-aboard on the dock, stepped forward and said, "If I see him anywhere near your boat, I'll call the cops, Ron."

As we drove home, Carol worried that the guy might do something to *Lastdance* to retaliate.

"I don't think so. I could really see fear in his eyes. Besides, we seem to have plenty of friends there to watch the boat."

She held my hand and said, "I don't like it here. I wish we had gone back to Chesapeake Bay."

"Carol, this could have happened anywhere. We haven't even been out on our first real cruise yet; let's give it a chance."

"We've been to the Sand Hole, and look how crowded it was."

It was obvious she wasn't happy, but I knew it had more to do with her love of Chesapeake Bay than her dislike of Long Island Sound. From the first moment we entered the Chesapeake where the mouth of the Susquehanna met the Elk River, she connected to the bay. And because she was part Cherokee, this connection became more profound after she read Mitchener's book, *Chesapeake*, which highlighted the early Native American presence and influence on the bay.

We drove in silence for a few minutes, and I remembered the vow I made to myself when we first reunited for this second chance at a life together.

"Carol, if you really want to go back to the Chesapeake, we'll go as soon as we can get the boat ready and time off from work, but we're paid up for the season here and we'll also have to pay for a marina in Maryland."

I squeezed her hand and said, "Hey, what the hell, it's only money. We can afford it, and I don't want you to be unhappy, but it would be easier if we sailed there next spring."

The inevitable tears welled up in her eyes. "You'd do that for me?"

Without taking my eyes off the road, I said, "I would do that for you and not give it a second thought if it made you happy."

She kissed my cheek softly, knowing that I loved the way it would linger and make me feel.

"Okay," she said, "let's make the best of it here and sail home in the spring."

It wasn't lost on me that she emphasized the word home. In many ways, it made sense, considering we bought *Lastdance* in Annapolis and that was her home port. As we drove home, a plan developed in my mind.

"I have a better idea! Except for the one haul-out we did in Florida, the boat hasn't been out of the water since we bought her. Let's sail to New Jersey in the fall and haul her for the winter at Lockwood's. We can do maintenance and put on new anti-fouling paint then sail to the Chesapeake in the spring!"

Carol was ecstatic, and her enthusiasm became contagious. By the time we got home, we agreed that it would be great if we could get a slip at our old marina at Kent Narrows and be with our friends again. Then, sitting in front of the fireplace drinking wine, the anticipated barrage of questions followed as we looked at the chart book.

"How long will it take?"

"Could we be on the Chesapeake in time for Memorial Day in Baltimore?"

"Do you think John & Gail might come with us?"

I laughed. "Slow down! You're like a kid planning your first trip to Disneyland."

She ignored me and went on. "I'm going to call Gail. No, wait, maybe you should ask John about it first?"

I kissed her then said aloud, "Stop! One thing at a time! I'll call Mears tomorrow and find out if they have any open slips. If they do, we'll put a deposit down before we do anything else. Okay?"

"Okay, but can you ask if they have any on O-Dock?"

I smiled. "Yes, Baby. I'll try to get one on O-Dock if they have it."

As we continued to look at the charts, I thought, *I love when she gets like this, so animated, so excited and lively.*

As was often the case when she awaited news from me, she was peeking from the front window when I came home from work and was on me as I came in the door.

"What did they say?" she asked. "Is there an opening?"

I went through my almost ritual pretension at being hurt. "What, no kiss, no hello, just what did they say?"

She slowly put her arms around my neck and kissed me softly, then said in a jovial voice, "Hi, Baby. Welcome home from the coal mines, I love you. Now what did they say?"

"I put a deposit on a slip on O-Dock, three spots away from our old slip!"

"Yippee," she yelled.

She hugged me again and I thought, *There it is again, the childlike innocence in the woman's body.* I held her in my arms and looked into her eyes.

"Are you really happy?"

She said, "Oh yes, I'm so glad we're going back."

"That's all that matters to me, but I'm happy we're going back too."

With those words, her exuberance evolved into passion and her next kiss was laced with desire, not just joy. I felt her tongue sensually probing but she stopped and with a sly smile said, "I have to go up and get out of these clothes and get dinner started. Wanna come and watch?"

Holding her in my arms an hour later, I said, "So much for getting dinner started." Then, looking at the clock, I asked, "Chinese or pizza?"

She rolled onto her side and said, "I'm hungry...whoever delivers faster."

We never had any more problems at the marina with the electrical power thief and although we found sailing conditions on Long Island Sound to be good, we also found that many of the anchorages were not as nice as we had remembered from our days there in *Ursaorion.* Places that had been secluded, were now crowded. Some of the nicer anchorages were full of moorings for which overnight fees were charged, and even from Stamford, the more secluded eastern end of Long Island was too far for a weekend cruise.

Our first long cruise wasn't until July with John and Gail in *Tranquility*, now based in Stratford, twenty miles to the east. Charlie and Val were coming from New Jersey in their new trawler, *Belle Amie,* so the plan was to rendezvous at Duck Island Roads, then stay at Brewers marina on the Patchogue River, which was for us, a fifty mile trip. We left Stamford at seven in the morning under an overcast sky, southwest winds of fifteen knots and temperatures in the low sixties. A slow-moving cold front was approaching, and the forecast was for northwest winds at twenty-five knots and heavy rain by evening, so we wanted to get in well ahead of the nasty weather.

We passed the Norwalk Islands shortly after eight o'clock with Carol huddled in the lee of the dodger. I knew she would have liked the warmth of our cabin but she wanted to keep me company and wouldn't budge without a good reason so I asked her to make coffee and calculate an ETA at Duck Island.

Going below, she said, "I'll try to raise *Belle Amie* and *Tranquility* on the VHF okay?"

"Good idea, but do the ETA first so you can pass it on to them if you do make contact."

Ten minuets later, she handed up a mug of hot coffee and asked if I was okay.

I said, "Hell yeah, I'm having fun. We haven't dropped below seven knots since we left so stay below and keep warm."

"Okay," she said, "but I'm passing up your harness."

"Thanks, Baby. I'll be fine, but if the wind picks up I'm going to put in a reef and will want you up here to help."

She blew me a kiss and closed that hatch. It slid open a moment later and she passed out my harness saying, "Put it on and hook up, or I'm not leaving."

I did as I was told, and only when I clipped myself in, did she go below.

I was having fun! *Lastdance* was on a broad reach, which was her best point of sail, and we were rocketing along at over seven knots. As we passed between Stratford Point and Stratford Shoal at ten-thirty, Carol came on deck wearing her harness. The wind was holding steady at fifteen knots and it had warmed considerably when the sun came out but the waves were getting slightly bigger with each passing hour.

"I need to go pee," I said. "Clip on and steer 090m."

I pointed out the lighthouse at Middle Ground and said, "That tug and barge behind us are coming up fast. He's south of us but keep an eye on him, he may turn toward us if he's going to New Haven."

She smiled and offered a snappy salute. "Aye aye, captain! Now go pee before you wet your pants; you've been up here all morning."

At one thirty, we heard Charlie calling us on the VHF, "*Lastdance, Lastdance, Belle Amie* calling."

We hadn't seen the Tremel's since we moved to Florida four years earlier, and it was exciting to hear them calling us!

Carol answered, "*Belle Amie, Belle Amie*, this is *Lastdance*, switch and answer channel 72."

A moment later, they were talking as if we had never left New Jersey.

I said, "Tell them we're coming up on Falkner Island."

She did, and Charlie replied that they had just passed inside of Falkner.

"Ask if he heard from John!"

The radio crackled back, "John is a few miles ahead of us."

I looked through the binoculars and could see *Tranquility*, but *Belle Amie* was still hidden behind Falkner Island.

"Tell him I think we're about an hour and a half from Duck Island Roads, and we'll see them there."

Carol did, then signed off. "I really miss them. I'm so excited," she said.

"So am I," I replied. We shared some wonderful times with them and were looking forward to rekindling our friendship.

At two twenty, we passed close to the Kelsey Point breakwater at the entrance to Clinton Harbor, and ten minuets later, Carol rounded up into the pocket behind the Duck Island jetties. Our sails thrashed loudly as they luffed, and all eyes were on *Lastdance* as we came into the lee of the island with Carol on the helm and me rolling up the jib. She started the engine and I dropped the main as she held our bow into the wind and a few seconds later, horns blared from *Belle Amie* and *Tranquility* who were anchored and waiting for us.

Duck Island Roads is an area inshore of two large stone jetties that extend out at right angles from Duck Island, offering shelter from the sometimes tumultuous conditions on Long Island Sound. From there, the entrance to Westbrook and the marina is less than a quarter mile away through a narrow cut in the beach. John suggested we stand by until he weighed anchor, then we'd all quickly motor in together ahead of the nasty weather coming our way.

By four o'clock, we were secure in our assigned slips and enjoying a boisterous reunion on the dock with a gallon jug of margaritas supplied by *Tranquility*. Twenty minutes later, we all huddled in the warm cabin of *Belle Amie* as a line of severe thunderstorms barreled through with heavy rain, wind gust to forty knots, and numerous nearby lightning strikes. Charlie said, "Guess we timed this just right!"

As we joked about the many times we had waited out thunderstorms together, I surveyed the happy faces and considered how good it was being with these friends again. I smiled, relishing the camaraderie we shared.

Bill's Seafood was a loud but fun restaurant with a colorful sing along band that kept us cheerfully engaged throughout most of the evening. After an excellent seafood dinner and many pitchers of beer, we sang along with Bill's Band until they took one of their infrequent breaks. It was then that we told our friends of our plans to go back to Chesapeake Bay. We were pleasantly surprised when John and Gail said they would consider joining us. They said they enjoyed Long Island Sound, but like us, they found it expensive and crowded. John also thought it was a good idea to haul out in New Jersey in the fall, and we agreed to sail down together in October. With that behind us and the band back on stage, we returned to the revelry. I watched Carol get right into the thick of it and I thought how I loved watching her sing and laugh like this, so uninhibited and carefree.

The next morning was windless, chilly, and overcast, so we motored the short distance to Essex, docking at Essex Island Marina where Carol and I visited in *Ursaorion* twelve years earlier. The plan was to go to dinner at the Griswold Inn, then to the Tap Room to sing bawdy sea shanties. While having drinks aboard *Belle Amie*, we told the story of how Carol had been called on stage during our first trip there. Everyone laughed and being in a silly mood, Carol suggested we take our yellow souwester rain hats to dinner, and put them on before entering the Tap Room.

I smiled. "Hell yeah, let's do it."

We had a wonderful dinner, and then like a gang of bank robbers, we stood at the entrance to the Tap Room, donned our salty souwester hats and walked into the warmth and pandemonium being unleashed on stage by a trio of musicians. Nothing! No reaction whatsoever. Not a single person even took notice of our headgear. Undeterred, we sang along and drank more than our share of dark ale until it got close to the bewitching hour when the ferry stopped. As we walked to the waterfront, Carol, still eager to party, urged us to go back, certain that we could get a ride with someone.

I laughed, "Come on, Baby. The party's over."

Departing from Essex the next morning, we sailed under main and jib down the Connecticut River, then into Long Island Sound. The forecast was for a sunny day and southwest winds at twelve knots, diminishing by late afternoon to five. We were bound for Watch Hill, Rhode Island in Little Narragansett Bay twenty miles away where we agreed to rendezvous with *Tranquility* and *Belle Amie*. Clearing Old Saybrook lighthouse at eleven forty, we fell off the wind until we were steering southeast. Then, once in open water, the wind increased and *Lastdance* gathered speed as we made for the deep cut between the Connecticut River Bar marked by Red "8" and Long Island Shoal.

In expectation of seeing a submarine entering or leaving the submarine base in Groton, I went below to get my camera. A moment later, *Lastdance* heeled a little more. Glancing at the instruments, I saw that the wind had increased to thirteen knots, which on this point of sail, quickly got us up to seven knots. Still below and fumbling with my camera bag, I smiled as I heard Carol unfurling the staysail on her own. Instinctively, I almost asked if she needed help but stopped myself. This was another first in a fifteen year series of first for her and I believed that any comment by me might diminish her sense of accomplishment. Making a change in the sail plan without running it by me might seem trivial to a blue water sailor, but I thought it was a big achievement for Carol. I had more confidence in her than she did in herself, and I knew she needed to push the envelope a bit in order to reach her full potential.

"I'm coming up, want anything?"

"No thanks, Baby," she replied.

Returning on deck munching a donut, I didn't say a word about the staysail until bursting with curiosity, Carol said, "I unfurled the staysail."

I looked up at the wind indicator and the set of the sails. "Good idea." Seeing the barest hint of a smile on her face, I smiled inwardly and went back to my donut. As I finished the last of it and knowing what her answer would be, I asked if she wanted a break.

She replied, "No thanks, Baby. I'm okay."

I thought, *She'd make a lousy poker player because she telegraphs her every mood. No thanks means leave me alone I'm having fun.*

Moments later, I shouted excitedly, "There, look there!" I pointed off our starboard bow while reaching for my camera. Carol looked and for the first time in her life, she saw a submarine underway.

The first thing she said was, "Who has the right of way?"

"Trust me, he does whether he does or not."

We just left Bartlett Reef a mile to port and steering 085m for North Dumpling Light in Fisher Island Sound. The inbound submarine had come through The Race, and I figured she was steering about 000m as she made her way to the submarine base in Groton on the Thames River.

Watching his bearing, I saw that it was quickly drifting left.

"Hold your course; we're going to cross well astern of her."

As we closed the distance, Carol asked, "Is that like the one you were on?"

"Only in that it's a submarine. Mine was a diesel, this is nuclear."

"What's the difference?" she asked.

I chuckled. "The difference is that this one can run for years underwater and mine had to surface and run the diesel engines to charge batteries, not to mention creature comforts. That boat has showers and everyone has their own bed."

She looked at me strangely. "Ah right, I forgot. When we went on the submarine in Baltimore, you explained about sharing a bed with two other men." Then she laughed. "I'm still not sure I want to know what else went on in those submarines."

We watched the dark, sinister shape cross our bow not more than a half a mile away. Carol asked, "Why did you ever want to be in them?"

"Truthfully, I'm not sure. My dad took me to a Navy Fleet Week in New York when I was a kid, and when he asked me which ship I wanted to go on first, I saw a sleek looking submarine. I pointed to it and said, 'That one!' I've been hooked ever since."

She glanced at me with a forlorn look, then her eyes got glassy. "I always worried about you, wondering if you were underwater and all. I was afraid for you."

As she steered, I moved behind her and put my arms around her waist and kissed her neck. "If it's any consolation, I always thought of you when I was at sea. Thirty-seven years ago, my submarine might have been right where that one is as we returned from sea. I would have been thinking about you, just like those guys are probably thinking about their girlfriends and wives right now."

I pressed my cheek to hers and could feel her tears. Then, as I often said when the painful part of our past came up, "Come on, it's okay, Princess. We're together again and that's all that matters now, right?"

She turned her head and kissed me, then said, "Right!"

I reached up and caressed her. Then, becoming aroused by touching her, I unbuttoned her blouse and said, "I love you more than life, Carol."

She started to say she loved me also, but stopped in mid-sentence and blurted out, "The camera! You wanted to take a picture of the submarine."

"Ah shit," I murmured, but continued to kiss her neck. "Screw the submarine."

She responded by laying her head back against my shoulder and with a soft laugh said, "No, Baby. Not the submarine. Me!"

Letting out an exaggerated moan, I said in my best authoritative voice, "Okay, that's it, no more hanky panky! There's too many rocks and shoals about. We need to pay attention!"

She laughed and gently caressing my cheek, she asked, "Not even a little?"

Again I moaned, but said jokingly, "No, the captain has spoken, not even a little!"

"Well then, let go of my boobs and you can take the wheel; I need to go pee."

I took the helm and she stepped aside without making any effort to button her blouse. Then, as she started to go below, she looked at me seductively. "Promise to do that again later?"

I chuckled and thought, *She could seduce me on the moon wearing a spacesuit, and here she was in shorts and an open blouse. How was I supposed to even think straight?* I looked at our speed, my watch, then the chart. It was one thirty and we had just nine miles to the entrance of Little Narragansett Bay. At this speed we would be there around three o'clock, then another half hour of motoring in the channel to the anchorage at Watch Hill.

With mounting desire, I looked at the chart again and thought, *Without much of a detour, we could anchor in Chocomount Cove on Fishers Island for an hour.* Then I remembered I had agreed to anchor first so *Tranquility* and *Belle Amie* could raft to us. I wondered where they were and if there was time for us to stop and then still be at Watch Hill before them. After looking at my watch, I hailed *Tranquility* on my handheld VHF. "Hey, John, where are you, amigo?"

"We're inshore of you, just past the entrance to New London. Did you see that sub?"

Looking over my shoulder, I saw them off to the north.

"Shit." I said out loud, then spoke into the radio, "Okay, I see you, *Tranquility.* Yeah, we saw the sub. We'll see you at Watch Hill."

Then, in a final effort to linger behind for a while, I asked. "Are we the anchor boat today?"

"That's affirmative, *Lastdance,* that's what we agreed on."

"Okay, John, see ya in the anchorage, *Lastdance* out."

I put the radio in its holder and again murmured, "Shit."

From below, Carol called out, "What's wrong?"

"Nothing, Baby. I was just thinking about anchoring off Fishers Island for a bit."

She came into the cockpit and laughed. "Anchor off Fishers Island for a bit? For a bit of what, you pervert?"

I took her hand as she sat beside me, her blouse still unbuttoned. "A bit of you! You make me crazy!"

"Good, I like to make you crazy."

Then, resting her hand on my thigh, she asked, "So are we going to anchor?"

"No, they're just a mile behind us, and we're the anchor boat today, so we have to get into Watch Hill first."

She pouted. "That's too bad. You have me in the mood, for a bit!" She then patted me gently, kissed my cheek, and buttoning her blouse, said, "We'll save it for later; now pay attention to where you're going."

She was right. Fishers Island Sound can be a challenge to navigate; especially, on weekends when hundreds of recreational craft ply its busy waters. We were coming up on North Dumpling Rock, and I asked her to take the helm so I could study the chart.

A few moments later, I asked, "What are you steering?"

She said, "About 085m."

"Okay, Come to 080m and keep an eye out for Red "20" and be sure to leave it to port!"

"But we're entering port, red should be to starboard!" she replied.

I smiled. "That was a test. It's good that you questioned me, but you have to remember, the adage red right returning means from seaward inbound. Even though we're going into a port soon, we're not yet in the channel to that port, we're still in a ship channel and we're headed outbound in it so the red markers are to port. That's why I tell you to always keep looking at the chart to help visualize your surroundings."

It was a lesson and she took it in stride, which was another thing I loved about her: her eagerness to learn.

The most protected anchorage for us was in the small bight formed by the town of Watch Hill and Napatree Beach. The beach was a slender peninsular that ran easterly for more than a mile, offering good protection from the ocean on its southern side. The harbor was small but nearly empty, so I told Carol to pick a spot that would allow us to swing 360° on a 10:1 ratio of anchor rode to depth. She looked at me, and I could see that she knew another test was in the works.

Looking at the chart, she slowly circled *Lastdance*, calling out depths as we got closer to shore. There was deep water to within twenty yards of the sandy beach, and as I looked aft, I could see her doing the calculations in her head. She picked a spot in ten feet of water that would allow us to swing a full 360° yet not get closer than fifty yards to the beach in order to give us some room in case we dragged. Pointing us into the wind, she yelled, "Stand-by to drop anchor!"

After gathering a hint of sternway, I let go our big forty-five pound CQR anchor, then let out chain as we slowly backed down. After the anchor was set, I rigged a bridle to the chain rode, then ran the eyes through port and starboard hawse pipes to our large centerline cleats.

At the same time, Carol shut down the engine, raised the bimini, and went below to make drinks. As we waited for *Tranquility* and *Belle Amie* to come into the harbor, I toasted her. "To my first mate, a perfect job of anchoring!

We touched glasses and I said, "It really was, Baby. I couldn't have done better myself; you've got us perfectly positioned."

I kissed her softly, then more passionately. She said, "Down, boy, here they come."

I laughed and we got up to take their lines and fifteen minuets later, with plenty of fenders rigged, *Tranquility* and *Belle Amie* were snugly rafted on either side of us.

Rafting was fun for socializing, but being the anchor boat was a double-edged sword for me. The seaman side of me liked being on the boat with the anchor already down. If a squall blew up in the night, we could stay put and not have to break away in the dark to anchor independently, which the rafted boats might have to do. On the other hand, my vanity didn't like *Lastdance* to be in the middle, hidden from view of appreciative eyes in an anchorage. Nevertheless, safety always won out over my pride because we also preferred using our ground tackle, which was a lot more suitable for rafting than that aboard *Tranquility* and *Belle Amie*.

Another good aspect of being the anchor boat in a raft-up is that once secured, drinks and snacks quickly materialize and everyone gravitates to the boat in the middle. That day, in the wake of our stimulating teasing after the submarine sighting, I was eager to be alone with Carol, not entertain friends. I gave her a suggestive look to go below. She smiled seductively, letting me know that she was as eager as I was to continue with the afternoon's playfulness. Then, to our amusement and frustration, our friends emerged from their cabins with trays of cheese, dips, and crackers and began climbing over lifelines to join us aboard *Lastdance*. Carol looked my way and shrugged her shoulders, but the move accentuated her already enticing cleavage and intensified my passion. I half-seriously contemplated taking her by the hand and going below, but instead, I resigned myself to a couple of hours of sweet anticipation.

After cocktails and dinner, Carol and I mischievously scurried into our cabin and hastily undressed. Standing before each other, time seemed to slow down and as I stared at her, my mind raced back to when we made love the very first time. I reached out and touched her face, gently tracing my fingers over her lips.

She whispered, "I remember too."

I said, "It's almost scary how we are so in tune with each others thoughts!"

Her eyes moistened and she said, "Hold me, Ron."

I did, and we stood, embraced, swaying slowly to the music drifting over from *Tranquility*. She looked up and we kissed softly until she took my hand and led me to our bed, kissing tenderly and moving only by the gentle rocking of the boat.

Our friends called out to us a few times to join them for a nightcap, but we ignored them, giggling as we wondered what they were thinking. At one point, I heard a muffled voice say, "I hope they're alright."

I yelled out an assurance that we were alive and well, but that we were out for the night. Charlie laughed and yelled out, "Perverts!"

We feel asleep in each others arms to the sounds of the surf on the other side of the beach. When I woke with the morning sun, she was still in my arms and almost in the same position.

After breakfast, we all went ashore and explored the town. Afterward, Carol and I strolled off alone along the long narrow beach. At Napatree point, we sat on a big log, looking out onto the Atlantic Ocean. Carol talked about reincarnation and that she was certain we had been lovers before and would be again in our next lives. I wanted to believe it, but I didn't. Nevertheless, I listened intently to her because she made it sound so interesting.

As she talked, a fog enveloped us. It became so thick we couldn't see more than a few feet in front of us. I said, "This happens a lot according to the cruising guide; maybe we should head back to town."

She said in a serious tone, "No, please let's stay. It's like our own universe, just us surrounded by water we can't see, and the fog is the ether of our own world forming." I almost broke her flight of fancy by saying it was just fog. Instead, I put my arm around her shoulder and let her go on. In the distance, the Watch Hill Point lighthouse sounded its horn in a forlorn cadence, and I drew her closer to me as she talked of an afterlife and aliens. An hour later, the fog burned off, and with it, the magic that Carol had woven for us. We then headed back in silence to meet the others for lunch.

Block Island is thirteen miles in the Atlantic from Watch Hill. The thick fog the day before served as a warning of what we could expect, so we agreed to leave mid-morning and, because we had radar, *Lastdance* would lead the way. We motored out of Little Napatree Bay in single file, under a clear sky. Once away from Middle Ground Breakwater, Carol manned the radar to see how land masses would appear on the small CRT screen and I

pretended to be sailing blind as she called up bearings to important reference points that were easily discernable to her on the radar.

There was a series of reefs and rocks between the eastern end of
Fishers Island and Watch Hill Point with several narrow passages between
them to the sea. I elected to use the bigger channel that ran along Napatree beach where Carol and I had strolled the day before. From Middle
Ground, I could already see Red "6" at Napatree Point Ledge about a
mile away, but I wanted Carol to get comfortable with using the radar
so she continued to call out course corrections to bring me directly to the
buoy. From there, she switched to Red "2" near Gangway Rock. This was
Watch Hill Passage and once through it, there was nothing between us and
Block Island other than pleasure craft, work boats, ships, submarines, and
ferries.

"Piece of cake," I said aloud.

Carol came on deck to look around. "Wow, it really looks different
from up here!"

"Yeah it does, but you did great on the radar. The bearings you gave
me were right on the money, so if we had been in fog, we wouldn't have had
any problems navigating other than being nervous."

She smiled. "Thank you, Baby."

I kissed her then said, I'm steering 130°m, but even with this clear
sky, there's a haze on the horizon and we can't see Block Island. Put the
radar on the sixteen mile range and get me a bearing to it, then check for
any moving targets and see if you have John and Charlie on the screen."

When she came up she said, "Block Island doesn't look anything
like it does on the chart. Is that because the radar only sees the side facing
us right?"

I said, "Right. Newer radar would show more of the island and
do it in colors, but this is fine, especially if you reference a chart to see the
highlights."

She read from a pad. "I got a bearing of 007° to the center of the
island, and there are five targets in front of us, but the blips are small. John
and Charlie show up bright and clear right behind us."

"Good job, but what kind of bearing is that to the island?"

She hesitated, then said, "A relative bearing, right?"

"Right, but what if I wanted the bearings in magnetic so I could easily steer a course by compass?"

More hesitation, then, "I'd have to add it to our course, right?"

I smiled. "Are you telling me or asking me?"

"I'm telling you!"

"Okay, but what if it you add the relative bearing to our course and it comes to more than 360°?"

Without hesitation, she said, "I subtract 360°!"

"Good girl, very good! Now take the helm, I need a break."

When I returned, she asked, "Why don't we use the GPS?"

I smiled. "We do use it all the time, but I still like to plot things out on a paper chart. The main thing I use the GPS for is to get our speed over ground and a latitude and longitude position, which I then plot along our DR track that we lay out on the chart. Besides, the GPS can't see, it only gives us a course to steer, which can take you right over an obstacle if you don't check the track line against a chart. Also, GPS is more accurate than the charts, so there can be mistakes as a result of errors that were made when the charts were drawn many years ago. Radar plotting sees the land mass as it really is so we know exactly where we are, not to mention being able to track moving targets."

She said, "I understand." She then came closer and pressed herself against me. "Mmmm, I love when you talk boat talk like that!"

The wind came up out of the north and we eagerly raised our sails. Carol killed the engine and we moved along at five knots steering 135°m, but we were still unable to see Block Island. John called me on the VHF saying he thought visibility had diminished, and that we seemed to be going into a fog bank. I agreed and told him I had us about six miles out, but still couldn't see Block. I then suggested he close it up a bit and try to keep me in sight. "I'm slowing down and turning on my running lights."

He said, "Affirmative."

A second later, Charlie who had been listening in, confirmed his agreement.

"We're running into fog, Carol. Do you want to man the radar or stay on the helm?" She said she'd stay on the helm, so after I furled the jib halfway to slow us down. I went below to scan the radar for targets and set up a guard zone, which would sound an alarm if anything came within two miles of our position. *What else?* I thought.

"Ah," I said aloud. "The fog horn."

I passed up the horn and told Carol to blow one prolonged and two short every two minutes and to listen for other boats.

"Okay, but it's really getting thick."

I checked the radar. John and Charlie were right behind me. Block was right where it should be at a range of just under five miles now, and there were eleven targets at the entrance to Great Salt Pond. I watched closely and guessed that four of them were entrance buoys and the rest were boats waiting for the fog to lift before negotiating the narrow channel into the harbor.

Going back on deck, Carol looked a little nervous and I could see why. John's running lights were visible behind us but when I looked forward, it appeared like we were sailing into a wall of cotton.

"Wow, you weren't kidding, this is like soup!"

"Are we okay, Ron?"

"We're fine. We're making just three knots and there is nothing ahead of us on radar until the entrance channel. She looked at her watch and blew the horn. I smiled. "Good girl" Then added. "If this doesn't lift, we're going to change course and wait it out a half mile north of the channel.

I went below and scanned the radar. A boat was coming our way directly from the channel entrance and moving much faster than anyone should have been in that visibility. I tracked him at three minute intervals and plotted his relative motion. He was drifting south of us, but I continued to watch him until I was sure he wasn't a threat. Carol sounded the horn again. I looked at my watch, she was right on time. Again, I thought, *Good girl.* All the other targets seemed to be stationary so I called *Tranquility* and *Belle Amie* on the radio. I told them of my plan to get close to shore to wait for the fog to lift north of the entrance. When they both responded, I went on deck just as Carol blew the horn again.

Twenty minutes later, we slowly approached the island and began to hear the baritone fog horn from Harbor Neck. Both the GPS and radar had us at a position half a mile north of the channel and about half a mile off the coast, but we still couldn't see it! John and Charlie closed on us, and we sat in the gentle swell waiting for the veil of fog to lift. Waiting with heightened senses, we heard the surf softly breaking against the rocky shore and fog signals being sounded by unseen various boats. Still, we saw nothing of the island.

Shortly after noon the shroud began to lift. First imperceptibly, but enough that the shoreline became barely discernable. Then in increments, as if pages of translucent paper were being turned to expose a landscape.

"I see the lighthouse, over there!" Gail shouted as she saw the entrance light tower.

Twenty minutes later, the fog fully dissipated and we entered the channel into Great Salt Pond under a bright blue sky.

Great Salt Pond is also known as New Harbor. It's located on the northwest side of the island and is the primary destination for recreational boats. It is completely enclosed and protected from the Atlantic except for its narrow entrance, which is on a northwest-southeast axis. The island itself is almost teardrop shaped and Great Salt Pond is located about two-thirds of the way toward the top. There are marinas and about a hundred moorings at the southern end of the harbor, but all were occupied when we arrived, so we looked for a place to anchor at the edge of the mooring field.

A large powerboat named *Classic Wine* was tied to a mooring about twenty yards upwind of us and as I prepared to drop our anchor, the owner yelled out, complaining about us being near him.

"Hey, bud, you're too close to me. You gotta move!"

I replied, "I'm going to put a hundred feet of chain out, captain, and we won't be leaving our boat unattended tonight." Then I added, "Besides, we're downwind of you, so you've got no reason to be concerned."

He grumbled something to a women standing beside him, then retreated to his cabin.

The wind kicked up to twenty-five knots and our anchor held fine throughout the night. In the morning, we woke to a flat, calm sea and totally windless day. *Tranquility* and *Belle Amie* had anchored on the opposite side of the mooring field and were waiting for Aldo's breakfast boat to make its way around the harbor, selling its warm buns and croissants. Carol and I had a breakfast appointment ashore with Keith, a college classmate of mine, so we hailed the water taxi by VHF radio and left *Lastdance* at nine o'clock.

After a great mini-reunion with Keith, we returned by water-taxi by eleven o'clock, but *Lastdance* was gone! After confirming we were in the right place, we then assumed our boat had been stolen, but the water-taxi driver said it might have been towed to the special mooring.

I asked, "What the hell is the special mooring?"

He said, "It's sometimes used by the harbormaster or Coast Guard."

Carol snapped, "Take us!"

The special mooring was at the northwestern end of the harbor near the U.S. Coast Guard Station and sure enough, *Lastdance* was there with the Harbormaster's boat alongside.

He apologized, but said, "You were dragging anchor; I had to tow you here."

"Dragging anchor, my ass, I had a hundred feet of chain out with a forty-five pound CQR anchor at the end of it. We sat rock steady throughout that blow last night. How could we suddenly drag anchor this morning in a dead calm?"

"Sorry, captain, but I have to respond to all complaints."

Carol shouted, "Complaint, who complained?"

He looked in his clipboard and said, "*Classic Wine.*"

"That son of a bitch!" I yelled.

"That sniveling bastard whined the minute we dropped our anchor yesterday. He saw that we didn't move all night through a twenty-five knot blow, but then called you the minute we left our boat this morning in a dead calm!"

We were furious, but once we calmed down, we cast off from the special mooring and headed over toward *Tranquility* and *Belle Amie*.

Suddenly, I yelled, "Bullshit!"

I put the helm hard over and made straight for *Classic Wine*.

"Where are you going?" Carol asked.

"To tell that guy what an ass he is."

"Ron, come on, please, let's just go by John and Charlie."

I glared at her. Then not wanting to take it out on her, I said, "We will, but right now I've got to vent to that bastard."

There were several people on *Classic Wine* when we glided down her starboard side, not five yards away. An overweight bimbo in a ridiculously tight bikini shouted into the cabin. "Michael, the sailboat is back!"

The captain came on deck, put his hands on his hips, and glared at us. Then he said, "Guess you didn't learn."

My blood boiled, but Carol shouted, "You know damn well we didn't drag."

He yelled at the top of his lungs. "So what!"

That did it! I yelled back, "So what? I'll show you so what, you dickhead."

I motored ahead and took a position a hundred feet directly in front of him. With the engine in neutral, I stormed forward and let go the anchor, then yelled for Carol to back down slowly! This time, she offered no objections as she backed us down toward *Classic Wine,* which now had four people standing on the foredeck watching us.

I snubbed up the chain twenty feet from their bow amidst their loud shouts and raucous objections.

I said to Carol, "Don't worry, we're only staying long enough to break his balls."

She said, "I'm not worried. After he made that comment, I don't care if we break his balls all night."

I laughed. "We might just do that!"

I wasn't done having my pound of flesh. I rigged our outdoor speakers on our stern rail, facing them aft, then went below to look for an obnoxious CD.

Carol shouted. "Mary Lou! Get the Mary Lou asshole song!"

"Yes!" I yelled. "That's perfect, way to go, Baby!"

Rummaging through our CD case I found it and then cranked the stereo to maximum volume. I think Fred Campbell wrote it but we had a version by Mary Lou and The Untouchables. It was perfect, and once it began, Carol and I sipped iced tea with smug faces and a real good feeling

in our hearts as we entertained *Classic Wine* and her odious crew with the
asshole song.

> *Were you born an asshole?*
> *Or did you work at it your whole life?*
> *Either way it worked out fine*
> *'Cause you're an asshole tonight*
> *Yes you're an A-S-S-H-O-L-E*
> *And don't you try to blame it on me*
> *You deserve all the credit*
> *You're an asshole tonight*
> *You were an asshole yesterday*
> *You're an asshole tonight*
> *And I've got a feelin'*
> *You'll be an asshole the rest of your life*
> *And I was talkin' to your mother*
> *Just the other night*
> *I told her I thought you were an asshole*
> *She said, "Yes, I think you're right"*
> *And all your friends are assholes*
> *'Cause you've known them your whole life*
> *And somebody told me*
> *You've got an asshole for a wife*
> *Were you born an asshole?*
> *Or did you work at it your whole life?*
> *Either way it worked out fine*
> *Cause you're an aaaass...hole tonight*

They were beside themselves, literally going nuts, and we thought
the Michael guy was going to have a heart attack. Carol was hysterical
laughing, which infuriated them even more, but the best was when the
bimbo in the tight bikini covered her ears and shouted, "Make them stop,
make them stop!"

We laughed even harder, and Carol leaned over to me and said,
"This was almost worth getting *Lastdance* towed."

After a dozen renditions of the song, we decided to leave before the harbormaster showed up, so with Carol on the helm, we weighed anchor and moved near *Tranquility* and *Belle Amie* for a night of hysterical laughter as we told and re-told the story.

Chapter 23
West Bound

Days later, we departed Block Island bound for Three Mile Harbor in Gardiners Bay some thirty-one miles away on Long Island's north fork. I considered motoring past *Classic Wine* and playing the asshole song just once more, but I wasn't even sure if anyone was aboard. Also, being early, I didn't want to annoy innocent bystanders on nearby boats. Soon after getting underway, we ran into a series of rain squalls, but the wind remained steady at twelve knots from the northwest and *Lastdance* sailed well as she reached through the bright blue Atlantic.

Whenever we saw dolphins, Carol would yell for glee and then play Enya's beautiful and haunting music on the stereo, believing she had attracted them to us in Florida that way. We also saw sharks, sometimes several at a time and we'd both instinctively move away from the rail of the boat. In between burst of warm sun, we were pelted by occasional squalls with driving rain but we sailed on, alternating between foul weather gear and t-shirts. Once past Montauk, we entered Napeague Bay and sailing south of Gardiners Island, we crossed tracks with *Tranquility* and *Belle Amie*, who had departed from Block Island much earlier.

The next several days we explored Three Mile Harbor, Coelces Harbor on Shelter Island and finally, the old whaling village of Greenport, which is nestled on the south side of Long Island's north fork. Greenport has a fair share of restaurants and pubs, but the main attraction for us was Preston's. It is the quintessential nautical antique store, as if the word store could describe the size and scale of maritime memorabilia under their roof.

In the morning, we prepared to get underway in light winds and a clear sky, our destination being Mattituck about twenty-seven miles away. The weather forecast had been good the previous night but as Carol got things ready topside, I checked NOAA weather one last time and stopped in my tracks. There was a severe thunderstorm warning until ten o'clock. "A line of severe thunderstorms is moving east on Long Island Sound with high winds, sometimes greater than forty knots, with hail and violent cloud to ground lightening. At this moment, the line extends from the south shore of Long Island to Danbury, Connecticut and is moving east at thirty-five miles per hour!"

Looking at the chart, I quickly calculated that it would be on us in less than two hours. *Damn, it's a good thing I checked.* I went on deck and looked west. The sky was sunny. I called over to Charlie and John.

"Did you guys hear the forecast?"

John said, "Yeah, southwest winds ten to fifteen. Why?"

I told them what was coming our way. They instinctively looked to the west, but the skies still looked clear and bright.

John looked at his watch. "If we don't leave soon I'll never make it through Plum Gut.

Plum Gut is a deep narrow waterway separating Long Island and Plum Island. The currents there can run as much as six knots, which is one knot faster than *Tranquility* can sail or even motor.

I asked, "How much of a window do we have?"

John said he'd check, and Charlie and I went to listen to the forecast again. A few moments later, we all agreed that we should wait and see what the line of storms was doing.

Carol took the initiative to do some calculations, and after plotting the storm line, she came on deck saying, "If we left now we'd be right in Plum Gut about the time the storms were due to hit. I say we stay put!"

"Thanks, Baby. Good work."

John came back on deck. "Maximum ebb is in two and a half hours, so we can wait a half hour, okay?"

We all agreed to wait half an hour to see if the storm line dissipated. In the meantime, we'd get our boats battened down for bad weather.

The urgency to leave was based on having a favorable current through Plum Gut and only a weak unfavorable current between there and Mattituck. Ideally, we should have left hours ago. We would have had a favorable current the entire way but no one was interested in a pre-dawn departure. Right now, the current was still flooding but would soon be slack, then would begin to ebb making it increasingly difficult for us to run Plum Gut or make decent time to Mattituck.

The eight o'clock forecast stated the line of severe thunderstorms was now moving more north-northeast toward the Connecticut shore. *Lastdance* and *Belle Amie* could easily handle the strong currents but it would have been a struggle for *Tranquility,* so we made the decision to depart immediately. I walked back to our boat and told Carol to start the engine.

"We're leaving?" she asked.

"Yeah, the storms are moving over to the Connecticut side, so we should be fine."

"Okay, you're the captain, but just tell me, do you have your nagging sense of doubt about going?"

I looked at her and thought, *She knows me so well.* I answered truthfully, "Yeah, I do but start the engine, you take her out."

We left in single file and proceeded east in a twelve knot southwest breeze. I took one last look to the west and detected a subtle darkening of the sky and made a mental note to look back frequently. With the current against us until we got into Plum Gut, *Tranquility* could barely make four knots so Carol slowed down as we approached the green buoy off of Hay Beach Point. I looked back again and could see the sky was definitely darker now.

Carol followed my glance astern and frowned. "We should have stayed; we could have left on the next tide or even tomorrow."

She was right; this was no place to roll the dice with the weather.

I went below and turned on the radar. When it warmed up, I scanned at its maximum sixteen mile range, but saw nothing in the way of bad weather. The storm line was probably just out of range on the Connecticut side of the sound. We passed between Red "2" and Green "3" west of Long Beach Point and I told Carol to go a few hundred yards past Red

"2", then come to 070°m. I looked to the west. The sky was now darkening fast, and I thought, *shit!*

"*Tranquility, Tranquility*, this is *Lastdance!*"

John answered. "This is *Tranquility*. Yeah, I see it."

I told him to stand-by while I checked the radar. Carol, thinking that we might be turning back, slowed to idle speed. I thought, *Good girl.* One look at the radar and I knew we had a problem. In less than ten minutes, what had only been land masses and a few boats, now showed a solid wall of rain stretching across the entire sound. I said out loud, "Damn, so much for moving toward the Connecticut side."

From the cockpit, Carol said, "The sky is getting pretty dark. Is it coming this way?"

"Yeah," I said. "Give me a minute; let me plot it."

Turning back was out of the question. It was four miles to Greenport, which would take an hour for John. The storm line was moving east at forty miles an hour and would be on us in thirty minutes. Even at maximum speed, it would be more than a half hour for us. We needed a place to anchor quickly. I looked at the chart and said aloud, "Damn, even Orient Harbor might take too long." I went on deck and told Carol to crank it up and get on 070°m again and put some distance between us and the channel.

"*Tranquility, Tranquility*, this is *Lastdance!*"

"This is *Tranquility*."

"John, this thing is moving very fast and looks like a solid wall on the radar. I figure we're gonna get whacked hard in about twenty minutes so I'm gonna anchor off Long Beach as soon as I gain some distance from the channel."

"Roger that, *Lastdance*, we're right behind you."

A second later, Charlie came on and said he was doing the same.

Before signing off, John said, "Let's keep the radios on seventy-two and not bunch up when we anchor guys."

Carol looked back toward the channel. "Is this far enough?"

I looked up at her and saw that the sky almost looked like night behind her. "Yeah, Baby, this is fine."

Without further word from me, she turned a hundred eighty degrees and headed *Lastdance* into the wind. I went forward to drop the anchor, silently cursing myself for not following my instincts.

"Depth?" I asked.

"Eighteen feet," she replied.

I signaled for reverse and dropped the anchor, letting out chain as Carol backed down. I stopped the windlass with a hundred feet of chain out, and a few seconds later the rode became taught as our big Bruce anchor set. We stopped abruptly, then sprang forward slightly by the catenary effect of the chain.

I signaled for more throttle, and Carol ran the engine up and the rode again became taught. I then let another hundred feet of chain rattle out over the bow roller. Still in reverse, *Lastdance* jerked to a halt again. I locked the windlass and quickly put the bridle through both hawse pipes, fastening it to the chain, then let out more chain until the bridle took the strain. We had a two hundred feet of chain out, which gave us more than a 10:1 ratio of rode to depth. I believed *Tranquility* and *Belle Amie* were anchoring far enough away that we could all safely swing a full 360°, but just in case, I called them on the radio to tell them how much chain I had out.

Carol kept us in reverse, and with the bridle now on, she began taking bearings on two large trees ashore. The bearings remained constant.

She said, "We're holding!"

"Leave it in reverse a few minutes longer, but throttle down to idle, then put it in neutral and leave it running. I'll get the bimini connector rigged. You get the foul weather gear out and turn the anchor light on."

From the look of things, visibility was going to drop to zero, so I turned on the GPS to track our position in case we dragged. I thought, *We're as ready as we can be; I hope it's over quickly.*

The western sky was now almost pitch black and the wind had increased steadily. As an afterthought, I peeked down the companionway and said, "Make sure all the ports are closed and dogged!"

Then, glancing at the radar screen, I thought, *Geez, it really does look like a moving wall.* Carol returned to the cockpit with our foul weather gear and we hastily bundled up. The wind began to sing loudly in the rigging and *Lastdance* tugged on her anchor as the first loud crack of thunder sounded and the sky lit up as a bolt of lightening hit somewhere near Greenport. Several other strikes followed in quick succession, and I thought, *Shit, shit, shit, I hate lightning!*

Then it was on us! *Lastdance* heeled over thirty degrees as she was hit with a blast of wind peaking at forty-seven knots on my anemometer. Torrential rain followed and visibility instantly dropped to zero, swallowing up *Tranquility* and *Belle Amie* in the maelstrom. As they disappeared from view, I silently wished them luck and again cursed myself for departing the safety of Greenport. Lightning strikes were all around us, and the sound of thunder was almost eclipsed by the sound of the rain pelting down on our little ship. This was where Carol and I parted ideas of what sailing should be like.

Huddling together in the cockpit, I knew I'd be happy to sail forever in that mythical place called "Perfect," where the sun always shined and the wind was always blowing out of the right direction at ten to fifteen knots. Carol, on the other hand was fascinated with the unrestrained violence nature could serve up once in a while. I sat in the flimsy shelter of our dodger, anticipating every lightning bolt was destined to target our boat or me personally. Carol, on the other hand, looked about with wonder, as if she was in the safety of a well-grounded brick house!

The wind blew steady at thirty knots with gust to over forty as it backed and veered violently through an arc of almost ninety degrees. Because the changes in wind direction were so rapid, *Lastdance* swung forcefully with each shift, and I wondered if a small riding sail would dampen the motion. I switched my thoughts to how the Tremels were making out, but their boats were still lost from sight in the driving rain. I opened the companionway hatch enough to look at the radar screen. They and most of the surrounding land masses were lost in the almost solid rain clutter on the screen as the storm hovered over us.

Amidst the wild cacophony of thunder, pelting rain, and wind screaming in the rigging, Carol glanced at the GPS and yelled over the noise. "We're holding!" A moment later, a bolt of lightning hit the water in a deafening explosion a hundred yards from us, and she excitedly said, "Wow, did you see that?"

I yelled, "See it? Hell, I felt it." Then I thought, *She is absolutely nuts, or she just doesn't understand the destructive power of lightning!*

I looked at the compass and averaging out the swings, I figured our heading was still pretty much southwest. Carol once again said the GPS had us in the same spot. I peeked below at the radar screen and could see the density of the rain was diminishing and land masses were now discernable. As if expecting my next question, she said, "The wind is down to twenty-five!"

As quickly as the storm hit us, it was over. *Tranquility* and *Belle Amie* became visible as the rain slowed from a deluge to just a downpour and the radio soon crackled with John's voice calling.

"*Lastdance, Lastdance, Tranquility* here."

"*Tranquility,* this is *Lastdance.*"

John said, "Good thing we weren't in Plum Guy when that hit; the water is too deep to anchor and I never would have been able to motor against that wind."

Charlie added a ditto to the conversation, and I replied that we were lucky, but we should have waited it out.

"Roger that," John said, "roger that!"

The sky was brightening to the west and our radar showed nothing further coming our way. After listening to NOAA weather once more to confirm it was truly over, I called out to *Tranquility* and *Belle* Amie. "I'll be weighing anchor in ten minutes."

Just then, I saw John waving frantically to the east. I saw a tug and barge emerging from the rain and rapidly bearing down on him. He blew his horn five loud blast to signal danger and began calling on the VHF on channel 13, then 16, but the tug didn't respond. I thought, *Son of a bitch, this is exactly why I got so far away from the channel.*

We stared in horror as John frantically tried to signal the tug to no avail. Then, with just a hundred yards to spare, the tug suddenly changed course and swept past *Tranquility* with not so much as a bye your leave. John flipped him off as did Charlie and I, but the idiot in the wheel house was either on drugs or asleep and never once acknowledged John's calls or even our obscene gestures. If he had been coming south through narrow Plum Gut, he would have hit one or all of us.

As we weighed anchor, the sun brightened in the sky and we stripped out of our wet foul weather gear. Forty minutes later, we rounded Orient Point and turned west. Carol removed her damp T-shirt and lay on her back while I manned the helm. I thought lovingly, *God, I love looking at her.*

Then, out of the blue she asked, "Can satellites see me?"

I laughed, "We've just come through a raging storm and you're wondering if satellites can see your boobs?" Then I added, "I once read they could read the headlines on a newspaper from up there so I'm sure they can easily see those puppies. You probably have everyone at the NSA and CIA in heat right now!"

She smiled. "Wake me when we get there or if you need me!"

"If I keep staring at you like this, I'll need you long before you fall asleep!"

She smiled again. "Promises, promises."

Smiling, I thought, *Oh yeah, wench, I'll show you promises, promises.* Just then, NOAA's forecasted wind shift to the northwest materialized and my thoughts turned to sailing. When I slowed the engine to idle, Carol opened her eyes and asked, "Everything okay?"

"Yeah," the wind shifted so I'm going to raise sail."

"Do you need me?" I leaned forward and fondled her. "I told you, I always need you!"

She smiled and asked, "Where are the others?"

"Charlie passed us and is way ahead. John is still way behind."

"Oh why didn't you tell me Charlie went by; they might have seen me like this?"

"I don't think so; he was pretty far off when he passed us. Anyway, I have to go below. Can you take the helm for a few minutes?"

She stood and looked around to be sure our friends couldn't see her, then stretched and yawned.

"What are you trying to do to me, woman?"

"I'm just stretching!" she replied.

I laughed. "Stretching my ass, you're driving me nuts."

I considered just drifting a while before raising our sails, but then I figured John would assume we were having trouble and come close to investigate.

Reading my mind, Carol patted me and said, "I know you're frisky, but *Tranquility* is right behind us so save it for later."

Fifteen minutes later, I gazed at the passing coast and Carol sleeping in the shade of the dodger as *Lastdance* flew westward at six knots under a full press of sail.

We passed Rocky Point and then Horton Point. Many years before, all of us once stopped for a swim on a blistering hot afternoon, tethered to our craft in the fast moving outgoing tide. A two o'clock, with my thoughts back to the present, we hove-to off Mattituck inlet and doused our headsails. Carol woke, put on her t-shirt and took my place at the helm. She started the engine and after yawning several times, she signaled for me to drop the main.

Mattituck is a quaint village with a totally protected anchorage offering free dinghy tie up and showers to visiting boats. I always looked forward to a stopover here, but inexplicably, Carol didn't like it but couldn't say why. For most big boats, the town can only be accessed from the north shore, but small boats can enter from Great Peconic Bay through a creek that doesn't connect with the anchorage, but either approach is close enough to walk to town.

The inlet on Long Island Sound is marked by a twenty-six foot tall flashing light and two channel buoys just inside the jetties, but it's still difficult to see. Green "3A" is six miles southeast of the hundred-foot-tall lighthouse at Horton Point and one mile due north of Mattituck, making it a perfect waypoint for finding the inlet. Once in the inlet, the channel makes a ninety degree turn to the northeast about four hundred yards inside the jetties. Even looking at the chart, it takes confidence to realize you are not going to run straight into the beach dead ahead.

From the turn, the narrow channel runs about one and a half miles past commercial docks, then pretty homes until it ends at the small rectangular harbor. *Belle Amine* was anchored and waiting for us, and we rafted to her starboard side. Charlie and Valerie had a batch of margaritas prepared and while waiting for John and Gail, we launched into our respective versions of the storm. Half and hour later, *Tranquility* came in and rafted to *Belle Amie's* port side and we celebrated our arrival with several bottles of wine, telling and re-telling the big storm story.

I woke the next morning to the sound of wind howling through the rigging. Carol lay snuggled to me and cold air was blowing down the open hatch above our bed. I reached up and closed it.

She mumbled, "Oh thanks, Baby. I'm so cold."

I drew the comforter up over her shoulders and, after wrapping my arms around her, she let out a soft sound of contentment as my body heat enveloped her.

"Is that better?" I asked.

"Yes, wonderful. You're always so warm, my hot-blooded Italian."

I put my leg over hers and even covered her feet with my own and she purred like a kitten. "I love being so close to you."

Then, a particularly strong gust of wind rocked the boat and screamed through the rigging. Carol said, "What's going on out there?"

"I don't know, but I'd better go check; it sounds nasty."

Leaving the warmth of our bed, I instantly felt the cabin's chill so I fired up the propane heater and put on a pot of coffee. Glancing at the wind indicator, I saw it was blowing twenty-three knots, so after first reaching for a t-shirt, I decided on a sweatshirt instead. Then once on deck, I replaced the companionway screens with hatch boards so the cabin could warm. John was on *Belle Amie* talking with Charlie over coffee so I joined them.

"What the hell is going on? This wasn't in the forecast last night. Geez, I'm showing twenty-three knots!"

Charlie laughed and passed me a cup of hot coffee. "Maybe it wasn't in the forecast last night, but it was this morning. Clear skies and temperatures in the sixties with the wind at twenty-five knots out of the west today and tomorrow, maybe until Friday!"

I exclaimed, "Just what we need, twenty-five knots of wind right on the nose."

John looked at his watch and said, "Yeah, plus the current turns against us in two hours, and it's what, twenty-five miles to Port Jefferson? I say we stay here another day." Charlie and I agreed, and with that settled, we went back to our respective boats after first agreeing to go into town for lunch.

Back on *Lastdance*, the cabin was toasty warm. I poured coffee from the pot into a thermos, then undressed and climbed back in bed with Carol. She let out a soft squeal as I snuggled close to her. "Brrrr, you're so cold."

I told her about the weather and that we decided to stay in Mattituck another day, which made her happy. I said, "I thought you didn't like it here."

She snuggled closer. "I don't, but I'd rather be here in Mattituck instead of out sailing in this crap. Can I sleep longer?"

I kissed her nose and said, "Sleep all morning, Princess, but we're all going into town for lunch, okay?"

She smiled and said, "Mmmm, sounds like a plan, now snuggle closer and let me hold you."

We found a great little place in town for lunch, and after a couple bottles of wine, we walked around the small village before returning to the boats. John and I then took a ride in his dinghy to see what the conditions were like at the inlet and found them to be ugly. It was very windy and big waves were forming high crest and deep troughs at the seaward ends of the jetties. We wondered if conditions would be the same the next day. If so, would there be enough water in the troughs to keep from slamming into the bottom of the relatively shallow channel on our way out? We turned around and went back to the anchorage, gathering on *Lastdance* for a captains meeting.

I said I'd leave if the wind was less than twenty knots, but I was going at high tide to minimize the chances of hitting bottom in the trough of a wave at the inlet. We checked the tide tables. High tide was at 5:30 in the morning. It would be five feet above mean low water, which, according to the charts, was seven and a half feet, for a total high tide depth of about thirteen feet. Also, with a strong west wind blowing water out of the sound for two days, there might be even less, so I decided to stick with my plan and leave close to high tide. John said *Tranquility's* draft was a foot less than *Lastdance* so he was going at 7:30 a.m.

Charlie laughed and said, "A pox on both your houses, if it's blowing twenty knots, I'm staying here another day!"

In a brilliant sunrise the next morning, I quietly cast off our lines. As Carol slowly motored away from *Belle Amie*, Charlie, ever vigilant, stepped out of his cabin and said softly. "Good luck, you guys, see ya in Port Jeff."

I waved and we glided silently down Mattituck Creek. It was only sixty-two degrees, but the forecast called for it to warm up to the mid-seventies by noon. We both had foul weather gear on and I felt a little guilty waking Carol so early, but I was really concerned about those deep troughs at the inlet and wanted every margin of safety.

The wind in the anchorage was only twelve knots, sometimes gusting to fifteen and I hoped it would be about the same out on the sound. Carol and I had frequently sailed in twenty-five knot winds, so we knew *Lastdance* could easily handle those conditions with a reefed main and a staysail. The immediate issue for me was clearing the inlet. Afterwards, we had to contend with a two knot unfavorable current and with the wind out of the west; we'd be tacking the whole twenty-five miles to Port Jefferson, so we'd be clawing for every mile we gained westward.

As we approached the ninety degree turn in the creek, a commercial fishing trawler signaled her intention to overtake us to port. I signaled an acknowledgement and smiled as Carol slowed so the trawler could more easily pass us. The captain waved as he went by. We returned his greeting, and before Carol fell in behind him, I looked at his draft markings. He drew six feet, a foot more than we did, which made me feel more comfortable. "Stay at this speed. If there are big waves at the inlet, we can watch how the trawler takes them."

The channel is almost four hundred yards long and a hundred yards wide, but the navigable part is just one hundred feet wide. The waves entering it had a chance to dissipate somewhat, but even before the stern of the fishing boat was out of sight after making her turn, we could see her begin to pitch. When we made the turn, we saw just how much she was pitching as she approached the ends of the jetty. I thought, *Maybe I should rethink this?*

Moving forward at dead slow, we watched the trawler as she reared up the face of a steep wave, then slammed down into the trough. I instinctively looked at our depth. It read fourteen feet, so even if the waves were eight feet from crest to trough, we only had six feet under us and we drew five feet. I considered turning around, but I didn't really think the waves were bigger than six feet. Carol asked what she should do.

I said, "Go to four knots." I looked at the wind speed. It was at a steady twenty knots. "Do you want me to take her out?"

She said, "Maybe you should?"

"Let me see what this trawler does." Watching the trawler, the waves and then the chart, I saw that the deeper water was actually a bit east of the jetty.

"Look at him, he's playing!" I said. "The waves are coming at an angle to the inlet from the west and he increased speed and turned right into them, that's why he's slamming so hard. Stay at this speed and, instead of turning northwest like he did, go straight out and take the waves at an angle off our port bow. We'll ride up the face of the wave and instead of leaping off the crest like he's doing; we should then slide down the back of it." Then I added, "Stay on the helm; you've done this before in Florida and in much bigger waves. Just don't let the jetties intimidate you!"

Fifty yards from the entrance, Carol said with a tinge of urgency in her voice, "Maybe you should take it!"

"Only if you really want me to." I replied.

"I don't know; I'm just nervous."

"Carol, are you going to do it or not?"

She took a deep breath. "I'll do it!"

We were pitching more with every passing second, and as we approached the ends of the jetties, I said, "I hope these waves aren't bigger than six feet!"

I held on tighter to the steering pedestal as Carol prepared to navigate the first big wave. It slammed first into the west jetty with a resounding crash sending spray twenty feet in the air. Then it hit us, then the east jetty. We slid off the crest into the trough, and I watched the depth gauge display: 13, 12, 10, 8, 7. A split-second later, it immediately began to rise 8, 9, 11, 12, then 14 as we rode up the face of the next wave. I thought, that was close, just two feet to spare under our keel.

Carol steered *Lastdance* through half a dozen of those until, suddenly, we were in twenty-five feet of water, then thirty, and the waves began to flatten a little. She held that course until the depth showed fifty feet.

"Okay, why were the waves a little bigger back there?"

She instantly replied. "Because as the depth decreases, the waves slow down and build higher?"

I smiled and kissed her cheek. "Are you asking me or telling me?"

"I'm telling you, smartass!"

I smiled again. "Good girl, I think I'll keep you! Now head her up; let's see if we can sail in this crap."

Carol yelled, "Heading up!"

She brought *Lastdance* into the wind and I raised the single-reefed main as the boom shook in short arcs from the luffing sail. She put the engine in neutral then turned to starboard and fell off the wind onto a port tack until the main filled with a resounding snap. I sheeted out a bit and *Lastdance* lurched forward, gathering speed until she was making three knots. A moment later, I unfurled the staysail and our speed rapidly increased to six knots until we'd crash into a wave and lose momentum. *Lastdance* sliced through the smaller waves, but some of the larger breaking ones would almost stop us, pouring a foot of solid water across our foredeck. The sea in front of us was streaked with whitecaps and spindrift, but we were making headway and although there were some white knuckle moments, the boat was under control.

"Let's see how high can you point?"

Carol came left a few degrees at a time until the staysail began to luff, then she fell off until it filled again, and the tell-tales were streaming straight back. I trimmed the main and looked back at her and asked, "How high?"

"330!"

I said, "Oh, that sucks! Okay, it is what it is. Let's see what kind of progress we can make to the west." The wind increased to twenty-six knots, and I estimated the waves to be mostly six footers, occasionally bigger, but *Lastdance* was sailing well as her clipper bow continued to slice through them.

At eight o'clock, the temperature was still in the sixties, but the day was warming and conditions were now forecasted to improve as the low pressure system moved off the coast. We were actually having fun, but our angle of heel and the constant pounding into the steep waves were tiring so we took turns steering a port and starboard tack each. After two series of tacks, I plotted our position and saw we were making two miles west progress on a starboard tack, then losing a mile on the port tack.

I said aloud, "The rhumb line from Mattituck to Port Jefferson is twenty-five miles. If we were sailing it, we'd be make Port Jeff in four hours, but with the wind from the west and current against us, it's going to be a long day. Are you okay with that?"

I looked at her for an answer. Her hat was off and her hair was flying about wildly. She had one leg propped up on the starboard cockpit combing and her foul weather jacket was open.

She said, "What?" I repeated myself. She yelled at the top of her lungs. "Arrgghhh! I love it, of course I'm okay. This is fun."

I laughed and said loudly over the sound of the wind and waves, "What a wench!"

She pursed her lips in a mock kiss. "You're not too bad yourself, wencher!"

It was nine o'clock, and remembering that John said he was going to leave two hours after us, I became concerned that they might have had a problem in the inlet.

I reached for the VHF. "*Tranquility*, *Tranquility*, this is *Lastdance*."

A moment later, the radio came alive. "*Lastdance*, this is *Tranquility*."

"Morning, John, where are you, amigo?"

"Ah, let me check the chart. Ah, we're motoring and coming up on a green buoy at Roanoke Point Shoal. Where are you, *Lastdance*?"

I looked at my last plot, then the GPS and chuckled into the radio.

"We should be about three miles off your starboard bow on a starboard tack. We're making two miles west on starboard tack, then we lose a mile on port, but we're having fun!"

John said, "We tried sailing but couldn't make any progress. Then a wave pooped our dinghy and broke our davit, so we gave up and we're now motoring." A moment later, he added, "We're making about three knots and getting pounded but I'm looking at an ETA of around four o'clock. The current becomes favorable about noon so maybe we'll do better than that. Gail says she thinks she sees you. Are you coming toward Long Island?"

"That's us. We'll probably get pretty close before we tack so camera time okay?"

"Okay, *Lastdance*, see ya later. *Tranquility* standing by on channel seventy-two."

I took the helm while Carol scanned inshore with the binoculars. She spotted them off our port bow. "Wow, we've been out here since six and they're already almost even with us."

"Yeah, but they're motoring and we're sailing, but if you want to, I'll crank up the engine."

She laughed. "No way, I'm having fun. Besides, this is a challenge now. We're going to sail right into the harbor, okay?"

"Hell yeah, sounds good to me, Baby! Get the camera ready and get a photo of them when we get close, then I'll tack and you can take the helm."

The morning warmed considerably, and as it approached noon, the current diminished and we began to make better progress to the west on starboard tack, not losing ground on port tack. By two o'clock, the wind dropped to a steady fifteen knots and our speed fell to five knots. I shook out the reef in the main and we went back up to six knots, but we were still being hammered by waves, which grew steeper as the current then opposed the wind. Although not losing ground, we were still only making about three miles of west progress with every two tacks. I figured our ETA to be about seven o'clock and thought it was time to take out the jib.

It's difficult to explain how just one or two additional knots of speed can make such a difference but with the jib out, *Lastdance* surged forward and propelled herself off the crest of the smaller waves. Carol yelled, "Wow, seven point five, seven point eight. Way to go, Baby."

"See if you can point a little higher. She smiled as she came into the wind another five degrees to a course of 325°m. We were not only sailing faster, but we were sailing closer to our destination. I recalculated our ETA.

"If we can keep this up, we can be in by six o'clock, which means we'll be sailing in a favorable current for the rest of the trip!"

I asked her if she was tired.

"Yes, but I still want to sail into Port Jeff. Are you tired?"

"Yeah, but it's one of the best sails of my life; let's press on!"

John called us on the radio at four o'clock to say they were anchored in the sand hole behind Mount Misery Point. "When will you be in?"

"I'm thinking about six, John."

He asked incredulously, "Have you been sailing all day?"

Before I could answer, Carol, who was on the helm yelled out, "Hell yeah, this is a sailboat, John!"

John chuckled. "Okay, *Lastdance*, Gail says you guys must be tired, so we'll have drinks waiting for you when you get in, then plan on having dinner with us."

"Roger that, *Tranquility*, much appreciated. We're exhausted, but having fun. See ya in about two hours."

At 5:50, we sailed into Port Jefferson on a starboard tack with all three sails flying. John and Gail waved as we came through the narrow entrance and then headed up into the wind to douse sails. We came alongside *Tranquility* which was anchored in the small cove surrounded on three sides by sand dunes almost a hundred feet high. It had once been a quarry, but now it was a sheltered anchorage for weary sailors like us. John and Gail took our lines, and we took pride when they laughed and said, "You guys are nuts!"

With the boats securely rafted together, we went below to wash up before joining them for drinks and dinner aboard *Tranquility*.

There is nothing that can describe our sense of satisfaction and accomplishment and once below deck, I gave Carol a big hug, a different kind of hug. There were always loving hugs of course, but this one spoke of camaraderie that only comes from winning hard fought battles together. She was a good sailor. More importantly, she was a dependable shipmate with plenty of mettle! As I waited for her to wash up and change blouses, I wrote down my feelings for her at that moment in a hokey but sincere note on a paper napkin.

Dearest Carol...

You know you have captivated me since we were kids. I can't help it, I look at you and I see your beautiful face and smile, alluring eyes and sensuous body, all beg-

ging me to caress and kiss you. But today, the real woman in you showed herself. You are all things to me and it is your inner beauty and strength that I love so much.
     Forever & Always,
     Ron

I gave it to her, half-expecting a cute response. I should have known better. As she read it, tears filled her eyes and she softly put her arms around my neck and told me how much she loved me and how much that note meant to her. We remained embraced for moments, whispering sentiments about how we were soul-mates forever until the spell was broken by John's voice booming across our deck.

"Come on, margaritas are ready. What's going on down there?"

We laughed and kissed gently, then went up to join our friends.

We talked about the day over drinks and dinner. John said it must have been tough tacking so often in those conditions and asked how many tacks we made.

I said I lost count during the twelve hour sail, but to journey the straight line distance of twenty-five miles between Mattituck and Port Jefferson, we actually logged sixty-two miles as we zigzagged up Long Island Sound. We probably tacked about thirty times, which was not noteworthy on a crewed racing boat in a tacking dual, but was not bad for a middle-aged married couple in blustery conditions.

Exactly one month later on September eleventh, the lives of thousand of Americans changed forever! I went home to find Carol crying softly as she looked out our bedroom window. There, from our vantage point high on the crest of a ridge, we could see thick black smoke billowing from the World Trade Center. I put my arms around her.

She said, "Those poor people in those buildings,"

Then, crying harder, she shouted, "What is wrong with those bastards? The news showed Palestinians dancing in the streets right here in New Jersey! Do we know anyone working there?"

"Yeah, Ed Reilly."

In an anguishing tone, she said, "Oh no. Oh no, Ron," and then turned and buried her face in my shoulder.

Ed survived the tragedy, but we avoided sailing west because even weeks later, we could still see smoke rising from where the World Trade Center once stood. It was upsetting and made us angry, so we pointed our bow eastward where during a late September cruise to the historic whaling village of Cold Spring Harbor, we reviewed our year on Long Island Sound. Then, after a good meal at the same restaurant we'd dined in years earlier, we strolled leisurely back to *Lastdance.*

"Any thoughts on where you want to go next weekend?"

She laughed. "We're not even finished with this weekend, but I don't care. Wherever you want to go is fine with me."

She pressed closer to me said seductively, "Right now, I just want you to take me to our bed."

The next morning we ghosted around the spit of land protecting the small inner harbor from the wider expanse of Cold Spring Harbor proper. We sailed under the high cliffs of Cove Neck with the stereo playing *Con Te Partiro* and I steered with one hand on the helm and one around Carol's shoulder as she sang along with Andrea Bocelli and Sarah Brightman. I told her she was my best friend and how much I loved her and that it was truly magical being with her. As I whispered these things to her, she showered me with soft kisses.

We cleared Whitewood Point on Lloyd Neck and set a course for Stamford. As we sailed in the freshening breeze, our mood became more lighthearted and we took turns talking about the things we wanted to do back on Chesapeake Bay.

Laughing lecherously, I said, "I want to be the only boat at anchor on the Corsica River like we used to and have my way with you on deck in the moonlight."

Carol laughed. "You pervert, I knew you had an ulterior motive!"

"Yes, but it doesn't make be a bad person, does it?"

She smiled. "No, it doesn't. I love how you want me." Then she added, "Thank you, Ron. I'm really happy we're going back. I promise we'll go to an empty anchorage the very first weekend, and you can have your way with me on one condition."

"What's that?" I asked.

With a mischievous look, she said, "If I can then have my way with you!"

I smiled and said, "Deal!"

The following weekend we met John and Gail to discuss our sail south. Amid wine glasses and dishes overflowing with pasta and calamari, we planned on a napkin how we'd sail to New Jersey. With average temperatures at the end of October dropping into the fifties and less than eleven hours of daylight, we decided the sooner we made the trip the better and agreed to sail down the following weekend.

Carol's excitement level rose dramatically, and while I went to work, she immersed herself in preparations to sail *Lastdance* to New Jersey. The most important decision was where we would haul out for the winter. John was going to Morgan where we first met them. We opted to haul at Lockwoods, which was also on Cheesequake Creek. Once we confirmed they could haul us, Carol prepared tide and current tables for the trip, and when the big day came, all that remained was to take a small bag of clothing and some stores for the two day voyage.

She spent Friday with Rhonda, who'd driven down from Connecticut in order to give us a ride back to Stamford, when I got home from work. Once in Stamford, we took Rhonda for drinks and dinner, and afterwards we sat on *Lastdance* sharing a bottle of champagne, lamenting how she should have spent more time sailing with us that summer. She promised to visit us on Chesapeake Bay, and after she and Carol exchanged a tearful hug goodbye, Rhonda embraced me and in mock seriousness asked, "Are you guys staying at anchor tomorrow night?"

"Yes we are. Why, do you want to make the trip with us?"

She laughed. "Yeah right, not unless you can get a hotel. So what will you do for heat?"

"Damn," I exclaimed. "I forgot the heater!"

Rhonda smiled. "Carol didn't! At least she didn't forget to put it in my car."

Then, looking at Carol, who had a bit too much champagne, she added in a chiding voice, "But I guess she forgot to bring it down to boat! Come on, I have to get home; walk me to my car, and I'll give you the heater!"

When I returned to the boat, Carol was already in bed basking in the warmth of our electric heater, which would have been useless at anchor. I thought, *We would have frozen our butts off tomorrow night without this.*

Tranquility was twenty miles east of us in Stratford, so they departed before sunrise. Several hours later, we said goodbye to friends at our marina and with the morning temperature in the low fifties, we motored out to the Stamford breakwater. The wind was northwest at twelve knots which was good, but we lingered at Red "32" south of Shippan Point and called *Tranquility* on the radio.

John replied immediately. "*Lastdance*, this is *Tranquility*"

"Morning, John, where are you guys?"

"We're out in the middle of the Sound about four miles west of Oyster Bay and freezing our asses off. Where are you?"

"We just left Stamford and steering about 245°m. We'll look for you as we close on Execution Rocks. We'll call you every half hour until we hook up."

An hour later, we spotted them off our port bow and drew alongside them by the time we reached Hewlett Point off Manhasset Bay. The day warmed considerably and Carol took the helm as we approached the Whitestone Bridge. We then spent the next several hours sailing *Lastdance* down the fast-moving currents of the East River. It was exciting as we raced past tall buildings until we approached New York Harbor where our mood became somber. Faint wisps of smoke still drifted upward from the embers and rubble of the World Trade Center and we sailed in silence with tears on our cheeks and rage in our hearts. I took the helm and sailed us away from the site of so much mindless carnage and destruction. Carol sat under a blanket with her back to the cabin. Her eyes were fixed on the forever changed skyline until it was lost from view when we sailed under the Verrazano Bridge on a southwest heading paralleling the Staten Island shoreline.

With the sun just sinking below the horizon, we rafted to *Tranquility* in Great Kills Harbor. An hour later, we were savoring dinner ashore in the Marina Café. The next day we motored the last six miles to South Amboy and as *Tranquility* continued up Cheesquake Creek, we waved goodbye and turned into the small tributary that would take us to Lockwood's

Marina for the winter. As we approached the dock, Bill Lockwood looked up and waved. Being the first time he'd seen *Lastdance*, he gave an approving nod to our little ship as we slowed to a stop.

With *Lastdance* hauled and dry-docked for the winter, we focused on our plans to go to Hawaii for Thanksgiving. It would be our first visit in twelve years, and in addition to spending the holiday with Christopher and his fiancée, Michelle, we were going to a luau hosted by our friends, David and Linda. As usual, Carol's level of excitement was at peak intensity. Nothing about her ever reflected complacency. Each trip was a new experience, each sail, a new adventure, and it brought me joy to see the intensity of her enthusiasm.

Chapter 24
Brain Tumor

"Ron, please come home, I'm really scared. Something happened!"

"What happened? Are you okay, Baby?"

"I'm okay now, but something weird happened. I think I passed out."

I asked where she was right then.

"I'm sitting on the bed."

"Okay, don't move; I'll be right there."

I was glad I drove to work that day and didn't have to walk home. Still, once in my driveway, I raced up the steps and found her safely in bed, but crying softly.

She saw me and extended her arms. "Please hold me; I'm so scared."

I sat on the bed and took her in my arms. "What happened?"

She sobbed uncontrollably and asked me to just hold her a few minutes. Seeing she wasn't physically injured, I silently held her and let her cry until she was ready to talk. In between bouts of tears, she explained that she felt fine all morning, then, as she was about to go into the shower, she heard her dead grandmother's voice loud and clear. *"Do not go in the shower, Carol Lee, go to the bed now!"* She said it was so real that she got scared and shouted, "Who's there?"

The only reply was her grandmother's voice again. *"Carol Lee, do not go into the shower; go to the bed now and lay down now!"*

"Geez, Baby, why didn't you call me?"

"I was going to, but the voice was so powerful, I got really scared and went into the bedroom. As I sat on the bed to call you, I was overcome with the smell of flowers, then everything went blank. The next thing I knew I was lying across the bed crying, and that's when I called you, but I don't know if I passed out or not."

"I should take you to the hospital or call a doctor."

"No, I'm fine, just stay with me a while, okay?"

I said, "Don't worry, I won't go back to work, but I really think you should see a doctor."

"No, I'm really fine; just lay down with me and hold me."

I stayed home the rest of the day and she seemed perfectly well, so much so that she sweet-talked me into taking her out to dinner. I dried her remaining tears and said, "Okay, we'll go to Casa Bella; I'll make reservations!"

She laughed. "Wow, Casa Bella. You really must be worried about me."

There were no other occurrences and as the week went by. The event was mostly forgotten, but every now and then, I'd think about it and wished I had called a doctor.

Three weeks later, I was returning from a business trip to Germany, eager to get home as my flight raced westward across the Atlantic. I missed Carol and was really looking forward to our Thanksgiving trip to Hawaii. I hadn't been thinking about her strange experience weeks earlier, but as I walked down the jetway into the terminal, I had a strange premonition that something was wrong. Then, at the foot of the ramp on a small bulletin board was a note with my name on it.

I read it, and it changed my life forever. It simply said, "Call your daughter, Carol is in the hospital." I didn't have a daughter; this must be a mistake, but then I realized it meant my step-daughter. In a panic, I called Jennifer. All she could tell me was that Carol had a seizure at work and that she was still in the emergency room and to come right away. I found my limo driver and told him to take me to New Brunswick instead of home, and within an hour of landing, we were racing south on the New Jersey Turnpike.

I found Nancy and Jennifer and they took me to Carol. When I entered the small emergency room, my heart sank when I saw her. She had an IV in her arm and a frightened look on her face. I knew this was serious.

Carol was a nurse and been hospitalized before and she didn't scare easily, but this was different. I could see that she was visibly afraid and disoriented.

She cried when she saw me and angrily asked, "Oh, Ron. Where have you been?"

"I was in Germany, Baby. My flight just got in and I came here as fast as I could."

She seemed confused. "You were in Germany?"

"Yes, for a week. It's okay. I'm here with you, and I promise I won't leave."

I calmed her and eventually met with the ER doctor who said they were going to keep her for a couple of days to run some neurological test. All they knew was that she had a seizure of some kind and a CAT scan hadn't revealed much. Two days later, they did an MRI and the news was devastating. He believed it was a brain tumor. From its diffused nature, the neuroncology team thought it might be a glioma, possibly a GBM, a glioblastoma multiforme. I stayed with Carol in the hospital, but in between tests, I'd go home and spend every chance I could on my computer, researching brain tumors. The more I learned, the scarier it got, and one site summed it up with frightening brevity.

"Studies have shown that patients with glioblastoma multiforme survive longer if they are under age 40, have a good performance status and have had gross total resection of the tumor. Overall, the survival of patients with glioblastoma after surgery alone is 14 weeks. With surgery plus radiotherapy, median survival increases to 40 weeks, justifying the time and effort involved."

I read it repeatedly and cried as I thought, *14 weeks survival time. 40 weeks with surgery and radiation.* It didn't say anything about being cured! I found many other sites, and all said similar things. The overall three-year survival rate was less than five percent. Then, only if there had been full surgical removal of the tumor followed by radiation and chemotherapy, but chemo was relatively ineffective against GBM brain tumors. Wherever I looked, all I could see were the words *14 weeks survival.* I stared at the screen and cried again.

It became obvious to me that the key for any chance of survival was full surgical resection. Without that, she could be gone in months or even weeks. I cried constantly as I stared at website after website, looking for a glimmer of hope, an experimental trial somewhere, anything. There was promising work being done by a doctor at Duke University, but every source of information emphasized that full surgical resection was the key to survival regardless of what follow-up treatment was performed.

I met alone with the head of neurosurgery and he told me they were pretty sure it was a glioblastoma, but they wouldn't know for certain until they got a pathology report. He then dropped the bomb on me. He said he was confident he could remove about thirty percent of the tumor. By this time I knew all that any layman could possibly know about GBM tumors.

I exclaimed, "Thirty percent? She'll be dead in months; you have to get it all!"

He went into a lengthy explanation about the tumor being diffused and having an intertwined tentacle-like structure, which made it impossible to fully remove it. I couldn't believe what I was hearing.

Somewhere in his explanation he uttered the words, "She has very little chance of survival."

My knees got weak. I thought, *What the hell is he talking about? Carol was fine a few days ago. We were just getting ready to go to Hawaii for Thanksgiving and our life was good and we had plans. How could this be happening to her?* He then told me we had to make up our minds quickly because the tumor was growing fast and she required surgery at the earliest possible date.

The doctor outlined the circumstances to Carol. I could see the fear in her eyes as he explained the diagnosis. I interrupted him before Carol could ask about the prognosis, which I knew she would do.

"Okay, doctor, thanks. We'll want to discuss this alone. We'll let you know our decision."

I took him by the arm and ushered him out of the room, but not before he again cautioned me about speed being of the essence and said he had scheduled surgery for the next day.

Surprised that he scheduled surgery without our consent, I said, "I'll let you know what we decide, but tomorrow is out; I want to get a second opinion!"

He seemed to take that as a personal affront, but I didn't give a shit.

Once I was alone with Carol, she cried and said she was really scared. We held each other for a long time, but as much as she needed me there, I knew she was doomed unless I could find a surgeon who could remove the entire tumor. I explained in very guarded terms that the odds for full recovery improved as a greater percentage of the tumor was removed and that I wanted to get a second opinion. I knew as a nurse, she would want to do that, so there was no problem in telling her I'd have to be away for a day to find other surgeons, then send them copies of her MRI's.

On the way home, I stopped off at the hospital records center and picked up three copies of Carol's MRI's, Then for the next twenty-eight hours straight, I explored the internet for brain surgeons across the country. After an arduous search, I identified three of the best doctors in their field: one at UCLA, one at NYU, and the third at University of Cincinnati Hospital. I immediately sent out overnight letters to them, each with a copy of Carol's MRI. Each doctor got back to me by the end of the next day. All three said that they felt certain they could do a full resection of the tumor, but that Carol needed the surgery almost immediately and none of them could fit her into their schedule.

I was devastated and angry. My wife was going to die because these guys were busy! I then questioned Carol's surgeon at the hospital.

"Why are these doctors saying they can remove the whole tumor and you're saying you can only get thirty percent of it?"

He again went into a lengthy discussion, saying they had not actually examined Carol and a lot of other crap. I grew more impatient and desperate by the minute. Then I remembered a conversation I had with our friend, Ed Butler, several years earlier in Florida!

We'd been sitting around at the tiki bar and Ed told us that his wife, Christine, once had a brain tumor. It hadn't been malignant, but it had been in a location that was life threatening, and they found a surgeon who saved her life when all others said they couldn't remove it. I immediately called Ed in Tennessee and explained Carol's situation. He could be a man of few words and just said, "Doctor Tew, Ron. You want to take Carol to Doctor Tew in Cincinnati! I researched the hell out of brain surgeons for

Christine. He is one of the best in the country. As far as we're concerned, he saved her life!"

I sat numbed before replying.

"Ed. He's one of the guys I contacted. He can't see her in time!"

There was silence, then he said, "Stay by the phone, Ron, stay right by the phone!"

A half hour later, Doctor Tew called me. He introduced himself, and without any further preamble, he said, "If you can't have her here by eight o'clock tomorrow morning, I can't see her."

I hesitated.

He then said, "Mister Ieva. Can you have her here by then or not?"

I wasn't even sure how far Cincinnati was, but I said, "Yeah, we'll be there!"

I looked at a map and thought, *Shit, Cincinnati is four hundred miles from here. That's at least an eight hour drive.* It was almost five in the afternoon. I could pack a couple of bags and be at the hospital in two hours, then on the road by eight. If I drove straight through the night, we could be there by four in the morning. As I raced back to the hospital, I wondered if Carol would be up to the trip, then I thought, *She'd have to; this was her only chance.*

I was scared and not even sure if this was the right thing to do, but three of the top doctors in the country said they believed a full resection was possible, and this ass in New Jersey was talking about a death sentence. Ed was right. He did more due diligence when buying anchor chain than most people did buying a boat. *This is the right thing to do. There's no more time to explore; I have to go with Doctor Tew.*

Carol was asleep when I got to her room. "Baby, wake up, it's me."

She opened her eyes and began to cry. Then putting her arms around me, she asked, "Where have you been all day?"

"I've been checking out surgeons, remember?"

I silently held her for a few minutes. Then, holding her hand, I told her everything I'd learned about glioblastoma brain tumors. I concluded by telling her about the three doctors who were confident they could do a full resection. I could see the fear well up in her, but she now needed to be fully aware of her prognosis.

As I wiped her tears away, she whispered, "Am I going to die, Ron?"

Fighting back my own tears, I said, "No, Baby. You're not going to die!"

I told her it was very serious, but that one of the surgeons from out of town said he could remove the tumor and would see her tomorrow morning. She quickly went right to where I knew she would go. "Does he take our insurance?"

I didn't know, but I lied. "Yes, I checked with our insurance, it's all okay" Then I added, "Carol, you have to decide right now, but I'm going to tell you, if you make the wrong decision, I'm going to ignore you. You have to have this operation and quickly before this thing becomes inoperable."

She was scared. "I don't know what to do, Ron."

"Listen to me. The doctor here says he can only remove thirty percent of the tumor, in which case you have no chance of beating this. Doctor Tew and two other top surgeons said a full resection is possible if done immediately."

She asked, "Is he coming to New Jersey?"

"No, we have to go to him."

"Where is he?" she asked.

"He's in Cincinnati. We have to be there by eight tomorrow morning or he can't fit you into his schedule."

"Oh, Ron, how far is Cincinnati? How did you find this guy? Are you sure he's good?"

"I'll explain everything in the car. Right now, we need to go! You've got to trust me on this, Baby. The three surgeons I found online are among best in the country, and they all felt confident they can do a full resection. Doctor Tew is the guy who saved Christine Butler."

She seemed shocked. "You spoke to the Butlers?"

"Yeah, Ed got us in to see Doctor Tew. Carol, I'm so sorry, but if this is a GBM and it isn't totally removed, you have no chance of surviving. None! Do you understand me? You will die within six months, a year at most. Please, Baby. Please trust me."

I put my arms around her and she cried convulsively. She needed to cry, and she needed me to hold her. I needed it as well, and as we hugged, I rocked her in my arms. Then, after just those few minutes of self-pity, her inner-strength returned.

She said, "Okay, call the nurse. I'm sure I need to be discharged by a doctor."

I hit the call button, but no one came, so I went out to the nurse station and said I was taking Carol away.

The nurse on duty said, "You can't do that, sir, I'll call the doctor."

The doctor came in and said, "She is a very sick woman. She'll have to be discharged by her own doctor."

I said, "Okay, thanks," then went to her room. I dressed Carol and wheeled her out over the protest of both the nurse and doctor who said they were calling security. An hour later, we were speeding away from New Brunswick in Carol's little red sports car, westbound for Ohio on Interstate 78.

It had been a long week and a difficult day, but with several naps along the way, we parked in front of The Mayfield Clinic at five forty in the morning. Now that we were here, it was impossible to sleep and we talked about the lunacy of the situation. If it wasn't so serious, it would be comical. Ten hours earlier, Carol was in a comfortable bed in a modern hospital; now we were sitting on the doorstep of some clinic in Cincinnati! I could see that she was sacred and still not sure this was the right decision. I told her that if she wasn't comfortable with this doctor, I'd take her right back to New Jersey, but in my mind, I knew that would be a death sentence.

At seven forty-five we went inside. The door was open, but there was no receptionist so we took a seat and nervously waited. Then at eight sharp, Doctor Tew came into the reception area. He was tall, with the kindest eyes imaginable, and he broke into a wide grin as he approached us. "I see you made it. You must be Carol!"

The rest of the morning, his staff did tests, including another MRI and an in-depth interview with Carol regarding her history of possible symptoms. At first she said there had been no symptoms other than the seizure and the strange event when she heard her grandmother's voice. But, as they questioned us further, it became apparent that little events we barely noticed over many months had been going on and were indicative that the tumor had been there a while.

At the end of the day, we met with Doctor Tew again and he laid it out for us in a caring but straightforward manner.

"The tumor had grown since the MRI you did in New Jersey just a week ago. Based on its nature among other things, it's very possible that this is a glioblastoma."

He explained that there were four grades, the worst being very aggressively malignant and that only a pathological test could determine that for certain. In any case, it had to be removed quickly.

He then took her hand and said, "Carol, rather than do a biopsy, I believe you must have surgery immediately. I'm confident that I can remove the entire tumor as it now exists, but any delay could change that." He went on to tell her about the risk of surgery and possible deficits, which included some memory loss and loss of sight in her right eye.

Carol acknowledged him, and then said, "And of course death, right?"

"Yes, Carol, that's true for any surgery, and this will be a very serious operation."

I sat dumbfounded, and then blurted out. "What the hell are you talking about, death?"

Carol held my hand and said death was a risk in any operation, then politely told me to be quiet. She asked the doctor if he would briefly describe the procedure. He hesitated an instant.

"Doctor, I'm a registered nurse. I'd like to know how you'll do it."

As he described the process, I got lightheaded and nearly fell off my chair. Nancy, the nurse practitioner steadied me and the three of them had a chuckle.

"Anymore questions, Carol? Ron?

Carol asked, "When can you do the surgery?

"The only time I can fit you in is tomorrow morning. I'm going to leave you and Ron alone to decide what you want to do."

Carol took his hand. "There's no need to leave us. I want you to do it!"

Suddenly for me, everything was happening too fast. "Hold on, Carol. We need to think about this!"

Still holding Doctor Tew's hand, she took mine and said, "You did your job, Baby. Now this man has to do his. I've made my decision."

After doing pre-surgical tests, we then got instructions from Nancy and walked out of the clinic into the late afternoon sun. We got into the car, and I didn't know what to say, so in a shaky voice, I asked, "Are you okay, Baby?"

She burst into tears and hugged me. "No, I'm not okay. I've got a fucking brain tumor and I'm scared. Please hold me."

We sat in the car a long time, maybe half and hour, and only the ringing of my cell phone broke the silence. It was my boss, Dan, calling to see how Carol was and to tell me our company had arranged a corporate apartment for us in Cincinnati.

"Okay, big guy, tell Carol we're all pulling for her!"

He gave me the number of the agent and told me to use it for as long as we needed, then said to call if there was anything else he could do. I thanked him and hung up, disbelieving. When I told Carol what Dan had said, she cried again.

"Are you hungry?" I asked.

She laughed. "Yes, I'm hungry! I haven't eaten since last night. Let's get something to eat then find the apartment."

The apartment turned out to be less than a fifteen minute drive from the hospital and afforded us a lot more comfort than a hotel room, especially since we'd been told we had to remain in Cincinnati for five days after the surgery. Sleep was almost impossible that night. I tried to comfort Carol, but somewhere between leaving the clinic and our late afternoon cheeseburgers, she put her fear aside, and as we lay embraced in bed, it was clear she was doing more to comfort me.

"I'm scared, Ron, but I want you to know if it doesn't go well tomorrow, these have been the happiest years of my life. I wouldn't have missed them for anything."

I held back tears and said, "Please don't talk like that. Everything is going to be okay." Hiding my fears from her, I silently prayed I was right.

The sun was rising when we arrived at the hospital the next morning, and after going through the insurance preliminaries, Carol was checked into a surgical suite. We were brought to a small private room, and she was told to undress and get in a gown and that someone would be in shortly. A few minutes later, a nurse came in, took some blood, and set up an IV port. Then we were alone. Nervously, I asked her if she wanted the TV on. "No, Ron. Just hold me and talk to me."

I held her tightly in my arms and fought back tears as I told her how much I loved her, then talked about all the things we were going to do in the future.

She said again, "I just want you to know you've made me so happy all these years and I love you."

"I love you too, Baby. You've made me the happiest man on earth."

I took her in my arms again, and we cried quietly together and through my tears, I begged her to come back to me. A moment later, they wheeled her away. I was sure I'd never see her again, then I got angry at myself for having so little faith. *She will be okay!* I thought.

I went to the surgical waiting room. The receptionist told me the operation was scheduled to be as long as ten hours, so there was little point in waiting at the hospital all day. Nevertheless, I felt I had to be there for Carol, and as morning became afternoon, I grew increasingly apprehensive. With each passing hour, surgeons of other patients told family members all went well, and by late afternoon, I was totally alone in the waiting room. I'd received periodic progress reports from a hospital representative, which I was thankful for, but more than ten hours had passed and I was sure something was wrong.

Sitting there alone, I thought of the years that had been stolen from us and about what could have been had we not drifted apart. Then I got angry because we hadn't just drifted apart, we were driven apart. I knew my thoughts were selfish, but they were mostly about what I could have given to Carol, the places we could have gone to, and the life we could have shared. I blamed her parents, but in my heart I knew they did what they thought was best for her. Then, for the first time, I looked to myself. I realized it had been in my power to keep her. I could have resigned from the academy and married her or simply married her and taken a chance that the marriage wouldn't be discovered. Then I thought, *So what if it had been discovered. I wouldn't have become an officer, but I could have still remained in the*

Navy, and we could have still lived a wonderful life. I cried. *What had I been thinking back then?*

Doctor Tew came in shortly before six. As he approached me, he broke into a big smile. "We got it all." He put his arm around my shoulder and repeated himself. "We got it all, Ron. She came through it very well."

"Is she really okay?" I asked, as I fought back tears.

He said, "She did really well throughout the entire operation. There were no complications, but we'll have to evaluate her condition in the morning to see if she has any deficits from the surgery."

Doctor Tew stayed with me a long time and talked with me about Carol and our fairy tale romance.

I asked, "Why were you so sure you could do a full resection while the doctor in New Jersey said he could only get thirty percent of it?"

"I can't speak for him, but my lack of experience early in my career would have also limited my own ability to get it all. I don't know, maybe he's done fifty of these; I've done perhaps a thousand, and bless the brave soul who was my first! It's getting late, I have to go. I'll check in on Carol several times a day, then I'll need to see her before you leave town next week."

He looked at his watch. "You should be able to see her in an hour or so."

I gave the doctor a big hug. "Thank you for saving my wife's life, doctor."

When I saw Carol she looked so helpless. Her face was bruised and swollen as if she had been beaten with a club.

She offered me a faint smile. "How are you, Baby?"

Hot tears rolled down my cheek as I took her hand in mine. "You've just been through ten hours of surgery and you're worried about how I'm feeling? How do you feel?"

She smiled. "I feel like crap. They just drilled a hole in my head and scooped out a piece of my brain, how do you think I feel?"

Fighting back new tears, I said, "Don't forget about the titanium plate they screwed into your skull."

She offered another smile. "No, I'll never forget about that."

"I was so scared, Carol. I thought I'd never see you again after they wheeled you away to surgery."

She patted my hand and comforted me when I should have been comforting her. A nurse came by and told me Carol had to rest, so I said I'd be back first thing in the morning. I kissed her gently, and she smiled, then pulled my hand to her cheek and closed her eyes and sighed softly. "Mmmm, I can't wait until we can sleep together again."

I drove back to the apartment in the rain thinking of how destiny saved Carol's life. The fact was, Doctor Tew saved her life, but had Ed Butler not intervened on her behalf, she surely would have died. My mind wandered back to that day in Fort Lauderdale when we met Ed, and it occurred to me how Carol played a crucial role in saving her own life.

I had come home from work, and as I walked through the courtyard gate toward our apartment, I heard Carol's voice out by the pool area. I strolled back and found her sitting and laughing with three guys, sipping beers.

She saw me and yelled out, "Oh, it's Ron! Hi, Baby. Come here and meet our new neighbors!"

After introductions, I went inside and changed, then brought out five more beers. Sitting at the table, I got briefed on how the impromptu party got started. Ed, his brother-in-law Lou, and their friend Tory had been checking out places to move their boat *Skirt Chaser.* As they tried to measure the distance between pilings in one of the slips at our property, Carol invited one of them aboard *Lastdance* so they could more easily hold the tape measure. She then brought out some iced teas, then beers, and proceeded to tell them what a great place Laudonnaire was and how we always cooked out and had a great time. The long and short of it was that based on her warm and friendly nature, they decided to rent the slip. That was the beginning of our friendship with them, a friendship that eventually saved her life.

Carol's kids drove out from New Jersey, which really boosted her morale. While she recuperated in the hospital for two more days, they shared the apartment with me, so when Carol was discharged, it was almost like coming home for her. She was weak and unsteady on her feet, but the measured attention of everyone and the sounds of her grandchildren was what she needed.

As hard as everything had been until now, a long and difficult road was ahead, beginning with getting Carol up to walk every hour. Having the apartment made everything so much easier because, although these short walks from the bedroom into the living room were tiring, it was better than walking in circles in a hotel room. The kids went back to New Jersey and we stayed on another three days until her post-surgical follow-up with Doctor Tew. He checked out her incision and performed some tests, and after referring us to a doctor at Memorial Sloan-Kettering Hospital in New York, he gave her his blessing to go home.

As we drove north on Interstate 71 toward Columbus, Carol burst into tears. "I'm so sorry to put you through this."

I got angry and pulled to the side of the road. "Damn it, Carol. Don't ever say that again!"

She reeled back from my angry shout. I felt bad that I yelled at her, but I was hurt and thought that she didn't understand how deeply I loved her. I sat there with my hands on the steering wheel and fumed.

Fighting back tears, I said. "I love you more than my own life, and if I could have taken that fucking thing out of your head and put it in mine, I would have."

She cried. "I'm so sorry, Baby. I know you would have done that for me."

Holding her in my arms, I said, "This isn't over; maybe the worst is yet to come. You can't be thinking this is a burden on me or you won't fight as hard as you're going to have to. Do you understand that?"

She nodded, and we sat there holding each other for a long time. I picked up her chin and looked into her eyes. "Are we in this together or not?"

Again, she nodded.

"Say it out loud; say we're in this together."

She smiled, and then shouted at the top of her lungs, "We're in this together!"

"That's my girl. Now can we get back on the road? We have a long way to go."

She wiped the tears from her eyes, giggled, and said, "Aye aye, captain!"

CHAPTER 25
WORST YEAR OF YOUR LIFE

Two weeks later, we met with Carol's neuroncology team at Memorial Sloan- Kettering Hospital in New York. Doctor Malkin headed up the group. Doctor Nolan and Nurse-Practitioner Eileen Tiernan rounded out the team that would manage Carol's post-surgical treatment. After explaining that she would be undergoing six weeks of radiation, Doctor Malkin then addressed the limited chemotherapy options.

We knew from our own research that chemotherapy was relatively ineffective against brain tumors due to the inability of these chemicals to penetrate the blood brain barrier. Carol asked about aggressive clinical trials. They told us about one trial that was showing some success. It used two existing chemo chemicals in concert, but we were cautioned that Carol might not qualify to participate in the trial. If she did, she would be in for a very tough time of it. We were given a package of material about the trial and details about the two drugs and their side effects, then set up a date to begin radiation in January.

After looking at the MRI's, Doctor Malkin said Carol's surgery was magnificent. He said to minimize the chance for a reoccurrence, the radiation would hopefully kill any remaining cancer cells. Radiation would be five days a week for six weeks, but could be done at the Sloan-Kettering affiliate in New Jersey. If Carol participated in the clinical trial, it would have to be carefully monitored, so it would be administered in New Your City. Even though I knew the statistics, I said, "Doctor, you keep using words like hopefully and minimize, what about cure?"

Carol interrupted me. "Ron, we know what the statistics are; let's just focus on the treatment!" Then looking at Doctor Malkin, she said, "I know what the odds are, but I want to live, and I'll do whatever it takes. I don't care if you have to pour battery acid on this damn thing; I can take whatever you dish out!"

The doctor smiled. "Good, you're a fighter. That's the attitude we'll need to beat this!"

He went on to tell us that because of Carol's good general health, age, and the full resection performed by Doctor Tew, she had a better chance of surviving than the statistics suggested. Before leaving, we set up a schedule for monthly MRI's, and the doctor gave her a prescription for a hairpiece. Carol stared at it a moment and pushed it back to him.

"I'm not going to need that; I'm not going to lose my hair!"

He tapped his finger on the prescription. "Carol, between the radiation and chemo, you're going to look like a cue ball. I'm sure you and Ron are okay with that, but many patients find that it helps their overall attitude to—"

She stopped him in mid-sentence. Fighting back tears, she said, "Doctor, I'm not going to lose my hair!"

She poked me in the chest and said, "He manages everything for me, and that's his job. Doctor Tew took the damn thing out of my head, and that was his job. You're going to treat me from now on, and that's your job, but I need a job. I need to be in control of something, and I'm going to control my hair!"

Doctor Malkin smiled. "Like I said, you're a fighter. Okay, we'll see you next month, but I'm going to tell you up front. Between the radiation and chemotherapy trial, this is going to be the worst year of your life! But, as I said earlier, you're in excellent general health and the surgery was very successful. I don't think I've ever seen anyone with a better chance of beating this."

When Carol was taken away to have blood drawn, Eileen passed me the hairpiece prescription. "Here, just in case she changes her mind."

It was all frightening for both of us, but, of course, more so for Carol. As we drove home, I promised I would be there for her no matter what happened and I would keep checking on the latest research. Once again, her concerns unselfishly focused on me. She fought back tears. "What about your job? You're going to have to take me for radiation every day for six weeks, then into the city for MRI's, then chemo. How are you going to take so much time off from work? What will they do?"

"Carol, stop it right now! The only thing that's important is you beating this thing. Nothing else matters! The only thing that's important about my job is the medical insurance. If they fire me, I can retire, so we'll still keep the insurance. Even if we have to, we can sell the boat and the house. I want you to tell me that you believe me that nothing else matters! Tell me, damn it!"

She cried and said she believed me, but I wasn't convinced, and I silently resolved to speak with my boss about what kind of support I could expect from work.

Dan saw me coming in the building the next morning and called me to his office.

"Hey, big guy, how's Carol?"

"She's in big trouble, Dan! This thing only has a three percent survival rate, and I need to be fully engaged in the fight with her. I'll be up-front with you. I'm going to need a lot of time off, and I can't do any traveling. I'm going to need my medical insurance, so if you want to replace me, I understand, but I'll do anything to keep employed for the insurance."

He stared at me. "Are you through babbling?"

I was taken aback, but I answered him. "Yeah, I guess so."

"Good, because I thought you were going to fall on your sword or something. Come on, let's go see Paul."

Paul was Dan's boss and headed up the global marine division. He and I started at the company thirty years earlier as service engineers. I counted him as a friend, but he was also a hard-nosed businessman, and I wasn't sure where this impromptu meeting going.

Paul asked about Carol's situation, and I repeated what I'd told Dan.

Then Dan said, "PD, Ron is of little faith. He's been chewing my ear off about not being able to travel or get in here at seven in the morning, so I thought you could tell him what we talked about."

Paul gave me his familiar reflective look, then said, "We understand the seriousness of this thing, so I'll be brief. Your first priority is Carol. You do whatever it takes for as long as it takes. Your job is not at risk. We'll do whatever we can to help, which includes Linda staying with Carol or taking her for treatments or whatever."

Dan interrupted, "The same goes for Barbara!"

Paul went on. "All I ask is that you do whatever you can to keep the business going. That means staying engaged with your team and customers by phone, teleconferencing, and email. In short, draw on whatever resources you need to get things done. You did a great job for us in Miami, and we think being flexible now is an investment in you, not a favor. Dan and I have no doubt that once Carol beats this, you'll be back to kick ass."

I had a physical reaction to that talk. It actually felt like a heavy burden had been lifted from my shoulders. I couldn't wait to tell Carol when I went home for lunch because I knew how much this concerned her. When I did tell her, she cried, but then asked me if I was making it up.

"Geez, do I have to get them to come here and tell you themselves?"

She said, "That would be nice, but no, I believe you, Baby."

When I told her that Paul's wife, Linda, offered to help with things she seemed to cheer up because they met in Miami many times and had really hit it off.

Carol was still very weak, but I felt that doing Thanksgiving at our place would cheer her up, so I invited the whole family over. She loved holiday gatherings, but after only a few hours, I could see she was exhausted. On my cue, everyone said they had to get going, and we were suddenly left alone again.

"I'm sorry I'm a party pooper, but I'm just so tired."

"Hey, you just had brain surgery two weeks ago! Don't worry about it! It's fine. We shared Thanksgiving with our family, and now we can be alone. Besides, I'm tired too, so how about we go lay down together?"

She smiled ever-so-slightly. "I always love to lay down with you, Baby."

I removed the cushions from the couch and lay down beside her and she fell asleep within a moment of taking her in my arms. I remember lying there, softly brushing her hair and wondering if she could really win this battle. I was eager for her to begin her radiation treatment, but before she could actually start, there were some preliminary things that had to be done. In December, we met with her Radio-oncologist, Dr Shupak. She had the bedside manner of an angel and Carol fully trusted this woman whose hands she would put her life into for the next six weeks.

The first thing that had to be done was to make a custom mask that form-fitted Carol's face. This had to be placed over her head and then clamped to the table to prevent even the slightest movement during radiation. When the mask was made, we returned to have Carol's head tattooed with three small dots. Once the radiation treatments began, she would be rigidly clamped to the table and lasers would be used to align the small tattoos so that the radiation beams could be precisely aimed at an exact location in her brain. This would focus maximum energy on the tumor site while minimize damage to surrounding brain tissue. With all of the preparation done, she was scheduled to begin radiation on Jan 2, 2002, for thirty-three sessions over the next six and a half weeks.

By the end of December, Carol said she was feeling well enough to go to Rhonda's annual Christmas party in Connecticut. I wasn't sure if she was up to it, but she had been cooped up in the house since we returned from Cincinnati, and I believed she needed to get out, see friends, and socialize a little. We stayed over, so it wasn't too difficult a trip and it was good to see her mingle with others including our friends Joe and Julie.

Driving back to New Jersey the next day she told me she had a lot of fun and said she heard me make plans for New Years Eve with Joe.

I said, "No, he just mentioned doing something with them." She didn't say anything. "Are you okay, Baby?"

"I'm fine, but I want to ask you a favor."

"What is it?"

She took my hand as if she were going to ask me to buy her a Rolls Royce or something. She said, "I'd like to go to Times Square for New Year's Eve!"

I laughed. "That's it? That's the favor?"

She looked at me through sad eyes and said she had always wanted to do that ever since we went steady back in Brooklyn, and that this might be her last chance.

I fought back tears. "Carol, don't go there. We'll do it because you want to do it, not because you're afraid this will be your last chance."

She held my hand in hers and patted me. "I'm sorry, Ron. I'm just so scared."

She quickly composed herself and asked, "Have you ever gone to Times Square for New Year's Eve?

"No," I said and smiled. "I guess that makes us both Times Square virgins. Let's go then!"

She smiled contently as we crossed the George Washington Bridge into New Jersey.

We drove back into New York on New Year's Eve. The events of 9/11 continued to instill fear in many New Yorkers, and hotel rooms were plentiful and inexpensive, so we got a room right in Times Square. After checking in, Carol wanted to go for a walk, but even using her cane, she became tired, and after only a few blocks, she asked me to take her back to the hotel. Staying out until midnight would be impossible, and I sensed her disappointment. Once back in the room she cried. I felt helpless to do anything but hold her and tell her it was alright.

She snapped at me. "It's not alright; I wanted to do this. I made you spend so much money on this hotel and I can't even walk two blocks!"

She tried to pull away, but I pulled her closer to me. "You disappoint me, but not because we can't be out there for New Year's. You disappoint me because you don't have any confidence in me. I keep telling you, nothing is important to me except you winning this battle and being happy."

Becoming suddenly angry, I lost my temper and yelled at her. "Damn it, Carol. I know you might not beat this! It scares me and makes me want to cry every minute of every day, so in my fucking world, nothing else is even remotely more important than making you happy. Why can't you understand that?"

My outburst surprised us both. I squeezed her tight. "I'm so sorry, Baby. I didn't mean to yell at you. I'm just so scared for you. Please forgive me."

We sat there on the bed comforting each other until she said, "I'm okay, but my legs feel weak; help me get into the bathroom."

While she was using the toilet, I opened the window drapes and began laughing my ass off. "Holy shit!" I said aloud. "Holy shit!"

She called for me to help her, and when I opened the bathroom door, she said, "What's going on? What was so funny?"

I laughed again, and holding her arm to steady her, I said, "Come with me."

We walked to the window and there in front of us was a spectacular view of Times Square, facing north, with throngs of people already packed in like sardines. To our right, not fifty yards away and almost at our eye level, was the famous ball.

"Oh my God!" she said. "We have grandstand seats!"

I held her tightly and said, "Happy anniversary, Princess. Thirty-eight years of going steady!"

We kissed softly and she asked, "How did you arrange for this incredible view?"

"I didn't; we just lucked out."

It was true, but I don't think she ever fully believed me, but who cares; we spent New Year's Eve in Times Square together.

As we apprehensively prepared to begin Carol's radiation treatment, I recalled a painting I had seen in a nautical museum. It was of the S.S. President Roosevelt standing by a disabled and sinking British freighter in a severe storm. As conditions grew worse in the tumultuous seas, the only comfort the crew of S.S. Antinoe found was from two signal flags that S.S. President Roosevelt had hoisted from her yardarm. They were the international code flags for the letters A, flown over the letter I, which meant, "I will not abandon you." I decided, that would be our rallying cry and printed out an 8" x 10"copy of the painting and mounted it on top of our television. I then explained it to Carol with tears in my eyes.

I clasped her hands in mine and said, "A over I, Baby, A over I."

As the radiation treatments progressed and Carol became increasingly weaker, she began to lose weight and became more dependent on a cane, then a walker to get around. After the second week of radiation, we went for her January MRI and we were hit with staggering news. There was a small spot not far from the original tumor site. I asked the doctors what could be done. They said, "Right now, nothing! We'll need to wait until the next MRI and see what effect the radiation has on it."

Panicked, I said, "We can't wait. What about surgery?"

Carol squeezed my hand. "Ron, you're scaring me. Let's just do what Doctor Malkin says."

Everyday was torture, and as we wondered what was going on inside Carol's head, she again offered me as much comfort to me as I gave to her.

She said, "At least we're doing something, right?"

"Yeah, I guess we are," I said without much conviction.

She was right, of course. Doing the radiation every morning made us feel like we were fighting back, not just passively letting things happen. When her hair began to thin, she was disappointed over losing that fight, but she quickly bounced back. One night while in bed, she blurted out, "Have you have had sex with a redhead?"

I looked at her as if she was crazy. "What did you say?"

"You heard me. Have you ever had sex with a redhead?"

"No, I haven't."

"Did you ever want to?"

I laughed. "I guess over the years I've sometimes fantasize about the image of a fair-skinned woman with flaming red hair."

Slowly facing me, she said, "Good, because I want to get a hair piece, and we may as well make it flaming red and fulfill your fantasy."

"What's this all about?" I asked.

She said, "As hard as I've willed it not to happen, my hair is thinning. I haven't even started chemo yet, so call Eileen and get the prescription for a hair piece."

I said, "Don't be mad, but Eileen gave it to me back in December."

She punched my arm. "Oh you stinker, you!"

"Hey, I put it away and never said a word to you. I've never had sex with a bald woman either, so I'm happy to leave it in the drawer."

"You won't mind me being bald?" she asked.

"Carol, I'd rather have you bald than see you with a hairy chest, but you have to be comfortable with whatever you do. How much can a hair piece cost, a few hundred dollars? Let's just get it, then you can use it if you want to. Okay?"

"Okay, I'm going to keep up my will power battle, but let's buy it."

She got one in her natural color which she never once used because she never did lose her hair. The other hairpiece was flaming red, and she never used it outside our bedroom.

At the end of the fourth week of radiation, we did another MRI. This one was the scariest. I held Carol's hand as we silently waited for the results, both knowing that her odds of surviving a recurring tumor were worse than the initial one. I thought to myself, *What is taking them so long?*

A split-second later, Carol asked aloud, "What is taking them so long?"

I smiled, thinking, *We are surely connected in some mysterious way.*

Fifteen minutes later, Doctor Malkin came in, and we could tell from the look on his face that it was good news.

"You're not out of the woods, but it's half the size it was a month ago, so it seems the radiation is having an effect on it. I'm really encouraged by how you're responding!"

It was great news, but the following weeks went by slowly, and once radiation was finished, a sense of helplessness crept in. Once again we felt like we were doing nothing. In spite of her weakened condition, Carol remained positive. She focused on doing peripheral things such as researching nutritious diets for cancer patients, sometimes putting menus together for me to prepare meals from. It helped her to be proactive, and if nothing else, she was convinced it contributed to winning the battle she waged with her hair, which hadn't thinned anymore than during the early weeks of radiation.

The March MRI was cause for celebration. There was no evidence of a tumor! We were more than elated because in addition to being life-threatening, a tumor might have also disqualified her from participating in the chemotherapy trial she was scheduled to begin in April.

The chemotherapy consisted of using two agents; BCNU and Temador. These were both existing drugs for brain tumors but hadn't been used in concert before. The BCNU was administered intravenously during regular visits to Sloan-Kettering in New York City. The Temador was taken orally at home in cycles lasting as long as fourteen days. She was also on Decadron, a steroid to control brain swelling, and Nupergen, a drug to help maintain white blood cell counts, which I had to administer by injection into her belly.

Doctor Malkin was right. It was becoming the worst year of Carol's life. Seizures were scary for both of us at first, but we learned to deal with them. Between March and July, however, Carol needed seventeen transfusions, mostly blood platelets, but also whole blood. The chemo was devastating, and I watched her deteriorate a little more each day. Where she was once vibrant and full of life, she was now a frail, emaciated woman who could barely stand without my help. It broke my heart to leave her in the morning to go to work, and it broke my heart to see her this way when I came home in the evening, but not once did she complain or ask, *"Why me?"*

Due to her low blood counts, I was afraid to touch her for fear of bruising her. For the same reason, sex was out of the question. In the scheme of things, that wasn't an issue for us, but physical intimacy had been a very important part of our relationship, and we both missed sharing the emotional closeness. I'd touch her gently and trace my fingers over her lips, then embrace her as tenderly as possible. Still, she'd sometimes bruise. Yet, when the doctors talked of removing her from the trial because of the effect it was having on her, she begged them not to.

Struggling to hold back tears, she became emotional and said, "I still have my memory and I can still read. I know chemo doesn't do much for brain tumors, but whatever it's doing to my body, it must be doing something to the damn cancer cells, right?"

Doctor Malkin said, "Maybe, but your blood counts are not rebounding fast enough; I think we should stop."

Carol stared at him fiercely. "Stop? I don't want to stop! I've been in really bad storms on our boat, you know. You can't just stop! If you just stop when it gets too rough you'll fucking sink the boat, so don't ask me to stop!"

We all laughed at her colorful retort, but he explained that the strict trial criteria would prevent them from keeping her in it if her conditioned worsened.

Her answer to that was, "Well, I just won't get any worse, damn it! Besides, how the hell can I get much worse and live?'"

Somberly, he said, "That's exactly my point, Carol." His words sending a chill through my body.

Carol's condition remained just barely above the minimum criteria for the next two months, so they kept her on the trial and she dealt with it heroically. Her MRI's continued to be squeaky clean every month, which as she put it, "That is the point of the whole damn exercise, right?"

Chapter 26
Back to Chesapeake Bay

In April 2002, Doctor Malkin left Sloan-Kettering and Doctor Nolan took over Carol's case. By then, she was seriously debilitated from the combined effects of radiation and the aggressive chemo program. She was frail and had lost almost fifty pounds, but she was determined as ever to make the voyage with me to Chesapeake Bay at the end of May. I suggested delaying the trip until she was stronger.

She said, "Stronger, my ass. You know what the statistics are of me beating this. I'm probably going to get weaker, not stronger, and I want to make this trip!"

Then she softly pleaded, "Please, Baby. It may be my last chance to sail on our boat."

I didn't want her to talk like that, but I knew she was being realistic, not pessimistic, and if things didn't go well, I didn't want to deny her a chance to sail once more.

I took her in my arms. "Okay, but Doctor Nolan has to give his approval."

Carol's monthly MRI was scheduled for May 18, so we planned a departure date for the following week along with John and Gail in *Tranquility*. Also, we wanted to join our old marina friends for their annual Memorial Day raft-up in Baltimore so we'd be sailing straight there from New Jersey. *Lastdance* was launched on May 3, and in between work and taking care of Carol, I hanked on her sails and got her ready to leave. I'd brief Carol each night on how the work was progressing and she'd excitedly question me to be sure I didn't forget anything. I could see that even stuck at home, the process of spring launching had a positive effect on her.

She was unusually quiet as we drove into New York for her MRI. We were both quiet during this monthly ritual because, with each test, we feared the news we might be given. Once there, we went through our routine of doing the MRI and blood work in the morning and then had lunch. Afterwards, we'd wait for the results at two o'clock in Dr. Nolan's office. As with almost every month since her surgery, the doctor came in with a big smile, saying the MRI was squeaky clean. The bad news was her blood counts were borderline and she was very weak. We'd have to follow up with more blood test in a few days.

The doctor questioned the wisdom of her going anywhere on a boat, cautioning us that with her counts so low, even a small bruise could become serious.

"Carol, I don't think you should make this trip!"

She fought back tears and said more as a statement than a question, "Isn't quality of life important?" Then she added, "If my blood counts are the concern, what if we did a test everyday along the way?"

Dr. Nolan asked, "Can you do that?"

I jumped into the conversation. "Yes we can! We're stopping every night. I'll find a lab in each port. We can do a test, and they can fax you the results. If at any time you feel she shouldn't go on, I'll take her home or bring her here, and I'll continue to give her Nupergen injections!"

I could sense Carol's level of anticipation increase as Doctor Nolan pondered this proposal. He looked at her, and seeing her face full of hope, he then smiled and said, "Be gentle with her! Remember, blood work every day and have them faxed here without fail. Eileen will give you the prescriptions."

Upon leaving the hospital, there was no mistaking the small bounce in Carol's step. It was as if she had been injected with an invigorating serum that nourished her body and spirit. She held my hand tightly as we drove home, and we talked about the voyage and the stopover in Baltimore. I told our friends in Maryland we were returning to the marina but made no mention we might be joining them for the Memorial Day weekend. Carol was now bubbling with excitement about surprising them and talked jovially about sneaking up on them and blasting loud music with our flags flying. It was really good to see her so energized.

After a brief internet search, I found blood labs and taxi companies in the three ports we planned on visiting. The night before departure,
we had dinner with John, Gail, and Charlie, who was making the trip
with them as far as Cape May. The forecast was for northwest winds, which
boded well for a southerly sail and contributed to our good mood and camaraderie. It felt good to watch Carol share in the fun, and we joked with
her about not being able to drink, but she didn't care. She was going to sail
to Chesapeake Bay, and that's all that mattered to her.

Back on *Lastdance,* we needed two heaters to warm the boat, and
as we prepared to go to bed, Carol hummed a cheery tune, something she
hadn't done since being diagnosed seven months earlier. I was happy to see
her spirits so high, but she still looked frail and her movements were slow
and carefully calculated for fear of bruising herself. I put my arms tenderly
around her and said, "I love you, Princess."

She leaned her head back against my shoulder and held my hands to
her breasts. "I know you do, Ron. I know that with all my heart; it's what
enables me to deal with this." She asked, "Would you do something for
me? Would you put on the Anne Murray CD and play "Could I Have This
Dance", and dance with me?"

I smiled. "Yeah Carol, of course. I'd love to dance with you."

And there on our little ship in the thirty-ninth year since I asked
her to go steady, I danced with my beautiful wife. She tired quickly and
couldn't finish the dance, and I wondered if she would still be with me the
following spring.

The alarm clock sounded at five in the morning, and I jumped up
to stop it from waking Carol. I turned up the heaters and put coffee on and
went on deck to get the boat ready. I promptly fell on my ass with a loud
thud!

"Ice?" I yelled.

It must have sounded terrible below and Carol called up, "Are you
okay, Ron?"

"Yeah, I'm alright, but I can't believe it; there's ice on deck."

Being extra careful removing the sail cover and rigging the halyard,
I mumbled, "Ice, damn it; I can't believe there's ice in May!"

I went below for coffee and something to eat and found Carol up and about. Even though the cabin was toasty warm, she was bundled in jeans and two sweaters.

I said, "You look really cold. I can get us out of here alone, go back to bed."

She growled, "Coffee, please! Am I still the first mate on this ship or not?"

I smiled. "Yes you are, Baby. Yes you are."

"Good," she said. "Then stop giving me shit about going back to bed, and get the donuts." I passed her the donuts and sat beside her. As we quietly ate, I looked at the clock. It was almost six. It was time to radio *Tranquility*.

Gail answered. "John is on deck. Are you guys ready?"

Before I could answer, Carol yelled out, "We were born ready!"

Gail laughed. "Okay, we'll see you in the creek in ten minutes. *Tranquility* out."

Slipping lines, we glided silently into Cheesequake Creek as *Tranquility* went by. It was very cold and like us, they were all bundled in ski jackets and watch caps. John called out, saying, "Can you believe this. The temperature was only thirty-one degrees when I got up."

Then Gail asked, "Where's Carol?"

I pointed to the pile of blankets against the cabin top just as she poked her arm and head out and waved. "Here I am!"

Then, with the blaring horn of the bridge opening, we stood out into Raritan Bay.

Carol impatiently asked if we could sail.

I laughed. "Is it okay if we leave the inlet first?"

She pouted. "It just seems warmer when we sail."

"If you're cold, let me take you below?"

"No, I'm alright, really."

Once clear of the inlet, I came to 090°m, a course that would take us to Flynns Knoll and Sandy Hook Channel.

I said, "I'm just going to get clear of Conaskonck Point before I raise the sails."

"Can we see the house?" she asked.

The house, being our old house on Matawan Point on the west shore of Keyport Harbor.

Remembering how much Carol loved the place, I said we should be able to see it in fifteen minutes, and I'd let her know when we could. We were sorry we sold it, but it was a hard commute for me to work, and we would have eventually sold it anyway when we moved to Florida. Matawan Point soon came into view, and slowing the boat to a crawl, I then turned north so Carol could see the house without having to get up from under her blankets.

Knowing why I turned the boat, she said, "Thank you, Ron."

I passed her the binoculars. She looked for a moment, then said, "Remember how we'd sit out back and look out over the bay?"

"Yeah I remember." Then thought to myself, *I also remembered how carefree life was for us then and wondered if would ever be that way again...I knew it wouldn't.*

Saddened by those thoughts, I quietly headed the boat into the wind and prepared to raise sail. Carol asked if I needed help, but I told her the wind was light and I could manage.

Then, as an afterthought, I said, "You can take a few hours steering later when it warms up, okay?"

She seemed satisfied with that. "Okay, I'd like that."

A few minutes later, we were sailing at a gentle five knots on a beam reach. She smiled as soon as I killed the engine, and as she often did when we began to sail, she said, "Ahhhh, peace and tranquility!"

We sailed silently and Carol slept until the boat's motion changed when we encountered the ocean swell after rounding Sandy Hook.

Waking, she jokingly asked, "Are we there yet?"

"No, Baby. We're only at Sandy Hook. We still have twenty-four miles to go for Manasquan."

She said, "I gotta pee. How long will it take?"

"We're doing six knots, so maybe four hours if the wind keeps up, but it seems to be veering to the north, so we may slow down some."

She sat up. "I can't wait four hours."

Before I could protest, she declared. "I'll be careful, I promise!"

"Carol, I can furl the jib and let the main luff and help you."

Adamant, she said, "No, I'll be okay, I promise. I'll hold on with two hands." Then, smiling, she added, "Just keep the boat steady, or do I have to show you everything?"

I growled, and she stuck her tongue out at me, then smiled softly and blew me a kiss.

With the wind almost due north, the boat wasn't heeling much, so I said, "Okay, but be very careful. Remember, one bad bruise and this trip is over for you."

I watched nervously as she went down the companionway ladder, but she negotiated the steps easily, and as promised, she walked to the head holding onto handrails with both hands. When she was done, she said she was going to stay below awhile to warm up, but to call her when we got to Shark River. I knew she must have been feeling tired, and I was relived that she was getting out of the cold and doubly pleased when she gave me a chocolate donut. Later, the wind dropped to ten knots. I unfurled the staysail and we were quickly doing to six knots again.

With the sun higher in the sky, the air warmed considerably. After several hours of a near perfect sail, I called Carol when we approached Shark River. She came on deck after first making a cup of instant soup for me, and as she passed it up, I smiled, thinking, *Even sick and weak, she is always thinking about me.* I watched her climb the steps, and I only felt comfortable when she sat safely beside me. Turning her face up to the sun, she said, "Oh, it's so nice up here in the sun; it feels warmer than down below!"

A moment later, she asked if she could steer. I gladly said I could use a break to use the head.

She said, "Wow, you've been holding it all this time?"

I laughed. "No, I peed down the scupper and rinsed it with the water jug."

In an exaggerated tone of disgust, she said, "Oh gross. Is that what they taught you in the Navy?"

I laughed and said, "Hey, I remember you peeing in your foul weather gear once!" Then I added, "And you don't want to know what they taught us in the Navy."

When I returned to the cockpit, she said, "I love it when we have all three sails flying. Can I keep steering?"

"Of course, just tell me when you get tired."

"I promise I will." Then she asked, "Where is *Tranquility?*"

Pointing astern, I said, "See that boat way back there. That's them!"

John was several miles back and way inshore of us. That would put us in before them, giving us time to get secured in our dock and go to the blood lab before they got in.

Approaching Manasquan Inlet, Carol said, "We're almost running on this course; we could easily sail in the inlet when I turn west and come onto a reach."

I glanced up at the wind indicator. The wind was still north at eight knots.

"Let me know when you want to do it, but you look really tired. Are you feeling okay?"

"I feel weak, but I want to do this."

She bore off for a while to get well clear of the north jetty, then began a slow steady turn to starboard until the boom moved to port with a slight jolt. I trimmed the sheets, and we smoothly came to a new heading of 318°m, aligning nicely with the channel.

"Do you remember when we came in here in *Ursaorion?*"

"Even with only half a brain left, I could never forget that day. I was so scared we would go on the rocks, it was so rough!"

I considered my own fears that day and how fickle the sea could be because it was totally different today with this gentle northerly breeze. Back then, onlookers must have expected us to be rolled over by the crashing waves at the mouth of the inlet. Today, however, we must have been a pretty sight with all three sails flying as we moved noiselessly through the water. As we ghosted up the inlet, a fisherman on the south jetty looked up and waved. We waved back at him, then a look of recognition came over Carol's face. "Oh my god, it's George!"

It was an unlikely place to encounter her ex-spouse, but there he was, fishing pole in hand, mouth agape as he watched in disbelief as Carol skillfully handled our beautiful ship under full sail. I was pleased for her that he witnessed how well she was doing health wise, but also that she could so easily sail *Lastdance* in tight quarters. It was the first time I had ever detected even a hint of smugness in her voice as she said, "Oh, I'm so glad I'm on the helm right now!"

Still smiling, she waved and said, "Hi, George." Then looking at me, she said quietly, "He didn't think I was smart enough to handle the lousy workboat we had."

When Gull Island was abeam, Carol headed up *Lastdance* and I furled the headsails and then dropped the main. A few minutes later, we tied up to the T-dock at the Brielle Yacht Club. There was still no sign of *Tranquility,* so after calling a taxi, I called John on the radio and told him we were going to have Carol's blood drawn. The lab was a short ride away in Manasquan. We were even able to have the taxi wait for us, and we were back on *Lastdance* thirty minutes later. Carol's kids arrived shortly after that. It was a great get-together. We were also joined by our friend, Jane, and Charlie's wife, Val, and after two rounds of drinks, we all marched off to the Sand Dollar restaurant for dinner.

We departed early the next morning for Atlantic City, fifty-four miles down the coast. The winds were northeast at twelve knots the whole way, and Carol seemed to be drawing strength from the voyage. She even relieved me on the helm every couple of hours until we arrived at Absecon Inlet in mid-afternoon. We stayed at a small marina on Clam Creek opposite the expensive casino marina where Carol stayed when she helped deliver *Ursaorion* ten years earlier. The area was reminiscent of the village in *Popeye.* There were rickety old wooden houses, restaurants, and a pier, but the marina was well-maintained and friendly.

After going to the blood lab in the morning, we then made the thirty-six mile run from Atlantic City to Cape May. It was another near perfect day of sailing, and we were treated to several pods of dolphin swimming alongside *Lastdance.* Carol said they were a personal escort for her, and as she had often done in years past, she asked me to put Enya's "Caribbean Blue" on the stereo. She shouted with glee as the number of dolphins increased until moments later, they were all around us. It sent a chill up my spine as they almost surrounded *Lastdance* and swam along with us. Carol looked at me with her best "I told you so," stare. She asked me to take the helm and when I did, she sat with her arm over the side humming along with Enya. I suppressed my tears as I watched her derive so such joy from these creatures.

We arrived in Cape May where Val was waiting on the dock to join us for dinner at the Lobster House. While everyone had drinks before dinner, Carol and I went off in a taxi to yet another blood lab, returning within the hour to join our friends in the restaurant. We had a great meal together, and Carol even threw caution to the wind and took a sip of wine when we made a toast to her for making the voyage.

Before turning in for the night, John and I met to discuss the next day's sail, which would take us from Cape May to Chesapeake City on the western side of the C&D canal. It was going to be the longest and most difficult part of the passage, a total of sixty-four miles in all. We agreed that a five o'clock departure would give us a fair tide most of the way up Delaware Bay. Also, listening to the weather forecast, we were encouraged by the predicted twelve knot southwest winds, which would speed our journey.

Waking at four in the morning, I tried my best not to wake Carol, but she sensed me leaving our bed and insisted on helping me. After a quick breakfast and a chat with John, we got underway before sunrise and motored through the Cape May Canal in the subdued light of dawn. To our surprise, we were greeted at the northern terminus by four-foot waves and fifteen-knot wind from the northwest, not southwest. Entering Delaware Bay, we began to tack our way north into the teeth of the opposing wind and waves. Carol huddled under blankets against the cabin top, and I worried that she was getting jostled around and suggested we turn back and try again the next day. She reminded me that all her blood work had come back with good counts, then laughing, she took sarcastic jab at me. "Unless this is too rough for you, Baby!"

I responded by letting out a wild yell. "Arrgghh."

Pressing on, we made less than four knots and *Tranquility* even less. The problem was the opposing wind and current was setting up big steep waves that broke over our bow, sometimes bringing *Lastdance* to almost a complete stop. We had a five-hour current window and although we looked forward to diminishing waves once it changed, we would lose the fair current, which would slow our already poor progress, putting us further behind schedule.

Finally, after a hard fought battle up Delaware Bay, we entered the C&D canal more than twelve hours after leaving Cape May. The current was against us and ran as much as two knots, but we made it to the anchorage in Chesapeake City by eight o'clock. The anchorage, like the canal, is maintained by the U.S. Army Corps of Engineers. It's located on the waterway's south bank and is dredged to a depth of fifteen feet and offers good protection from the wakes of tugs and large ships passing less than fifty yards away.

Even in the fading light I could see the lines of exhaustion on Carol's face as she stood to take the helm so I could get the anchor ready. She motored slowly through the crowded anchorage and found a hole with enough room for us to anchor and have *Tranquility* raft to us when they arrived.

Carol called out, "Eleven feet," as she brought *Lastdance* to a stop.

I nodded and she slowly backed down with only the sound of sixty feet of anchor chain running out over our bow roller. I would have preferred more scope but the crowded conditions made that impossible so we took extra care to be sure the anchor was well set. Killing the engine, Carol sat back against the cockpit combing, too tired to get our drinks or even return to her favorite position against the cabin top.

There were several restaurants and bars along the anchorage perimeter, one of which had a live band playing. Under any other circumstances, Carol would have insisted on going ashore after dinner, but not tonight. I didn't think she could even stay awake long enough for John and Gail to arrive. Going below to make myself a drink, I asked her if she wanted anything. She didn't answer. She was sitting up behind the helm, already snoring. I sat beside her and lowered her head to my lap, then covered her with a blanket and softly stroked her hair until *Tranquility* came alongside.

Gail heated up a big pot of soup, and after waking Carol, we went aboard *Tranquility* for a simple but delicious meal of thick-crusted Italian bread, soup, and wine. We discussed the day's sail and agreed that if the wind had been southwest as predicted it would have made all the difference, and we would have arrived in Chesapeake City four or five hours earlier. That's the uncertainty of sailing though, and like it or not, it's the variables of wind and tide that make it so challenging.

It was forty-seven miles to Baltimore. That meant another long day on the water. Being slower than us, John said he wanted to leave at dawn in order to get in before six in the evening. Carol was exhausted, so I said we were going to sleep late in the morning and would try to catch up to them. We agreed to keep in touch by radio, and by ten o'clock, Carol and I were back aboard *Lastdance* and sound asleep.

Shortly after dawn, I heard *Tranquility* cast off lines, the muted sound of her engine fading as they left the anchorage in the early morning mist. I rolled onto my side and kissed Carol's shoulder, then put my arm around her and drew her close to me. Even in a deep sleep, she snuggled closer to me, and I closed my eyes and before falling asleep again, I tried to will away the deadly thing that might still be in her head.

I woke later, feeling refreshed for the first time in days. The sky was a brilliant blue and the sun was already warming the cabin. After coffee and biscotti for breakfast, I gently woke Carol and told her that I was getting underway and that she should stay in bed. I expected her to protest and became mildly concerned when she said, "Thank you, Baby. I'm so tired, I want to sleep."

Raising the anchor as quietly as possible, I then slipped out of Chesapeake City, turning west into the canal, then Elk River, which would soon open into the increasingly wider expanses of Chesapeake Bay.

Carol peered up the companionway at ten o'clock. "Good morning, Baby. Is there any coffee?"

"Good morning. Coffee is in the thermos!" I replied.

She handed the cup up and came on deck, then gave me a kiss and cheerfully thanked me for letting her sleep in.

Looking around, she shouted, "Oh, we're on the bay!"

Then laughing, she shed tears of joy, put her arms around my neck, and said, "Welcome home, Baby!"

By mid-afternoon, the wind came up from the south at eight knots as forecasted. Nevertheless, we sailed close, hauled at four knots, our excitement increasing as we approached Baltimore and our old friends, most of whom we hadn't seen in years. The wind increased and we overtook *Tranquility* on the Patapsco River, waving as we passed them close aboard. Approaching the Key Bridge twenty minutes later, I pointed out Fort Carroll, and as I had done many times before, I said, "They named it after you."

As always, she smiled and said, "Well, they spelled it wrong; see what you can do about getting it changed, buster!"

We laughed, and I held her close to my side as we sailed *Lastdance* over the spot Francis Scott Key wrote the Star Spangled Banner from the deck of his ship as the British bombarded Fort McHenry three miles away.

Continuing past Canton, then Fells Point, we approached the Inner Harbor and Carol took the helm as I prepared our holiday flags for a grand entrance. I called Jane on her cell phone, and she confirmed that no one knew we were coming.

"Okay, that's good. We'll be coming around the aquarium in about ten minutes. *Tranquility* is about half an hour behind us; we'll see ya soon."

I raised our large flags up the full height of our mast, and we immediately caught the attention of everyone who could see them. A large American flag was at the truck, followed by a POW flag, then one flag for each of the services my family had served in...Army, Navy, and Marines. A blue Naval Academy flag followed, then a red and white striped Navy rattlesnake flag with the words "Don't Thread on Me," and lastly, a Vietnamese flag consisting of a yellow field and three horizontal red stripes.

Carol loved watching them fly in the breeze and I had to caution her to keep an eye on her course. I went below and readied the stereo, then came back on deck with just minutes to spare as Carol steered a more westerly course toward the Inner Harbor along its south boundary. Looking around to be sure it was clear, she then came to a northeasterly course, steering right for the anchorage under the World Trade Center. We could see the eight boat raft up with *Bliss* in the center and recognized *Seawoof* and *Tiami,* but the other five boats were new to us. Seconds later, with *Lastdance* heeled over smartly, I put a CD on the stereo and cranked up the volume as the song "Southern Cross" came on. Aboard the rafted boats, heads turned in our direction and faces peered at us until over the din of music, we heard Gene's voice: "Holy cow, it's *Lastdance!*"

It was an exciting reunion, especially for Carol. Once we were rafted to *Seawoof*, everyone came over to greet her, but their surprise at her frail condition was unmistakable. Where she had been so demonstrative and animated in years past, she was now reserved about hugging and kissing due to her concern over infection because of her low white cell counts. I made a mental note to explain it to several friends in private later on.

Tranquility soon entered the anchorage and came alongside us, and once secured, we introduced John and Gail to everyone. With Carol chatting away with friends in our cockpit, I felt liberated enough to embark on a bit of a binge now that we were settled in. Gail noticed me let loose and whispered to me that she would keep an eye on Carol and get her to bed if I overdid things.

I could see she was tired, but she wouldn't take a break. She was having fun for the first time in more than seven months and nothing was going to deter her. As night fell, the wind piped up to sixteen knots and some boats in the anchorage began to drag their anchors, but even that was exciting for her. Then, as one of the sailboats was trying to re-anchor, a large dinner cruise ship collided with it. Fortunately, no one was hurt, but it could have been a disaster, especially if the ship had hit our raft up! Carol, who would normally worry about stuff like that, simply found it entertaining, and given all she had been through, I understood.

The next day, our friends Pete and Rhonda drove down from Connecticut to spend Memorial Day with us. Rhonda had visited with Carol several times over the past months but Pete hadn't seen her since their Christmas party and I could see that he, like the others, was taken aback at her appearance. Still, when someone made a motion to go ashore to the Mexican restaurant overlooking the harbor, Carol was first to second it. Then, while five of us consumed margaritas, she became intoxicated with the festival atmosphere and life that abounded around her. I knew this was good for her, and I was glad we came.

Monday morning, we weathered a thunderstorm while still at anchor, and when the weather settled down, we sailed to our marina on

Kent Island. Carol was happy John and Gail had moved their boat to Chesapeake Bay, especially now that *Tranquility* and *Lastdance* were side-by-side on the same dock. We were anxious to explore, but no one more than Carol, who seemed to draw spiritual strength from this beautiful body of water. She was still on chemo, however, and she required periodic transfusions, so most of our sailing depended on how she was feeling, but even on good days, we were limited to short sails where I could quickly get her medical attention if needed.

The chemo continued to take its toll on her health and we spent much of that summer at Sloan-Kettering in New York for treatments, tests, and transfusions. Then, with mixed feelings, the chemotherapy was over. It had beaten the hell out of her, but at least there had been a sense we were fighting the disease. We had done all there was to do except go for monthly MRI's and hope the damn thing didn't come back. As Carol's strength slowly returned, I got her to the boat more often, sometimes even if it was just to stay at the dock. The more time she spent aboard *Lastdance*, the stronger she became, and we started doing more frequent overnight trips.

In the fall we did weekend sails to St. Michael's and Annapolis, but it was the Corsica River that she wanted to visit most at that time of year. It was there that we first experienced and marveled at the phenomena of thousands migrating geese. Like that first time, we now sat in our cockpit and drank wine, but as I held Carol close to me under a blanket, I couldn't help but wonder if she would be with me the following year.

Stifling my tears, she asked, "Are you okay, Baby?"

"Yeah, I'm fine. There was just something in my eye."

Chapter 27
Greece

In 2002, over drinks in a quiet anchorage on a hot July night, John raised the idea of doing a sailing charter in Greece. It continued to intrigue us all summer, so at the Annapolis Boat Show in October, we investigated several charter companies. Carol was beside herself with excitement.

"I can't believe we're going sailing in Greece."

"Carol, it's not a done deal; don't jump the gun on this."

She laughed and said to Gail, "Oh, he's so full of crap. He doesn't put this much time into anything unless he's already made up his mind."

Then in a moment of uncertainty, she turned to Gail. "We are going to Greece, right, Gail?"

Gail said, "I don't know; it's up to the men. They know about this stuff."

Carol pouted. "Why can't it be up to us? Then they can deal with the details."

Gail laughed. "Sounds good to me, Carol."

We were skeptical about chartering a boat five thousand miles away, but the sexy saleswoman beckoned to us like a mythical Greek siren and the contract was signed by the third glass of ouzo.

Carol looked at Gail and snickered. "So much for them knowing about this stuff, huh? All it took was some ouzo and that woman's long legs and big boobs and they signed on the dotted line."

Except for occasional seizures, Carol's general health and appearance continued to improve and the monthly MRI's showed no signs of a reoccurring tumor. Nevertheless, we both knew the statistics were heavily stacked against her long term survival, so when an opportunity arose for me to take an early retirement, I jumped at the chance. Before discussing it with Carol, I considered the career and economic implications. There were none to consider because if she survived, we would get by financially, and I could always go back to work if we needed money. Even though the thought of losing her was more painful than I could bear, the possibility that she might not survive made it clear to me what I wanted to do; spend quality time with her while she is doing well. I put in my papers and they were approved with a totally unexpected bonus; my company added a one year consultant contract at my current salary.

After her initial joyful response, Carol then questioned why I was really doing it. She became gloomy, unrealistically blaming herself and her illness for ruining my life and career. She began to cry. "You're only doing this on account of me. I've ruined everything!"

I held her by her shoulders and shook her. "Carol, stop it. We've been through this already. It could have just as easily been me who got sick. What would you have done then? Answer me! I'll tell you, you would have done everything I've done for you and more, right? You know that's true! This is not about sacrifices, it's about what I want to do, what I need to do. Baby, please don't take this away from me!"

I brought her to the dining room table and opened the folder I'd prepared.

"Look at these numbers. Firstly, the company will keep paying me for a year as a consultant, then my Navy pension kicks in soon. We can do this and still get by, okay? It'll just mean dinners at Arby's instead of Aldo's and twelve dollar champagne instead of the forty dollar stuff, but we can do it."

Through tears she laughed. "Where is Aldo's?"

I laughed with her. "There is no Aldo's that I know of wench. You know what I mean. I want to do this, Baby. It's what we always talked about long before you got sick, right? We can spend all our time sailing, even sail to Florida for the winter. I have a ton of air miles, so we can still travel, maybe go back to Italy. Wouldn't you like that?"

She said, "Yes I would." Then she added, "Can we still go sailing in Greece if you retire?"

"Yes, of course we can still go to Greece."

Since her brain surgery, things came slow for Carol. If she focused hard enough though, she could grasp most problems, so after going over our financials, she came to accept that we could retire somewhat comfortably. I acknowledged that we'd have to move out of the big townhouse we were in, but that was something else we could turn into a plus. We could move somewhere on Chesapeake Bay. More importantly, I convinced her of what she already knew in her heart for years; that being able to sail *Lastdance* with her was infinitely more important to me than a career. I held her face in my hands and dried away the tears on her cheeks.

"Are we okay, Princess?"

She placed her arms around my neck, kissed me. "Yes, Baby, we're okay!"

The specter of a recurring brain tumor hung over us like a cloud everyday. As optimistic as we tried to be, we knew that there was a high probability that the cancer could return, so we wanted to spend as much time together while Carol was well and vibrant. This was one of the main reasons I wanted to go to Greece and I was determined to make it a wonderful experience for her. With her strength improving almost daily, we delved into charts and cruising guides about sailing the Greek Isles. We read *The Odyssey* together, which mythically took place on the Ionian Sea where we would be sailing. We were like two kids given free reign by our parents to plan a vacation except we were adults and our playground was the land of Calypso and Odysseus.

Spring arrived and Carol was well enough to assist me with de-winterizing *Lastdance.* Other than trips to Sloan-Kettering, we spent most of April and May sailing Chesapeake Bay. During the last few weeks before leaving for Greece, I could see she wasn't happy with her wardrobe for the trip, and as she sorted through her clothes for the third time, I asked, "What's wrong?"

"Nothing is wrong."

"So then why have you packed and unpacked three times?"

"I know money is tight, but I wish I could buy a few new things to wear in Greece."

I smiled. "Like what?"

"Like some sexy tops and bathing suits. Everyone in Europe dresses so sexy, especially on the beach. I'm sorry, Baby. I just want to feel sexy again."

I pondered what she must be feeling. If anyone deserved to feel sexy, it was Carol. She was so naturally beautiful but in the past year her body had been ravaged by brain surgery, months of radiation and chemo and she never once complained.

I took her in my arms. "Carol, you are an incredibly sexy woman. You know I feel that way about you, but since when do you need my approval to go shopping for anything, let alone sexy clothes?"

Pointing to her head, she asked, "Do you still think I'm sexy since this?"

"Yes I do! You are the sexiest woman I've ever known. Have you forgotten what you do to me all these years?

"Yes, but that was before I got sick."

"Oh, really? What about yesterday when you were trying on bras for the trip?" I tapped her head and said, "Must be short term memory loss, huh?"

She put her arms around my neck. "Mmmm, no, I haven't forgotten about yesterday."

I kissed her and told her to be ready to go shopping in an hour, and I surprised myself at how such a small gesture could make her so happy.

I hated shopping, but on that day, I took immense pleasure in her delight. It truly made me happy to see her so excited each time she came out of the dressing room to get my opinion, whereupon I'd nod, then look at her lecherously until she smiled. In the end, she only bought a few blouses and two bathing suits, but she was bubbling with joy. Each top clung to her seductively and had a deep V-neck revealing her generous cleavage. The bathing suits were also very sexy! One had such a deeply plunging neckline that I laughingly questioned how it contained her. The other had toggle style buttons down the front, which even when closed, left wide gaps, revealing glimpses appealing flesh. I watched her jovial demeanor at the check out register and was angry at myself, thinking, *She requires so little to make her so happy; why wasn't I the catalyst for this modest shopping spree?*

As we drove home, I asked, "So, do those things make you feel sexy?"

She replied, "Oh yes, Baby. They do, very much."

John and Gail had already been exploring the Aegean side of Greece when Carol and I joined them in Athens. We went to the Acropolis, had drinks on the roof garden of our hotel, then enjoyed a magnificent meal in a Piraeus waterfront taverna I'd been to many times in the past when there on business. The next day we drove seven hours through mountains and along the Corinthian coast to the charter base in Pelaros. We provisioned in Levkas, and after loading stores and gear aboard *Joie de Vivre*, our forty-foot Beneteau, we went to dinner and began our week long quest for the perfect baklava! We all loved baklava, but no one more than Carol who at the end of every meal, would always ask us all in turn, "Are you going to finish yours?"

We set sail the first morning for the island of Skorpios where we anchored in a small cove off the beach house made famous by the photo of Jackie O romping nude in the sand. Floating in the Ionian Sea is easy because the density is so high, it's nearly impossible to sink. As we floated like corks in these comfortably cool waters just yards from shore, Carol wanted to do a replay of Jackie's famous frolic on the beach and no doubt would have had there not been guards on the island.

On the island of Meganisi, we discovered the village of Spartahori where we were treated to Greek table dancing! From the harbor, we trekked up a small but steep mountain to the village, which consisted of homes, shops, and tavernas. There we found hilltop mama, a seventy-eight year old table dancer. For reasons having to do with village women of yesteryear carrying water urns on their heads from wells at the foot of the mountain, they now commemorated those days by dancing with a heavy table on their heads.

It made no sense to us, but after a demonstration by mama, they asked for volunteers. Of course, it was Carol who first jumped up to try it. Being concerned about her brain surgery, I told her she shouldn't do it, which was the wrong thing to say to her, especially when she'd had too much ouzo. She tried it and did pretty well and was forever pleased to be able to say she had been a table dancer in Greece. Gail tried it next and almost balanced it for the ten seconds required to win a bottle of ouzo, but fell short by just one second.

We sailed from Spartahori the next morning, tacking our way through the Straights of Meganisi in light fluky winds. Once south of Levkada, however, we found a strong westerly breeze and *Joive de Verve* kicked up her heels and we made seven knots on a starboard tack bound for Kioni on Ithaca sixteen miles away. Carol would sit up on the bow for long stretches at a time looking for dolphin and if John and Gail were reading behind the hard dodger or below deck, she would casually sun herself and I'd alternate between burning desire for her and simple admiration of her innocent loveliness.

Kioni proved to be a wonderful town with excellent tavernas and we tied up alongside *Horn*, a sixty-four-foot cutter just back from a three year global circumnavigation. Roman, the captain of *Horn* and author of a book about the voyage, befriended us and invited us aboard for a tour of his vessel. As he showed us around, it was difficult not to gawk at the slinky woman in a very skimpy bikini on the boat. Roman introduced us to her, but like his book, it was Croatian so totally unintelligible.

Roman liked Carol. He flirted with her openly, making several subtle comments about how well she filled out her bathing suit.

She whispered to me. "Of course he has the hots for me; his girlfriend is barely ninety pounds soaking wet."

Not to miss a chance to rekindle our long standing squabble about the metric system, I said, "Carol, we're in Europe, it's kilos, use kilos!"

She poked me and laughed. "Smart ass. Pounds or kilos, she's all skin and bones!"

Nodding to the open button on her bathing suit top, I said, "You're showing."

"That's okay," she whispered. "When he tries to convert these puppies from pounds to kilos, he can eat his heart out!"

She was clearly feeling good about herself and I was glad we did the last minute shopping back home. As I often did, I laughed inwardly thinking back to the first week she moved in with me when she asked for permission to wear a simple V-neck blouse.

A strong front was forecasted for the next day, so we departed Kioni early and sailed to Sivota, a fjord-like harbor on Levkada. We took shelter there, and it proved to be a good call because the storm was a nasty one. We were no sooner tied to the seawall when we were hit with thirty-five knot winds and torrential rain. Still, it was much worse outside the harbor where winds exceeded forty-five knots and several maydays were heard while we comfortably savored fresh calamari in one of the many tavernas along the waterfront. From Sivota, we sailed to the caves on the southwestern shore of Meganisi. Here, the water is so clear, that even in the darkness of the caves, enough light filters through the water to make it appear like a lighted pool at night.

Incredibly, the depth gauge showed seventy-one meters almost right up to the shore. That was more than two hundred feet, far too deep to anchor the boat, so we agreed to take turns with one couple exploring the cave in the dinghy while the other couple waited aboard the boat.

After a week aboard a forty-foot boat with another couple, I instantly sensed an opportunity to be intimate beyond the bounds of our small cabin on *Joie de Vivre*. We rowed in first with Carol sitting in the stern of the dinghy facing me. As I propelled us toward the gaping hole in the high rocky cliff, she looked at me so seductively I could barely row the boat.

I said, "When John said we'd have to take turns rowing to the cave, this was your first thought too, wasn't it?"

She stared at me with an incredibly sultry look and said, "What was my first thought?" Then, with her eyes locked on mine, she slowly opened several buttons on her bathing suit. I missed the water with an oar and nearly fell backwards. After eighteen years, I was still completely captivated by her.

"You know what!" I exclaimed.

She pulled the strap down off one shoulder. "No, Ron. I don't know what you mean. Tell me."

She was teasing me and doing a good job of it.

I said, "Your first thought was that we could be alone right?"

She didn't answer, she just stared at me. Then, with the dinghy only yards from the shadow of the cave, she pulled down the strap from her other shoulder and lowered the bathing suit to her waist. Looking at her, I felt the same overwhelming emotions I did when I first saw her naked forty years earlier as teenagers in my bedroom.

I stopped rowing and we coasted into the darkness of the grotto.

"Carol, I don't want you to think it's just your looks I'm love-struck with. It's you, Baby. I love you so much I feel like I'm going to explode sometimes."

Kneeling in front of me, we embraced tenderly, and as we kissed, she smiled coyly and said in a soft purring voice, "Please don't explode yet."

Then, removing her bathing suit, she gently slipped into the water. It was true, the cave was dim, but the water was almost like a lighted pool at night. My gaze followed her shimmering body until she surfaced and turned back toward me, beckoning with her eyes. I went in after her and we embraced, kissing passionately and as we floated in the glowing waters in a cave on the Ionian Sea.

Greece made Carol happy and it was difficult to believe that as vibrant as she looked, she was still a very sick woman. She loved sailing among these beautiful islands, but she also loved the zestful pursuit of life that Greeks embraced. Back in Athens, my former business associates took us to a spectacular dinner where we ate and drank by the sea. My friend, Michael, our manager in Greece, knew Carol from his business trips to America and always teased me that I robbed her from a cradle.

During dinner, he quietly said to me, "Ron, it is finished, she is well, no?"

I looked at him only briefly, but said nothing. He understood.

"But excuse me, she is beautiful and full of life. Look at her smiling; she captures everyone."

"I know, Mike, but it could be back tomorrow or next year or in five years; it's always there. We have to live with it."

Looking genuinely sad, he said, "I will say prayers for her, my friend, I promise to do that for you and for her."

Our Greek odyssey ended all too soon, but it was a priceless gift we had given to ourselves. It brought Carol respite, pleasure, and happiness at a time when the uncertainties of her illness must have been frightful for her. But, even as we flew home, she was already excitedly talking about sailing on Chesapeake Bay again. I silently added resilient to the many adjectives I used to describe her.

CHAPTER 28

ON THE BAY AGAIN

Within days of returning from Greece and still tired from the long trip, we went to *Lastdance*. I was content to stay at the dock. Carol wanted to get away for several days before the hectic Fourth of July weekend in St. Michael's, so we sailed to the Corsica River. There, we lounged around, happily recounting our Greek adventure and talking about more serious life issues. We were both feeling helpless regarding her healthcare because, from a treatment perspective, there was nothing to do but go for monthly MRI's. I continued to search the internet for innovative treatments or new discoveries, but there was nothing new. In the meantime, we tried to be positive and appreciate the gift of life, taking comfort in each others arms and the tranquility of a peaceful anchorage.

On the third morning, I asked if she wanted to forget about going to St. Michael's with our friends and just spend the holiday weekend alone.

She smiled. "You want me all to yourself, huh?"

"I want you to be happy, that's what I want!"

"I know, but let's go to St. Michaels. I'm ready to be around friends. Think they'll be wind today?"

"I don't know; I haven't listened to the forecast yet. Why don't you check it out while I start breakfast?"

NOAA offered a good forecast of clear skies with west winds of twelve knots. A few moments later over a breakfast of scrambled eggs, bacon, and grits with hot coffee and cold orange juice, we discussed our plan for the day.

It was only eight o'clock and our friends twelve miles to the south hadn't yet departed Kent Narrows. We knew we'd still be the last boat into the anchorage at Saint Michael's, so there was no point in rushing. Still, I was antsy from sitting at anchor for three days. As we moved slowly down the Chester River in the light morning breeze I said aloud, "A west wind means good north-south sailing."

Carol looked up from her book and smiled knowingly. "Go for it; we're in no hurry."

I laughed. "How did you know what I meant?"

She laughed back. "Ha, I know you like a book."

"You don't mind?

"Of course not," she replied. "It's beautiful; let's go around the island!"

It's almost twenty miles longer going around Kent Island and up Eastern Bay, rather than the much shorter route through Kent Narrows, but it is a nicer sail, and as Carol said, we weren't in a hurry.

I said, "I hope the wind gets as high as the forecast said it will."

Carol just smiled and continued to read her book.

The wind did pick up as we rounded Love Point. By noon, we were just south of Thomas Point Shoal, and it was blowing nicely at fourteen knots from the southwest and Carol took a turn on the helm. We were sailing on a comfortable reach at six and a half knots so I unfurled the staysail and after trimming all three sails, we increased to a steady seven and a half knots. At times like this I could see how much she truly loved sailing. She stood on the cockpit bench looking so intense and vibrant, I almost forgot how sick she had been, and I placed great value on all the extra time she had been given so far.

Once we turned into Eastern Bay and came to a northeast heading, the boat slowed and Carol turned the helm back over to me for the more sedate downwind run.

As I settled in for the six mile run to the Miles River, Carol sat behind me and massaged my neck. A few moments later, she put her arms over my shoulders and pressed herself against me. I smiled as I felt her bare breasts against my back and her soft lips kiss my neck.

She whispered, "I love you, Ron. Can I just hold you like this?"

We sailed silently for a long time and Carol remained in that position until she seemed to go limp. I became alarmed for an instant, thinking something was wrong.

"Carol, are you okay?"

She mumbled a sleepy acknowledgement. "Oh boy, I fell asleep."

She came into the cockpit and I put my arm around her shoulder.

I said, "It was so good to feel you against me like that."

She sighed. "It felt good for me too, Baby. I love feeling your skin against mine. I'm sorry I fell asleep; I had something else in mind for you."

She kissed me tenderly. "But it's too late now, there's the raft-up. Be a good boy and I'll surprise you later."

We lived aboard *Lastdance* the rest of the summer, enjoying life at the marina and sailing all over Chesapeake Bay. Then, while on a cruise to Cape Charles and still several days away from Kent Narrows, we began hearing the first reports of Hurricane Isabel, a Category V storm. We searched the charts and cruising guides for nearby hurricane holes, but after tracking the movement of the violent storm, we decided we had time to make an overnight run for our marina. As when sailing offshore, we took turns sleeping during the day, but both of us remained awake in the cockpit at night as we raced up the bay at seven knots under a full press of sail.

We beat Isabel by thirty hours, but as tired as we were, we immediately began preparing *Lastdance* for the approaching storm. Long lines, heavy chafing gear, and big fenders was the rule in Florida, and we now applied it on Chesapeake Bay. When the work was over, we had sixteen lines securing *Lastdance* to the dock just eleven hours before Isabel made landfall in North Carolina with hurricane-force winds that extended to the Chesapeake. The storm surge poured into the mouth of the bay, causing extensive flooding everywhere, most notably on the western shore in Baltimore's Inner Harbor and Annapolis where it crested over the first floor of downtown bars and restaurants.

When it was over, *Lastdance* and most of our marina did well except for several boats that had been on the hard and were re-floated by the eight-foot storm surge. Red Eyes Dock Bar, our favorite haunt, was damaged by wave action when the normally sheltered Kent Narrows became exposed to the Bay and sheltering land masses became submerged by the rising water. Afterwards, the water receded rapidly, and we counted ourselves lucky to have survived yet another hurricane.

With fall approaching, we investigated places to relocate to and eventually settled on Virginia Beach near Oceana Naval Air Station. Once settled in, we contacted Ken, a sailing friend who we had last seen a year earlier on the Patuxent River. We were happily surprised to discover that he and his girlfriend, Carrie Lee, lived in the same apartment complex we had just moved into. It was nice to have good friends nearby because I was regularly traveling to New Jersey for consulting projects and I knew Ken and Carrie Lee would look after Carol, which lessened my concerns about her being alone.

We liked Virginia Beach, even when jets took off from the Naval Air Station all hours of the night. I bought Carol a metal detector and we'd drive to the beach every morning and walk along the shore as she searched for pieces-of-eight she was certain lay just beneath the sand. With every disappointing false alarm, she became even more enthusiastic in her efforts to find a pot of gold, but mostly we'd just walk and talk about the places we were going to sail to in the summer. During one of those talks, we decided to bring *Lastdance* down in the spring and after looking at several marinas, we choose one in Little Creek where Carol had once joined me aboard *USS Boulder* for brunch so many years before.

Carol was beginning her third year in remission and her general health continued to improve, which was important to ultimately beating the disease. The doctors told us to ignore the statistics, but that was impossible when you had a disease with a ninety-seven percent mortality rate. Those numbers hung over our heads like the Sword of Damocles, and the longer she did well, the more we feared the numbers, so we made the best of every day, taking increasing pleasure and comfort in each others arms at night. I also looked for opportunities to do things that I knew Carol would take delight in.

Returning from a trip to Camp Lejeune to visit Christopher and Michelle, we got in the car to head back to Virginia Beach, I asked, "Ya wanna go to Florida?"

Without hesitation, Carol said, "Sure!"

She thought I was kidding until I turned south on Route 17 instead of north. Her directional senses were one of the things that suffered from her brain surgery, but she knew enough to question me about the turn.

"Where are you going?" she asked.

I squeezed her hand. "Florida!"

She looked at me incredulously. "Are you kidding?"

"No, but we're in no hurry, so I want to stop in Calabash."

"What's in Calabash?"

"I'm not sure." Then I explained that Jimmy Durante used to end his show by saying, "Goodnight, Mrs. Calabash, wherever you are!"

She said, "So?"

"So I'm just curious about it. They also have a special kind of cooking there. Calabash style seafood, and I want to try it."

"Ron, you're nuts! We have to go home. We don't have enough clothes to go to Florida."

I laughed. "What do we need, a few pairs of shorts, some t-shirts, some underwear, bathing suits? Besides, we have to go; I arranged a surprise for you there. Relax, enjoy the ride; in two hours we'll be having Calabash seafood right in Calabash!"

There wasn't much to the town of Calabash, and Calabash seafood turned out to be nothing more than fried fish and shrimp. It was good eating, but unless I missed something, we could get a similar meal just about anywhere. The trip to Florida, on the other hand, turned out to be great. We drove along the coast stopping in Charleston and Beaufort, South Carolina, then jumped on I-95 only long enough to get us into Florida. There, we returned to US 1, taking it all the way to Fort Lauderdale, stopping at beach-front motels and local seafood restaurants whenever Carol got tired or hungry.

In Fort Lauderdale, David and Linda threw a big party for Carol and invited all of our friends from southeast Florida. Then in Miami, Mike and Liz took us out on their new boat, and instead of Carol tiring, each day seemed to revitalize her. When we left our hotel in Miami, Carol fully expected us to get on I-95 and head for home, but I turned south on US 1 instead.

She said, "Now what?"

"Did you forget the surprise?" I asked. She seemed confused. "Remember I said I had a surprise for you in Florida?"

"I thought seeing our friends was the surprise."

"You have no imagination. They must have scooped it out with your brain!"

She laughed and said, "Someone must have scooped out your brain! Are we were going to Key West?

I laughed. "Key West? Are you nuts? We can't hang around here all month, we have to get home, but first, we have one more stop to make."

Two hours later, we pulled off US 1 at Key Largo. Carol sat silently staring at the colorful sign. *Dolphin and Marine Mammal Research and Education Center - Swim with the Dolphins.* I looked at her. She said nothing, but tears were trickling down her face. I looked at my watch.

"Its eleven forty-five. You have an appointment for the one o'clock swim. We should go inside and sign in and see what you have to do to get ready."

Carol sobbed like a little girl. "You did this for me?"

"No, Baby, I did it for me because nothing gives me as much pleasure as seeing you really happy. Nothing!"

She put her arms around me so hard we banged heads.

Jokingly, I said, "Hey, you've got a titanium plate in there. Be careful, you'll hurt me!" Looking into her eyes, I added, "I mean it, Carol, it gives me so much pleasure when I can do something to make you happy."

We kissed and talked about the magic we'd always felt for each other until looking at my watch again, I said, "Come on, get your sorry ass in there; you have to listen to a class or something."

I watched Carol in the class. She was beside herself with excitement, but paid careful attention to everything the speaker said. I spoke to one of the trainers and told her about Carol's brain surgery and asked if it would be a problem.

She said, "Quite the contrary, the dolphins will in all likelihood be drawn to her. They sense brain injury and anomalies."

I looked at her with obvious skepticism. "Get out!"

She smiled and said, "You'll see!"

Carol's group came out to the lagoon, and each person took their place on a small float. The trainer told them to splash the water and dolphins immediately swam to them, shooting up the float until their bodies were about two-thirds out of the water. Everyone but Carol was startled and jumped back. She just stared in amazement, then without waiting for any guidance from the trainer, she touched the dolphin's head. The dolphin made a squeaking sound, then two of the other dolphins withdrew from the adjacent floats and came to Carol! The trainer I had talked with looked up at me and smiled knowingly. Admonished by the trainer on the float, the two wayward dolphins returned to the other guest. Over the next half hour, she gave out the names of the dolphins and made everyone participate in a series of swimming exercises with them. In almost every case, several dolphins would leave their assigned people and swim to Carol and vie for her attention. She'd pet them, calling each by name, which amazed me due to her short-term memory problem.

All the time Carol was in the water with the dolphins, her big, radiant smile never once left her face. She was the most childlike and innocent I'd ever seen her, and I marveled at how she interacted with these powerful, gentle creatures. I was so happy for her and rebuked myself for not taking her there years earlier when we lived in Fort Lauderdale. I found myself fighting back tears, not sure if they were from the joy of seeing Carol swimming with dolphins, or because I was afraid this would be her last time.

We were enjoying life in our new home in Virginia Beach and Carol's health continued to improve. We cherished our time alone, most especially on long walks on the empty beach at Fort Story where we spent countless hours talking. Evenings we'd finish dinner, and after clearing the table, we'd break out charts and review the plans to sail *Lastdance* to Little Creek in the spring. We kept expecting things to warm up, but by late March it was still pretty cold and our departure was only three weeks away because our contract at Kent Narrows expired on April 15.

We spent the night aboard *Lastdance* huddled together in bed with the heater on high and the sound of rain beating against the cabin top above our heads. In the morning, the heavy downpour stopped, but it was cold and overcast and the NOAA forecast offered more of the same for the rest of the day.

Over breakfast I asked, "Do you want to delay leaving another day?"

She said, "No, what am I married to a fair weather sailor?"

"No, wench, but I'm worried about you getting chilled and wet."

"Let's go. There's no hazardous weather coming, just this rain crap, right?"

She was right. Aside from the rain and chilly temperature, the wind was forecasted to be northwest at only twelve to fifteen knots, perfect for a broad reach down the bay.

"Okay, smart ass," I said, "let's go!"

We departed Kent Narrows around eight o'clock and for the next seven hours, we sailed through a series chilling rain showers that pelted us from behind. We averaged six knots over forty seven miles to Solomon's Island and Carol stood her share of tricks on the helm as we took turns warming below deck with the propane heater and hot soup.

At three thirty, we arrived off Drum Point, and instead of anchoring by Molly's Leg in Solomon's Island, we decided to take a berth at the Patuxent Naval Air Station marina so we could plug in and get electric heat for the night. In another era, the basin had been a seaplane base and was sheltered on all sides except for its entrance which faced due north toward the river. We were cold and tired and opted to tie up to the T-head rather than take a regular slip farther to the west, which offered more protection. I reasoned that the forecast was for continued northwest winds, and that we could more easily slip away in the morning from the T-head, so we came alongside, our port side to the floating dock, our bow into the wind.

We straightened up the boat and hung our foul weather gear to dry in the warmth of our cabin. Carol prepared some snacks and opened a bottle of wine, and we toasted the first leg of our trip. Later on, I made my signature risotto with shrimp, which we enjoyed with another bottle of wine. Then, with the wind howling outside, we listened to Do-Wop tunes on the stereo and slow-danced in our small salon.

Carol whispered in my ear, "Are you trying to seduce me?"

I smiled. "No, I'm just dancing with you."

She looked at me in mock disbelief. "Just as I suspected, you are seducing me! Okay, take me to bed, captain!"

Later, as she lay in my arms, we talked about plans for the next day and wondered if we could get in early enough to meet Ken and Carrie Lee for dinner. The wind piped up in stronger gusts and *Lastdance* took on a subtle pitching movement. Carol joked how the rise and fall of our bow would have been nice a half-hour earlier during our lovemaking. She then brazenly asked, "Mmmm, maybe we can try again?"

Then she smiled and kissed me, snuggling closer as we were gently rocked to sleep.

An hour later, I woke to a harsher motion as *Lastdance* pitched more violently. The wind was howling louder in the rigging, and from experience, I guessed it was blowing twenty-five knots. I got up to look at the wind indicator.

"Damn," I said aloud, it was a steady twenty-three knots, gusting as high as twenty-eight, and it had veered more to the north. The entrance to the basin was now a funnel for waves rolling in from the river and they churned up the enclosed basin like a washing machine.

Carol called out from bed, "What's going on?"

I told her the situation we were in, then turned on NOAA weather and opened the chart book. The weather report offered poor news. The wind was predicted to be steady tonight and tomorrow at twenty-five knots from the north-northwest with gust as high as thirty-five.

Looking at the chart, I saw that the entrance was actually on an axis that was east of north, 015°m to be precise. I stuck my head out of the companionway hatch and saw that the waves causing all the fuss were really not more than one or two feet high and that the wind was actually north-northwest as NOAA said, which fortunately, was keeping us off the bucking T-head floating dock.

Our dock lines were taut, and I could see them stretch each time the wind gusted, but Carol had wisely doubled up the bow line, which was now taking the brunt of the load. We had also rigged fore and aft springs, so I felt if I added chafing gear, they would all be fine. I had no idea how well the dock cleats were mounted, so I made a mental note to try adding another bow line to a separate cleat on the dock or better yet, to a piling.

Returning to the warmth of the cabin, I was momentarily taken aback as I caught sight of Carol standing over the chart in the warm glow of our oil lamp.

"What?" she asked.

I smiled. "You look beautiful standing there with all hell breaking loose on deck."

She laughed. "Well, you're naked too, buster, and you didn't look so cute mooning me while you were peeking out the companionway."

I laughed. "Okay, pay attention; we're going to be in for a rough night, but if I put chafing gear on the lines and rig another bow line to the piling, I'm sure we'll be fine as long as the wind remains out of the northwest to keep us off that floating dock." Carol quickly sized up our predicament. "And if the winds come from the northeast, we're screwed?"

I looked at her more serious, "Yeah, not only could the waves get bigger, but we'll be getting slammed against that dock and fenders or not, we'd be in real danger!"

She calmly looked at me and said, "So what's the plan, captain?"

"First thing, we get another bow line on. I don't think I can pull the boat against this wind, so you'll have to come on deck and use the engine to get us close enough for me to get a line around the piling. You'll have to be careful not to get too close to that dock; it scares the hell out of me!"

She put her hand on mine and without any false bravado, she said, "I can do that."

"Good girl, I'm sure you can. Let's get this over with."

I told her once we got another bow line on, we'd then put chafing gear on all the other lines. After that, all we had to do was monitor the wind all night to be sure it continued to keep us off the dock.

She asked, "What do we do if it shifts?"

"We cast off and motor to the far side of the basin where we can anchor in the lee of the big seawall."

Carol nodded then said, "Why don't we put out the rest of our fenders on the port side just in case?"

I thought, *I should have thought of that. If the wind did shift, it could buy us extra time to get away.* "Good idea, Baby!"

I patted her ass. "Let's get some foul weather gear on and do this, so I can get you back into bed!"

She smiled seductively. "Does that mean you're rested?"

On deck, the wind was howling like a banshee and my face stung from the pelting rain. *Lastdance* pitched wildly; her bow rising and falling in a great arc but at a different frequency than the floating dock beside us. The awkward movements of the dock and boat was disorienting so I put a harness on before carefully going forward. Once on the bow, I made the new line fast to our second bow cleat, and Carol started the engine.

She signaled for me to wait, then went below and turned on the foredeck light and then returned to the helm. I smiled and thought, *In spite of the brain surgery, the important stuff still comes naturally to her. Remember to thank her for that.* It was almost impossible to yell over the noise of the wind, so I walked back and told her she'd have to maneuver *Lastdance* using her own judgment, then added, "But watch me carefully."

She nodded, then saying it as a statement but sounding like a question, she said, "If we get too close, I'll just back off on the throttle and let the wind blow us off!"

Again, I smiled. She had confidence, but was wise enough to seek affirmation. Still smiling, I nodded.

She smiled back and shouted, "Okay, let's do it!"

Going back to the foredeck, I looked aft and could see Carol engage the gearshift. She then waited to see if the throttle in idle was enough to move us forward. It wasn't. She gave it a little fuel and slowly turned the helm to port and we crept forward, but the bow wouldn't come into the wind. She applied more throttle and ever so slowly, we began to swing left, bringing the pulpit dangerously close to the piling, which seemed massive as I rode the pitching deck on its five-foot rise and fall. Struggling to get a turn around the piling, I stopped for a brief instant to glance back at Carol. She had a look of steadfast determination on her face and I thought, *Almost everyone with her disease three years ago is now dead, but just look at her, handling our boat with my life in her hands and I thanked god she was still with me.*

I finally got the line secured to the piling and facing Carol, I signaled her to go to neutral. The instant she did, *Lastdance* blew away from the dock until the lines became taut again. I added chafing gear to the bow lines, and after killing the engine, Carol did the same to the stern line and both springs. Returning to the warmth of our cabin, Carol removed her foul weather jacket, saying, "Brrrr, it's so cold up there."

I stopped short and stared at her and thought, *My god, talk about form and function.* She was the image of both as she stood by the salon table in her foul weather pants and souwester hat, her bare breasts caught in the soft glow of the oil lamp.

Smiling, she said, "You like this look, huh?"

"Yeah I do! You look so sexy dressed like that. It reminds me of all the things you can be. Come here you old salt!"

With little sleep during the night, we were eager to get away from the churning basin in the morning so we departed early under a double-reefed main and staysail. The temperature was again in the forties and out on the bay the wind was gusting to thirty knots with six foot waves. Carol and the boat were handling the conditions well, but I wasn't. With a fifty-six mile voyage to the Rappannock River still ahead of us, I was already queasy as we raced downwind at six knots, often faster. It made little sense to spend the day getting knocked around like this so less than half way between Cedar Point and Point No Point, I motioned for Carol to come about. What took forty-five minutes of downwind sailing, now took us more than two hours of hard fought tacking to regain. Once we rounded Cedar Point again, Carol fell off the wind, and we raced forward on a starboard tack for Solomon's Island, this time staying at a marina on sheltered Back Creek.

We woke the next morning to a much nicer day with the temperature already in the low sixties and the wind a more reasonable fifteen knots out of the north. After getting underway, we rounded Cedar Point for the third time in twenty-four hours and began a comfortable downwind sail to Deltaville where Ken and Carrie Lee keep their boat, *Renaissance*. After dinner with them, Ken and I drank most of a bottle of his guava berry rum. I woke the next morning with my hair hurting and a mixed bag of weather, but with warmer temperatures and the wind now right on the nose out of the south. Once underway, we completed a long tack over to the Eastern Shore, but we only made three miles of southing, so we fired up the engine and charged batteries the last forty miles to our new marina in Little Creek, VA.

Keeping *Lastdance* in Little Creek afforded us the chance to sail in both bay and ocean conditions. Unfortunately, even the closest gunkhole was a long day's sail away and gunkholing is what we liked to do; sail four or five hours, then anchor somewhere, explore our surroundings, and spend time together. Also, my dad was hospitalized, so we had to limit our sailing to short overnighters because we were driving to see him once a week in Brooklyn.

Then, as mid-May approached and the weather warmed, Carol asked, "Have you given any thought about sailing to Baltimore for Memorial Day."

"Baby, we just sailed all the way down here a month ago!

Sensing a lack of passion in my objection she zeroed in for the kill. "Yes, but you're retired, and isn't that what we want to do, just sail around?"

I could see that she really wanted to go, and the truth was, so did I. We missed our friends and we thought Memorial Day in Baltimore would be a great way to see most of them at the same time. Also, we could easily rent a car there and drive to Brooklyn to see my dad.

"Okay, if we want to be in Baltimore before Memorial Day, we've only got a week to get the boat ready!"

We looked at a calendar and decided to leave Little Creek on Sunday, the twenty-third. That would allow for unfavorable winds or bad weather and give us an extra day because Carol wanted to spend a night in Annapolis.

Getting underway in a twelve knot southwesterly wind, we made it to Jackson Creek on the Piankatank River on a broad reach. The last time we had been there was in 1997, when we anchored there on our second night during our voyage to Florida. We drank wine in the cockpit at night and talked about all that had happened since then. There were now grandchildren, retirement, three relocations, and, of course, Carol's ongoing battle with a brain tumor. I looked at her and thought, *She is as beautiful now as she was then, but the strain of her fight is evident in her eyes. Where does she find the strength?*

Two days later, while on a mooring in Annapolis, we received a call that my brother, Bob, died suddenly at his home in New York!

I banged my fist on the salon table. "Give me a fucking break here!"

We made arrangements to leave *Lastdance* on the mooring, and where we originally planned on renting a car to visit my dad in the hospital, we now found ourselves driving north to attend my brothers funeral. Carol and Bob had been playmates during our early childhood, so she took this hard, but I also knew his death made her more aware of her own mortality.

We returned to Annapolis after the funeral and contemplated the tragic events of the last several weeks. With my dad in the hospital and my brother's death, we came to recognize more clearly that all of our family was up north and that maybe the move to Virginia Beach was ill-timed. There in our cockpit, we decided to move *Lastdance* back to our old marina on Kent Island where we could use her as a half way house, putting us in easy striking distance to visit family. The next day we drove over the Bay Bridge to Mears Point Marina. Not only did they have a slip available, they had one on O-Dock, a few slips down from where we had been just a month and a half earlier.

We were able to drive from Virginia Beach to Kent Island, get a good night's sleep, then drive to Brooklyn to visit my dad. We'd then return to the marina on our way home and get some sailing in to decompress from the stress of shuttle hospital visits. Then, two months later and just hours after returning to Virginia Beach from visiting my father, we were devastated with the news that he died.

Again, I raged to the heavens. "Why are you doing this? Carol with cancer, my brother and dad gone within two months. What is wrong with you?"

My mom was completely distraught and needed me to be supportive, but it was Carol, still in a fight for her own life, who became supportive for all of us. I don't know where she drew her strength from or what reserves she called on, but she was there for me, so I could be there for my family.

My dad and brother were veterans and had military funerals. They were buried just a hundred yards apart among long rows of simple but elegant military headstones, which had a profound effect on Carol. Previously, during times when she acknowledged the possibility she might lose her battle, she always expressed her desire to be cremated. Now, as the military honor guard folded the flag over my dad's casket, she surveyed the imposing ground where so many brave warriors rested.

Holding my hand, she whispered, "I would like to be here."

I looked at her quizzically. With tears in her eyes, she gave me the barest hint of a smile, then squeezed my hand. I closed my eyes, fully understanding what she meant.

With the losses of my brother and dad behind us, we spent the summer sailing around the bay. It proved to be cathartic for both of us, but it wasn't until the annual RWYB regatta in October that we really began to smile. This is a fun race around Kent Island in which some crews wear costumes. Bill and Jane aboard *Galena* wore elaborate eighteenth century English costumes, the kind where the damsel shows lots of cleavage, something Jane had no problem doing, much to the enjoyment of the men in the race.

Lastdance was crewed by Carol and Rhonda. I wore basic pirate garb, and my surreptitious plan was to have my attractive crew wear skimpy tanktops, shorts, navy hats, and neckerchiefs, but they mutinied. Instead, they came on deck wearing a more modest version that included t-shirts. Whatever the uniform, a race was not to be. When the starting gun sounded, the wind was barely two knots and the fleet drifted slowly backwards with the current. After an hour of sweltering in the sun, my crew mutinied once again and demanded we drop our limp sails and motor to St. Michael's for lunch.

I was sure the wind would come up, but Carol was having none of it. She cranked the starter, pointed south to Saint Michael's, and said simply. "Lunch!"

After being satiated with nachos and margaritas at the Carpenter Street Saloon, the wind did pipe up, and with a happier crew, we had a great sail up Eastern Bay, arriving at the marina in time for the post-race party with Carol's favorite band, Mama-Jama.

Chapter 29
Second Battle

After almost two years of relatively good health, I took notice of several signs that caused me to think something might be wrong. I saw Carol's left foot drag, but she dismissed it, saying she tripped on something. Then she dropped a knife while talking and didn't seem to know it fell from her left hand, but, again, she dismissed it. The stress of the previous three years since she was first diagnosed with a brain tumor caught up with me. I got scared, then angry. I didn't say anything, but inwardly, my mood darkened, and for the first time in my entire life, I felt on the verge of panic. It was August 2005.

Weeks later, we were on a sailing vacation with the Tremel's to the Choptank River where most of James Michener's novel, *Chesapeake* took place. We stopped in Cambridge and when all three boats were secured at the town marina, we prepared to go ashore for dinner. Carol dressed in a nice top and a pair of Capri pants with an elastic waistband. For reasons I cannot even now comprehend, I said, "I really don't like those elastic waist-band pants, would you change them?"

She casually said, "It's hot, Ron. They're comfortable."

Inexplicably, I fumed, then shouted, "Carol, why won't you change the fucking pants; they look like hell on you."

She stared at me in disbelief. "Are you feeling okay?"

"I'm fine, just change the pants!"

Staring at me incredulously, I saw the hurt in her eyes. Every instinct told me to embrace her and apologize, but I was out of control. "Change them!"

She began to remove the pants, but stopped. "I don't know what the hell is wrong with you, but no, I'm not going to be uncomfortable just because you have a bug up your ass."

I said, "Fine, then go to dinner without me!"

I looked on as she fought back tears. I knew I was being an ass; I knew there was no reason for my behavior, but I wouldn't relent and I didn't know why.

She left the boat and joined the Tremels waiting for us on the dock. I heard Gail ask, "Where's Ron?"

Carol replied, "He's not coming," and then she explained why.

As Carol, Gail, and Valerie walked ahead to the restaurant, John and Charlie came aboard to talk me into joining them. After a lot of discussion, I eventually agreed to go, and once in the restaurant, my irrational anger dissipated and we made up, not that Carol had anything to say she was sorry about.

She didn't say another word about my bizarre behavior, but once alone aboard *Lastdance*, I apologized to her profusely, telling her how sorry I was and that I didn't know why I became so angry over her pants.

She said, "It's the stress of everything catching up with you. I know you're still worried about me tripping."

In her way, she just snuggled closer to me, and I held her in my arms. I'd wake and I kissed her face and shoulder throughout the night, so much so that around three in the morning she said loudly, "Ron, you're forgiven!"

"I'm so sorry, are you sure, Princess?"

She kissed my lips softly. "Yes, Baby. I'm very sure; now save your kisses for the morning and let me get some sleep, okay?"

Several days later, after rafting together on beautiful LaTrappe Creek, we said goodbye to our friends and went our separate ways. *Tranquility* and *Belle Amie* headed for home and we sailed to Tilghman Island after a long day of tacking in a stiff northerly breeze around Sharps Island. We tied up to the dock at Knapps Narrows, and while chilling out with a glass of wine before showering, Carol fell in the cockpit without warning, coming within an inch of striking her head against a winch.

She downplayed the incident saying she was tired and that the drink went to her head, but I saw it happen and knew it was more than that. She had only taken a few sips of her wine and she didn't trip; it looked like her left leg just gave out. I thought, *Oh God, she's been doing so well, don't let it be back!* I put some ice on her thigh and arm, and she partially soothed my fears by doing an impromptu dance routine in the cockpit.

"I'm really okay," she insisted.

It was too late on Friday afternoon to call her oncologist, and I didn't want to scare her, so I let it go, but I made a mental note to call the doctor first thing Monday morning.

We went to dinner at Bay One Hundred, a wonderful little restaurant at the marina, and I did my best to conceal my concerns, but I was probably acting a bit too romantic.

"Are you trying to get in my pants tonight or are you still worried about me falling?"

I smiled and said, "Both."

"Ron, you know I love all the touching and attention, but you don't have to worry about me, I'm really fine, and as far as getting in my pants, take me, I'm yours anytime, Baby!"

I smiled, but I was clearly a lot more frightened for her than she was for herself. She was putting up a brave front, but then I thought, *Who knows, maybe she really did trip.* Throughout the meal, I rationalized that people tripped and fell on boats all the time. Then I thought, *No, I saw her simply fall over, and she didn't even seem to know she was falling. I will call Dr. Nolan on Monday.*

We walked back to *Lastdance* holding hands, and she looked up at the stars and talked to me about the book she was reading, *The Lost Book of Enki.* It was about extraterrestrials who came to earth almost half a million years ago. This was stuff she loved to read about, and I enjoyed hearing her go on with such enthusiasm and conviction. Her sensual movements at dinner and her invitation for me to get in her pants fueled my libido, but I was captivated by her monologue and wanted to watch her tell me about her theories as much as just hear them.

Back on the boat, we sat in the cockpit under the stars and sipped red wine and ate the last pieces of dark chocolate we brought aboard a week earlier. I watched her intently as she talked about Babylonians, Assyrians, Hittites, and people called Anunnaki, who I had never heard of before. Even after twenty years, I thought, *She is so exciting and beautiful. Look at her, even explaining extraterrestrials; her smile is radiant in the darkness.* Almost two hours passed and I barely said a word as I listened to her. We ate the chocolate and drank a bottle of merlot and I was getting sleepy, but when she asked me what I thought, all I could think of saying was, "I want you!"

She smiled and took me by the hand and we went below to make love softly and unhurried. Afterward, as she slept peacefully in my arms, I held her tightly and prayed that my concerns were unfounded.

While reading and drinking coffee in the cockpit the next morning, I heard Carol stirring below. I peeked down the hatch to ask if she wanted me to make breakfast or go ashore to eat, but I became instantly alarmed as I observed her shaking her left hand.

"What's wrong?"

"Oh boy, Ron. You're like an old grandmother. Nothing's wrong, Baby. My hand fell asleep that's all. So what's for breakfast, Granny Ron?"

I laughed. "If you showed some respect to the captain, I'd treat you to breakfast ashore, wench."

Climbing out of bed, she said mockingly, "Aye aye, captain, sir," but as her feet touched the deck, she gave me a sultry look, then slowly pulled on her shorts, her eyes never leaving mine. She lingered like that a second or two, then seductively pulled her blouse over her head, and with the buttons undone, she came to the companionway and said, "So what are we having for breakfast, Captain Bligh?"

I went below and poured her a mug of coffee. Then, after promising to take her ashore for breakfast, we went up to the cockpit to discuss options for the day. As she sat on the cockpit bench, she spilled some coffee. I became instantly concerned again. Visibly annoyed with my doting, she said, "Stop it! This is getting ridiculous. Look down at where you were sitting last night; there are wine stains everywhere! You spill crap too."

She was right, I was being silly. Besides, there was nothing I could do about it until Monday morning, so I promised I'd stop being a weenie.

I wanted to sail to our marina and go home so we could be ready to go to Sloan-Kettering if they could fit us in on Monday. Carol argued that our friends would be out sailing for the weekend and she wanted to rendezvous with them. The wind was southwest and forecasted to be ten to fifteen knots by late morning with the usual chance of afternoon thunderstorms. That would make for a great sail up Chesapeake Bay. If she still wanted to hook up with our friends, we could sail into Eastern Bay and call them on the VHF and find out where they were going.

Two hours later, we left Knapps Narrows and once clear of the "1" PA marker, we hoisted sail and set a course through Poplar Island Narrows for Eastern Bay. We had sailed through this narrow waterway which separates Poplar Island from the mainland many times, and as the restoration project on the island progressed, we observed it grow to enormous proportions as it advanced to the size it was in the 1800's. Carol threaded her way through hundreds of crab trap floats, which shouldn't have been in the narrow channel, but we didn't complain about them because we had thoughts of having steamed crabs ourselves Sunday night.

As noon approached, the wind remained southwesterly and built to the promised twelve knots. We were making six knots on a broad reach as we approached Red "4" which marks the juncture of Prospect Bay to the north and the Miles River to the south. I called *Seawoof* and *Bliss* on the VHF and Gene answered almost immediately and said they were headed to Shaw Bay for the weekend. I told him we were coming in from Eastern Bay. Within a moment, he called back to ask if we were off Tilghman Point, saying that they were all approaching the large triangular shoal in the Miles River. I looked to starboard and recognized several boats as they negotiated the deep water between the shoals off Bennett Point.

"Okay, *Seawoof*, I see ya; we'll see you in an hour. *Lastdance* out."

Once behind the long peninsular that juts down from the eastern shore of Prospect Bay, the Wye River runs almost due north between Piney Neck and Wye Neck. About half a mile from the mouth at Bennett Point, Wye East River breaks away from the main river and follows an easterly course along the southern side of Wye Island. It then joins with Wye Narrows, which follows a torturous route, first northwest then west, until it rejoins the main river. The result in a twenty square mile area peppered with countless well-protected anchorages. Shaw Bay is the largest and least protected of these, especially from northerly winds, but on hot summer nights, it's a popular for its cool breezes. With a forecast of only light and variables winds, it was our destination for the night.

It was a typical weekend raft up where everyone did their own thing. There were few sea nettles, so kids and adults alike swam while others lounged around or socialize all of which is what Carol loved to do. I watched her carefully, concerned she might fall as she moved from boat to boat, smiling and laughing, always gregarious, but she seemed to be doing fine. During dinner aboard *Lastdance*, she talked excitedly about the day, and I was glad I didn't rush her home because no one knew better than me how fleeting life could be, and I treasured every joyful day she could take pleasure in.

Later that evening, everyone gathered on *Bliss* and Jane brought out her basket of unusual musical instruments, then she played the steel drum which she has come to master. From the basket, Carol selected her favorite tambourine and she played it for the rest of the night as she sang and danced, sometimes to a tune only she could hear. I thought, *It is pure fun just watching her!* I still had the nagging concern that something was wrong, so I tried to stay near her in case she fell, yet not be so obvious that she'd notice. Hours later as we snuggled in bed, she said, "I always feel safe in bed with you. You put your arms around me, and I know no boogiemen can hurt me."

"That's because I love you, Princess."

She replied in a mocking tone. "I know you do." Then, in a louder voice she added, "I also know that's why you hovered over me all day! But Ron, but I mean it, I'm alright."

The next day I woke to a gray sky, which was not in the previous days forecast. I put some coffee on, then listened to the NOAA forecast: "A line of severe thunderstorms is expected to cross the listening area by late morning. Wind gust to fifty miles per hour, heavy rain and cloud to ground lightning. There is a seventy percent chance of continued scattered afternoon storms through six o'clock."

"Shit," I said aloud, "I just wanted to chill out today, and what exactly do they mean by late morning?"

Aside from lightning, which scares the hell out of me, the other problem I have with thunderstorms was that the wind was often unpredictable and could come at you from several directions as the storm moved. It could kick up a confused chop and small waves in no time, so the one place you didn't want to be during a thunder storm was in an exposed anchorage, especially rafted to other boats.

"Carol, wake up!"

After years of sailing together, she knew I wouldn't wake her like that unless there was a problem, so without hesitation or asking why, she climbed out of bed and rubbed the sleep from her eyes. I told her about the approaching line of storms and said the coffee would be ready in a few minutes. I wasn't sure if we had time to motor back to our marina ten miles away, but I knew that at the very least, we would break away from the raft up and find a more protected anchorage.

Preparing things on deck, my actions drew the attention of several of our friends. I told them about the weather forecast and as I came to expect over the years, the kindest of their comments was that I was being overly cautious. Moments later and still half-asleep, Carol came on deck and received a chorus of good-natured wolf whistles and exaggerated morning greetings. When the clamor abated, she smiled quizzically, saying to me that the coffee was ready and then to everyone else, "Good morning, guys." Still puzzled about the inordinate attention she had been given, she retreated into our cabin to fix a light breakfast for us.

Once below, she asked, "I look like shit. Why were they hooting and whistling?"

Pouring coffee, I smiled and said, "They're from Mars. A revealing tank top, no bra, big boobs will cause that reaction every time, Baby."

She shrieked in embarrassment and got so flustered, she spilled half her coffee.

I laughed. "I won't worry about the cause of that spill; now get the foul weather gear out and let's figure out what we're going to do."

Ten minutes later, we took in lines and fenders and as I readied our big CQR anchor, Carol motored slowly away from the raft up and out of Shaw Bay. The prudent thing would have been to go two miles further up the river, then re-anchor in narrow and well-protected Dividing Creek. I weighed the alternatives. The last forecast put the line of storms over Manassas, Virginia, moving west at thirty miles an hour. That would give us about two hours. I thought, *That's cutting it close, but we can be back at our marina with half an hour to spare.* If we stayed somewhere on the Wye, there was still a seventy percent chance of other afternoon thunderstorms that we'd have to contend with.

Carol could see I was pondering what to do and as she reached the mouth of Shaw Bay, she said aloud, "I say we anchor in Dividing Creek!"

She was right, but in the back of my mind was the thought that I wanted to get home so I could take her to see her doctor in the morning, so at the last minute, I said, "Come left, head for the marina; I'm going below to look at the radar!"

She came left, taking us south into the Wye River and increased throttle until we were doing six and a half knots. As she rounded Green "3" off Bennett Point shoal, I scanned the radar for storm activity to the west, and Carol increased our speed to seven knots.

I went on deck. "In a hurry?"

She said, "I don't want to get stuck out here or near the bridge if we get hit with the storm."

I said, "Don't worry. Once we're in the turning basin, we can tie up at one of the marina docks if we get whacked."

Half an hour later, the sky to the west darkened at an alarming rate, and we could see lightning flashes on the western shore of Chesapeake Bay. I went below and looked at the radar, but could barely distinguish the shore from the storm line at this point. Returning to the cockpit, I looked to the west again and said aloud, "Son of a bitch, how did that move so fast? Goose it up, Baby!"

Lastdance moved along at seven and a half knots, but the sounds of thunder were becoming audible over the noise of her engine.

We were in a race, but the greatest danger was not out here, it was getting hit with strong winds while trying to maneuver within the narrow fairways of our marina. I looked at the chart and told Carol if it looked like we were going to get hit, to veer out of the channel and be prepared to anchor. She looked down at the chart and pointed out Red "2" which marked the long shoal extending south from Hood Point.

"Yeah," I said. "Before we get there, you can only leave the channel on that side. Once we're past Red "2" you can only go out of the channel on the west side, okay?"

She nodded, and I walked forward to make sure the anchor was ready to deploy, but left the stopper on the chain to keep it from dropping on its own if we got bounced around.

The sky darkened ominously by the minute, but we were now in the turning basin south of the bridge with ten minutes to go until it opened. The radar showed the bold squall line off the western shore of Chesapeake Bay, less than ten miles away and moving at about thirty knots. It would be on us in fifteen minutes, which gave us time to make the bridge but was too risky to enter the marina.

I said, "We'll tie up at the fuel dock on the other side of the bridge."

As I readied dock lines on our starboard side, the bridge tender sounded the horn to signal he was opening. It was five minutes early. *Good man*. I thought *He knows the storm is approaching and is letting us through.*

As soon as the span opened, Carol accelerated quickly, and we raced through the narrow passage, giving the tender an extra loud thank you as he peered down from his perch in the tower.

"What now?" Carol asked.

"Go to the fuel dock!"

The wind suddenly increased from the west and we felt the first drops of rain. Seconds later, the sky was abruptly shattered with a bolt of lightning and a loud clap of thunder.

Carol yelled over the wind. "The fuel dock is crowded. I'm going to Red Eye's, okay?"

"Okay," I shouted, and as she turned, I put out our two big fenders, then stood by amidships to step ashore with lines.

I looked at her thinking that she should slow down because the west wind would blow us down onto the dock, but she was already doing it and she brought *Lastdance* to a complete stop parallel to the pier and about three feet off. A few seconds later, our fenders gently kissed the wharf right in front Red Eye's Dock Bar. I stepped off and quickly secured the bow and spring lines, then took the stern line from Carol.

"Is everything closed up?" I asked.

"Yes," she replied, as she killed the engine and stepped onto the dock.

We casually strolled inside. It was wall-to-wall with people who usually sat outside to catch the band. Brenda was tending bar and had watched us tie up and said, "Wow, Carol, good docking!"

I chuckled. "That's not all she's good at, Brenda. Two Yuenglings please!"

A minute later, the sky opened up with a torrential downpour and a blast of wind that blew tables and chairs over on the patio. Lightning and thunder was all about us, and one bolt struck the marina on the other side of the narrows.

Standing at the crowded bar, Brenda brought us two drafts and again complimented Carol's boat handling. "That was really good; way to go, girl, I'm impressed!"

I toasted Carol and our luck. "That was close, huh?"

She said, "Too close, I was really nervous. Next time, we should stay put okay?"

I sheepishly agreed. "Yeah, you're right. It was just as stupid of me to come through the narrows. We should have just anchored behind Hog Island or tied up to a pier on the south side of the bridge."

As I asked Brenda for menus, Carol took off her foul weather jacket. The level of chatter immediately diminished and eager eyes from men at the crowded bar stared at her. She was still wearing only the tank top and to add spice to the image, it was now thoroughly wet from perspiration. Also, the wide suspender straps from the bib-trousers were imparting completely unnecessary lift. She seemed oblivious to the sudden attention and I said nothing until our lunch arrived.

"Don't shriek like you did this morning, but do you remember what I had said about how men react to women with big boobs in flimsy tank tops?"

With just the hint of a brazen smile, she mischievously said, "Yup!"

I snickered and whispered. "You wench! And here I thought you were all innocence and virtue, oblivious to all the stares!"

She leaned toward me with her lips seductively close to mine. "I was oblivious at first, but when I realized they were looking at me, I was too embarrassed to make a big deal over it, then I found myself enjoying it."

She kissed me with a soft lingering kiss, then went back to her cheeseburger. I thought, *Talk about a complex nature. She absentmindedly presents an enticing image, gets embarrassed over it, and then becomes an exhibitionist to overcome her embarrassment.* I kissed her cheek. "With logic like that, you're definitely from Venus!"

As we ate lunch and critiqued our storm tactics, I struggled to find a complimentary way to tell her what I was thinking. "Carol, this place is a meat market. There are women in here a lot younger than you who spent hours putting on makeup and preparing themselves to come here. You haven't showered in two days, your hair is wet and wild, and you don't have an ounce of make-up on, yet there isn't guy in the place who hasn't checked you out!" Then I added, "I hope you take that as a compliment!"

She put both hands on my cheeks, kissed me. "I do, Ron, I do. Thank you."

An hour later, well fed and with the last of the rain and wind gone, we motored around the fuel dock and secured *Lastdance* safely in her slip.

There had been no further falling incidents since Knapps Narrows, but back at home Monday morning, I organized my thoughts as I prepared to call Sloan-Kettering. Carol again protested, saying she just tripped. Nevertheless, I called Dr. Nolan at nine sharp. He said he would scrutinize the MRI done in May and would schedule a new one. In my mind, he seemed concerned over my description of how Carol fell. When she asked me what he said, I told her he didn't think anything was wrong but would schedule an MRI.

Carol characteristically worried about our insurance and said an extra MRI might not be covered. I said impatiently, "If the doctor orders it, it'll be covered. If not, screw it, we'll pay for it ourselves!"

Dr. Nolan called back within the hour. He said the May MRI was squeaky clean and we had an appointment to do another one August 8."

I felt elated. "That's great, thank you, doctor!"

I told Carol we had an appointment and added, "I'm sure it's going to be okay, and a clean MRI will be a nice birthday present for you."

She laughed, "Birthday present? I hope I'm at least getting dinner out for my birthday!"

We drove into New York and did the MRI. By noon we strolled along First Avenue looking for a place to have lunch and wait for the results. Our usual routine was to eat lunch, then Doctor Nolan would give us the MRI report and do a brief physical exam. We were always nervous at this point, but now, other than Carol falling and the few other minor incidents, there were no significant signs that something was wrong. I began to think I overreacted and I felt bad, knowing I caused her unnecessary worry and fear. As in the past, Doctor Nolan came in with a smile on his face and said. "The MRI looks great, go sailing!" I thanked him, then reminded the receptionist to send a copy of the MRI to Doctor Tew in Cincinnati.

Carol took my hands in hers. "I knew everything was okay, but I really appreciate you worrying about me."

I saw tears welling up in her eyes and my own emotions let loose as tears rolled down my cheeks. "I'm so sorry I worried you; I was just so scared."

She squeezed my hands. "I know, Ron, but it's okay now." Then she added, "So where are you taking me for my birthday, huh?"

I smiled and said, "It's a surprise, but you'll want to have an overnight bag packed with a nice dress and sexy lingerie in it!"

We returned to Maryland and spent a quiet night on *Lastdance* where, on her deck and within the confines of her hull, we felt most at home. This good boat embodied the achievement of our childhood dream and characterized our entire relationship. We sailed thousands of miles in her, through good weather and bad and we shared all of our passions, joys, and fears aboard her. This night, there was much to reflect upon because the recent scare once again reminded us of how fragile life could be and there was no hiding the weak-kneed feeling we felt. It was like escaping unscathed from a violent car crash. I made no effort to conceal it from her that night, when overwhelmed with sadness that I could lose her, I fought back tears as I took her in my arms before we slept.

"I was so afraid it was back."

"So was I, Ron. So was I."

Doctor Tew called the next morning and said he concurred with Sloan-Kettering; the MRI was clean, so happily, with Carol's medical concerns put to rest, we sailed to St. Michael's for her birthday. I reserved a room and boat slip at a luxurious manor house resort and spa. Being retired, this inn would normally be out of our price range, but given the anxiety of the past week and subsequent good news, as well as it being Carol's birthday, we went a little crazy. Even though in years past we'd spent countless nights at anchor just off the inn's dock, for this occasion we had a chic room with a water view. The room was opulent with a romantic king-size sleigh bed, a working fireplace, and a spectacular view of the Miles River with *Lastdance* in the foreground.

Carol's present included being pampered at the luxurious spa for several hours, which she said she loved. Then, remembering our wager at Indian Key years before, she added, "And I didn't have to sail topless to get it!"

In the afternoon we strolled around the beautiful grounds, then took afternoon high tea at the water's edge. Later, we dined at the inn's elegant restaurant where Carol looked ravishing, wearing a long-forgotten black dress that she jokingly said she kept for emergencies. Sitting across the table from her, I was gripped by her innate beauty and vitality, and as we ate, I couldn't take my eyes off her. It was almost impossible to believe how sick and frail she had been, and I silently prayed that she would not ever have to endue that again.

As she often did whenever I seemed preoccupied, she asked, "Where are you?"

I took her hand and smiled. "Sorry, Baby. I was just thinking about how beautiful you look and how I'm going to have my way with you later."

She squeezed my hand. "Thank you, and that will be nice, Ron, but you looked sad, not seductive." Then she added, "It's okay; you heard the results. There's nothing going on in my head."

I smiled and told her the truth. "It wasn't that, honestly. I was thinking how beautiful you look tonight, but I was also remembering how sick you were just a year ago."

It was a balmy night, and once back in our room, I lit the gas fireplace and turned off the lights so only the soft glow of the fire illuminated the room. Carol called out from the balcony for me to put just a lamp on. Perplexed, I did as she asked. Then, retrieving the bottle of Verve Clicquot I had left to chill, I put on one of the plush hotel robes and joined her outside. Also wearing a hotel robe, she sat on a chaise lounge and motioned for me to join her. I poured the champagne, but I couldn't conceal my disappointment. "What happened to the sexy lingerie you were going to bring?"

She didn't answer. She touched my glass with hers and said, "Thank you for all this, I really love it."

"Happy birthday, Carol; I wish I could do this for you everyday."

"You do, Ron. In so many ways."

Then she stood, undid the plush robe and let it fall from her shoulders to the balcony floor. She left me breathless as she stood before me wearing a long sheer gown, the soft contours of her voluptuous body clearly silhouetted by the lamp in the room behind her that she shrewdly had me turn back on. We sipped our champagne on the balcony, then retreated to the four poster bed. Although I felt as romantic as if this had been our honeymoon, I still couldn't shake the nagging feeling that all wasn't well.

We began the fall of 2005 with a cruise to Fairlee Creek for Labor Day weekend. We rafted to *Tranquility, Broadway, Belle-Amie,* and *Galena* and later joined by Carol's friend, Ann, who drove down from New Jersey. Ann had last sailed with us five years earlier in Florida on a short cruise from Fort Lauderdale to Coconut Grove. Thinking back to that day, I smiled as I remembered how they had tantalized the all male crew of a training schooner on Biscayne Bay.

We had been approaching the Rickenbacker Causeway Bridge when I went below to make docking arrangements with the marina in Coconut Grove. As I scrutinized the cruising guide, we passed through the shadow of the bridge, and moments later, Carol tacked the boat, which I thought was unusual. There was no urgency in her voice as she and Ann went through the maneuver. Still, there was no need to tack so I asked, "Is everything okay?"

"No problem, Baby. We're just having some fun."

I then heard laughter by both of them, followed by what sounded like a chorus of muffled shouts.

Several minutes later, Carol tacked again. I heard her and Ann laughing, then the unmistakable shouts and whistling of men, followed soon after by Carol's voice calling out, "Ready about…Hard a'lee" as she tacked yet again.

I thought, *Okay, what the hell is going on?* I went on deck to investigate. Carol and Ann were behind the helm wearing the *Hooters* tank tops I bought for them in Miami the night before. A second later, loud shouting in a foreign language rang out as Carol sailed close down the port rail of an anchored schooner with dozens of shouting trainees. It was a sight. The schooner listed to port as the crew clamored to get a closer view of my crew.

Passing them for the third time, several voices in English urged them to take off their tops. Then, upon seeing me standing in the companionway, a collective burst of scowls and boos rang out. I smiled and waved as we drew away and said to my flaunting crew, "You can tack back and forth all afternoon, but if you wenches want dinner in Coconut Grove, we'd better be heading there soon."

Carol laughed. "Oh, okay, kill joy."

The girls turned and waved goodbye to their audience, jiggling one last time which caused a thunderous outburst from the crew of the schooner as it vanished astern. I shook my head laughing as I went below and even now, five years later, I smiled at the memory.

Throughout September, Carol seemed to tire easily but we'd been very busy with family events including our sixteenth wedding anniversary and Christopher's return from Iraq. We raced in another RWYB regatta, and at the end of October; we drove to Camp Lejeune once again, this time for the birth of a new granddaughter. A month later, but without Carol, I returned to see Christopher receive a Bronze Star for his combat actions in Iraq. It was unlike Carol to miss something like that, and even though I had seen no new signs of a neurological problem, it troubled me, but I chalked it up to nothing more than fatigue from too much running around.

In October, I received a phone call from my classmate and good friend, Jerry Mount. He had been following Carol's medical progress since 2001 and called to tell me that astonishingly, his wife Mary Lynne who he had been married to since our graduation from Maine Maritime Academy, had just been diagnosed with a glioblastoma brain tumor like Carol. I quickly brought Jerry up to speed on everything I knew, and we began a journey together, which as midshipman thirty-five years earlier, would have been impossible to even contemplate.

Jerry and Mary Lynne were confronted with the same dismal statistics that we first read about, but they were encouraged by Carol's three year survival. I told Jerry about the false alarm we had gone through in the summer, but that Carol still seemed to be doing well. We talked almost daily and discussed various treatment options and clinical trials, but it sounded like Mary Lynne was experiencing several secondary problems that Carol hadn't had to deal with. Nevertheless, we continued to talk frequently comparing notes and offering encouragement to each other.

By Thanksgiving, I noticed Carol was sometimes favoring her right leg. When I pressed her, she confessed that her left hip hurt. Till this day, I'm troubled that alarm bells didn't go off in my head. I was responsible for her, and I missed what, in retrospect, should have been a signal that something as wrong. Carol didn't want to even acknowledge a problem and quelled my fears by reminding me of the earlier false alarm I had raised.

"Ron, you bitch about aches and pains all the time. I'm fifty-seven years old and I sometimes ache. There's nothing more to it, so please don't worry about me."

In late December, we went to our annual Christmas dinner at a restaurant in Brooklyn with our friends John, Denise, Rich, and Lori. We were seated just a few minutes when suddenly, I sensed, more than saw Carol toppling from her chair. No one could get to her fast enough, and she fell to the floor. Even before she hit, I could see from the confused look on her face that she was unaware of what was happening, which reminded me of how she fell on the boat back in August.

She wasn't hurt, and as we rushed to help her up, she smiled at onlookers from other tables, handling them with humor and aplomb.

Pointing to me, she said, "Lucky him, huh? Guess I'm a cheap date, one glass of wine and bam!"

Looking at me, she said more seriously, "I don't know what happened, Ron. I suddenly felt off-balance and the next thing I know, I was on my ass."

I said, "Let's go home."

"No, I feel fine now!"

"Geez, Carol, you just fell off your chair. Let me take you home!"

"No, I'm fine. Please, I want to stay."

"Are you sure?"

"Yes, really. I want to stay."

I agreed to stay, but I could see that she was clearly not herself.

I called Sloan-Kettering in the morning, but since it wasn't an emergency, they told me to call Doctor Nolan Monday morning. I wanted to take her to our local hospital, but Carol insisted there was nothing wrong with her at the moment, saying, "We should wait until we talk to Doctor Nolan in the morning."

Other than the fall, Carol's only problem was increased fatigue and some pain in her left leg, but although she used her cane to walk occasionally, she downplayed the symptoms. Still, Doctor Nolan scheduled an MRI for New Year's Eve. Carol was looking forward to going out and told me to reschedule the MRI for after the holiday, but this time I held fast.

"No, damn it, you're a nurse and should know better."

Driving into Manhattan on the last day of December, we crossed the George Washington Bridge and I looked at the cars around us and wondered how many people were going into the city to celebrate New Year's Eve, whereas I had no thoughts of celebration, just an ominous feeling.

Two hours later, we sat nervously waiting for the MRI results. The attending doctor, who we had never met before, came to us with a poker face and simply said, "We'd like to admit Carol to the hospital; we're arranging for a room right now."

I was stunned but not surprised. "Admit her, why? What's going on?"

He said Dr. Nolan would give us the details, but the MRI showed the presence of a mass and some swelling and she needed to be admitted.

Later than night, we welcomed in 2006 alone in a hospital room, and instead of champagne, my wife and best friend was being pumped full of Decadron to reduce swelling of her brain, which was probably causing the pain in her hip.

On January second, we sat in the doctor's office, more fearful than ever before, and I held Carol's hands in mine as we waited nervously to meet with Doctor Nolan and Eileen. When they came in, I could tell by the grave look on their faces that it was not good news. It was worse than that, much worse; it was devastating. There was a new tumor, and between the August MRI, which was squeaky clean, and now, it had developed and grown in a way that made it inoperable! I was stunned and speechless for a moment. Carol began to cry, and I drew her close to me.

I said, "Inoperable? That can't be!" *We'd heard that bullshit once before, but that was a local hospital in New Jersey.* I shouted. "This is Sloan-Kettering! What the hell do you mean it's inoperable?"

Carol calmed me. "Let Doctor Nolan talk, Ron."

"No!" I shouted. "I don't want to hear what can't be done." Then, contradicting myself, I asked, "Why can't it be removed?"

Carol calmed me again, and Doctor Nolan explained that this tumor was incredibly aggressive. It had an irregular shape and had infiltrated her brain stem and simply couldn't be removed surgically.

With panic in my voice, I shouted, "Doctor Tew! I want the MRI sent to Doctor Tew!"

Eileen said, "It's already on its way; it should arrive this morning."

Then Doctor Nolan said, "We're going to leave you two alone for a while, then we want to come back to discuss options with you, okay?"

I kept current with all the latest treatment protocols, and I thought to myself, *What fucking options? There are no options. Doctor Tew is the only option!*

As the door closed, I turned to Carol. She looked terrified and collapsed in my arms in tears of despair.

I wanted to be strong for her, but I couldn't rally myself. I had read too much about how bad it was when the tumor infiltrated the brain stem.

I knew I had to get a grip on myself for Carol. I couldn't let her believe I was already giving up.

"Carol, look at me. Doctor Tew will do it again! Don't you remember they were so certain they could only get thirty percent of the tumor, then Doctor Tew said he could get it all?"

She smiled faintly. "Oh, Ron. I don't want to go through all that again, I don't think I can do it."

"You can do it, you have to do it. We have plans. You'll do it, Carol, I'll help you. I promise, Baby."

Doctor Nolan outlined several chemotherapy protocols that had shown limited success with a recurring glioblastoma, and he wanted to get started immediately with the most promising. The statistics were so heavily stacked against Carol I didn't believe a drug would work, but the idea of fighting back gave her a renewed sense of hope, and I remained outwardly positive in spite of my inner pessimism. She took her first dose that afternoon, and as I waited for her to finish, Doctor Tew called.

For the second time that day, our world collapsed. In spite of my blind emotional faith in him, intellectually I had already guessed what he would say. "I'm sorry, Ron, but it's inoperable. There are tentacles everywhere; it cannot be surgically removed." I sat stunned and disbelieving as he went on to tell me that she was in excellent hands at Sloan-Kettering and that all that could be done was to make her as comfortable as possible and try chemotherapy.

Driving home, Carol said she didn't want her kids to know how serious it was. I didn't argue with her, but I thought they should know. She insisted and made me promise not to tell them she was dying. I heard those words and began to cry so hard I had to pull the car off the road. As was the case so many times before, she comforted me when it should have been me comforting her, and I thought to myself, *To win the battle once, only to have the victory of her renewed life snatched away must be totally demoralizing. Yet, here she was being strong, trying comfort me.*

I vowed to be strong, but the first time I was alone, I selfishly felt sorry for myself and shouted yet again to heaven in a rage. "*Why are you doing this? You put that fucking tumor in her head the first time, then you took my brother and my father, and now you're doing it again to Carol. What is wrong with you?"*

The next ten months would be the supreme test of our love and everything we had come to trust and believe in. The large A over I card was once again in a prominent place in the living room. I made another one for the bedroom, but in a rare moment of resignation, Carol said, "You won't have to stand by me very long."

My temper flared and I was about to chastise her, but I let it pass. The rest of January, Carol's physical condition deteriorated from the combined effects of the chemo and Decadron, and she gained weight from the steroids. The tumor was also affecting her motor control, so walking became very difficult to the point where physical therapy was needed twice a week. I didn't want to demoralize Jerry, but I had to tell him what was happening on our end. He was devastated. First for Carol, then in his mind, it removed the one direct source of personal inspiration for Mary Lynne. After that, I don't think our conversations ever again reflected the hope we once shared for our women.

I was working two days a week at my old company to offset some of the medical cost not covered by insurance, but our neighbor, Father Vincent, a catholic priest, came over daily to spend time with Carol. We met Father Vinny when we moved to New Jersey. He was from the Upper East Side in New York and had been a U.S. Navy chaplain, so we had some things in common. Even before Carol got sick again, she would walk his dog, Duffy, with him and they'd talk about Carol's "search for truths," as Vinny called it. He'd say she was self-honest and a genuine searcher, something I knew about her from as far back as our childhood days in Brooklyn.

I could see that he was having an effect on her and that she was becoming increasingly religious in her thoughts and expressions. I wasn't sure how I felt about that because I was still blaming Father Vinny's boss for causing this travesty in the first place. Nevertheless, it gave Carol comfort, and I eventually came to fully support her return to the church and developed a deep appreciation for the daily spiritual comfort he gave her.

I didn't think it was possible to feel more despondent, but the result of the February MRI was bad. The chemo had no effect on the tumor, and it had spread into other areas of her brain. In reality, I wasn't surprised because Carol's physical condition had worsened considerably. I asked, "What's next?"

Doctor Nolan simply said, "Hospice."

I knew what hospice was, but I didn't grasp the full impact of the finality of that one word, but Carol did. Through tears she said, "No! I'm not ready to roll over and die. There must be something else to try."

The doctor said there were several other chemo agents available but none with better results than Temozolomide, the one she had just come off. He recommended staying with it another month, then added that sometimes one patient reacts far better to a drug than another and as long as Carol was tolerating the drugs, he could prescribe another agent the following month if the March results were not encouraging. We agreed but I continued to spend countless hours on the internet looking for a silver bullet.

By then, Carol needed full-time care. For reasons that had to do with her morale as much as physical comfort, she didn't want to use a catheter. She couldn't walk alone or go to the bathroom, which meant I had to transfer her from the bed or couch to the wheelchair, then to the toilet, then reverse the process. Doing this during the day, then again several times a night was exhausting and resulted in sleep deprivation for both of us. In her mind, she felt she was being a burden on me, and it also challenged her strong sense of independence. I could see this was going to be a source of contention because I'd catch her trying to get up on her own, which was dangerous.

One night in late March in the fog of sleep, I sensed movement. "Carol, is that you?"

I heard her voice, but wasn't sure where it was coming from.

"I'm okay, I'm using the walker."

My mind tried to register what she meant, and I opened my groggy eyes to see her standing at the foot of the bed.

"Oh no! Please, Baby. You can't do that. You have to wait for me!"

I should have got up to help her. I didn't. A moment later I heard a loud crash and a cry of pain. She had fallen in the small bathroom, partially blocking the door, and I had to remove it to get to her.

I struggled to lift her into the wheelchair, cursing and angry at her for not waking me and equally mad at myself for not getting up when I sensed she was up. Hours later in the emergency room, they confirmed she broke her ankle. This was serious due to the dangers of an embolism. When I explained her condition and the medications she was on, they decided to keep her in the hospital for observation. Ultimately, extensive surgery was required, after which she was put into a rehabilitation facility for several weeks. Initially, this gave me a much-needed break from the daily care giving, but with the knowledge that she was in a terminal condition from the cancer, the time apart robbed us of the intimacy that we both so desperately wanted and needed.

Her April MRI dealt us another crushing blow. The tumor had grown considerably. We made the decision to switch to another chemo agent, but that also meant an increase in steroids and its associated side effects. I felt that any benefit Carol was getting at the rehab facility was negated by the time we were spending apart, especially at night when for more than twenty years, we sleep embraced in each others arms.

"Carol, I want you to come home. I need you to come home!"

I began to tell her I was arranging for home physical therapy when she burst into tears and threw her arms around me.

"Oh, Baby. I want to come home so bad. I don't want to be a burden, but I hate being here."

We cried together, then talked for hours.

"I promise, Princess. I'll get you discharged tomorrow morning."

As I gathered my things to leave, Carol asked, "Please stay until I fall asleep."

I smiled at her. "Of course, Baby."

Sitting in the chair beside her bed, I held her hand and fell asleep myself. I woke at two in the morning, and once again tried to leave, but even in her sleep, she wouldn't let me go and whispered, "Please don't go, Ron."

I climbed into bed with her, and through the entire night, we never once let go of each other.

We followed Bill and Jane's winter voyage over the internet as they sailed *Galena* to the Caribbean. I'd look for Bill's weekly cruising blog and print it out for Carol to read, but more often, she'd ask me to read it to her as she sat by the window looking at the snowy landscape outside. Sometimes she would cry afterwards, saying how sorry she was that she wouldn't be able to go cruising around the world with me. It was during those times that we would just hold each other for hours and I'd recant our earlier sailing adventures as if reciting a storybook to a child. When we read that Bill and Jane would be arriving back at our marina in early May, Carol asked me to follow their progress as they sailed up the coast. Then, on the day they were sailing up Chesapeake Bay, she asked me to take her to Kent Narrows to welcome them home.

I didn't think it was wise at first, but other than going into New York for an MRI and chemo, and her stay at the rehab center, she had been stuck in our condo for months and could use the diversion. So, early on May 12 we drove to Maryland and arrived just in time to see *Galena* enter the fairway to O-dock. As I pushed Carol's wheelchair down the dock, she began to shout and wave excitedly. Bill and Jane waved back, but I could see the stunned looks on their faces when they realized who she was. When they departed in October, Carol had been voluptuous and full of vitality. Now, seven months later, she had gained over seventy pounds and was in a wheelchair, and regardless of how excitedly she waved, she was clearly a sick woman.

Bill and Jane secured *Galena* in her slip and after composing themselves, they came ashore and greeted Carol with cheery hugs. Watching this reunion, it didn't go unnoticed by me how Carol carried on without embarrassment or awkwardness at her condition. There was no vanity or self-consciousness; these were friends who had come home from the sea, and she was just happy to see them. In that moment, I discovered and marveled at yet another facet to her beautiful character.

CHAPTER 30
LAST VOYAGE

Through unrelenting and painful physical therapy, Carol was again able to move around in our home with the aid of a walker. She lost much of the weight she had gained from steroids, but she was still in constant pain. It was no surprise that after a long and difficult winter of suffering and bad news, she tried to convince me to take her on our annual sail to Baltimore over Memorial Day. I agreed, but only if she promised not to move about, even once on the boat, without my assistance.

Departing a day earlier than our friends so we could have time to ourselves and get a good spot in the anchorage, we arrived in Inner Harbor and motored gingerly among tourists in dragon headed paddle boats. Then, selecting a spot where imaginary lines from the World Trade Center and aquarium intersected, we anchored *Lastdance* and settled back to watch the show around us.

In previous years, we'd go to exhibits at the aquarium where Carol always insisted on seeing the dolphins first, as if they were old friends. From there we'd tour the *USS Torsk*, a decommissioned submarine of the same class I had once served in and each year, she would ask the same questions about that time in my life. Afterwards, we'd stop at one of the many outdoor bars where after one or two margaritas, the woman in her would emerge, and she would become devilishly seductive with me. Then, just as quickly she would display her childlike curiosity again as we strolled the science center at the far end of the harbor promenade. Regretfully, we could do none of that this year. She couldn't go ashore or even shuffle among the boats that rafted to *Lastdance* the next day. Nevertheless, after a painful winter of chemotherapy, it was good for her to get out on the water among so many friends who came aboard to greet her.

Carol couldn't have alcohol, so I made her virgin margaritas, and she became drunk with the passing extravaganza that was Inner Harbor on a holiday weekend. I was glad I brought her! The symphony of sounds and aromas from nearby boat grills and restaurants ashore was a magic elixir for her. There was no wind on the morning we departed and Carol's disappointment at not sailing almost overshadowed the benefit of the voyage, but not quite. Later, as we motored down the Patapsco River, we approached the old fort south of the Francis Scott Key Bridge. As I had done countless times before, I said. "See that fort, that's Fort Carroll. It was named after you, but they misspelled it."

She said nothing.

"What, you don't believe me?"

She looked at me and offered a sad smile, then took my hand. "Promise you'll take me sailing once more before the summer ends, no matter what."

"You know I can't promise that, Baby. You're really sick."

Then, acknowledging the implication of her words and fighting back tears, I said, "Okay, I promise, but not until you say you believe me that they named Fort Carroll after you!"

Tears filled her eyes. "I believe you, Ron. I believe you."

At the end of June there was no doubt Carol was in extremis. Even the most promising experimental chemo failed to produce any results, and her physical condition worsened as the loss of motor control on her left side became more acute. Still, she had experienced several rebounds in the past, so there was no way of knowing that the Fourth of July weekend would be her last voyage aboard *Lastdance*. It was the name she had chosen above all others ten years earlier, but it was a name that now broke my heart.

We left home early Friday morning for the drive to Maryland. Saint Michael's was the destination for the Independence Day raft up with our marina friends, and Carol seemed happy with that. As we drove south, however, her talk turned to celebrations that might be going on in Annapolis that holiday weekend. I made a mental note to ask her about it later.

Right now, my thoughts were on how I was going to get her safely aboard the boat. Carol needed a wheelchair most of the time, but could sometimes walk short distances with a walker, but that wouldn't be possible on a narrow finger pier.

As I pushed her wheelchair onto O-Dock, she spotted our friends Bill, Gene, and Jeff sitting on our dock box sipping rum. She called out to them.

"Hey, get off my dock box unless you've got a beer for me!"

They hadn't seen Carol since Memorial Day weekend, and they gathered around her, but it was Gene who ran to his boat to get a beer for her. It was an awkward moment for everyone, but only briefly as Carol's cheery demeanor put everyone at ease. Gene returned with a cold Corona and Carol readily accepted it.

"You really know how to treat a woman, Gene." Then motioning to me with her bottle, she said, "Captain Bligh here won't let me drink at home!"

Everyone laughed and as others heard her name mentioned, they came off their boats to greet her, and as often happened, an impromptu dock party began.

Nothing could have been better for Carol, but after a half hour, I could see she was tiring. I suggested we move the party aboard *Lastdance*. I knew she'd need to use the head soon, and I didn't want it to become a crisis because it was so hard for her to move about. I asked for help, but she said she wanted to board on her own. Before I could say anything, she looked at me and softly pleaded, "Please let me do this. It's not the beer, Ron. Being here gives me strength, really!"

"Okay, but someone has to walk in front of and behind you, I'll be on the boat as you step across!"

She laughed and said, "Okay, you old fuddy duddy."

Then with Bill in front of her and Jeff behind her, she got out of the wheelchair and carefully walked down the narrow finger pier, boarding *Lastdance* under her own power. I thought, *God, I hope I'll be as strong when my turn comes.*

Once aboard, she laughed and turning to everyone she said, "Hey, I just gotta pee. I hope the party isn't over!"

Half a dozen friends came aboard and partied on as I guided Carol below. Once in our cabin, Carol began to cry softly.

Embracing her, I asked, "What's wrong, Baby?"

"Nothing, silly, I'm just so happy to be here on our boat again."

She then put her arms around my neck and said, "It would be nice to go to Saint Michael's with everyone, but I'd really rather go to Annapolis alone with you. Can we do that? Do you think our friends will be mad?"

I smiled. "Of course we can go there. I've been considering the same thing, and don't worry, no one will be mad."

I hugged her tightly and fought back tears.

Carol loved the Chesapeake's many faces. Sailing its broad expanses and exploring its hidden rivers and creeks filled her with a sense of history and she delighted in the times we were the only boat in an anchorage. On such nights we used to lower the bimini and share intimate evenings in our cockpit under a canopy of stars. We'd sip red wine and make out like a couple of kids, then talk for hours about things like life, destiny, and aliens. It was Annapolis she loved most though, and depending on her mood, we might enjoy the town from a mooring in the harbor or be right in the thick of things by bringing *Lastdance* along the seawall at City Dock. From there, we could dine and pub crawl the evening away, then watch tourists as they strolled the bustling waterfront. Mooring or seawall, she had always been as excited entering Annapolis as the very first time we called there in 1994. I was certain this Fourth of July weekend would be no different.

As our friends bound for St. Michael's awaited the bridge opening, we headed out the north channel, bound for Annapolis in a twelve-knot northwest breeze. Carol took pleasure from the boat's motion and the warm sun, and as she often did, she thanked me for the conditions as if I had ordered them up just for her. We rounded Love Point, then came to a broad reach and glided down the bay toward Annapolis ten miles away. Carol took a brief turn at the helm, but was happy to simply sit back and survey our surroundings as we surged through small waves.

An hour and forty-five minutes later, we headed up at the yellow flashing light southeast of Greenbury Point. Dousing our sails, we then motored toward the Naval Academy, racing several boats for what we were sure would be the last mooring.

"Hurry," she said excitedly. "I don't see any open moorings."

I smiled as I increased the throttle and thought, *Even now, with her body ravaged by cancer and chemo, she is so childlike in her excitement over a place she's been to countless times before.*

As soon as we rounded Sycamore Point, it became evident that our race wasn't necessary. There were several open moorings, and knowing what her answer would be, I still asked, "Which one do you want to take?"

Ignoring my question, she said, "Can we go in and check for an open slip?"

I smiled as I motored through the mooring field and entered City Dock. We went past occupied slips across from Pusser's and the Fleet Reserve Club, then looked for an opening along the seawall, but it appeared to be fully occupied as well.

Carol's disappointment was obvious.

I said, "Sorry, Princess. Looks like we have to take a mooring."

She smiled. "It's okay; it's not your fault."

Continuing on toward the turning basin, we passed a docked sport fisherman whereupon Carol shouted, "Ron, there! There's an opening, go there, go there!"

I saw the opening along the seawall between the sport fisherman and a large trawler. It looked tight, and I tried to judge if we could safely squeeze between them. From my experience working for the Annapolis Harbormaster, I knew the bulkhead slips were forty-feet long, but the bow of the sport fisherman protruded slightly into the open space and the trawler's transom gave us no room to spare on the other end.

Deciding we could fit, I rigged our dock lines, and all that remained was to figure out how to do it. Fortunately, the wind was almost southwesterly, so I thought if I could position us between the two boats, the wind would blow us in between them as long as I maintained our fore and aft position. *Lastdance* has two large and intimidating anchors overhanging her bow, and these got the undivided attention of the trawler skipper. As I maneuvered into position, I thought, *Who better to keep and eye on things up forward.* Carol helped by telling me how our stern was lining up with the bow of the sport fisherman, so I gave it a try.

As anticipated, the wind got hold of us, and with the throttle in idle, using forward and reverse as needed, *Lastdance* blew down between the two yachts until we struck softly against the bulkhead. I threw the bow line ashore, then stepped ashore with the fore and aft spring lines and quickly secured them to the center piling. Carol threw me the stern line, which I promptly secured, then I walked bow line to a piling between us and the trawler. Carol was elated and clapped her hands with joy. As I stepped back aboard, she stood on weak legs and hugged me as if I had just fought off ten thousand Persians at Thermopylae.

Telling her she deserved a beer for her help, I went below to get a cold Corona for her and a Gosling on the rocks for me. Then, sitting in the cockpit, we surveyed what would be our home for the next two days.

I chuckled. "The trawler guy never cracked a smile. I guess we made him nervous."

Carol touched her beer bottle against my glass and said, "Cheers, Baby. You did good, and we're going to have fun, so forget the old grump. This is a great spot. We're right in the thick of things!"

I smiled and thought, *Ever since we were kids, she always said she wanted to be right in the thick of things.*

She was right. We were in the thick of things and lucky to find such a good slip. This is the center of the historic district, where six streets converge on the large traffic circle at the foot of Main Street. There, a small park sits at the terminus of the narrow finger of water protruding into downtown Annapolis. This is where sailing ships and fishing boats have docked since the founding of the town in 1649 and now serves as a center for visiting yachts. Looking north, the dome of the state capital building can easily be seen, and the history of America's first capital abounds in nearly every building between it and the harbor. Although Carol was too weak to leave the boat this time, it didn't diminish her enthusiasm for any of the sights and sounds of this vibrant town.

The finger docks and slips along the seawall were occupied by boats from all over the east coast and even a few from overseas. Even the dinghy dock was fully occupied by tenders from anchored and moored boats in the harbor, and sailors and tourists alike meandered city streets that came right down to the waterfront. I made another drink for myself and brought up an iced tea for Carol, and as we people-watched from the comfort of our cockpit, she pointed out lean looking midshipmen from the Naval Academy in crisp white uniforms. She smiled and said, "I remember back in the day when you looked like that," and then took my hands in hers and kissed my lips. Looking into my eyes, she then reminisced about an exciting night in a Manhattan hotel when I was a midshipman on leave. The memory was wonderful, but it saddened me for an instant until she added with a chuckle.

"I was just in high school. My father would have shot you if he found out."

I laughed. "Just imagine what he would have done if he found out about our first time back in Brooklyn. Hell, you were only in junior high school then."

Later in the evening, in a town where we once ate every meal ashore, Carol was now confined to our boat and in constant pain as we watched fireworks and listened to the Naval Academy band. We talked for a long time about all the things we'd done, and I asked if she had any regrets. She thought for a moment, then said, "The tree. I always wished you had carved our names inside a heart on the tree on 74th Street."

I remembered the day. I tried to do it, but Mr. Savino, whose property the tree was on, came out and took my knife and threatened to tell my parents if I ever came back. I thought about how such a small thing meant so much to her, even then as her life ebbed away. An instant later and to Carol's shock, I took out my rigging knife and began to carve our names in our beautiful teak cockpit table.

She shouted, "Ron, are you nuts. Oh no, Baby, please don't do that!"

Tears filled her eyes, but I could see that she really liked it and she said softly, "Oh, why did you do that, Ron?"

I took her hands in mine and said simply, "Because I love you."

She kissed me softly. "I love you too, with all my heart and soul."

Carol exhausted herself with excitement and fell asleep in my arms by nine o'clock, but not before she whistled at two midshipmen walking along the dock. I sat there for a long time holding her, leaving only to get a blanket from below to wrap her in. She felt so frail in my arms and tears welled up in my eyes. Still, I couldn't suppress a smile as I remembered the night ten years earlier in the Middleton Tavern, not fifty yards away. There, she nimbly removed her bra from under a sweater and donated it to a group of fraternity boys on a scavenger hunt.

It was getting late and I woke her with a kiss. "Come on, Princess. Wake up so we can go to sleep."

She laughed. "You always say that!"

I could see she was in pain as I helped her negotiate the steep companionway steps, but once below, I closed the hatch and laughed.

She said, "What's so funny?"

I told her I had been thinking about the time she gave her bra to the frat guys in the Middleton Tavern, and she laughed with me. "You did that from under a sweater. How did you do that?"

She smiled and kissed me. "It's a women thing; you'll never figure it out."

I helped her into bed, and as we had done for twenty-one years, we faced each other and embraced. With tears in her eyes, she said, "Thank you for taking me here; I really had a nice time today."

"So did I, Princess. It was the best day of the summer."

I kissed her goodnight and she smiled, saying softly, "Goodnight, Baby. I love being on our boat with you."

Waking early the next morning, I sat in the cockpit with a cup of coffee and a book. How different everything looked in the light of day. As the city slowly came to life, early morning joggers ran by the dock, and street cleaners emptied trash cans filled by tourist the night before. An occasional dinghy puttered in from the anchorage carrying sailors eager for breakfast at Chick and Ruth's where the Pledge of Allegiance is said over a loudspeaker every morning. I grew angry at it all because I knew Carol wouldn't be here with me this time next year, and I thought, *Why her? Why not that guy there, or this woman jogging? Why not me?*

We spent the day reading and relaxing, sometimes answering questions about *Lastdance* from curious tourists, the most common being, "How far have you been?"

When Carol told folks from Arizona we'd been from Maine to the Florida Keys, they couldn't believe it.

"You mean just the two of you out on the ocean, Honey?"

Carol beamed with pride. "Yup, just the two of us!"

I bought sandwiches for lunch from our friends at The Big Cheese, a fantastic deli and cheese shop that we had been patronizing for years. The owners knew of Carol's condition and asked for her. I told them she couldn't leave the boat, so they surprised us at the end of the day by stopping by to say hello and gave her a piece of her favorite cheese, a delicious blend of mascarpone cheese with layers of pesto sauce.

Carol insisted we should dress up a bit for our holiday dinner. I wore my best khaki shorts and a crisp white shirt; she wore her silky red lounging slacks I liked so much and a very sexy red tank top. When she called me to help her into the cockpit, I looked at her, and as always, she took my breath away.

"The lady in red, huh?"

She smiled. "Like it?"

"I love it. You look beautiful!"

I set the cockpit table with a white tablecloth and candles, and after helping her get on deck, I opened our favorite champagne and we toasted Independence Day and then each other. I brought up the shrimp risotto I made for dinner and added some of the mascarpone cheese to it. Then, over the remaining champagne and a bottle of wine, we dined al fresco in our cockpit, as pedestrians walked past, some gawking as they saw our feast. Later, I brought out dessert, a large portion of tiramisu I'd secretly purchased at the cheese store earlier in the day.

Carol said, "This is the best restaurant in town and serves the best risotto by the most handsome cook, how will I ever pay for it because my cheap husband didn't give me any money?"

I smiled. "You'll have to wash dishes lady because nutten is free in this joint."

"Oh, I don't do dishes, mister; I had something else in mind."

Then putting her hands behind her head, she closed her eyes and slightly jiggled her breasts for me.

"Oh, you wench! Don't do that. I've been frisky as hell since you came out in that outfit."

She took a sip of wine and said, "And I've been frisky knowing that you've been frisky seeing me in this outfit, so help me go below and get me out of it."

Since she became sick again, our lovemaking had none of the wild abandon we shared during better times. Nevertheless, it was as intimate as it had ever been, but by medical necessity, it was ever so tender, which made it even more intense. Carol was a sexual creature, and even in this dreadful state of health, she needed to share herself with me as much as I needed to be with her.

We departed the next morning with the sun glistening off the dome of the Naval Academy chapel, and it broke my heart to know that Carol would probably never be back. The wind was fourteen knots from the northwest and would have made for a good but lengthy sail around the south end of Kent Island. Carol's fatigue was evident though, and I was eager to get her home, so I headed north under power.

"Why aren't you raising the sails?" she asked.

"I'm sorry, Baby, but you really look tired. Sailing around Bloody Point will take too long, and I don't want to spend the day tacking to Love Point against this wind because it'll be very uncomfortable for you."

Her eyes pleaded with me and she simply said, "Please, Ron. I'd really like to sail today."

Knowing the unspoken words were that she would probably never get to sail again, I choked back tears. "Okay, Princess. Of course we'll sail."

An hour later, as we sailed down the bay, I held her in my arms with only the sounds of the wind and waves. Suddenly, Carol sat bolt upright and said loudly, "What's that noise?"

After all the years of sailing together and my endless pleadings with her to be specific when questioning noises, here she was doing it again.

"What noise?" I snapped. I was then immediately sorry for losing my patience, but not to be reprimanded so abruptly, she said, "The noise that doesn't sound like our dinghy slapping against the water as we tow it. That noise, smart ass!"

Oh shit, I'd done it again! I looked astern, and sure enough our dinghy was gone.

As tired as she was, she took the helm while I scanned the miles of empty bay behind us with binoculars. "There it is, way back there. Can you come about while I tend the jib?"

Without answering me directly, she called out, "Ready about." Then she shouted, "Hard a'lee," as she put the helm hard over, bringing *Lastdance* smartly about. A moment later, she had us close-hauled and making almost seven knots back up the bay. I got the boat hook and positioned myself at the rail and asked if she was okay as we rapidly approached the dinghy.

She said, "I'm fine. I'll bring us alongside it on the starboard side." Then she laughed. "Just get the damn thing on the first try."

In an instant, she had us right on it, and as it bumped gently down our hull, I snagged it with the boathook and pulled on the painter like mad to cleat it before it became taut.

"I got it!" I shouted. I put the boat hook down and finished securing the painter. "It's secured!"

She laughed again. "Are you sure?"

I said, "Yeah, I've got it. I don't know how it came loose."

I knew full well our dinghy had come undone in the past and that it was sloppy knot tying on my part that had been the cause, so I was somewhat sheepish about it. My introspection was jolted by her sweet voice calling out softly, "Stand by to jibe, Baby."

I repeated her command.

An instant later, she said tiredly, "Jibe ho," then brought our little ship smoothly through the maneuver.

The boom swung to leeward, and I trimmed the sails until we were once again sailing south on a broad reach down the bay. I could see she was exhausted and before taking over the helm, I brought up a blanket for her. A moment later, she was snuggled in my arms, wrapped warmly in the blanket as I steered a course for home. I kissed her lips, and as she opened her eyes, I could see tears forming.

"What's wrong?" I asked.

She looked into my soul. "Who will listen for noises and look after you when I'm gone?"

I felt a terrible overwhelming sadness, and through warm tears of my own I said, "You will, Carol. You will."

She patted my hand, then with both of us silent in the knowledge that this would probably be her last sail, we glided down the bay with all three sails spread like the wings of an angel taking her home.

CHAPTER 31
GONE IN THE BLINK OF AN EYE

Three days after returning home, Carol had a massive seizure. Her face became contorted and she could barely move her left arm and leg, and she had all the symptoms of a stroke. I called EMT, and after a quick triage exam, they stabilized her and took her to the emergency room of our local hospital. I followed in my car, barely able to see the road through my tears because I believed she was dying.

Once in the emergency room with her I could see that she had improved considerably. I made the doctors aware of the brain tumor, and after several test and hours of waiting, they concluded that it had been a seizure, not a stroke. Still, they admitted her for observation for a few days. A few days turned into five, and all I could think of was getting her out of there where, due to the chemo, she was very susceptible to infection. I also wanted her to be home with me so I could hold her at night as she slept. I felt that she needed to know I was with her as much as she needed any drugs.

It broke my heart to see her completely confined to a wheelchair, and over the next two months, Carol struggled through a home rehabilitation program several days a week. There were days I cried and thought in resignation, *What's the use?* Amazingly though, she never relented, and as she vigorously applied herself, I began to see slow, steady progress. It wasn't without a price in pain for her, but within the first month, she was able to use the walker as she regained some use of her left leg and arm. I urged her not to push herself so hard, but in one of the few times in our lives when she was truly angry at me, she shouted, "Ron! I read something a long time ago and I liked the way it sounded and what it meant." Catching her breath she went on. "I'm only going to say it to you once." Then, in a quivering voice she shouted, "I will not go quietly in the night! Do you understand me?"

I choked back tears, wondering if I would have her courage if I was in her situation or would I just surrender. I told her I understood and promised never again to deny her the fight she so desperately needed to wage.

One night while sitting on the couch, she suddenly turned off the television and asked me to hold her. I became concerned.

"Are you okay, Baby. What's wrong?"

She took my hands in hers and said, "I'm alright. I just want to tell you something." Hesitating to catch her breath, she squeezed my hands and said, "I want you to know I'm not afraid of dying." Then through tears, she added, "The thought of not being here makes me so sad and I'll miss the kids and you so much, but I really believe I'm going to Jesus and he will look after me."

Through tears I said, "Why are you telling me this, Carol?"

She held me tight and whispered, "I just wanted you to know I'm not afraid."

It was as much her tone and how she said it, as what she said, and I truly believed her. One of my paramount concerns for her had been this very subject, her fear of dying. Perhaps she sensed my anguish and she now felt compelled to ease my burden. *That would have been her way*, I thought. Whatever the reason, a huge physical and emotional weight had been lifted from me, and it was clear that Father Vincent had brought her to a good place. Weeks later, during another infrequent moment when we spoke of death, Carol held my hands and quietly said, "I promise I'll live through our anniversary."

I fought back tears, and for the first time, I acknowledged openly what I simply couldn't bear to concede before, that she was dying and that her fight was ending.

"Carol, it's not important; it's just a date on a calendar. It's only important for you to be comfortable and to know how much I love you."

My tears flowed freely, "Please don't leave me, Carol. Please don't leave me."

She put her arms around my neck and drew me to her, then patted my back. We remained like that for a long time, giving immeasurable comfort to each other by a simple embrace.

We hadn't wanted to participate in even an in-home hospice program, but caring for Carol became increasingly difficult. I had long since stopped going to work even two days a week, but I wasn't equipped with the knowledge and training she now needed. Pain management had become a major issue, and it was clear to me that only a hospice program could provide her with the care and medications she required. After a particularly bad night, I went to her and with reluctance in my voice said, "Carol we need to talk. You need more help than I can give you. I've read up on the in-home hospice program. They can have someone here twice a week and a nurse on call around the clock. I'll still be here all the time, Princess, but you were in so much pain last night, we need professional help."

She looked at me with a deep sadness in her eyes that broke my heart and all she said was, "Okay, call them."

Hospice proved to be everything we'd ever heard about them. They came regularly and were caring and compassionate. Most importantly, their nursing skills quickly alleviated most of the pain and discomfort Carol had been regularly enduring. I was provided with a host of medications that included powerful pain patches and morphine, anti-nausea medications, and even prescription stool softeners, all of which was meant to address quality of life issues. The downside to this was the effect on her morale. Even though her pain became manageable most of the time, in Carol's mind, crossing the threshold from treatment to hospice meant the fight was almost over. I tried to minimize that by keeping her on the latest chemo plan prescribed by Doctor Nolan, a binary program of Gleevec and Hydroxyurea. Because insurance didn't cover both hospice and treatment cost, it meant we had to pay for the expensive chemo ourselves, a fact which I had to conceal from her.

In August, we had a small family birthday party for Carol. As with the time when we welcomed Bill and Jane home from their voyage, she showed no uneasiness about her condition and eagerly urged me to take photos of her with our family. Maybe that doesn't seem like a big deal, but my experience with most women had been that if a single hair on their head was amiss, they'd scream if you even touched a camera. Not Carol; she was as comfortable that day as any other, and though it pained me to see her that way, I admired her strength of character and her lack of self-absorption and vanity.

I knew September would be the last time I could take her to Sloan-Kettering by car. She had lost almost the full use of her left side and was quickly losing her cognitive ability. Even Doctor Nolan and Eileen were surprised at her condition, and he was reluctant to prescribe another round of chemo.

"Ron, I can't say how long she has. Maybe days or weeks, but it's imminent. This is doing nothing for her, and you really should be thinking about an inpatient hospice facility."

I struggled to speak. "I know you're right, but she still asks for her chemo and dutifully notes down the dosage and time she takes it in her medical journal. I just can't take her out of the fight. It's all she's got."

Back at home when she'd ask me to take her to the bathroom, I charged her a fee of a soft kiss on my cheek. With my arms around her waist, I lifted her from the wheelchair, and when she kissed my cheek, I said, "I love you, Princess. You'll always be beautiful to me," then I kissed her passionately on her lips. As I lifted her one night though, she suddenly threw her full weight backward, straining my back unbearably.

"Carol," I yelled. "Damn it, this is hard enough, don't do that!"

She remained silent.

"Carol, do you hear me, stop it, I can barely hold you up!"

She suddenly leaned forward without even acknowledging my pleas. It happened several times and only when the hospice nurse was at our home and witnessed it, did we come to see what was happening.

Carol was having seizures, most likely induced by the pressure I was putting on her spine when I lifted her. After taking her to the bathroom, it happened just after I put my arms around her in a bear hug and applied pressure. The nurse and I got her into the bed and went into the living room.

"Ron, you can't help her here any longer; she needs full-time professional care."

Hot tears flowed over my cheeks, and I tried to protest, but she was right; I was now doing more harm than good.

"I have an idea," she said. "We can admit her for a week as part of a caregiver respite program. That will give you a rest and get her the care she needs, then we can evaluate her condition at the end of the week and make a decision."

"What decision?" I asked.

She took my hand and I could see her eyes glass over. "Ron, I'm not a doctor, but we know she is dying; she may not survive a week. At some point very soon, there will be little to nothing you can do for her. Do you understand that?"

I didn't want to, but I did understand and I cried unashamedly. When I composed myself, I went in to talk with Carol. "I'm causing the seizures by lifting you, Baby. That's why you're throwing yourself backwards."

Her immediate concern was for me. She said, "I'm sorry, Ron. I can't help it; I don't even know its happening."

"I know, it's okay, but I can't lift you for a while, so to help me, we can get you into what they call a caregiver respite program. They'll admit you for a week so I can get some rest, then you can come home."

Then, in an attempt to ease her mind, I added. "They also said the insurance will cover it once every six months."

I didn't know if she bought it, but it was mostly true except I knew she wouldn't be here to take advantage of the program in six months and it made me choke on my words.

She looked into my eyes. "Are you telling me this is for your benefit?"

I couldn't lie to her. "No, it's as much for you as it is to give me a break, but you'll come home again, I promise."

"Don't make promises you may not be able to keep, Ron. I'm not stupid." After hesitating a moment to reflect, she added. "Okay, I'll go."

By the end of the week, Carol was in pain and slipping in and out of consciousness. She couldn't chew solid food, and when I attempted to feed her soft foods, her body rejected even that. Then, when she began to reject liquids a few days later, the hospice representative spoke to me. I was faced with the painful realization that she wasn't going to be coming home. "Ron, we can manage her pain here and be certain she is comfortable. It's the right thing to do. It's not a choice you're making. She needs to be here!"

I agreed and signed the papers, but I felt I was letting her down, that she belonged at home. She was nearly comatose though and couldn't take in any food or water, and I even had to stop giving her the chemo because she couldn't ingest the capsules. I wanted them to do something, but the doctors said there was nothing to be done. Her brain was shutting down her body functions. They counseled me to stop trying to give her water, saying her body could no longer process it and I was causing her discomfort.

I shouted. "This is my wife! Damn it, how can I stop giving her water?"

Your mind accepts what's happening, but emotionally, you're just not prepared for the finality of it. As compassionately as he could, he said. "Mr. Ieva, your wife is in the process of dying, and everything you're seeing is part of that process."

They gave me a brochure to read. As I read it, I recalled our first meeting with Doctor Malkin when Carol asked how she would likely die if the treatments didn't work. It was all here, the slow decline into a coma, the brain shutting down body functions until finally the heart or pulmonary system simply stopped working. There would be no resuscitation or CPR to revive her. The tumor would simply take over the brain and her life would end. I let out a deep cry of anguish and felt that the air would never stop leaving my lungs. *Oh God, how could this be happening to her?*

The next few days she slipped further away, communicating only by hand signals; one squeeze for no, two for yes. She was in there, but just barely, yet I knew she could hear and understand me. I stayed by her side constantly, moistening her parched lips and putting cool compresses on her face, never letting go of her hand except to go home for a brief nap and a change of clothes when one of the kids was with her. Holding her hand, I'd read and pray aloud for her until I couldn't bear it, then I'd leave the room and cry uncontrollably.

On September twenty-ninth, I went home for a change of clothes and returned with a split of champagne. Although almost completely co-matose, I held Carol's hand for hours, talking aloud about our wonderful life and how happy she had made me. When I said I hoped that I had given her happiness and a good life in return, she squeezed my hand twice, then paused, then twice again, then repeated the sequence several times. I like to believe that she meant she had been very happy and that she wasn't just repeating herself. As the night wore on, I sometimes rambled about sailing or talked about our teenage years. Every now and then, I'd ask her a question about what I was saying, and she always responded with the correct signal.

When the clock struck midnight, I embraced her and softly kissed her dry lips.

"It's after midnight, Baby. It's September thirtieth. Happy anniversary, Carol. I love you!" Her hand squeezed mine in constant rapid pulses.

Then, as a test of her awareness, I said, "Yup, we're married fifty years!"

Her squeezing immediately stopped.

"Oh I'm sorry; I mean we're married five years."

Still, there was no response, just the feel of her soft hand in mine.

Then I said, "Oh, I remember now, we're married seventeen years!"

She immediately squeezed my hand in rapid pulses. I kissed her and said, "You know I was only teasing you right, Baby?"

Two squeezes. Yes

"Are you mad at me for teasing you?"

One squeeze. No.

"You know I love you right, Baby?"

Two squeezes. Yes.

The barest hint of tears pooled at her eyes, and I dried them away, then kissed her tenderly, hoping she could feel my lips.

"Are you tired, Carol?"

She squeezed once. No.

"Do you want me to talk to you?"

Two squeezes. Yes.

Then, oblivious to whether her mind was awake or asleep, I talked for hours until I no longer got a response. Only then did I sleep sporadically in the chair alongside her bed.

There were many visitors during the day. David, Rob, Jennifer, and Nancy were there of course. Also my mom, Brother Tony, and Victoria came out from Brooklyn to wish Carol a happy anniversary. She was more sluggish in her responses than she had been just the day before, and her breathing was labored, but she was still able to answer questions with hand squeezes. When I was alone with her, I begged her to remember me and look for me in heaven or in another life or place. I knew she believed in those things, so I promised I would never forget her in this life or stop looking for her in the next. I begged her, "Please, Carol. Please wait for me."

On Sunday, Jennifer and Nancy relieved me so I could get some rest. When I returned, I could see that her condition worsened considerably. I sat by her side holding her hand and monitored the symptoms she was exhibiting. Her breathing became increasingly labored and she no longer used hand signals in response to my questions. Disbelievingly, my soulmate and best friend of nearly fifty years was dying before my eyes.

Tormented beyond belief, I watched the great love of my life slip away. I was powerless to help her and could only hold her ravaged body tightly in my arms. I told her repeatedly how much I loved her and how much joy she had brought to me. I recounted our last twenty-one years together and reminisced aloud about the splendor of our childhood together. I didn't know if she could hear me but I begged her not to leave me. Knowing she believed in an afterlife, I again pleaded with her to wait for me. I cried because I was losing her, then I laughed at some funny memory from years past that she had gifted to me.

I read Psalm 23 to her repeatedly and prayed that she could hear me, but when her breathing became even faster and more shallow I knew I was about to lose her. I sat on the bed and held her in my arms, crying as I gently rocked her. I wanted her all to myself, to have these precious few minutes alone with her so I could tell her my most intimate feelings. Then, feeling guilty that maybe she wanted her children there, or that they'd want the chance to be with her one more time, I called Jennifer, who lived only moments away. Crying, I said, "Jennifer, you need to come here fast, she's really bad. Her breathing is very rapid and shallow!"

Putting down the phone, I took Carol in my arms and again promised her I would look for her in a next life and pleaded for her to wait for me. If she could hear anything, I wanted her to hear those words. Jennifer arrived, and together we held her, telling her repeatedly that we loved her and were there for her, hoping that she could hear us and know she wasn't alone. Her breathing suddenly slowed dramatically, then stopped. And in the blink of an eye, she was gone.

CHAPTER 32
SAILING WITHOUT CAROL

Hundreds came to Carol's funeral, some from as far away as California and Florida. Flowers from Singapore, England, Germany, and Greece stood alongside those from our old neighborhood in Brooklyn, and they over-flowed into the hall and lounge. Boat friends who we'd known for a decade, but seen only in shorts and t-shirts, arrived wearing suits and ties, but with boat shoes as a silent tribute to Carol the sailor.

As she requested, I buried her in Calverton National Cemetery, not far from my father and brother in a field of heroes beneath precisely aligned military headstones. As I said goodbye, I took comfort in knowing I'd be there with her one day and that my name would be engraved on the other side of her headstone as is custom in a National Cemetery. I smiled and thought, *How fitting that will be; our names on the same headstone, like a mirror image of our lives together.*

Suddenly it was all over; the viewing, the church, the burial, and finally the ritual gathering of family and friends at our home. A part of me wanted it to go on indefinitely, but it ended, and everyone but my son departed. The next day, even he was gone and I sat alone disbelieving. I looked around at her photos, the A over I card I had made for her and the hundreds of old get well and more recent condolence cards that had arrived from all over the world, and I cried through the night. I thought, *This is where she spent her last year, sick and dying, and I didn't want to be there.*

In the morning, I gathered some things and fled, knowing the only place I might find some comfort was aboard *Lastdance* where we shared eleven years of extraordinarily happy times and adventures together. I drove to Maryland, and three hours later, as I walked down our dock, I began to cry uncontrollably. When I got within ten paces of our little ship, I stopped, unable to take another step. I stared at the large blue script on her stern, *Lastdance*. A chill ran up my spine and I wondered why she ever wanted that name. Did she have some kind of premonition, or was it simply as she said, a song from our childhood to tell me that she indeed saved the last dance for me. I should have insisted we name the boat after her; maybe I could do that now. "Yes," I said aloud. "I'm going to rename the boat Carol Lee!"

There was the briefest moment of peace with that decision, but still, I couldn't take another step. With tears on my cheek, I turned and drove three hours back home without setting foot aboard our boat.

As I prepared to go to bed that night, my arthritic shoulder hurt terribly. I had already taken a sleeping pill and a pain killer to no avail. In the past, I would lay behind Carol and put my arm around her, and as her body bore its weight, the pain would ease. With that in mind, I tried a pillow, but found it too small. Then I tried a large cushion from the couch, which worked. So much so, it reminded me of how it felt to hold Carol. I began to cry. Then, more for my emotional benefit than anything else, I said aloud, "Goodnight, Baby. I love you."

Unbelievingly, I heard Carol's voice reply, "I love you too, Ron."

I sat upright so fast I strained my back. I turned the lights on and looked around the room thinking, *That was not in my head, I heard her voice loud and clear!* My shoulder pain was gone and I slept like a baby, wanting to believe that her spirit was with me. By the next morning, however, I was already rationalizing the event, thinking that the combination of grief, sleeping pills, and pain killer was the cause.

One week after Carol's burial, the furthest thing from my mind was the Annapolis Boat Show. Nevertheless, I went because I now needed to buy an auto pilot. Although just a collection of electronics and motors, it represented the very last thing I wanted in the world, something to replace Carol. I went only to vendors selling auto pilots, but I still felt guilty, as if even my presence there somehow made me disloyal to her. I fought back tears as memories of being at the show with her countless times flooded my mind. I knew I could save a thousand dollars buying an auto pilot at boat show prices, but still, I slinked around feeling ashamed and thought, *I just buried her. What am I doing here?*

I found the unit I wanted for $3900, which was a good price, and I hurriedly conducted what I felt was tainted business, then left quickly as if I'd done something terribly wrong. I was still numb and disbelieving that she was gone, and as I drove home, I drove right by our marina and *Last-dance,* not stopping because I knew I'd still be unable to go aboard her. Still driving, I searched for a radio station and heard the very end of a song that soothed my grief. I only heard a few words, but it had a spiritually healing effect on me. They never mentioned the artist or the name of the song, but I searched for weeks afterwards, even looking on the internet, and I began to wonder if I'd actually heard it.

That night, I took a sleeping pill to ease my grief. I considered taking several more, maybe even all of them because I missed Carol so much and I wanted to go to her. In the morning I sat in front of my uneaten breakfast and looked at her place on the couch where she spent much of the last year of her life and I cried. Sometime later the phone rang. It was Met-Life. They had managed Carol's long-term disability insurance, and the woman asked if I was Mr. Ieva, Carol Ieva's husband. She said there was a matter of her disability survivor benefit. Annoyed, I told her we elected not to have a survivor benefit and that I had already mailed them a death certificate and to please leave me alone.

I heard her flipping through papers, then she spoke again, asking me to confirm my Social Security number. I immediately thought this was some kind of scam. I said I didn't want to give that information out over the phone and was about to hang up when she stated my correct number. I searched my memory. I remembered helping Carol fill out the forms years earlier, but I distinctly told her not to check off a survivor benefit so we would get a higher payment, which we needed back then for medical expenses.

"As I was saying Mr. Ieva, the benefit is small so there will be a lump sum payment, which we will mail to you within the week."

"How small?" I asked.

"Ah, let me see, the benefit amount is four thousand eighteen dollars and thirty-eight cents."

Stunned, I said, "How much did you say?"

She repeated herself then went on to say, "We at Met-Life are sorry for your loss, please accept our sincere condolences, have a nice day."

I was dumbfounded. There was no way Carol could have known what her survivor benefit would be or what an auto pilot would cost. She must have made a simple mistake on the form or disregarded my advice and did what she considered best. Either way, I realized Carol just bought me the auto pilot.

A week later, I drove to our marina. All I wanted to do was sail away in *Lastdance,* but I had to take the difficult first step of going aboard. I stepped onto her familiar deck and began to cry softly. Then after opening the companionway hatch and going below, I immediately felt Carol's presence. She was there in our boat. I could hear her laughter and see her sitting at her place at the salon table. As I sat there, I heard voices on the dock; people were arriving to begin their weekend, but I didn't want to meet or speak with anyone. I just needed to get underway and out sailing, so I cast off and motored into the Chester River. I considered sailing to Annapolis where Carol would want to go, but then I remembered the wonderful sail we made to the Corsica River in *Ursaorion* during our first fall on Chesapeake Bay. The wind was light but from the northwest. *Yeah*, I thought, *I'm going to the Corsica!*

Almost twelve years to the day after that first magical sail and twelve days after Carol lost her long and courageous fight, I anchored *Lastdance* on the Corsica River. I watched the geese and sipped wine alone and thought of the countless times in years past when Carol sat beside me for hours. I wanted this to be a cathartic cruise to recapture memories of happier times, but of course it was really a very bittersweet journey, much more bitter than sweet. The river, geese, and wine were the same, but I underestimated how much I would miss holding her and seeing the wonder in her eyes. I was overcome by grief and realized that sailing would never again be the same for me. It was true that I'd always wanted to sail, but the real joy had been in sharing it with Carol. I knew nothing would ever fill the empty place in my life or on our boat that had been occupied by her for so many years. Now, because of her passion and zest for life, I think about her more on an exciting close reach than on a gentle run, but it's never the same.

Fall became winter and I immersed myself in what I came to call Carol projects. I scanned hundreds of photos of her from old albums into my computer, then produced a variety of photo journals from online publishing sites and literally filled every room in my home with her photos. Nothing helped. And then, for what would be the first of many morose nights, I found myself sitting on my bed in the dark, holding my pistol in my hands and thinking, *This is a way to go to Carol.* I didn't think I was seeking an escape from my grief, I just saw it as a way to be with her. At that point I got professional grief counseling through hospice and began having weekly afternoon tea sessions with Father Vincent.

In March, just when I began to pull out of my depression, Jerry called to tell me Mary Lynne died. For reasons I couldn't explain, I knew the only thing to keep myself from crashing in despair was to drive to Michigan to be with my friend. We had been through a lot together, so maybe it was a mutual support thing; in any case, it seemed to work and we promised to do a healing sail in the spring aboard *Lastdance*. I drove home sensing there would be no more nights in the dark with a loaded gun and that maybe I could even make some forward progress.

In early spring during a talk with Father Vincent, I told him I wished I could believe Carol was in a better place. He said I would one day, but only if I accepted Jesus into my heart.

"How?" I asked.

He simply said, "Ask Him. Ask Jesus."

The next day while driving to *Lastdance,* I came upon a billboard not far from my home on Route 70. It was black and had but two words in bold white letters: "Ask Jesus."

What the hell? I felt blasphemous for that thought, and as I drove along, I thought of Father Vincent's words the day before and now the sign. The urge became overwhelming and I spoke aloud, "Please, Jesus. Please tell me she's in a better place and that she knows I love her."

I felt foolish. There was nothing! No lightning or thunder, just the loud intrusion into my thoughts by an obnoxious rap song on the radio. I hit the scan button to change the station. Astonishingly, there was the song I had heard weeks earlier and had searched in vain for. I had switched the station at the very instant it began.

May the angels protect you
Trouble neglect you
And heaven accept you when its time to go home
May you always have plenty
Your glass never empty
And know in your belly
You're never alone

May your tears come from laughing
You find friends worth having
With every year passing
They mean more than gold
May you win but stay humble
Smile more than grumble
And know when you stumble
You're never alone

Never alone, Never alone
I'll be in every beat of your heart
When you face the unknown
Wherever you fly
This isn't goodbye
My love will follow you stay with you
Baby you're never alone

Well I have to be honest
As much as I wanted
I'm not gonna promise the cold winds won't blow
So when hard times have found you
And your fears surround you
Wrap my love around you
You're never alone
My love will follow you stay with you
Baby you're never alone.

The song was "Never Alone" by Sara Evans. For me, the words were haunting but comforting. I wasn't a religious man, but at the moment I asked Jesus for help, I received a reply and no one could have convinced me that it wasn't a message from Carol that she would always be with me.

In May, Jerry and I spent a week aboard *Lastdance* sailing to Annapolis where I drank too much rum and Jerry ate too much ice cream. We spent long days on Chesapeake Bay talking about Carol and Mary Lynne and pondered what the future might hold for two crusty old sailors without our women by our side. We looked inwardly and discussed what the odds were of this happening to us; our beautiful wives both coming down with the same rare and deadly disease and dying just months apart. *Was there a common denominator, something from our past that brought this on us?*

Months later, Bill came by and showed me his new tattoo. It was a mermaid caught in an anchor rode, and it made me remember when I got my sailor girl tattoo in Hawaii. When Carol saw it, she confessed she was disappointed the face didn't resemble her. I remembered thinking, *What an idiot I was; it would have been so thoughtful to use Carol's likeness for the face.* Years later, she sometimes prodded me about getting another tattoo, one of a mermaid using her likeness, but I never got around to it. Now, looking at Bill's mermaid, I could think of nothing else.

I came up with a drawing using several of my favorite photos of Carol, then searched for a tattoo artist who could do it well. After several months, I found Patrick. He grasped the concept immediately and using a breathtaking photo of Carol's face and torso, he designed a tattoo that I liked immediately. Now, more than a year later, my only regret is that I didn't do it when she was alive to see it. Although it may sound silly, in a way she is truly part of me again, and I will wear her likeness until this earthly body is dust for the ages.

With my new tattoo and *Lastdance* loaded with stores, I prepared to sail south for the winter. My wedding ring had become increasingly tight over the past few years, so much so that I couldn't remove it. As I gained weight, it became so tight, it actually hurt, and I thought I should have it expanded before sailing away for six months. I went to a jeweler to have the ring expanded without damaging it, but he said it had to be cut off.

"Look at your finger, mister, it's already discolored."

I explained that my wife died and I couldn't bring myself to cut it. He told me I could really hurt my finger if I didn't cut it off soon, then added he could do it right there. He explained we would then wait a few weeks for my finger to return to normal, at which time he would resize the ring. I told him I'd have to think about it and went home.

I talked to Father Vinny, and he told what I already knew. "Ron, what would Carol say?"

The answer was clear, she would tell me to cut the ring and resize it and not cause injury to my finger. The next day I had it cut off, but immediately felt terrible about it. Whatever progress I was making in moving forward through my grief was lost, and I slid back in into depression. Then, after three days of being miserable, I had a dream in which I woke to find Carol in my arms, sleeping the way she always did, facing me and snuggled in my embrace. Suddenly, her eyes opened wide and she simply said, "We really love each other!" She said nothing else, but I could actually smell her breath and remember thinking it was comforting and familiar. Then she evaporated as I woke, only to find myself waking again, as if I had been having a dream within a dream.

Whether from Carol's spirit or some deep recess of my mind, I can't say, but it's the third message to bring me comfort. I wish with all my heart that I fully believed in an afterlife and that Carol was truly looking over me, but I just can't fully embrace the concept. Yet, I'm envious of people who do because I know it would ease my pain immeasurably.

Many months later, while engaged in my own battle with cancer, Carol's daughter, Nancy, called to tell me about a vivid dream she had. In it, she came upon a large sailing ship at a dock with many billowing sails. The sky was clear and brilliant and the huge ship floated on cobalt blue water that sparked like diamonds in the morning sun. Nancy approached the ship, and there on a small platform high up on the mast, she saw a little girl. When she called to her, the child turned and it was Carol, exactly as she looked in a photo Nancy had once seen of her mom at about age ten, a photo which I've had for more than fifty years.

The ship was beautiful and looked like an old clipper ship, and Carol was the only one aboard. When Nancy asked what she was doing on the big ship, Carol replied. "I'm waiting for Ronnie." Nancy kept trying to tell her how much she meant to her, but all Carol kept talking about was her how she needed to get the ship ready for Ronnie. In the dream, Nancy didn't know if Carol told her, or she just knew it, but the ship was on Lake Erie.

The rational side of me thought the dream had been generated subconsciously deep in the mind of a grieving daughter, but then I thought, *Carol hadn't called me Ronnie since we were kids; how would Nancy know that?* I rationalized that Carol could have mentioned it over the years, but then Nancy asked me what the significance Lake Erie might have been.

I said, "You don't know? Your mom was born near Pittsburgh, near Lake Erie!"

I wish Nancy's dream had been my own; I think it should have been! Even if it was just a subconscious creation of her own mind, it's a vision of what could be, and that gives me great comfort in itself, but also because it also reminded me of an event a time long ago, maybe when we were as young as Carol was in Nancy's dream.

I was building a raft in front of my apartment building with my friend Johnny Spezicatina. We were going to put it on my wagon and take it to the harbor, then float across to Staten Island. Carol had been watching us hammering planks all afternoon, her face clasped between her palms, but saying nothing. Then, while arguing over where to put a board and apparently disgusted with the flimsiness of the raft, Johnny said, "This is a piece of shit; I ain't going in the ocean on it!"

I called him a chicken and he walked away, but before I could utter another word, Carol said, "I'll go with you, Ronnie!"

I want to believe there is a connection between Nancy's dream and that raft. That the raft is the sailing ship and that Carol is truly waiting for me, just like I asked her to do in the hospice room.

In the end, I didn't rename *Lastdance*. Carol had chosen that name above all others, even her own, and I couldn't bear to change it now. Friends from Maine to Florida would always associate *Lastdance* with us, and I didn't want to alter the connection. She had touched so many people in her life, but especially during her years of sailing. And although most would remember her for her fun loving nature, beauty, and passion, all would remember her at the helm of *Lastdance*. They would also remember her courage because she chose to fight the good fight against long if not impossible odds, and she did so with the knowledge that the struggle would be very painful, and that in the end, she would most likely lose the battle.

Now, through all the grief, loneliness, and missing her so badly that I'm on the verge of tears almost every hour of every day, she can still make me smile. The memories of her laughter are infectious, the swell of her breasts exhilarating, her scent intoxicating. And though I'll never really hear her laugh again, or kiss her breasts, or become drunk with her scent, I will surely smile at the memory of those things and so much more that she gave to me unconditionally.

I sail and live aboard *Lastdance* alone now. I sometimes move about the boat forgetting the auto pilot is engaged and turn, half-expecting to see Carol at the helm. Other times I go forward to weigh anchor and give the hand signal for slow ahead, forgetting she isn't there to respond, and I hang my head and fight back tears. At quiet anchorages with her presence drawn around me like a soft blanket, I look at our photo albums and relive those moments forever frozen in time as well as the events surrounding them. I take notice that in every one of the hundreds of photos of us together, we're always touching in some manner, always holding hands or an arm over a shoulder or a hand resting on a leg. I think. *That was us, always needing to be connected somehow, always touching.*

She's gone. A beautiful life has ended, and I cry when I consider the enormity of her loss. I also smile, believing she is with me here aboard our little ship, and when I hear her voice saying, "Who is going to listen for noises and look after you when I'm gone?"

I know the answer: "You do, Carol. You do."

I borrowed the opening and closing lines from a poem by Mary Frye and tried to capture that feeling by writing a poem for my wonderful wife and best friend. It now hangs in the salon of *Lastdance*. Sail on, Carol. Sail on!

Carol's Song

Do not stand at my grave and cry, I am not there, I did not die
I am a wind to drive our ship; I am your strength for the long night's trick
I am a star unseen in day, I am a compass to guide your way
I am shipmate to calm your fears; I am a spirit to dry your tears
I am a dolphin's cry of glee; I am a light on the dark stormy sea
I am your angel always near; I am now a memory, vivid and clear
Do not stand at my grave and cry, I am not there, I did not die